OPEN
WOUND

OPEN WOUND

THE LONG VIEW OF RACE IN AMERICA

WILLIAM McKEE EVANS

UNIVERSITY OF
ILLINOIS PRESS
URBANA AND
CHICAGO

The publication of this book was made possible, in part, by a grant from the Center for Community Action in Lumberton, N.C.

⬯ This book is printed on acid-free paper.

Library of Congress Cataloging-in-Publication Data
Evans, William McKee.
Open wound : the long view of race in America / William McKee Evans.
p.   cm.
Includes bibliographical references and index.
ISBN 978-0-252-03427-5 (cloth : alk. paper)
1. African Americans—History.
2. African Americans—Southern States—History. 3. African Americans—Civil rights—History.
4. Racism—United States—History.
5. United States—Race relations.
6. Southern States—Race relations.
I. Title.
E185.E93   2009
973'.0496073—dc22
2008032904

Dedication

To a White-bearded Fiddler,
an Unrepentant "Scalawag,"
and to a Tradition

When I was doing research for *To Die Game* in the Reconstruction records of the National Archives, I was thrilled to come across a reference to an individual whom I had actually known. The Union Army in 1867 was organizing the first elections ever conducted in North Carolina according to universal manhood suffrage. One Radical officer, in a letter to another, marked "for your eyes only," recommended a certain Dan'l McNeill, a youth of "firm Union convictions," who could be trusted as a Republican poll watcher.

McNeill was a distant relative of mine. As a youngster I thought that he looked like Santa Claus because of his long white hair and beard. When he came to visit, he would arrive carrying a fiddle case in one hand and a jug of homemade whiskey in the other. I remember him saying to my father, "Now I shall play for you a tune that was played at your great granddaddy's enfare [wedding feast], 'Bonaparte's Retreat.'" "Bonaparte's Retreat"! To me he was like an ancient bridge to some twilight world of the past.

In 1861, McNeill's father had been expelled from the Presbyterian Church, on charges of heresy and immorality, after he had publicly opposed secession. In 1867, McNeill himself had also been expelled from the same church on the same charges, after he had begun work for the Freedmen's Bureau. He was later readmitted to fellowship, only to be kicked out again in the 1890s after he joined the Populist Party. This time he did not return.

My father used to chide him for his stubbornness. He should be thinking of the hereafter and become reconciled with the church to which his family had been long devoted. McNeill replied that, though his religious views were not orthodox, he did not worry about the hereafter, "because," he added curiously, "I am the son of a believer." He seemed to think that his father, who had once rescued him when he had fallen into the hands of the Confederate Home Guard, would always stand by him.

He died at age eighty-seven, and his grandnephew came to bring us the news. He said that his uncle may have overexerted himself the week before when he had been planting an apple orchard. When asked why, at his age, he was planting so many trees, McNeill had replied, "Things have gotten to the place where there is hardly a man left in this county who can sit you down to a decent cup of cider."

I dedicate this book to that unrepentant "scalawag" Dan'l McNeill, who celebrated the music of his ancestors and who planted trees that some new, unseen generation might enjoy their fruit. And to those genuine Southern rebels who stood by him.

Contents

Acknowledgments   ix

Interpretive Overview   1

Prologue: Race and the Human Race   7

PART 1   The Colonial Period

1. How the American Racial System Began:
   Atlantic Slavery Becomes Market-Driven and Color-Defined   13

2. Anglo Americans Adopt the Atlantic Racial System   24

3. The Construction of Planter Hegemony, 1676–1776   36

4. The Era of the American Revolution: The Challenge
   to Slavery and the Compromise   50

PART 2   The Antebellum Republic

5. The Old South's Triumph   65

6. The Old South's Crisis and the Emergence of the
   White Solidarity Myth   75

7. Emancipated but Black: Freedom in the Free States   93

8. The Planter and the "Wage Slave": A Reactionary Alliance   109

9. King Cotton's Jesters: The Minstrel Show Interprets Race
   for the White Working Class   120

10. The War of the Cabins: The Struggle for the Soul
    of the "Common Man"   130

PART 3   The Racial System Challenged and Revised

11. The Republican Revolution and the Struggle for a "New Birth of Freedom"   147

12. Reconstruction: The Radical Challenge, 1865–77   163

13. Between Slavery and Freedom: The Conservative Quest for a Halfway House   175

PART 4   The Racial System in a Rising Superpower

14. The Age of Segregation at Its Zenith: The Racial System in a World of Colonialism   189

15. Radical Challenge, Liberal Reform: African Americans Gain New Allies   199

16. The American Century, the American Dilemma   210

17. The Black Freedom Movement   221

18. The Racial System in the Age of Corporate Globalism, Technological Revolution, and Environmental Crisis   235

Notes   249

Index   321

Acknowledgments

Like all books, this book has its own history. As World War II drew to a close in Europe, I was a twenty-one-year-old soldier on the Rhine. A group of us were listening to the radio one night and we heard "Lord Haw Haw," a Nazi commentator with an elegant British accent. He reported on some race riots in the United States and gave them a white supremacist spin. In our Jim Crow army, his words hit home with some listeners and we started arguing. Some said that blacks were getting out of hand. Harmony was restored when we tuned to an American commentator who said nothing about race and gave an upbeat version of the news. But it was the argument that I remembered.

Later, when I was a student and aspiring historian, the question of race somehow informed everything I wrote. It seemed the dark counterpoint to the traditional narrative of American history. By the late 1960s, the book of record on the subject was Winthrop D. Jordan's *White over Black*. To me it said that racial prejudice, like sin, was a part of human nature, certainly the nature of white people.

I did not believe this. But I had already discovered that it is easier to shoot down somebody else's argument than to come up with a better one. I rashly decided that while Jordan and others had *described* racial prejudice, I would *explain* it—how historically it came about.

If racism was indeed a universal human flaw, as some writers seemed to think, I would have to look for manifestations of it in ancient times and worldwide. The literature was staggering, much of it in languages I could barely read or didn't know at all. Fortunately, my son, Daniel G. Evans, strong in languages, helped me. Still it seemed that I was trying to drink the ocean.

At one point, I was about to give up when Edmund S. Morgan sent me an encouraging response to some rough writing that I had showed him. I also received early encouragement from Immanuel Wallerstein, Moses Finley, and Charles Verlinden. But the project only took real shape in Timothy Breen's National Endowment for the Humanities seminar in 1978. In 1980, the *American Historical Review* published an early part of my project as an article, "From the Land of Canaan to the Land of Guinea: The Strange Odyssey of the 'Sons of Ham.'" That gave me momentum. Later, I presented a paper to the Southern Historical Association, a rough projection of how I thought the racial system developed in the Americas. The comments of the panelists, David Brion Davis, George Fredrickson, and Carl N. Deglar, were sharp and insightful, and I came away smarter and encouraged. My project further matured in Orlando Patterson's National Endowment for the Humanities seminar at Harvard.

My student assistant, Todd Menzing, later a history professor himself, read several generations of the manuscript; and my student Ursula Markham, later assistant editor of *Central European History*, gave valuable criticism. The faculty and students of the Cal Poly, Pomona, chapter of Phi Alpha Theta allowed me to try out fragments of my project at our meetings. My colleagues David Levering, Anthony Brundage, David Smith, John Moore, Joseph Block, Ralph Schafer, William Smith, John Lloyd, Lydia Gans, and Saul Landau read parts or all of the work and offered suggestions. Our history department arranged my teaching schedule so as to give me unfragmented time to write, and it also allowed me more than my share of the department's travel funds.

In order to make the project more manageable and reduce it to a more publishable length, I eventually accepted the advice of Otto H. Olsen, who over the years kept up with my project, to restrict it to the American racial system. Later, I also took the advice of Brian Kelly, who thoroughly critiqued the manuscript, to compress the chapters dealing with the Old World and Latin America.

Latin America, with its shared history of racial slavery, provided an illuminating counterexample to the way racial ideology unfolded in the United States. I learned about the different way race played out in these countries from my colleagues Donald Castro and José Vadi, who read and criticized part of the manuscript. I observed Latin American racial patterns firsthand during vacations spent in Puerto Rico and Brazil, in Afro-Mexican villages on the Costa Chica of Mexico, and in the Afro-Cuban neighborhood around the Martin Luther King Baptist Center in Havana.

I am indebted to scholars and others who have reacted to my ideas after reading all or parts of the manuscript. Timothy B. Tyson, especially, offered extensive criticism. Others who have read the entire manuscript and made especially valuable suggestions are George B. Tindall, John Niven, Gary B. Nash, William J. Billingsley, Junius Scales, the Reverend Robert Zuber, Mac Legerton, and Jack P. Maddex. For critiques of particular chapters or short passages I am indebted to Raymond Gavins, Joseph Miller, Vernon Burton, Peter Kolchin, Louis Harlan, David Gillespie, Iris Tillman Hill, Philip Curtin, Steven Hahn, Oscar Berland, Robin Blackburn, Herbert Shapiro, Michael Tadman, Merton Dillon, Peter Wood, Robert Korstad, Dan Carter, Hans Trefousse, Walter Jackson, Leslie Rolland, Warren Williams, and Staughton Lynd. I especially appreciate the suggestions and encouragement of Glenda Gilmore.

A sharp and encouraging editor can certainly improve a manuscript. Laurie Matheson, senior acquisitions editor at the University of Illinois Press, got me to clarify my argument, especially in the early chapters, and showed me where I could divide long, unwieldy chapters into more focused ones. Sometimes it was a case of "Why didn't I think of that long ago?!"

For their help in preparation of the manuscript I owe many thanks to Donna Botash Tec, to Alejandra and Santiago Ocampo, and to Agustin Ortega.

Most of all, I want to thank Jerome Van Camp for his vital criticism, advice, and ideas over the years of the production of this work, and for his editing—which sometimes included rewriting, sometimes even writing—as well as for his help with the many tasks in the preparation of the several generations of the manuscript.

Interpretive Overview

In 1776, the Continental Congress launched a new nation, but a nation with an open wound. From the outset the nation had a system of mutually reinforcing ideas, practices, and institutions that disadvantage people of color. Over the centuries the racial system has changed. Old ideas and practices have given way to new ones, and white behavior and attitudes toward black people have changed in important ways. Yet the system has continued from slavery to segregation to resegregation in jobless ghettos. So, while many black Americans have escaped from a three-hundred-year-old mudsill stratum of American society and recently some have indeed risen to positions of influence, the imprint of slavery on the nation is still visible.

Through decades of American history, African Americans remained virtually invisible to whites. From the beginning, however, whenever the nation has faced a crisis, the same question has emerged: What about the blacks? In recent times, during World War II, the Cold War, and the so-called war on terror, as the nation has competed for the leadership of a largely nonwhite world, blacks have been by no means invisible to scholars. Nothing has more occupied scholars than particular components of the nation's racial history. Many excellent studies have illuminated particular aspects of this history: works on slavery, peonage, segregation, constitutional rights, white racial attitudes, the black freedom movement, the causes of black unemployment, among other important aspects. What is needed now is a long view of how American racial institutions and ideas began and how and why, over time, they have changed.

Certain studies have approached the centuries-old persistence of the white-over-black shape of American society, finding causes in "human nature." Such early twentieth-century historians as U. B. Phillips thought that the lowly jobs held by African Americans could be explained by their limited mental capacity. In the 1950s and 60s, however, when blacks took to the streets, the theory of their inferiority fell into disfavor. But then a prominent school of white historians, stressing psychology and culture, held that the problem lay not with the nature of blacks but with the nature of whites. Whites' prejudice derived, not from the way they *treated* blacks, but from the way they *perceived* them. These scholars thought that black had always been a color that whites associated with disagreeable things and that this limited their ability to fully accept black people. Two narratives but one conclusion: the status quo. Because of either the nature of blacks or the nature of whites, American society was likely to remain racially stratified.

Yet, in other times and places black people and white people have not always interacted as they have in the United States. The first task of the present study is, therefore, to demonstrate that the attitude of American whites toward Africans derived, not from their unchanging reactions to color, but from a new type of slavery that appeared in the new Atlantic World of the 1500s. It differed from the then traditional Old World slavery in two ways: slaves produced commodities for the market, and slaves were taken almost exclusively from sub-Saharan Africa. Now a master was motivated by profit. A slave was recognized by color. This appearance of market-driven, color-defined slavery, and a legacy of anti-African lore that came with the Atlantic slave trade, were the beginnings of what came to be called "American racism." If one can establish that this self-reinforcing system of ideas and practices had a beginning, one can also venture the prediction that it will have an end.

Those who locate the origins of the American racial system either in the nature of blacks or in the nature of whites are not only mistaken about how it began, but they also underestimate the significance of the changes that have taken place. Important changes occurred at three historical moments when the racial system entered a crisis phase. The first was during the War for Independence, when American slavery became a threat to the struggle for American freedom. The second phase of crisis came during the "irrepressible conflict" over slavery, culminating in the Civil War and Reconstruction. The latest crisis occurred during the Cold War when a Jim Crow nation set out to "lead the free world," which was then seething with revolution and colonial revolt by people of color. Each of these crises opened a window of opportunity for idealists who challenged the defenders of the racial status quo. Each of the ensuing conflicts resulted in a compromise that changed the way whites treated blacks, but fell far short of Thomas Jefferson's vision of human equality.

But how is one to explain why change has taken place only at discrete historical moments? Why the relatively changeless behavior and ideas of whites during the long decades between these crisis phases? To ask such questions is to probe the secrets of power. An important part of this study is an effort to illuminate these periods of near stability by the theory of "hegemony," or the idea that a governing class achieves firm control, or "legitimacy," by popularizing a consensus ideology, which advances its own agenda. These beliefs are accepted as self-evident by common citizens, even though they may actually conflict with their own self-interest.

People with power have the means to mold the way a society views the world. They can establish their own outlook as orthodox or the mainstream view. They can make the views of their challengers heretical or even turn the opposition into solitary voices crying in the wilderness. They can establish the language of normal political discussion. The normal words and phrases used have inherent biases validating their position. Hegemony is complete when ordinary citizens do not perceive the limitations imposed by the belief system of their society, neither its assumptions, its restrictions on subject matter, nor the biases inherent in the words they use. Instead, one normally assumes that public discourse is framed by self-evident truths.

In the antebellum American republic, the people whom the abolitionists called the Slave Power established a hegemonic North-South consensus of racial ideas. The planters and their northern business partners, the commodity brokers and bankers, held this hegemonic ideological power. The commodities that slaves produced provided two-thirds of the nation's exports, making planters the richest class in the country and their northern allies the second richest class. The defense of slavery was thus critical both to the prosperity of the planters and to the accumulation of capital in the North.

The Slave Power was most vulnerable in the North, where slavery had been abolished in the wake of the War for Independence. Slavery was serving less and less the self-interest of most Northerners, indeed of most Southerners as well. More and more, it was harming their interests. As the unavoidable tensions caused by slavery mounted, the Slave Power "played the race card," in the latter-day phrase, with an intensity never seen before, saturating the nation, above all the North, with the message that blacks as slaves were happy and useful, but when free were lazy and dangerous. To convey this message they mobilized every vehicle of culture: the political rally, the newspaper, the church, the school, and most vividly the minstrel show. The formative American nation was thus thoroughly indoctrinated with an ideology of race.

The Republican revolution overthrew the Slave Power. But the Republicans did not complete their revolution in the South. During the struggles of Reconstruction, they repudiated their Radical contingent and finally came to terms with the former Confederates, leaving them in local control and allowing them to restore plantation production based on half-free labor. By the turn of the twentieth century, the new national corporate establishment, after defeating the challenges of the Farmers' Alliance movement and the Knights of Labor, finally established a corporate hegemony that continued into the twenty-first century. Also by the turn of the twentieth century, the ex-Confederates had finally crushed all opposition and achieved a "solid South." The age of segregation had begun.

Although the corporate elite in the North used free labor, they retained most of the racial ideology of the antebellum nation. They endorsed segregation in the South and tolerated its labor system, half free for blacks and little better for many whites. In the North, industrialists continued their "white only" hiring policy of the antebellum era. This policy helped keep black workers on the plantations and made possible a vigorous revival of southern commodity exports. Also, just as at the beginning of the racial system, planters in the West Indies had used a few less-debased whites to control many blacks, now industrialists used a few more-debased black strikebreakers to control many whites. The racial ideology of the antebellum regime was well suited to the needs of the new northern leaders. Indeed they built on it with so-called scientific racism.

The racial system showed increasing instability as the nation moved toward globalism. World War I opened industrial jobs in the North to black workers for the first time, giving rise to a process of black urbanization and the appearance of the more assertive "new Negro." The racial system became more unstable with the stock market crash of 1929 and the Great Depression of the 1930s, which created the first important split in the American elite since the Civil War. In response to the Great Depression, one faction, the New Dealers, favored economic and social programs. They began a reform movement. In the New Deal movement, African Americans came together with such other previously marginalized groups as the "new immigrants" and organized labor. Civil rights once again became a political issue.

After World War II, American leaders positioned themselves as the leaders of the "free world." At the same time, through the Atlantic Pact, they gave military support to the European powers that were trying to suppress the freedom movements in their colonies. The struggle of the "free world" against the "Communist slave world" precipitated the Cold War ideological crisis of the racial system. The black freedom movement saw its moment and seized it. The movement brought down the "white only" signs, opened the polling booth to black Southerners, and restored vitality to the Fourteenth and Fifteenth Amendments. By the late 1960s, more than half of African Americans had escaped from the bottom layer of society that they had occupied for three hundred years.

The black freedom movement came to grief when it moved from abolishing the legal disabilities that African Americans suffered to addressing their disproportionate poverty. Civil rights made slight demands on the nation's resources and enhanced its political image. But programs to provide jobs and to combat poverty required resources the nation's leaders wanted to use for their increasingly costly military ventures. Indeed social programs already in place were eroded ever more as the "welfare state" was displaced by the "national security state." In the backlash against social programs, new racial stereotypes appeared, Sambo the servant being replaced by Willie Horton the criminal and by the "gangsta rappers." The plight of the black poor and other poor people worsened with the "information revolution," which privileged a quality education out of the reach of most people and facilitated the outsourcing of jobs to low-wage countries.

The nation's growing gap between rich and poor signals a new crisis in which, for the first time in three hundred years, the line of class is more sharply drawn than the line of race. Historically, African Americans, however, as the last hired and first fired, have been the "miners' canary," the harbingers of coming trouble. In the misery, chaos, and high incarceration rates suffered by African Americans of the inner city, one may see some of what lies ahead for the rest of American society.

Prologue
Race and the Human Race

When Americans think of slavery, they think of black slavery. In other places, at other times, it was not always so.

Seville, c. 1626: In Lope de Vega's play *Slave of Her Lover,* set in the Seville of the playwright's day, Alberto is asked if he has a black slave for sale. "By no means would I deal in that business," he replies. The business he spurns is not the slave trade itself. Indeed, at that very moment he is offering for sale a Muslim slave. It is the black slave trade that sparks his indignation.[1] For Lope de Vega and for his audience, the respectable view was still the medieval one that for enslavement to be legal the victim had to be a captive taken in a war against "enemies of the faith," which currently meant the Muslims. Black Africans were not legitimate captives taken in a crusade.

Charleston, South Carolina, c. 1825: A mob broke up a slave sale. The dealer had put on the auction block a youth who appeared to be white. "I was whiter than he was," the youth later recalled, "and the peoples was a going to put him in prison."[2]

Between Seville in the seventeenth century and Charleston in the nineteenth, the justification of slavery had changed. In Seville it was still religion. In Charleston it had become race.

The colonizers brought a harsh form of slavery to the Americas, one that was a minor and peripheral institution in the Old World. In the Old World most slaves continued to serve in wealthy households and in local economies. But in the American colonies, overwhelmingly they worked in gangs on plantations, producing commodities for the gigantic and lucrative new Atlantic market.

Distant market forces drove overseers to turn a greater profit, often for absentee investors.

Slaves in the Old World continued to come from many places. But in the New World, as the native peoples died in apocalyptic numbers from the diseases that their conquerors brought, planters replaced them with Africans, who had more disease resistance. Black skin took on a new meaning powered by the new Atlantic market.

From this harshest form of exploitation, justified by race, the United States has inherited a racial system of interacting ideas and practices that mock the nation's ideals of equality and democracy, and perpetuate racial inequality and conflict. Yet from the outset of the Republic, during times of crisis, some Americans—the Quakers, the abolitionists, the Freedom Riders—have seized the initiative and challenged the racial system. Such rebels have reduced the system's scope and authority but have not yet managed to abolish it. They have been inspired by a tradition that stretches back to the ancient world, a belief in the unity of the human family and that nowhere was there an enslaveable "other."

The medieval view still present in Lope de Vega's time, that one could lawfully enslave only an enemy of the faith, was itself a doctrine that theologians had devised to manage tension created by an even older and more radical idea, that of a single human family. For example, the Essenes, a pre-Christian Jewish sect, "denounce the owners of slaves, not merely for their injustice in outraging the law of equality, but also for their impiety in annulling the statute of Nature, who, mother-like, has born and reared all men alike, . . . although this kinship has been put to confusion by the triumph of malignant covetousness, which has wrought estrangement instead of affinity, and enmity instead of friendship."[3]

And Saint Paul, while conceding the rights of "them who according to the flesh are your masters," reached out to all humanity with an idea that seemed to preclude an enslaveable "other": in Christ "there is neither Greek nor Jew . . . , Barbarian, Scythian, bond nor free" (Colossians 3:11). As late as the fifth century, Saint Augustine had warned, "Whoever is born anywhere, . . . however strange he may appear to our senses in bodily form and colour . . . , let no true believer doubt that such an individual is descended from the one man who was first created."[4]

God had made humankind one. Missionaries still hoped to carry this message "beyond the rivers of Ethiopia," the distant headwaters of the Blue and the White Nile.[5] Through centuries of bloody conflict and slavery this vision of humanity's original unity would never be entirely extinguished.

Such a view of humankind was not faring well in Augustine's day. The church, now allied to the Roman state, was involved in the bloody power struggles that afflicted the dying empire. The elite classes, having maintained their distance from the Christian movement for two and a half centuries, had flooded into the church, bringing their slaves with them. Theologians now decided that, if in Christ there was neither "bond nor free," in the real world of sin there were both. "True believers," if born free, should not be enslaved. But there were also "enemies of the faith," who should be enslaved. There was debate about who these included, but likely candidates were pagans, Jews, and the strange-looking barbarians who lived beyond the Roman frontier.

For most believers the sweeping apostolic vision had narrowed. Medieval artists, using black-white symbolism, often depicted Jews and, later, Muslims with black faces. And they drew hideous images that they called "Ethiopian demons."[6] Yet, despite the prevalence of these new divisive beliefs, the old idea still persisted. Balthazar, for example, one of the Three Wise Men who brought gifts to the baby Jesus, was often depicted as a black African.[7]

Even in the harsh environment of the colonial New World, where slavery became market-driven and color-defined, this ancient view of human unity did not disappear. It was the inspiration of Bartolomé de las Casas in Mexico, and of the Jesuits in Paraguay as they struck back at the slave catchers who raided native villages.[8] In the eighteenth century, the same ideal stirred to action the English abolitionists.

Again it surfaced at the time of the American Revolution. The planter/merchant elite had split over how to deal with new assertions of British authority. Rebellious "Patriots" and accommodationist "Loyalists" argued about "liberty." Their debate popularized this ideal and their war demonstrated the vulnerability of their slaveholding society. More people listened to Quakers and others who asserted that all human beings shared "the inner light." The northern states began to phase out slavery.

In 1862, a Confederate army crossed the Potomac. "Copperhead" mobs rioted behind the Union lines and killed army recruiting officers. More people then listened to abolitionists, who proclaimed a "God who will break every yoke and let the oppressed go free." Before the year was out, the nation's war objective changed from bringing the slave states back into the Union to letting "the oppressed go free."

At the beginning of the Cold War, when the American government set out with a Jim Crow army to lead the "free world," it precipitated a revolt against its racial practices at home. While white mobs attacked black protesters and bombed homes and churches, there were also in this crisis whites who responded in a different way. There were those who glimpsed the broad vision of humankind that Martin Luther King saw from "the mountaintop." Some whites joined the civil rights demonstrators and helped bring down the "white only" signs. On television, real African American images replaced the "jumping Jim Crow" ones of the minstrel show. Yet, at the beginning of the twenty-first century, a disproportionate number of African Americans are still trapped in the bottom stratum of American society.

From the beginnings of the American nation, racial ideas have functioned to justify inequality. At three historical moments, a national crisis has opened a window of opportunity for people opposing racial ideas and practices. These dissidents have mobilized the forces for change by evoking the ancient vision of a universal human family. Each of these movements achieved a historical advance, but none swept clean. Each ended in a compromise, leaving behind a residue of ideas that were overhauled to justify the new racial status quo. Most recently, many of these old ideas have been revised to explain the scandal of urban decay and social misery in the ghettos of the world's superpower.

Part 1
The Colonial Period

Chapter 1

How the American Racial System Began
Atlantic Slavery Becomes Market-Driven and Color-Defined

     Omar ibn Saíd was on the run. Taken prisoner in Africa, Omar ibn Saíd was now on the run in America. His African captors had sold him "into the hands of the Christians, who . . . sent me on board a great ship. . . . to a place called Charleston in the Christian language. There they sold me to a small, weak and wicked man called Johnson, a complete infidel, who had no fear of God at all." He had escaped from Johnson and during his flight taken refuge in a church. "A lad saw me . . . and informed [his father] that he had seen a black man in the church. [His father] and another man . . . on horseback came attended by a troop of dogs. They took me."[1]

The lad told his father that he had seen a black man in the church. But at no point does Omar ibn Saíd call himself black or his captors white. Where he came from, the all-important difference was religion. In America, it was color. In his homeland, most masters bought slaves to be house servants. In America, masters mainly bought slaves to produce plantation commodities for the European market. The American racial system began in a market-driven and racially defined type of slavery, which had begun before there was a single English colony. The European conquerors had discovered a bottomless market in Europe's growing addiction to sugar, rum, and tobacco. They had also discovered that stable plantation production of these commodities was not possible without black slaves, who had more resistance to the killer diseases that had devastated the American natives whom they had enslaved during the early decades of the conquest. From these two discoveries a historic mutation occurred in the ideology of slavery that would later be called racism.

When the institution of slavery crossed the Atlantic, large changes took place. For centuries, most slaves had been white, and European Christendom had justified their enslavement as the proper fate of "enemies of the faith." Now in the rising Atlantic World, above all in the plantation colonies, slavery became black slavery, justified as the proper fate of black Africans. In the Americas, there was a radical shift in the purposes for which slaves were exploited, in the way their labor was managed, in the geographical areas from which slaves were drawn, and, finally, in slavery's justifying ideology.

But none of the dominant features of slavery in the Americas was new. What was new was their dominance. First, the shift in the purposes for which slaves were exploited: Their most common use in the Old World was as household servants and as workers in local economies, for example, in the shops of artisans. Most of the household servants were women, who sometimes doubled as concubines. This form of the institution fostered ties of kinship between master and slave. But even for other slaves, the ideology of paternalism held out the prospect of eventual emancipation and full integration into a larger society defined by religion.[2] Another important use of slaves was as soldiers, who often served to control nominally free but severely exploited peasants. Rulers indoctrinated these slaves with an esprit de corps that resembled the paternalism of the patriarchal household. They also systematically instructed them in the official religion. Such slaves looked forward to eventually being mustered out as free men and fully integrated into the religious community.[3]

A minor use of slaves in the Old World, their exploitation in work gangs, became the dominant use in the Americas. In the Old World, these slaves rowed galleys, toiled in quarries and mines, or worked on plantations in some Mediterranean lands. Not only was "gang slavery" unusual in the Old World, far from mainstream society, but it made no discernible impression on the traditional ideology of the institution, on the idea that slaves were quasi or inferior members of the master's household; and, like his own children, they were being taught the true religion. Gang slaves could not look forward to improving their lot in life; and, unless ransomed, only death brought emancipation. This most debased type of slavery in the Old World became the standard type in the New.

The Mediterranean Origins of the Plantation

Between the 1300s and the 1600s, the use of gang slaves expanded with the rise of plantation production.[4] Sugar plantations had their beginnings in the crusader kingdoms of the eastern Mediterranean. From there they spread to the western Mediterranean. As sugar production spread westward in the Mediterranean, the plantation labor force reflected the full ethnic and racial variety of infidels and heretics offered by Mediterranean slave traders, who justified their business by religion.[5] Christians and Muslims, nevertheless, bought and sold fellow believers. White and black traffickers sold victims of whatever color. From the western Mediterranean, plantation production spread to the islands along the West African coast, and finally, in the 1500s, to the New World.

Wage, or "free," labor was emerging in the home countries of the European colonizers at the same time as plantation slavery was expanding to the New World colonies. In the American colonies, diseases lurked to which Europeans had little resistance. The lure of a quick fortune tempted some free workers to the plantations, but not to work as field hands.[6] Moreover, the first colonizers, Spain and Portugal, chronically suffered a labor scarcity at home. Few colonists were available, bound or free.

The Apocalypse

At the outset the *conquistadores* appeared to have a ready source of labor. During the early 1500s, Spanish and Portuguese planters enslaved thousands of the American natives. But by the end of the century, these populations had been decimated by an apocalypse of overwork, abuse, and epidemics of diseases that their conquerors had introduced.[7] Slave catchers had to raid farther and farther away from the plantations. Without labor, all the vast "open resources" of the New World would escape the conquerors' grasp.

During this century of death, planters had been experimenting with the labor of sub-Saharan Africans, who had some resistance to the most devastating plantation killers: yellow fever and malaria. Even these slaves died in fearful numbers but survived longer than either American natives or Europeans.[8] The growing demand and high prices for sugar, rum, and tobacco in Europe provided many planters with the capital to buy the more expensive Africans. The larger and well-capitalized planters imported evermore African slaves and thrived. In the 1600s, when the English began to found colonies, their planters also began to buy black slaves. By 1700, black slavery had become the core labor force in plantation societies from Brazil to Maryland.

Free Labor versus Coerced Labor in the Atlantic Economy

The plantation system had gained new energy when European capitalism burst its medieval constraints and encompassed the Atlantic. Mediterranean plantations had been early capitalist enterprises. But these small beginnings were dwarfed by the scale of plantation production in the Americas.

In the narrowest sense, a capitalist society is one with a market economy and a wage-labor system.[9] Such societies in the 1600s existed in only a few countries, notably in the Dutch Republic, in England, and in several city states.[10] But capitalists from these countries and elsewhere were creating a great international market system that encompassed the Atlantic.

Wherever the shock waves of the market system were felt, customs were being transformed, human relationships changed, ancient values dissolved. The hitherto unheard-of luxuries that now became available inflamed traditional elites with an acquisitive zeal that matched that of the capitalists themselves. Victorious African rulers sold captive warriors—and sometimes their own subjects—as slaves. Scottish chiefs drove their kinsfolk from their ancestral lands and replaced them with sheep. Everywhere, paternalistic restraint, responsibility toward relatives and compatriots, gave way to the demands of the market.[11]

As Immanuel Wallerstein has shown, the capitalist market economy from its inception fostered the growth of two polar opposite but complementary methods of managing labor.[12] The core of the growing Atlantic economy was northwestern Europe. There, employers more and more needed skilled, strongly motivated labor. Increasingly they encouraged such workers with wages. Forms of coerced labor were falling into disuse.

In the early 1600s, the wage, or free, labor system flourished especially vigorously in the Netherlands, where high wages were attracting immigrants from all over Europe. By midcentury its highly skilled, multinational population had achieved world hegemony in technology.[13]

But capitalists also needed low-cost raw materials; and, in the countries that produced them, suppliers managed labor differently. Especially before the Industrial Revolution, raw materials could be produced most cheaply by unskilled workers endlessly repeating the same elemental operations. Each piece of timber destined for the shipyards of Amsterdam was cut and hewn like the previous one. Each basket of ore was removed from the mine exactly as had been the one before. Each ratoon of cane was planted like the last. All work could be quantitatively measured, all easily supervised. The only worker motivation required was that of animal survival.

Thus in the raw materials–producing lands, which formed a broad periphery around the core countries of northwestern Europe, a very different way of managing labor was emerging, the reverse image of the labor system used in the Dutch Republic. This new coercion of labor took several forms: the so-called second enserfment taking place in eastern Europe, the *encomienda* and *hacienda* systems of the Andean highlands and Mexico, and the plantation system of the greater West Indies, an area extending from Brazil to Maryland. There were many local variations in these labor systems, but from Peru to Poland they shared one common feature: coercion, not wages and the prospect of upward mobility, was the norm of labor.[14]

In a far-flung international division of labor, some commodities were produced by workers who were comparatively free and privileged, others by those who were debased and coerced. But in the 1600s, people in Europe rarely experienced this stark polarity. Half a continent separated the consumption-oriented Dutch worker, innovative and full of initiative, from his labor opposite, the Prussian serf, who required a few blows of the knout to get him moving. But by the 1700s, the polarity of the modern world became delineated with unmistakable clarity in England's mainland colonies, where the immigrant from the core countries confronted the slave from sub-Saharan Africa, where the difference was drawn in black and white.

This confrontation ultimately resulted from the discovery that Europe was an insatiable market for plantation commodities and the discovery that Africans, having more resistance to plantation diseases than either American natives or Europeans, were a basis for stable plantation production. Slavery had been multiracial since the days of the pharaohs. Now in the Americas it became black slavery.

Why No White Slaves in America?

As the Atlantic black slave trade expanded, the slave traders of the Mediterranean continued their religiously justified traffic in infidels, heretics, and pagans, of whatever color. During the early 1400s, most slaves sold in Western Europe had been shipped through the Mediterranean from the longtime slave export area around the Black Sea. Many of these were Slavs, and the ethnic term "Slav" had become the root word for slave in most Western European languages. The age-old image of a clownish, groveling slave, the so-called Sambo stereotype that Americans came to associate with blacks, had become attached to Slavic peoples.

But then, toward the mid-1400s, these eastern slaves began to grow scarce in the markets of Europe. Viable governments had emerged in Poland and Russia, reducing Turkish slave raids. Most captives the Turks still took in the Black Sea area they now sold within the Ottoman Empire itself.

Meanwhile, by the mid-1400s, the Portuguese had opened a sea route to a new slave export area, the Guinea Coast of Africa, previously inaccessible to Christian Europe. The Atlantic slave trade had begun. Atlantic traders were offering Africans on European markets in competition with the Slavs that the Mediterranean slave traders were offering. By the time Columbus sailed, most slaves in Western Europe were black.[15]

But then the racial composition of slavery in Europe again began to change. During the 1500s, as Old World diseases devastated American natives, the Atlantic slave trade in Africans was more and more diverted from Europe to America. By 1600, Africans who could be sold in Spain for only 80 ducats were bringing 150 or more in America.[16] Meanwhile, the Turks, in their ongoing conquest of the Balkans, had saturated their domestic market with captives and were now exporting their surplus to the West. Once again in European markets, Bulgarians, Serbs, and other eastern slaves were becoming more numerous. Later, a reversal of Turkish fortunes also put more white slaves on the market. After the Austrian victories of 1680, about two thousand Turkish, Greek, and Slavic captives were sold at Cadiz in Spain.[17]

Why did these white slaves not land in the cane fields of the labor-starved West Indies? For one thing, the Catholic monarchs of Spain discouraged sending to the colonies, where their power was insecure, anybody, free or slave, suspected of heresy or adhering to a rival religion. This suspicion fell on slaves arriving in Spain through the Mediterranean.[18] At first there were violations of official Spanish religious policy. In 1506, a royal order expelled some Muslim slaves from Hispaniola and imposed a fine of a thousand pesos or a hundred lashes on anyone who in the future would import such slaves. In 1543, other Muslim slaves were expelled from Mexico.[19]

But the laws of the market were more compelling than the laws of Spain in keeping light-skinned slaves out of the New World. First, distance was an important influence on the profits of a slave trader. The greater the distance between source and market, the greater the mortality of his cargo and the greater the shipping cost of his survivors. In the 1500s, most African captives came from the Guinea Coast. But most Caucasian ones came from the Black Sea area or from the Dalmatian coast. Both of these slave export areas were more than double the sailing distance to American markets than was the Guinea Coast.

Also, while blacks and whites in the Mediterranean countries enjoyed approximately the same life expectancy, whites sold for more. Their prices were increased by their greater prospect of being ransomed, either by their families or by ransoming societies. These were Muslim or Christian charitable organizations, which arose from centuries of conflict between Christendom and Islam. They ransomed freeborn fellow believers.[20] In practice this meant whites, since sub-Saharan Africans were rarely either freeborn Muslims or Christians.

In America there were no ransoming societies. Even more, the prospect of an African surviving the initial "seasoning period" was about three times that of a European. No merchant was likely to transport a white slave, who would sell for more than a black in a Mediterranean port, thousands of miles to the Caribbean in order to sell him for perhaps one-third as much.[21] The fact that white slaves were thus not sold in the New World reinforced the American belief that only a black could be a slave.

The Mutation in the Justification of Slavery from Religion to Race

Before English colonization, racially defined black slavery and a system of mutually reinforcing ideas and practices had been evolving in Latin American plantation societies. Now an economic shift within Europe contributed further to this evolving racial system: in the 1600s, the century of English colonization, the hub of Atlantic commerce shifted from Catholic Spain and Portugal to northwestern Europe. In this new hub, free workers were becoming more numerous and assertive. It was here, too, that the Reformation had shattered the unity of medieval Christendom and had thrown into disarray the traditional assurance against enslavement, being a freeborn "true believer." Now religious fragmentation had made everybody in this part of the world enough of a heretic, a papist, a Protestant, or a dissenter to satisfy the religious scruples of some slave trafficker.

In this new hub of Atlantic commerce, workers now eligible, somewhere or other in Christendom, for enslavement under the religious rationale manned the ships and provided the soldiers and skilled craftsmen who made the new Atlantic commercial system work. Furthermore, planters needed loyal supporters for protection against slave revolt, and to these they conceded privileges. Without the cooperation of free workers, the great Atlantic wheel of fortune would come to a halt: no Africans sold to the plantations, no plantation commodities produced for Europe, no European trading goods exported to Africa to buy more Africans. But this wheel was oiled by a new doctrine: the assurance that no white man, regardless of his religious beliefs, or his lack of beliefs, could be a slave.[22]

Spain and Portugal were influenced by both the Atlantic black slave trade and the Mediterranean multiracial slave trade. So in these countries some ambiguity remained whether it was color or religion that made one a slave. In the larger Atlantic World, however, by the 1600s the idea that white skin made one free and black skin made one a slave was widely held. In actuality, even as late as 1631, Turkish slave catchers seized victims on the English coast.[23] Yet, while the English of that day would have regarded a black breaking rock in a Turkish quarry as a "slave," the Hollander or Briton working next to him was more likely to have been a "captive." Certainly no one called Captain John Smith, one of the founders of Virginia, an escaped slave. He was white, British, and he had been a "captive" of the Turks.

The color definition of slavery in the Atlantic World thus made white slavery disappear by definition. A white man who spent his last days chained to the oar of a galley, or toiling in a plantation work gang, was a "captive," a "convict," or a "temporary servant." This new language of color and servitude had implications that extended beyond the institution of slavery. As surely as coercion and debasement did not make a white worker truly a slave, so emancipation did not make a black one truly free.

The change from the traditional religious justification of slavery to the new racial one did not occur without conflict. The issue of what made one a slave first became evident in Spain and Spanish America. Present here was a strong undercurrent of Christian idealism. Some Christian idealists saw their mission in the empire as the spread of the Catholic faith. They did not wish to see it colonized by unbelievers, free or slave. But planters saw their mission as the profitable production of sugar and rum, a goal often in conflict with Catholic idealism.

As far back as Christian memory reached, whenever slaves accepted baptism they could expect better treatment and even eventual freedom. To be sure, planters could derive some comfort from the papal briefs of Nicholas II and Callixtus III, which granted to the Portuguese king Alfonso V the right not only to conquer "enemies of Christ," unbelievers and pagans, but also to "reduce them to servitude forever."[24] Nevertheless, for a thousand years and more, the baptism of an unbeliever had been celebrated as a joyous victory for the true faith.[25]

Better Treatment for "Brothers-in-Christ"?

If the traditional idea that slaves becoming "brothers-in-Christ" implied their better treatment, the profitable operation of plantations required their continuing debasement. Racial ideology provided an escape from this dilemma. Black slaves could change their religion but not their color. Racial ideology offered the possibility of rigid, caste-like lines of social stratification.

At the very beginning of the Atlantic slave trade, a racial version of the Hamitic myth, long current in northern Africa and southwestern Asia, now made its appearance in Christian Europe. In this late retelling of a biblical story (Genesis 9:21–27), the claim is made that Noah intended blacks when he cursed the descendants of Ham to perpetual slavery.[26]

During the 1500s, derogatory slave-trade lore about Africans began to appear in the cities and colonies, wherever Europeans were buying, selling, or exploiting African slaves, the same things that late medieval Muslim masters had said about the captives that the caravans brought them from beyond the Sahara.

Africans thus encountered most of the same racial prejudices in the colonial Americas that had been current in those Mediterranean countries where most slaves were black. But the results were different. In the Old World, most slaves could continue to look forward to mitigated servitude and even emancipation as they adopted the master's religion and assimilated the new culture. In Muslim countries, some black Africans thus became influential administrators, generals, some indeed mothers of sultans. Even their color, the telltale evidence of their *kaffir,* or pagan, origin was not, over the passing generations, indelible. Racial prejudice did not prevent high-status men from marrying black women.[27] No doctrines of permanent inferiority appeared.

The Impact of Capitalism on Slavery

In the Americas, where slavery was being modified by early capitalism, the story of racial ideas was different. Conversion was no longer a claim for better treatment, a step toward emancipation and full integration into the community. Most of the language of Old World paternalism, including a religious justification of slavery, crossed the Atlantic, but little of its substance. The overseer who supervised slaves, often for an absentee owner or trading company, did not regard them as inferior members of his extended family. He was likely to be a desperate individual, lured to a fever-infested plantation region in hope of eluding death from the "bloody flux" long enough to acquire a fortune that he could enjoy in Portugal, Holland, or some other civilized country. In his chaotic world, all that counted were results, profits. All else would be forgiven. Simon Legree was a creation of Harriet Beecher Stowe's literary imagination. But in the real world, such characters had an ancestry going back to the dawn of capitalism.

Slavery in the Americas often flourished in locations that were remote from the constraining influences of law courts, the church, or even the family. In the religious tradition, masters had often mitigated the servitude of baptized slaves and emancipated those they thought most worthy. These customs fared badly in lands where the conquerors saw open resources, yet their labor supply disappeared as rapidly as the burial ground grew. Their visions of wealth were threatened by amelioration and manumission. In the traditional view, slavery was a ladder leading upward to the true faith. But racial ideology broke all the rungs of the ladder, offering masters the prospect of keeping slaves permanently at the most debased level.

The Rise and Fall of Latin American *Castas*

In the broader society beyond the plantations, where Europeans scrambled for the Americas' open resources, the defining of status by color kept more people at the bottom producing wealth and fewer at the top competing for a share. The Spaniards and the Portuguese gave a great deal of attention to making racial distinctions in their colonies, to drawing color lines. They instituted a system of racial *castas,* which conceded the most privileges to whites, fewer to Indians, and virtually none to black people.

The system of castas, however, showed signs of disintegration from the outset. Spain and Portugal, with a labor shortage at home, sent few settlers to America, and these mostly young males. They mated with native or black women and thus produced new castas of mixed ancestry and mixed privileges. Subsequent generations produced even newer castas of even more finely differentiated shades of tan, each with its ratio of European, native, and African ancestry, and hence with an even more complicated claim to preference over other status groups supposed to be darker.

"In Spain it is almost a title of nobility to descend neither from Jews or Moors," wrote Alexander von Humboldt, following an extended tour of Latin America about 1800.

> In America, the greater or less degree of whiteness of skin decides the rank which a man occupies in society. A white who rides barefoot on horseback thinks he belongs to the nobility of the country. Colour establishes even a certain equality among men, who . . . take a particular pleasure in dwelling on the prerogatives of race and origin. When a common man disputes with one of the titled lords of the country, he is frequently heard to say, "Do you think me not so white as yourself?" . . . It becomes consequently a very interesting business for the public vanity to estimate accurately the fractions of European blood which belong to the different cast[e]s.[28]

The Conquest shaped the racial values and racial behavior that have become characteristic of much of Latin America: pride about things European, shame about things African or native. European racial features evoke conquerors, wealth, and power; non-European features, defeat, servitude, poverty, and humiliation. In the eighteenth century, Montesquieu remarked that Spaniards who had migrated to Latin America considered that they had "the sublime merit to be, as they say, *men of white flesh.* There has never been in the seraglio of the Great Sultan a sultana so proud of her beauty as the ugliest old dog in a Mexican city is of his whitish olive complexion, as he sits in his doorway with his arms folded. A man of this importance, a creature so perfect, would not do manual labor for all the treasure in the world; and would never choose, by common labor, to compromise the honor and dignity of his skin."[29]

But due to the scarcity of whites, a tri-racial multitude made its way into the militia, the lower ranks of the bureaucracy, and even the clergy. The white family remained numerically weak throughout the colonial period. A legitimate family eventually superseded the casual mating patterns of the conquest. Yet although racial mixtures varied from colony to colony and especially according to social class, few families could claim a racial purity that would stand scrutiny.[30]

The Conquest and the practice of slavery left Latin Americans with a tradition that links light skin with high status. They also have a legacy of derogatory lore about Africans that came with the slave trade. But unlike in the United States of the nineteenth and twentieth centuries, these pejorative ideas about Africans have always been whispered, not shouted from the political campaign stump. (In Latin America one was often talking about one's own acknowledged relatives.) Also, the predominance of the racially mixed family undermined any racial defense of slavery. For a militia captain or a planter whose mother or grandmother was black, it was awkward to cite African ancestry as a justification for slavery.[31] In Latin America, no clearly defined color line was consolidated.

By 1700, as the Latin American system of castas was disintegrating into racial convergence, a very different development was taking place in the English colonies of the North American mainland. There, the population was becoming stabilized into two caste-like status groups, identified as "white" and "black."

Chapter 2

Anglo Americans Adopt the Atlantic Racial System

Between the Jamestown settlement in 1607 and the War for Independence, the English who settled the mainland plantation colonies created a race-conscious society remarkably different from the class-conscious one they had left behind. In England the great divide had been between "people of quality" and "the multitude." By the time of Independence, however, a new mentality, later called "American exceptionalism," had appeared that minimized or even denied class distinctions. The mark dividing the haves from the have-nots was now color: slavery was black; freedom and opportunity white.

This society was different, too, from the one that had evolved in Latin America. There the status lines between the castas had become negotiable and were constantly shifting. In some colonies they were disappearing as racial blending progressed. But in the English mainland plantation colonies, two distinct populations had been established, joined by few ties of kinship and these not publicly acknowledged. Law and custom recognized just two racial colors, black and white.[1] And the decree of color was final.

This new social order had begun with the good business sense of English planters. Black slaves had been an option for them from the beginning, and they had bought a few.[2] But in the early years of colonization, slaves were scarce, expensive, and a risky investment in the deadly colonial disease environment. Planters had little trouble acquiring English workers as temporary bound servants, often just for the cost of transporting them. A few of these were freed Afro-Britons.[3] But overwhelmingly, planters had formed their labor force with white servants.

By the second century of settlement, however, a fundamental change had taken place: a large number of slaves had been imported from Africa. Almost all Africans were now being held as slaves. Most whites had become entirely free, many indeed landholders. Those who were still servants increasingly were people with skills.[4] Their servitude was regulated by indentures, or contracts, that specified the length of time they were to serve, under what conditions, and the "freedom dues" they were to receive upon completion of their terms. Most important, unlike in the early days of settlement when justice had been arbitrary, the terms of their contracts were now enforceable in colonial courts. A huge difference in status separated even these remaining servants from slaves.

Yet ideas about race and status that would become characteristic of the later South still did not form the mentality of ordinary white settlers. In the older colonies of the Atlantic World, the ideological equations—black equals slave, white equals free—had long existed. But for common settlers of England's mainland colonies the great divide was not yet between whites and blacks. It was still that of the old country: between gentlemen and commoners.

Revolutionary Changes in English Society

The early Tudor monarchs had confiscated the lands of their secular and religious opponents and distributed them among their supporters. This had furthered the growth of a class of market-oriented landlords who began to "enclose" as their private property what had been community lands.

The labor needs of these new landlords had been poorly served by large numbers of free tenants, and even less by villeins, as British serfs were called, who had traditional claims to the land and forest, and who stubbornly clung to time-honored patterns of work. So the new landlords freed the villeins and drastically downsized the rural labor force, retaining some selected workers whom they contracted for temporary terms.[5]

This modernization of agriculture and livestock production was a feature of "the English Revolution," which in the 1500s and 1600s held great promise for the future, but at a devastating human cost. For patriots, the freeing of the villeins was a soaring achievement, making England the land of the free. But urban-centered industries could not yet provide enough employment. So unemployment, homelessness, and crime also soared. If the thousands of emancipated but landless villeins wandering on the country roads and swelling the population of the cities were now "free workers," people at the time were likely to call them vagabonds or sturdy beggars.[6]

The large uprooted population of the British Isles, along with the social disruption that these homeless caused, gave an explosive force to English colonization. This nation, with two-thirds the population of Spain and scarcely one-quarter that of France, in the first half of the 1600s may have sent as many immigrants to America as the rest of Europe combined.[7]

The immigrants' pattern of settlement is startling. Of all the colonies one might choose in the early 1600s, those in New England enjoyed the best reputation. Health conditions there were as good as or better than in England, and land was still available. Yet only about 10 percent went to New England. In the southern colonies, on the other hand, health conditions were poor, life short. In the West Indies, conditions were even worse, life even shorter, and little or no land was available to survivors. Yet more than two-thirds of the English immigrants ended up in the West Indies. Most of the rest went to the mainland plantation colonies where, as in the West Indies, the majority died from disease during their initial, or "seasoning," period.[8]

American schoolbooks have stressed the freedom or, at worst, the temporary and contractual servitude of English plantation workers and the slavery of Africans. Yet in the early 1600s, if the uprooted English were free to sign or not sign themselves into servitude, why did they in such overwhelming numbers end up in the West Indies, where they had almost no chance of getting land but an excellent chance of getting a terminal case of "bloody flux"?

To make sense of this paradox, we must consider not what freedom in America came to mean a century later, but what it meant in Britain on the eve of colonization and during the period of the great "swarming of the English" in the early 1600s. During these earlier years, the new labor system of the entrepreneurial English landlords still bore some of the marks of the villeinage that it was replacing. Now the rural poor, "freed" from their hereditary tenure to the land, could bind themselves to a master for a term of years, at the end of which, competing with other unemployed workers, they would attempt to negotiate another term of years. This system of end-to-end terms of temporary servitude of workers intimidated by massive unemployment served well the new entrepreneurial class. It enabled them to get rid of inefficient, tradition-bound hands and build a labor force that was more flexible, more innovative, and disciplined by the threat of unemployment.[9]

The government's solution to unemployment was to make it a crime. In December 1591, on the eve of colonization, the clerk of the Middlesex county court noted that during the previous ten weeks, "71 persons, male or female, and aged fourteen or upward, were sentenced to be severely whipt and branded with a hot iron for being masterless vagrants."[10] And these were first offenders. When Margaret Archer and Joan Winston (or Wynston) were hauled into court, their cases were more serious. The two had been convicted of vagrancy once before. "Putting themselves 'Guilty,' both women pleaded pregnancy. Found pregnant by a jury of matrons, Margaret Archer was remanded. Found 'Not Pregnant' by the same jury of matrons, Joan Wynston was forthwith sentenced to be hung."[11]

With the onset of colonization, the English justice system took a different direction. Later in the same court, twenty-four convicted men and women "pleaded the King's special pardon, . . . under condition that they and each of them shall within two months go out of England . . . [to Virginia or] Barbadoes or some other part of America inhabited by the King's subjects, and do not return . . . for seven years"[12] No advance payment was required for a passage to the plantations. So the choice that many immigrants made was not between Massachusetts and Barbados, but rather between the plantations and the gallows.[13]

The Equality of Misery of Servants and Slaves

These colonists in a sense were free workers. They had more choices than those brought from Africa. They usually signed or put their X on contracts or indentures. Once in the colonies, indentured servants, technically their work contracts, might be sold at auction. In Barbados, for example, they were "being bought and sold . . . from one Planter to another or attached as horses or beasts for the debts of their masters, being whipt at the whipping posts." They worked under overseers in gangs that included slaves. Like slaves, they were sometimes branded on the face or forced to wear an iron collar.[14] Under a 1639 Maryland law, a runaway servant could be put to death.[15] Whatever their legal status, servants were being treated as chattel, or disposable property.

So much were they treated like slaves, beside whom they often toiled, that there were times when the colonial authorities were afraid that they would make common cause with slaves. A group of Virginia planters, having failed to recapture a band of escaped slaves, worried that "other negroes, Indians or servants . . . [might] fly forth and joyne with them."[16] There were also reports of Irish workers conspiring with Africans in Bermuda, Barbados, and Maryland.[17]

The one important difference between servants and slaves was that servants, if they survived their three-year to ten-year terms, might claim their freedom. Yet these terms might be extended for crime or for a myriad of religious and other infractions, or their masters might pressure them to sign a new contract before the old one was fulfilled.[18] The legal distinction between slaves and servants never completely disappeared. In theory only blacks served "forever." But in the disease-plagued cane fields of the Caribbean, and in the pestilent bottomlands of the mainland plantations, for most temporary servants, their servitude was forever.[19]

Allegations of slavery and reports of pestilence and death, reached the home country, making recruiting more difficult.[20] The "crimps," or recruiting agents, became more heavy-handed, especially in Ireland. Following thirteen years of war, 1641–54, and after extensive land confiscations by the English conquerors, Ireland suffered massive destitution and vagabondage. In 1654, the British Commissioners for Ireland ordered the governors of the military garrisons to turn over to a group of English merchants prisoners of war, convicts, and inmates of work houses, and by March of the following year 6,500 of these were sent to the plantations. The next year, 2,000 boys and girls, aged twelve to fourteen, were assembled in Galway for shipment to the newly conquered colony of Jamaica. The Reverend John Grace, a Catholic priest who visited the West Indies in 1666, "found 12,000 Irish slaves in Barbadoes."[21]

The Kidnappers

The activities of the "spirits," or kidnappers, were a growing scandal in England.[22] So long as severe unemployment persisted, however, there was little official recognition of the problem. If plantation recruiting agents operated outside the law, the end result was to solve the vagabond problem in England and the labor problem on the plantations.

When "spiriting" finally did begin to surface in the court records, the individuals being prosecuted were often charged, not with kidnapping, but rather with provoking a riot or some other offense against a suspected kidnapper. In 1657, for example, Sarah Sharp was charged with an attack on Katherine Wall, "tearing her by the hair of her head, and byting her arm" and alleging that Wall was "a common taker up of children, and a setter to betray young men and maydens to be conveyed into shipps, and hath at this time fower [four] persons aboard a ship where of one is a child about elevan years of age."[23] It would not be until later in the century, when English employers were beginning to feel the pinch of a labor shortage, that pressure would be brought to bear on the government to regulate and restrict emigration. It was only then that the government began a concerted campaign against the kidnappers.

The Upturn of the British Economy Diminishes Pressure on the Poor to Emigrate

In the late 1600s, a number of developments improved the conditions of the poor in the home country. For one thing, the rate of population growth slowed. The thousands of homeless died quicker and had fewer surviving children. Also the agricultural revolution, which originally had caused so much misery, now was converting England into a food surplus country.[24] Workers were thus becoming less plentiful, food more so. Then too, there were rapidly growing job openings, especially in the textile and maritime industries.[25] All in all, workers were now in a much stronger bargaining position.

Also the reexport trade in colonial commodities grew rapidly, and in the late century, England came to dominate trade in the Atlantic market's fastest expanding and most profitable products: sugar, rum, and tobacco. After defeating the Dutch in three wars, and after the formation of the Royal African Company, in 1672, England also dominated the Atlantic slave trade.[26]

Political events too accelerated England's economic development. A group of leaders, who were later called the "Whig oligarchy" and who were strongly committed to the expansion of English commerce and industry, consolidated their power during the second half of the 1600s. During this time, they inflicted military defeat on their Dutch rivals and reduced them to junior partners. Historically, the House of Commons had been their base of power. But, in 1688, with their "Glorious Revolution," they gained control over the crown as well. They were able to choose their king and queen. The resulting government was a pro-business consensus so stable that for the next hundred years the nation had virtually a one-party system.

The Glorious Revolution also had international consequences favorable to England's economic growth. By picking the leading political figure of the Dutch Republic to be king of England, the "Whig oligarchy" partially reconciled the Dutch to their new position as England's junior partners. This event also created political conditions favorable to the free flow of capital from the Dutch Republic, which had the world's largest accumulation of capital, to England, which, after 1688, had the most attractive conditions for capital investment.[27] English wages began to rise and continued to rise for a century. A labor surplus became a labor shortage.[28] The Elizabethan fear of overpopulation now gave way to what one scholar has called "an almost fanatical desire to increase population."[29]

Labor Shortage Brings Government Protection

As employers in the home country competed for labor, the authorities began to take measures to mitigate the shortage. In Bristol, for example, the city authorities in 1654 put strictures on persons "Inveighing, purloining, carrying and Stealing away Boyes, Maides and other persons and transporting them beyond Seas and there selling or otherwise disposeing them for private gaine and profit."[30] In 1664, the Registry of Servants Office was created. Now anyone who bought or sold unregistered servants risked kidnapping charges. Parliament began to hear the petitions of the victims.

With the changing attitude of the government, fewer and fewer servants were being shipped to the colonies, and their prices rose sharply. They "will no longer go on ordinary terms," complained a gentleman who was seeking workers for his plantations in the Leeward Islands. "And the Lord Chief Justice hath so severely handled the kidnappers, and so encouraged all informers against them, that it is very difficult to procure any. One of the kidnappers, a slopseller, hath been fined five hundred pounds sterling; and Mr. Bauden and Mr. Baxler, with several eminent men, have been in some trouble on this score; and poor Captain Winter is prosecuted and put into print."[31] While the seizure and forcible transport of Africans was increasing, these methods for recruiting English labor were sharply reduced.

Law Comes to the Colonies

Increasingly, the protection of law also reached the overseas plantations. And as colonial legislatures became concerned about the dwindling flow of servants to the plantations, they took measures to repair the slavish reputation that the colonies had in England. Virginia, for example, invalidated new indentures signed while old ones were still in force, thus preventing servants from being pressured into negotiating a new term while they were still subject to coercion by their masters. Maryland repealed its "Shamefull Matches" act "to prevent persons from purchasing White women [as servants] and marrying them to their slaves for the purpose of making slaves of them."[32] Now with the royal government taking an interest in what happened to English subjects overseas, and colonial governments taking steps to attract immigrants, the legal distinction between a temporary servant's rights and a slave's lack of rights became much more important.

Yet the favorable turn for the legal rights of servants did not bring a flood of English workers to the southern plantations. The opposite occurred. Planters found it harder and harder to recruit a sufficient number of servants.[33] More and more English workers shunned colonial labor recruiters and tried their chances at home. Those who still emigrated, furthermore, favored the northern settler colonies.

English employers were in a stronger political position than were colonial planters. With their new concern about the slavish conditions that their fellow countrymen suffered on the plantations, their insistence on stronger laws against kidnapping, and stricter enforcement by the courts, they were in a position to pass on some of the home country's labor shortage to the places where the problem had always been most acute, the overseas plantations.[34] But to do so was to threaten one of the most promising segments of the home economy, the lucrative reexport trade in plantation commodities.

The Upsurge in the Atlantic Slave Trade

The African slave trade provided an escape from this dilemma. Happily for employers in England and planters in the colonies, the Atlantic slave trade took a dramatic upturn in the mid-1600s. The estimates of Philip D. Curtin tell the story: 187,000 slaves arrived in the New World during the first quarter of the century, 182,300 during the second quarter; but then 368,500 during the third and 602,500 during the last quarter.[35]

Not only was the slave trade expanding sharply, but also more and more of these slaves were being brought to the English mainland plantations and transported in English ships as England came to dominate the trade. Until nearly the end of the century, the destination of the slave ships had been Latin America and the West Indies. Any slaves who ended up in North America or England were no more than the overflow from this trade.[36] But the sharp upsurge in the trade saturated Latin American and West Indian markets and transformed the overflow reaching North America from a trickle to a stream until, toward the end of the century, some slave ships bypassed Latin America and the West Indies altogether and unloaded their cargoes in the ports of the southern mainland.[37]

Why the steep upturn of the slave trade after midcentury, with all its sinister implications for the future? Behind this momentous development lay a conjuncture of events and a host of decisions. As important as these decisions were to the creation of a racially stratified society in the future United States, the men who made them acted from practical business concerns.[38]

The Relocation of Dutch Capital Spurs a Sugar Boom

Dutch investors, with an eye on the phenomenal market for sugar and rum that was opening up in Europe, decided to transfer their capital and advanced sugar technology from their insecure foothold in Brazil to the virgin lands of the Caribbean, where the climatic conditions for growing sugar cane were better and where Holland's great fleet could offer better protection. This decision created a sugar boom in the Caribbean, from which their sometime rivals, sometime allies, the English planters, especially benefited. As one English writer noted, "heither to the Collonies did not thrive, but were like to bee extinguish[ed] for want of provisions untill it happen'd that the Duch loosing Brasille, many Duch and Jews repairing to Barbadoes began the planting and making sugar, which caused the Duch with shipping often to relieve them and Credit when they were ready to perish . . . , this was the first rise of the plantation that made it able to subsist and trafficke."[39] The sugar boom was taking place in the West Indies, where the annihilation of the indigenous population was most complete, and where the fate of European workers had been not much better. The expansion of the sugar and rum market thus increased even more the demand for labor in the already labor-starved lands of the Caribbean.

The End of the Portuguese Slave-Trade Monopoly

In addition to the decision of the Dutch to shift their interests from Brazil to the Caribbean, the Spanish Council of the Indies also made a decision that would contribute to the phenomenal increase in the slave trade and hence contribute to English planters' turn from white indentured servitude to black slavery. The council decided to throw open for international competition the *asiento,* or contract, to supply Spanish America with slaves. The Portuguese, who had been supplying most of the slaves to the Americas, could no longer meet the ever-growing demand. Also, since Portugal had gained its independence from the Spanish Empire in 1640, that nation no longer had any special claim to the asiento, which had given them a virtual monopoly on the African slave trade.[40]

The decision of the Dutch to shift their capital and know-how to the islands and the Spanish decision to throw open the asiento had a sensational impact

on European shippers and investors. Thanks to the sugar boom in the Caribbean, slaves could be sold there for more than five times what they had cost
in Africa.[41] Thanks to the Spanish decision, the Portuguese could no longer
dominate the African coast and treat competitors as pirates. Without waiting
to see what nation would finally be awarded the asiento, investors from many
lands rushed into the business. Soon the Portuguese were confronted with
new competitors from Holland, England, France, Genoa, Denmark, Sweden,
Brandenburg, and New England. Free-for-all competition received another
boost in 1698 when the English government divested the Royal African Company of its monopoly over the English share of the trade, legalizing the slave
trade for upstart English shippers. By 1700, even South Carolina slave ships
appeared in the river Gambia in West Africa.[42]

Slave ships began arriving to the English mainland colonies more frequently,
their captains offering slaves at prices that large planters could afford. With
servant prices rising sharply, the larger tobacco planters began to buy substantial numbers of African slaves. These were still more expensive than servants.
But, with improved health conditions, they soon became a self-perpetuating
labor supply requiring no new capital outlay.[43]

The White-Black Demographics and the Color Line

The long delay in the introduction of significant numbers of slaves into England's
mainland plantation colonies influenced the kind of society that arose there. The
delay resulted in a demographic development strikingly different from that in
Latin America. As we have seen in chapter 1, the Spanish and Portuguese conquerors were a relatively small number of males who established their control
over large settled native populations. From the outset they mated with native
women, later often with African women. Before large numbers of white women
arrived, the original European settlers had already sired several generations of
people with varying shades of skin color and degrees of status.[44]

On the other hand, during the formative period of the English mainland
colonies, roughly the 1600s, the settlers were essentially a displaced English
rural population, about one-third of whom were women, brought into an
area with a very small and periodically shifting native population. The white
settlers were, therefore, from the beginning essentially endogamous; that is,
they married or mated with each other. Once they had made some adjustment to the disease environment, they were self-perpetuating, even increasing. Late in the century, to this original settler population from Europe was
added a displaced agricultural population from Africa that also consisted of

about one-third women. They too were essentially endogamous; and, after they had made an adjustment to the disease environment, they too were self-perpetuating and increasing.[45]

But in virtually no other way were these two populations alike. Unlike the earlier sprinkling of English-speaking, Christian Afro-Britons, the great majority of blacks now came directly from Africa and were originally different from the whites in language, religion, and custom. Yet, most of all, they differed in legal and economic condition.

American Freedom, American Slavery

The whites were free, or would become free, in a land where labor was scarce and resources abundant. For those who were still servants, America had become a land where the legal rights of a servant received more recognition as the arbitrary justice of early governors was superseded by the laws of colonial legislatures and the decisions of courts. More and more servants became "seasoned" to the disease environment and survived their terms. In some of the older settled areas in the lowlands, health conditions remained poor, especially for recent immigrants.[46] Yet higher and healthier land to the west was becoming available, as native peoples succumbed to Old World epidemics or were driven out by settlers. By the late 1600s and into the 1700s, many servants would find themselves free in a country where their labor was much in demand, where rich land was abundant and cheap, and where the livestock they acquired multiplied prodigiously in an unfenced wilderness.[47] Adam Smith was optimistic about the opportunities made possible by these fortunate circumstances:

> Every colonist gets more land than he can possibly cultivate. He has no rent, and scarcely any taxes to pay. No landlord shares with him its produce, and the share of the sovereign is commonly but a trifle. . . . But his land is commonly so extensive, that . . . he can seldom make it produce the tenth part of what it is capable of producing. He is eager, therefore, to collect labourers . . . , and to reward them with the most liberal wages. But those liberal wages, joined to the plenty and cheapness of land, soon make those labourers leave him in order to become landlords themselves.[48]

Liberal wages, cheapness of land, every colonist becoming a land owner. Certainly many colonists came to own land. But no slave did.

Freedom in America in the 1700s was key to everything else. To be free meant the opportunity to harvest the riches of a land that stretched away to the west seemingly forever. But to own slaves was to magnify by tenfold, or even a hundredfold, the wealth that one could gather in from this fertile land.

To command one's own labor was to prosper. To command the labor of others was to grow rich. To do either, one had to have white skin.

Latin Americans drew color lines. But those making these distinctions and their victims were often separated by little distance either in color or status and were indeed often connected by ties of family. In Anglo America, however, blacks and whites were separated by a chasm, bridged by few kinship ties and these unacknowledged. Long before segregation became a passion, it was a physical fact.

An English immigrant arriving in Virginia in 1700 was moving into a different social environment, moving from a land where rich families enjoyed the services of a few household slaves to one where rich planters worked many slaves in their fields. Slavery now had a new meaning: In England when one saw a coach-and-four driven by a black slave, one knew that the owner was a person of wealth and power. But in Virginia when one saw a plantation cultivated by scores of black slaves, these slaves were more than status symbols. They were the very source of wealth and power.

English mainland plantation society had taken on some features of the older plantation societies of Latin America and the West Indies. In these lands, whites had long ago formed ideas about race and status. They were imbued with the slave trade's legacy of anti-African lore. And they assumed that a black man was or was recently a slave, while a white man who was being treated like a slave was a "convict," a "temporary servant," or a "captive." But in the 1600s, not many slaves had arrived in either England or the English mainland plantation colonies, nor had many of the ideas that came with the slave traders. The settlers' ideas were still those of England.

In the plantation colonies, Anglo American ideology did not change overnight. But change it did. In England, the world was composed of "people of quality" and "the multitude." This distinction did not disappear from the Old South. But it became overshadowed by a more important distinction. The world of the Old South was divided between blacks and whites.

Chapter 3

The Construction of Planter Hegemony, 1676–1776

Mature slave-based societies presented an astounding paradox: People who by their own self-interest might be expected to oppose slavery were in fact the master's staunch defenders. In the fourth century B.C., Plato wrote, "Suppose some god should catch up a man who has fifty or more slaves and waft him with his wife and children away from the city and set him down with . . . his slaves in a solitude where no freeman could come to his rescue. What and how great would be his fear?"[1] A Greek master having trouble with his slaves could expect his mostly non-slaveholding neighbors to rush to his rescue. In another slave-based society, two thousand years later and a half a world away, the Virginian George Fitzhugh had the same expectation: "The poor [whites] constitute our militia and our police. [They] secure men in the possession of a kind of property [slaves] which they could not hold a day, but for the supervision and protection of the poor."[2]

Plato's fellow citizens thought that Greeks were more intelligent than the "barbarians" that they held as slaves, and that this superiority made all Greeks, rich or poor, equal and obligated to help each other. Fitzhugh's fellow citizens had a similar idea about white people. Yet in reality slavery by no means made free people equal. On the contrary it widened their differences in wealth and power. By commanding the labor of slaves, a master could multiply his wealth and power five times or fifty times over that of his non-slaveholding neighbors.

Slavery also increased the authority of the patriarch over his family, and inflated his masculine ego. Even his wife, as much as she might benefit from slavery, might find herself diminished. Mary Chestnut, whose husband was heir to one of the largest fortunes in land and slaves in South Carolina, confided to her diary, "like the patriarchs of old our men live in one house with their wives & concubines."[3] Also, Catherine Hammond, wife of a onetime governor and multiterm senator of South Carolina, was so upset by the situation on their Redcliffe Plantation that she returned for a time to her family of origin. Her husband and their son, Harry, were sharing the same slave mistress, Louisa. Louisa was also the elder Hammond's own daughter by another slave, Sally Johnson, thus the half-sister of young Harry.[4]

An entire community felt threatened when slaveholders flooded the area with hostile strangers. Many a free craftsman was undermined by a planter's slave craftsman. And by the 1850s, with the end of the Old South's westward expansion, planters expanded their domains *within* the South. More and more, only marginal land remained for plain white farmers and livestock herders, and increasing numbers of them were being reduced to sharecroppers. Why indeed did free citizens, from ancient Greece to the Old South, spring like watchdogs to defend slaveholding patriarchs? How is one to explain the final paradox of the Old South, where whites, two-thirds of whom owned no slaves, rallied to their leaders for a rich man's war that was a poor man's fight? How did they become so keenly sensitized to the slaveholder's needs, so anesthetized to the plight of the slave and even to their own well-being?

Over the centuries people have embraced myths that harnessed their energies to the objectives of others. To discover why they have done so is to probe the secrets of power. During his prison years, Antonio Gramsci contemplated the mystery of why individuals and entire social classes could be mobilized to advance agendas that were often injurious to themselves. He offered a theory of power that may illuminate some of the paradoxes of the Old South.

According to Gramsci, a dominant group may control a society simply by rewarding supporters and punishing enemies. But with no more than this, their rule is insecure, mere "domination." No matter how princely their rewards or how fearful their punishments, the power of such rulers is fragile. They cannot trust those they bribe or bully. Stable power, which he called "hegemony," or "legitimacy," requires much more, what would later be called "winning the hearts and minds." To accomplish this, an elite group can consolidate control by means of a hegemonic ideology that legitimizes their agenda and their authority and becomes a popular consensus accepted as self-evident truth by all classes.[5] Hegemony is achieved when common citizens look upon their leaders not as "they," but as "we," not as "those who govern us," but as "our government."

Planter hegemony began to emerge by about 1700, toward the end of the first century of settlement. It resulted from a realignment of social classes which, in the words of Edmund S. Morgan, pitted "white men of every rank against colored men of every tint."[6] Race replaced class as the norm of political bonding.

During the 1700s, planters and plain whites were allied by common objectives. But they did not yet express the idea that race was the basis for this political alliance. It was more than a century later, only after planter society had entered a crisis phase, threatened by an abolitionist challenge from without and by class tensions from within, that southern leaders began to articulate the white solidarity myth, the idea that white skin made one equal to any other white and superior to any nonwhite. It was only then, when the inequality of rich and poor had become glaring, that southern leaders expressed ever more stridently the notion that color made all whites equal.

The Rebellions

In the early decades of settlement, the settlers' world was composed of "people of quality" and "the multitude." The realignment of social classes in which race came to overshadow class as the norm for political bonding matured in the 1700s. The new order's origins were rebellions that swept the Greater Chesapeake, a region extending from the Albemarle Sound area of North Carolina across low country Virginia and Maryland to the Delaware River: Bacon's Rebellion in Virginia in 1676, Culpepper's Rebellion in neighboring parts of North Carolina in 1677, and perhaps the Glorious Revolution in Maryland in 1689. These upheavals each had causes that were immediate and local. But more generally, they resulted from unrest that was common to the entire region. Out of these upheavals ultimately would come a society that had replaced the whites' class conflicts between the rich and poor with a racial alliance, under planter hegemony, against the American natives and against the blacks, slave or free.

Before the rebellions, the Chesapeake's planter elite did not look on plain whites as the sturdy yeomen that they would become, whom, a hundred years later, the great planter, Thomas Jefferson, would praise as "the chosen people of God." To this colonial elite they were still the sturdy beggars that they had always been, England's surplus poor transported to the plantations as bound laborers.

These ex-servants were growing in number, some landless and footloose, others now farmers and cattle herders. They were class conscious and antagonistic toward the colonial elite who, in Gramsci's terms, "dominated" the region.

Already some of the paradoxes of the Old South were apparent. First of all, the southern colonies were more thinly populated than those in the North, yet suffered greater population pressure. A half-century of continuous plantation monoculture had already exhausted much land. Declining yields drove planters to seek virgin bottomlands for new plantations.[7] At the same time, an increasing number of former servants had growing livestock herds and sought forage on open range. Unlike in the North, open-range livestock production was possible because forage for animals was available, albeit in much reduced supply, during winter.[8] So long as population remained thin, therefore, southern pioneers could amass large herds.[9] But the bottomlands along the banks of streams, where cattle fed in winter on frost-resistant reeds, were favorite locations for plantations. With population growth, and even greater multiplication of livestock, the pioneer cattle herders were now likely to find in the bottomlands a fence with a planter's "No Trespassing" sign.[10]

Land hunger led to class conflicts. Prosperity for both planter and herdsman depended on an expanding frontier. When governments negotiated Indian treaties, these often caused frontier expansion to stall, giving rise to unrest, internal conflicts over land.[11] Out of these conflicts emerged the Old South, a society extraordinarily well armed and aggressive that usually ignored the treaty rights of the native peoples.

Bacon's Rebellion

Bacon's Rebellion encapsulates the main conflicts that gave rise to the Old South. There was a glaring disconnect between the way Virginia was governed and the growing number and power of the newly emancipated servants. Governor William Berkeley's council was a tiny circle of his friends and relatives that the colonists called the "Green Spring faction," named for Berkeley's plantation near Jamestown.[12] Even some substantial planters were not included in this circle.

The governor's main trouble, however, came from the now footloose former servants. "How miserable is the man," Berkeley complained, who governs "a People wher six parts of seven are Poore Endebted Discontented and Armed."[13] Their discontent was intensified by what lay beyond the frontier: an unfenced wilderness where they could raise gigantic livestock herds that would make them prosperous and perhaps even make them planters.

The solution to the land crisis, to the claustrophobia and class conflicts of the 1600s, seems simple enough: beyond the fall line of the rivers lay the Piedmont country of Virginia and the Carolinas. It was rich and, by English standards, virtually uninhabited. But there were obstacles to the occupation of this territory. In the first place, this wilderness belonged to someone. Much of it belonged to great speculators, often the more important tidewater planters. Some of it still belonged to Native Americans whose rights were secured by treaties with the English government.[14]

All settlers, rich and poor, were land hungry. But for many plain whites, land was a bitter class issue. This was because speculators preferred to lease their frontier land to tenants, who, having no money, paid rent with labor. They cleared fields, constructed buildings, and planted orchards, converting cheap frontier land into valuable plantation land. But the poor wanted to be independent farmers, not tenants. As they worked as tenants, as they improved the land, they were raising its price. They were reducing their prospects for becoming independent owners.[15] Their labor only enriched the speculators.

The poor preferred to ignore land titles, to simply occupy, or "squat," on wilderness land. But squatting was risky business. To occupy someone else's land often meant to lose the protection of the English government. It stirred the wrath of powerful speculators among the tidewater elite and caused trouble with native peoples, who were primarily farmers and raised little or no livestock. Thus they did not customarily fence their fields.[16] The pioneers, on the other hand, did little farming and raised much livestock. Like the seven plagues of Egypt, their ravenous herds descended on the unfenced fields. And as the pioneers' cattle fattened on the natives' corn, they created a problem of race relations.[17] Natives shot half-wild cows. Half-wild pioneers shot natives. Wars erupted. Both sides committed atrocities.

A movement led by Nathaniel Bacon sprang up along the Virginia frontier. Most of Bacon's followers were land poor, many completely landless. They had suffered many injuries in their conflicts with the natives. But they soon found themselves also in conflict with Governor Berkeley and the Green Spring faction. From this ruling circle the pioneers demanded not only protection from the natives but bloody retribution against them.

But Berkeley had commitments that conflicted with their demands. Some of the Green Spring faction had grown rich in the fur trade and in selling arms to the natives; and the haphazard settlement of the "back country" was setting off wars with them that disrupted the flow of furs.[18] Some among the governor's friends were speculators who resented the appropriation of their lands rent-free by squatters. Then, too, Berkeley had a commitment to the government in London, which was contesting with France for the control of North America. For reasons of imperial strategy it was important that native allies be cultivated, that treaties with them be observed.[19]

Berkeley and his circle, therefore, responded to the crisis in a way that outraged landless laborers, middling planters, backwoods herdsmen, and indeed most colonists. The governor's council proposed a heavy tax for the construction of more forts. Tax laws had a bad reputation in Virginia. Some had overcharged taxpayers and exempted the governor's friends, who had misappropriated the funds. Also forts had never stopped the natives' attacks on farms.[20] The governor's proposal, which colonists read as the status quo plus more corruption, ignited an explosion of anger. Bacon's followers took matters into their own hands.

The rebels, though drawn overwhelmingly from colonists who were land poor or landless, attracted supporters from the entire social spectrum. If the poor wanted land, the rich wanted more land; and a war against the native peoples was the way to get it. When the Bacon movement appeared to be sweeping toward victory, five members of Berkeley's own council became last-minute converts.

Bacon's followers now included both land speculators and their tenants as well as the squatters, both planters and their servants, and even their slaves. Many of the grievances of the poor now became so disruptive of the rebellion that they were placed beyond discussion. Nothing could be said about the class-biased taxes, or the exploitation of the labor of pioneer renters to enrich speculators, since the movement now included gentlemen who owed their fortunes to those very practices. Class issues had become too threatening to the success of the rebellion on which all pinned their hopes.[21]

But there was one issue about which all factions agreed: "Indians." For most colonists there were no "friendly Indians."[22] No matter whether native peoples were allied to England or to France, no matter whether they were true believers, heathens, or papists, they shot hogs and cattle.[23] They held a great deal of land. Land speculator and squatter alike could see that these people, their numbers decimated by Old World diseases, were in no condition to defend their land.[24] United on Indians, the Bacon rebels drove the native peoples from Piedmont Virginia, put Governor Berkeley to flight, and burned Jamestown.[25]

The Compromise

Within a year Bacon had died, an English expeditionary force had restored Berkeley, and some rebel leaders had been hanged. But at the same time, the government quietly acquiesced to the principal rebel demand: to allow settlers to deal as they saw fit with Indians and their property. The anger of the poor, once directed against the rich, was now redirected against the Indians. Indeed it was the colonial authorities themselves in the Carolinas who carried out the Tuscarora War in 1711 and the Yamasee War in 1715, precisely the kind of wars Bacon's rebels had demanded. Also during the rebellion, Berkeley himself had extended suffrage to all free white males.[26] Such was the class compromise: plain white males would get the vote and a share of Indian land.

Bacon's Rebellion and the co-option of Bacon's expansionist demands by colonial authorities gave a dramatic forward thrust to what might be called "Southernization," the creation and recreation on a moving frontier of an extraordinarily aggressive society in which whites, both planters and yeomen, stood together against outsiders, first the Indians, later the French, British, Spaniards, and Mexicans. So long as this expansion continued, the Old South exported westward its poverty and remained internally strong.

From Planter Domination to Planter Hegemony

During the years following the insurrections, colonial leaders began to look on the plain whites in a different way, no longer as a hard-to-control source of labor, but as a much-needed source of security. There was now a sharp rise in the number of slaves being unloaded on the shores of the Chesapeake.

As the number of slaves increased, the colonial elite began to write "black codes" to control slaves. In the early 1600s, slaves had been so few that no special laws were enacted to control them. Also in the early years, the distinction between white servants and slaves had been blurred by the "bottom rail" abuse and misery that they both suffered. White servants and black slaves had sometimes conspired together against their exploiters. The pejorative black codes and the now better treatment of white servants would strengthen the new racial alignment of social classes.

In addition, colonial authorities began to draw up racial laws spelling out legal distance between blacks and whites. These laws increased the status of plain whites, making it easier for planters to recruit them as a population of guards against their slaves, and as armed retainers in the conquest of Indian lands. A law in 1691, for example, prohibited whites from marrying Negroes, Mulattoes, or Indians; and a woman bearing a nonwhite child, in or out of wedlock, could be banished from Virginia. A law of 1705 provided for the confiscation of hogs, cattle, or other property acquired by slaves, to be used for the benefit of the parish poor whites. Edmund S. Morgan characterizes these and similar laws as a deliberate attempt of the authorities "to foster the contempt of whites for blacks and Indians."[27] The planter class wove these racial laws and court decisions into the new social fabric.

English "Sturdy Beggars" Become American "Sturdy Yeomen"

With the passing of the frontier, the long-settled parts of the South took on the appearance of stability and permanence. There were now few success stories about former indentured servants moving from a cabin in the wilderness to a plantation big house and to a seat in the House of Burgesses. In the eastern tidewater area, the wilderness had vanished. With it had vanished the great frontier herds, the principal resource of the plain whites. Land and slaves, those two critical factors of production that made plain people fancy, were now typically inherited.

The plain whites of the 1700s, however, were by no means poor whites. They were middling farmers. Although the pioneer life style had receded to beyond the Great Blue Ridge, the prosperity of Chesapeake society was still linked to the frontier. Planters/speculators and even prosperous farmers often could will to their younger sons land in the West. These heirs could migrate to the land of the second chance, where success stories were often reenacted.

Kinship Linked Yeomanry to Gentry

In the 1700s, family ties gave strength to the alliance between the planters and the plain whites. Planters were also often related to slaves. But these ties were not acknowledged while those to the yeomanry were acknowledged and celebrated. Family ties reached far because of the prevalence of the extended family in the South. In the 1700s, the extended family was as common in the South as the nuclear family was in the North. One study has found that this divergence originated in the deadly health conditions of the previous century, when children often survived the death of their parents and were reared by more distant kin. Thus, while "in New England one lived in a parental situation, in the Chesapeake area one lived in a kinship situation."[28]

The southern extended family may also owe much to the way wealthy planter/speculators amassed vast fiefdoms and then distributed them to their heirs. European families were sometimes torn asunder by the competition of heirs for the family estate. But some Chesapeake planters acquired so much land that they were able to leave plantations not only to all of their children but to more distant kin as well, a practice that has done no harm to that region's telescopic genealogical vision allowing one to recognize incredibly distant cousins. It also contributed to the solidarity of the extended family. Sons and cousins could think of themselves not as rivals, but as companions in a common venture.

Hospitality Converted Wealth into Power

The great extended families, or clans, were vehicles through which planters could win the loyalty of countless substantial farmers. The prevalence of such family names as Carter, Lee, and Meade indicates that many prosperous farm families were the junior branches of the great aristocratic clans. Proud farm families, without the slightest embarrassment, could accept hospitality or other favors from a gentleman they perceived as a relative. He in turn could call out a virtual army of plain kin to elect him to the House of Burgesses. Philip Fithian, tutor at Nomini Hall, the seat of Robert "King" Carter's estate, provided some details of that planter's hospitality: "this Family one year with another consumes 27,000 Lb of Pork; & twenty Beeves. 500 Bushels of Wheat, besides corn—4 Hogsheads of Rum & 150 Gallons of Brandy."[29] Undoubtedly most of the corn and pork, and some of the beef, were rations for the slaves. But one can be sure that Carter's numerous relatives and other guests consumed the other items of food and drink.

To an important degree it was the ideology of kinship and largesse, and the particular form of the family in the South, that enabled great slaveholders to control more territory than they actually owned. It was for this reason that Anne Arundel County, Maryland, was "Carroll country," that the falls of the Potomac was a Washington fief, that the Randolphs were a force to be reckoned with in the valley of the James.[30]

Plantations in Place of Towns

The gentry could usually count on the loyal support of many plain whites to whom they were by no means related, not even by the far-extending web of kinship recognized in the Chesapeake. To a considerable degree, the gentry controlled the infrastructure of their society; that is, they controlled the distribution of goods and services upon which people depended. Farming communities are normally urban-centered. Farmers go to town to market their crops and to purchase goods and services. In this respect the Chesapeake region differed sharply from the North, where towns had grown vigorously. Philadelphia was the second-largest city in the British Empire, and New York was nearly as large. But in Virginia and Maryland together, as late as 1780, only nine communities had more than a thousand inhabitants.[31] Plantations often took on the functions of towns, becoming focal points of exchange.

In the absence of towns, farmers delivered their tobacco crop to some great waterfront plantation where ocean-going ships called. When the planter saw a good opportunity to sell his own crop, he would also market the crops of less affluent neighbors.[32] It was also to the plantation that people came when they needed sugar, tea, rum, or virtually any imported item. These were purchased through the planter or his overseas "factor," or agent.[33]

Also, a southern yeoman, unlike a northern farmer, frequently did not have direct access to the services of skilled craftsmen. If he needed barrels for tobacco or required the services of a shoemaker, tailor, blacksmith, carpenter, brewer, distiller, or nail maker, he found these craftsmen on a large plantation, most often among the owner's household slaves.[34] For a family who did not wish to be looked on as "buckskins," whites who lived like Indians, it was important to enjoy the patronage of a gentleman.[35]

Credit was another tie that bound the plain whites to the great slaveholders. In a land where banking had not yet developed, if a farmer needed an advance, he had to have a patron. The prosperity of a Chesapeake farmer was fragile. One hailstorm could destroy his tobacco crop, a bitter winter his livestock. Yet if he had a friend who was a great planter, whose name was respected by the bankers of London, such a friendship could spell the difference between comfort and want.[36]

The Vigilant South

Planters and yeomen had originally drawn together during their conquest of Indian lands. On these lands, plantations had multiplied and the population of slaves had increased. Whites became watchful and armed. The planter William Byrd wrote in 1736 that there were "already at least 10,000 men of these descendants of Ham fit to bear arms, & their numbers increase every day as well by birth as importation. And in case there should arise a man of desperate courage among us, . . . he might with more advantage than Cataline kindle a servile war. . . . We have mountains in Virginia too, to which they may retire as safely, and do as much mischief as they do in Jamaica."[37] Plain whites saw the threat of a slave revolt as a danger to the community, not just to planters. Some yeomen owned a few slaves and hoped to own more. The people they most looked up to were planters. And many farm families, in their far-reaching web of kinship, regarded certain planters as "relatives." The defense of masters had become a civic duty.

Also, though the great pioneer herds had disappeared, whites still raised livestock in the unfenced woods. Few forms of property were more vulnerable to theft. Slaves on rare occasions were allowed to keep a pig or a few chickens. But overwhelmingly they lived on monotonous rations, consisting mainly of cornmeal and salt pork.[38] They sometimes varied this fare by killing and barbecuing half-wild livestock. When ordinary farmers rode at night with the slave patrol, they were protecting the property of whites against the misery of blacks.

"Muster day" dramatized the armed South. Planters, who in general were the militia officers, also supplied the barbecue and drink for these celebrations, and the community turned out. "Soldiers delighted in surrounding a pretty girl and firing their muskets in the air, while officers dashed about in glittering uniforms that bespoke social rank more than military prowess."[39] Officers sometimes made political speeches at these events and even marched their companies to the polls. Training exercises of the militia, and the related slave patrols, made clear that white men were armed. Muster days also were community pageants that highlighted the Old South's social structure: gentlemen gave orders and plain farmers willingly obeyed.[40]

Dissenters and the End of Dissent

For a time, religion in the Chesapeake South seemed to conflict with planter hegemony. Christians sometimes behaved as if they thought there was a power in the region that rivaled that of the great clans. Yeomen in large numbers deserted the planter-controlled Church of England and joined dissenter sects, especially the Baptists and Methodists.[41] In the beginning, dissent from the established church sometimes seemed to imply a different way of looking at society. In 1787, for example, the Ketocton Baptist Association, whose members lived in some seven northwestern Virginia counties along both sides of the Great Blue Ridge, "determined that hereditary slavery was a breach of the divine law."[42]

All dissenters by no means shared this view. But enough did to put their churches at risk. Elder John Waller was leading a Baptist service when several Anglican gentlemen and their followers invaded the meeting. Waller was "Violently Jerked off the Stage, [they] Caught him by the Back part of his Neck[,] Beat his head against the ground. . . . They Carried him through a Gate . . . , where a Gentleman [the sheriff] Gave him . . . Twenty Lashes with his Horse whip."[43] Religious leaders who were attentive to these lessons fared better. No slave driver or overseer could have matched the vigilance of the God that the Reverend Thomas Bacon, an Anglican minister, described to his black listeners:

> you can do nothing so secretly but he will know it, and that no place is so dark and private, but his all-piercing eye can see what you are doing in it: *For the darkness and the light are both alike to him.* . . . when you are idle and neglectful of your master's business,—when you *steal,* and *waste,* and *hurt* any of their substance,—when you are *saucy* and *impudent,* when you are telling them *lies,* and deceiving them, or when you prove *stubborn* or *sullen,* and will not do the work you are set about without stripes and vexations; you do not consider, . . . that what faults you are guilty of toward your masters and mistresses, are faults done against God himself, who hath set your masters and mistresses over you.[44]

In the dissenter churches, antislavery sentiment reached its high point just after the American Revolution, but thereafter it went into steep decline. Anglican and dissenter churches continued to disagree about theology, but on slavery dissenters ceased to dissent. If their celebrations continued to be more boisterous than the sedate services of the Church of England, these noises no longer disturbed the gentlemen who supervised religion, bought and sold slaves, commanded the militia, passed laws, or tried and hanged offenders. With the exception of the Quakers, all churches adapted themselves to a world in which the power of heaven was distant, that of the gentry close at hand.[45]

Planter Hegemony or *Herrenvolk* Democracy?

By 1776, the Chesapeake proto-South was already in place. Planters controlled the economic infrastructure of society. They held powers that in the North were distributed among large landholders, real estate speculators, exporters, merchants, bankers, and skilled craftsmen. They also occupied a large number of key positions in the legislative bodies, the judicial system, the militia, and such influential religious institutions as the Church of England vestries. Even where members of aristocratic families did not personally busy themselves in the machinery of social control, they often influenced the selection of individuals who carried out these functions.

Despite the prominence of the elite in the decision-making process, historians disagree about how to characterize power in Chesapeake society and in the later South. Did the gentry rule over the yeomanry or did they represent them? Did planters exercise hegemony, or was the Old South a *Herrenvolk* (master race) democracy?[46] These two approaches do not ask the same question. Hegemony concerns *who* ruled. Democracy concerns *how* they ruled.

Planter control over credit, commodity exchange, and access to skilled crafts-men certainly gave planters the means to reward or punish, the powers needed for domination. But they enjoyed hegemony, or "legitimacy." Such power re-quired more than the stick and the carrot. A ruling class must act with restraint and make concessions to followers, thus winning the loyalty of a sufficient con-stituency. Above all, the planters won the loyalty of the yeomanry by sharing with them some of the land conquered from the American natives. Beyond this basic concession, they won the yeomen's loyalty by providing them with competent leadership and treating them with respect, by extending lavish hos-pitality, even to distant kin, and by providing to everyone barbecue and drink on muster day and election day.

But hegemony—consolidated power—required an ideology: beliefs shared by those who lead and those who follow. Adam Smith expressed the objec-tive basis of the beliefs that integrated this original South: "civil government, so far as it is instituted for the security of property, is in reality instituted for the defense of the rich against the poor, or of those who have some property against those who have none at all."[47] It was black folk who had virtually no property at all and were most often property themselves. Chesapeake so-ciety was thus polarized between property owners, large and small, on the one hand, and slaves on the other, white "haves" and black "have-nots." In the 1700s, this clash of objective interests was not yet obscured by a strident racial ideology. Racial ideas had still not entered the political discourse of the Chesapeake proto-South. But they had entered its culture.

The men most knowledgeable about Africa were slave traders who brought ideas as well as slaves. They charged their victims with everything from can-nibalism to bad body odor. Their indictment included the legend that blacks had been condemned to eternal slavery by the Biblical curse on the "sons of Ham."[48] These ideas entered the folklore of white society. Also present, if not often expressed in the 1700s, was the equation of black with slavery and white with freedom. Accordingly a free black was not truly free and certainly not equal. This idea, along with the pejorative folklore, devastated the opportuni-ties of free blacks. They enjoyed little legal protection or success in the com-petition for resources. In time they were reduced to a caste-like proletariat.

Little of this ideology appears in the polite discourse of whites in the 1700s. Generations would pass before racial ideology would form the political ce-ment of a "solid South." A glance ahead makes this clear. In the 1820s, as the campaign to legalize slavery in Illinois moved to a climax, a free-state sup-porter at a political rally made "an able and eloquent" speech. He was followed at the podium by a slave-state supporter who made "three jumps, and each time exclaiming, 'I am a white man.'"[49]

This was not the political style of George Washington, Thomas Jefferson, or any of the Chesapeake gentry. During the century when the Old South was most stable, when a planter could still bequeath bottomland plantations to each of his sons, when a moving frontier still provided fresh pasture for a yeoman's growing herds, southern spokesmen said little about race. The early South was ideologically and politically integrated not by race, but by "democracy," an idea that excluded most people: white women, roughly half the white population but not fully empowered as citizens; blacks, nearly 40 percent of the Chesapeake South; and the American natives, who in the whole territory claimed by Virginia were probably equal in number to blacks.

Planter hegemony was never complete. In the underdeveloped areas of the East, and on newly settled frontiers, plantations were few. Here, voters sometimes rejected planter candidates and their policies, giving rise to so-called East-West conflicts. More generally, however, yeomen shared the expansionist objectives of their leaders. They were prospering and the future appeared bright.

The early South gained cohesion from outside threats. First, there were the Indians and the French, whose fur traders in the heartland of North America established a symbiotic relationship. This mitigated some tribal conflicts and stiffened native resistance to the advancing Anglo-American frontier. The British and colonist victory in the French and Indian War ended this threat.

But a more formidable threat appeared. The British took over the fur trade and adopted methods similar to those of the French in managing it. In addition, they began enforcing trade restrictions that depressed income from the tobacco exports of yeoman and planter, and they began taxing imports. In the Chesapeake region, supporters of the king were few. Whites closed ranks behind their colonial leaders.

Whites, to be sure, but what about the men and women who were invisible to Patriots, as they made speeches about liberty and the rights of Americans? When Patriot defiance brought a British invasion, colonial leaders learned how often a slave was an enemy within. If slavery had made black people invisible, the invasion brought them into full view.

Chapter 4

The Era of the American Revolution
The Challenge to Slavery and the Compromise

In the Declaration of Independence, Thomas Jefferson proclaimed that "all men are created equal . . . [and] are endowed by their creator with certain unalienable Rights." In Britain, Dr. Samuel Johnson retorted, "How is it that we hear the loudest *yelps* for liberty among the drivers of negroes?"[1]

Slavery was practiced in every one of the thirteen original states. Yet few Patriots saw any disconnect between what they said about liberty and how they treated black people. Black slavery was normal. For some Patriots, however, all men's "unalienable Rights" to "Life, Liberty and the pursuit of Happiness" evoked the ancient religious tradition that freedom was the natural human condition.[2] There were no slaves in God's original creation.

But long ago, mainstream Christians had come to terms with the fact of slavery in a world of sin. They knew that there were peoples who did not practice slavery, indeed peoples who had the most rudimentary class divisions of any kind. These, however, were "primitive" or "barbarous" peoples, not societies that they admired, like the Greeks and Romans. Wherever civilization had shone most brilliantly, it had cast its darkest shadows. And in those shadows there had always been slaves. A world without slaves was a fantasy of holy men, not a plan of ordinary people.

Yet if the idea that God made humankind one family and made them free was too lofty for people to live by, it was also too noble for them to forget. There had always been God-intoxicated prophets who would not let them forget. One of these in Pennsylvania in the 1700s was Benjamin Lay. Like many a critic of slavery before him, Lay did not blend unnoticed into the social landscape of his day. He rarely trimmed his white beard. He observed a strict vegetarian diet and wore only homespun clothes that he made himself. For his food and clothing he would use no materials that had resulted from the enslavement of a human being or from the death of an animal. One practice of this glorious eccentric was to storm into a church during divine services and to the scandalized worshipers announce, "I came to cry aloud against your practice of slaveholding."[3]

Technology and Abolition

As the century progressed, abolitionist harangues were becoming more common. Something had occurred, furthermore, that had never before happened in the history of the world. Not only were more and more people listening to the abolitionists but they included people of a very different frame of mind from that ancient line of prophets extending from Benjamin Lay back over the millennia to John the Baptist and beyond.[4] Many of those who now most clearly saw the virtue of free labor, and the evil of coerced labor, were those closest to the growing edge of technology. In the marvels of the Industrial Revolution, they had glimpsed a vision of the world transformed. The civilization that was to come would shine brighter than any in the past, and there would be no slaves except machines.

Many of these new opponents of slavery were Quakers, who both in England and America had an unusually keen interest in such earthly problems as the best way to recover lead from ore, how to bring light into a mine without causing an explosion, or how to deal with its poisonous gases. They were investigating the mysteries of electricity, were captivated by "useful improvements," such as watches, scientific instruments, and all kinds of mechanical contrivances.[5]

England, the wicked stepmother of American Patriots, was at the center of this scientific and technological revolution. But its shock waves extended far: to the French and Scottish Enlightenment and to the great minds of America, including the author of the Declaration of Independence, Thomas Jefferson.[6]

The Great Awakening

If the revolution in science and technology was forcing secular thinkers to take a new look at slavery, its impact on religious thinkers was equally great. In the English-speaking lands, especially, a vibrant upsurge of religious activity was redefining faith. There was an exciting rediscovery of John 1:9, a biblical text more often shelved and forgotten than remembered and quoted: "That was the true light of the world which lighteth every man that cometh into the world." This was the doctrine of the "inner light." To many, these words said that the light of God burns within every human being on earth, however much corrupted by the ways of the world.[7] This spark of divinity glowed in every papist, every Turk, in the blackest African and the wildest Indian. Nowhere on earth was there an enslaveable "other."

The "inner light" doctrine appeared sporadically in the dissenter churches of the 1600s, such as the Presbyterians and the Congregationalists, and these showed a fresh vitality. Even more, this doctrine appeared in the new religious movements: the Baptists, the Methodists, and the Quakers. The religious upheaval had its beginnings in those lands where the technological revolution and free labor were most successful. Indeed the artisans and craftsmen of the new evangelical movements were in no small measure responsible for this success. The resurgence of religion reached the English colonies in the 1740s as the Great Awakening.

Quakers, the First Organized Abolitionists

Antislavery sentiment was widely distributed across the religious spectrum. But only the Quakers, or Society of Friends, became solidly abolitionist. Only they succeeded more or less completely in pressuring their members, first by friendly persuasion, later by threat of "disownment," to withdraw from the slave trade and, finally, toward the close of the 1700s, to abstain from the use of slave labor altogether.[8] Also, during the closing years of the century, antislavery sentiment reached its high point among the Congregationalists, the Presbyterians, the Baptists, and the Methodists—but with very different results. In none of these churches did abolitionists gain the upper hand; and in the United States their influence, like that of secular abolitionists, declined after 1800 when the plantation South gained ascendancy over the republic.[9]

The antislavery cause seems to have suffered from the very success of these vigorously growing churches. As they swelled from tiny sects to major denominations with power and influence, they attracted converts who sought power and influence, including planters and merchants involved in Atlantic commerce. The more the Lord's work came to depend on slaves, tobacco, sugar, and rum, the more these churches became tongue-tied about slavery.

Among the Quakers, too, these same battles were fought. Until the second half of the century, their split over slavery resembled that among the other evangelicals. But the tension that slavery caused within their flock was more severe.[10] Much more than other groups they were committed to nonviolence, and to the doctrine of the inner light.[11] These were both good reasons to reject a labor system that required considerable violence and fostered a belief in racial inferiority. Since the opening of the sub-Saharan slave trade in the Middle Ages, slavery had been associated with prejudice against Africans, who, as part of the great human family, shared the inner light.

But, on the other hand, Quaker diligence, frugality, and innovation had contributed to their worldly success, to their steep rate of capital accumulation.[12] More than most other religious groups they were acquiring the means for investing in African labor and Atlantic commerce. In the early 1700s, they were as much involved with slaves, tobacco, sugar, and rum as the Congregationalists, Presbyterians, Baptists, and other dissenters.[13]

But the Seven Years' War came as a severe blow to Quakers who had risen to high places in government and trade. In 1754, the French and Indians smashed the army of General Edward Braddock and turned the westward march of Pennsylvania pioneers into an eastward flight of refugees.[14] In Pennsylvania, the Quaker-controlled Assembly demanded a reopening of negotiations with the French and Indians. But Governor Robert Hunter Morris bypassed the Assembly, declared war, and offered huge bounties for Indian scalps, those of both men and women,[15] whereupon the Quakers resigned from the Assembly.[16] Thus, after seventy-five years, Quaker control of Pennsylvania ended.

Their commitment to nonviolence not only forced the Society of Friends out of government but also forced them out of much Atlantic commerce. During the Seven Years' War, the government impressed ships for military purposes. The Atlantic trade now compounded the sin of slavery with the sin of war. This was too much for most Quakers.[17] First in certain local meetings of rural Pennsylvania, finally in the great yearly meetings in Philadelphia and London, Quaker farmers and artisans forced their more prosperous brothers to choose between some of the richest flesh pots of Atlantic commerce and the Society of Friends.[18] Many important persons were at this time "disowned," and joined churches with less demanding principles.[19]

The withdrawal of Quakers from government and from much of the Atlantic trade kept the Society closer to its original constituency of free farmers and skilled artisans.[20] The vision of a world without slaves gleamed in their meetinghouses even after it was fading from other churches. What had always been a fantasy of prophets, in the Society of Friends now became a plan of practical men and women.

Quakers were pacifists and tried to remain neutral during the War for Independence. But for all opponents of slavery, war gave the question an unprecedented immediacy. It brought home to all that slaves were by necessity an enemy within. Yet for the opponents of slavery, so long as the military conflict continued, there was a formidable obstacle: Thomas Jefferson, the author of the Declaration of Independence, and George Washington, the commander of the Continental Army, were large slaveholders. Even in the North, many Patriot leaders owned household slaves. For Patriots to attack slavery was to attack their own leaders at a time when British troops were on American soil.

The Strange Coalition against the African Slave Trade

Before armed conflict began, the opponents of slavery were able to attack, if not slavery itself, the Atlantic slave trade. It was dominated by the British. More important, when the opponents of slavery attacked the Atlantic slave trade, they found allies in an unlikely place, among some of the largest slaveholders in the land.

Many large slaveholders of the Chesapeake had their own reasons for hating the African slave trade, which had reached its all-time high on the eve of the independence struggle.[21] In this region, a century of tobacco monoculture had resulted in soil exhaustion and a partial conversion to mixed farming, and thus to free labor. Mixed farming was unsuited to slave labor, since it fragmented slave gangs and undermined discipline and efficiency. The demand for slaves had shrunk in the region. The great planters of the Chesapeake had become the sellers of slaves. Selling them on a soft market was made no easier by the fecundity of Chesapeake slaves, who probably had the highest rate of natural increase of any slave population in the world.[22] The British were dumping surplus slaves onto this already saturated market. Chesapeake masters, therefore, were as eloquent in their condemnation of the horrors of the "middle passage" as they were silent about those of the domestic slave trade.[23]

In the North also, where there was a growing stream of immigrants, the demand for slaves had diminished. Even in the Deep South, where the demand for slaves was strong, colonial leaders worried about British merchants' dumping large numbers of African captives in their ports. In the low country, the black population already greatly outnumbered the white. Whites remembered the Stono Revolt of 1739. They feared that the unrestricted Atlantic slave trade was creating a powder keg in the coastal areas.

The first objective of the abolitionists, Quakers as well as others, was thus the Atlantic slave trade. No feature of the system was more scandalous than this "nefarious traffic," which sometimes involved kidnappers and pirates. Slave traders regularly gave unwitting testimony about the middle passage every time they brought a ship into port.[24] No indictment of slavery by abolitionist preachers was more devastating than the stench of these overcrowded ships, or the degrading spectacle of slave auctions. Slave traders thus staged a living pageant of cruelty and greed witnessed by thousands.

In all of the colonies that became the United States, therefore, there was dissatisfaction with the Atlantic slave trade that brought together groups as diverse as abolitionists and large slaveholders. Yet when the colonial assemblies attempted to regulate this business, their measures were "disallowed" by the British Board of Trade, whose members seemed more concerned about the profits of the British merchants who dominated the Atlantic slave trade than about slave conspiracies in South Carolina, or about odd religious doctrines.[25] In 1774, the First Continental Congress, in retaliation against the British "coercive acts," pledged its provinces to boycott British products and a total discontinuation of slave imports. This pledge was reinforced with legislative actions by eventually all thirteen colonial assemblies.[26] Emboldened by such widespread sentiment, Jefferson, in an early draft of the Declaration of Independence, accused the king of violating the rights "of a distant people who never offended him, captivating & carrying them into slavery."[27] This indignant language went beyond the pragmatic and fragile consensus of the colonial leaders, and in the final draft of the Declaration, the question of the slave trade was passed over in prudent silence.[28]

Slaves, the Enemy Within

For the sake of colonial unity it was just as well that the slave trade was not included among the misdeeds of the king. The delicate consensus opposing the foreign slave trade by no means extended to slavery itself. British leaders recognized that slavery was the Achilles' heel of the American rebellion. Thus, when in November 1775, the Patriots forced the royal governor of Virginia, Lord Edward Dunmore, to take flight to a British ship, Dunmore was able to take his revenge. He issued a proclamation offering the slaves belonging to rebels their freedom if they joined "His Majesty's Troops."[29]

By the end of the war, all told, tens of thousands of slaves had, at one time or another, fled to the British lines.[30] But the British effort failed, because the imperial government never made a clear choice between two mutually exclusive alternatives: promoting a slave revolt or promoting the Loyalist Party, which included important slave owners.[31]

These contradictory policies eroded much of the political support once enjoyed by the royal government. Lord Dunmore, for example, while offering freedom to recruits for his "Ethiopian Regiment," stopped short of general emancipation and protection for the emancipated. As a result, the Patriots could threaten those who were tempted by the British offer of freedom that their desertion would "provoke the fury of the Americans against their defenseless fathers, mothers, their wives, their women and children."[32] In the end, out of perhaps 300,000 slaves in the Chesapeake region, Dunmore was able to assemble only about 1,000 at Gwinn's Island, where they were decimated by a smallpox epidemic.[33]

The British then abandoned the Chesapeake early in 1776, returning in 1777 and again in 1781, each time renewing their policy of hesitant subversion. Perhaps such important policymakers as the British Board of Trade did not really want a slave revolt, since British merchants enjoyed substantial profits from the commodities slaves produced both in British colonies and elsewhere.

As for planter Patriots, the class interests they shared with planter Loyalists were more fundamental than any differences they had about "loyalty" or "patriotism." This became clear in 1775 on the rice plantations of North Carolina when slaves armed themselves and took to the swamps. The Loyalists and the Patriots called a truce and restored the social order before resuming their battles with each other.[34]

Later in Georgia, the Loyalist governor Sir James Wright's attempt to subvert the labor system of his Patriot enemies outraged Loyalist planters as well.[35] At the beginning of the war, there had been both Loyalist and Patriot planters in the plantation low country. And there had been Loyalists and Patriots in the pioneer backcountry. British gestures toward the slaves wiped out the Loyalist Party in the low country, while their gestures toward the Native Americans wiped it out in the backcountry. The experiences of the war reduced the longtime antagonism between the two regions. Also, economic changes were bringing them more together: Pioneers were creating a thriving export economy of wood products as well as meat and hides from their giant herds. Indeed, prosperous yeomen had begun to buy a few slaves and to look to the planter elite for leadership.

By the war's end, the planters had reestablished control over their slaves and had resolved the differences between Patriot and Loyalist planters. They also had gained leadership over the entire white population of the Lower South: over the low-country east and the backcountry west. Thus while in the North and the Upper South, the war became a strong challenge to slavery, the challenge was weaker in the Lower South, and the planters actually emerged from the conflict with their power enhanced.

The Chesapeake Labor Crisis

War and the challenge of the "enemy within" strongly affected the Greater Chesapeake, an area extending from Delaware to the Albemarle Sound in North Carolina. Here, the British had employed their same hesitant subversion of slavery, but the economic situation was different: planters faced a labor crisis. The continuous cropping of tidewater land with tobacco had exhausted much of the soil and was forcing a conversion to mixed farming and small grains. This conversion fragmented slave gangs. Supervision costs rose. Discipline and efficiency fell.[36] Some planters grumbled that slavery was a system that required two overseers to watch one slave do nothing.[37] Unlike tobacco, the newer crops, corn and wheat, were not labor intensive. Furthermore, they did not keep workers busy twelve months of the year. A relatively inflexible and expensive slave labor force was now left standing idle during slack seasons. Slaves ate whether employed or not.

Ironically, as slave labor became harder and harder to use efficiently, vigorous population growth was making slaves more and more plentiful.[38] Criticism of slavery often came not only from evangelical preachers and the plain people but from planters themselves. George Washington commented that it was "demonstratively clear that . . . I have working Negroes by a full moiety [half] more than can be employed to any advantage."[39] The fragmentation of the slave gang had weakened controls and resulted in the dragging feet, the fumbling hands, the calculated stupidity of the worker who was compelled. So different was the spontaneity, the innovativeness, the seeming intrinsic intelligence of the worker who was free.[40]

Thus before the beginning of the cotton boom, which turned around slave prices, some Chesapeake masters thought that slavery belonged to the colonial past. The future belonged to the white yeomanry. Not only could yeomen drive out the British; their free hands could also transform backwoods America, already proud and independent, into an advanced and cultivated society.[41]

The War for Independence had heightened the tension between what Patriots said and what they did. They made speeches about freedom, and hunted slaves who had run away to join the enemies of freedom.[42] But now in the

Chesapeake, some planters, confronted with the inefficiency of their work gangs, concluded that slavery was a mixed blessing if not an affliction that an angry God had visited upon them for their sins. By the 1790s, the antislavery evangelicals reached the height of their influence. Religious or patriotic masters freed more slaves in the Chesapeake region than in any other area of the nation during the Revolutionary Era. Most of these emancipations took place in the generation following the Battle of Yorktown in 1781.

But after the turn of the century, unlike the North, the Chesapeake region turned back from the path of manumission. Chesapeake legislators put new restrictions on manumission and made them increasingly severe.[43] A definite reaction had set in.[44] People still spoke well of liberty and were still saved at religious revivals. What was happening was that the agricultural crisis of the Chesapeake was easing.

Victories over the British and their native allies were opening up, especially after the War of 1812, vast expanses of virgin cotton land in the southwest. By 1820, some 250,000 whites had left the Chesapeake, taking with them 175,000 slaves.[45] With the cotton boom, a surplus of slaves, which in 1790 was a problem, by 1820 was a valuable asset. With the demand by a fully mechanized textile industry in Britain and the invention of the cotton gin, the South's colonial-type export economy revived with renewed vigor.

Before the Revolution, people were not sure whether Maryland and Virginia were "north" or "south." These terms were relative, like "up" and "down." They were written with small letters and referred to directions on the map. No one knew where "north" ended and "south" began. But by 1830, everybody knew. The "South" was capitalized and referred to those states where the dominant class derived its wealth from the sale or exploitation of slaves. If there was still an Upper South and a Deep South, more fundamentally there was now a unified and prosperous slave South. Southern leaders were in a strong position to dominate the fragile new republic.

The North's Historic Compromise
Black Freedom Defined by White Masters

A far-reaching result of the War for Independence was the ending of slavery in the North and the appearance there of the "freedmen" or, more accurately, the "quasi freed people."[46] Although there had been a scattering of free blacks throughout colonial times, the emancipations beginning in the era of the independence struggle increased their numbers to about 10 percent of the nation's black population.[47]

The First Emancipation was a compromise between revolutionary demo-crats and slaveholders: emancipation was carried out, but on the master's own terms. This compromise produced a people depleted of any resources that they could pass on to their children. In this way they became virtually a hereditary caste, the "bottom rail."

In the era of the Revolution, many people in the Chesapeake region, and more in the North, took seriously the ideas for which they had been called upon to sacrifice. Pressure to emancipate came from below. But emancipa-tion came from above.[48] According to James Monroe, slaveholder and future president, emancipation should be carried out "on principles consistent with humanity, without expense or inconvenience to ourselves."[49] And so it was. The northern states passed emancipation laws. But these laws freed no liv-ing slave, as this would incur immediate expense either to the master, or if he were compensated, expense to the state. Those to be freed by law were the children that would be born to slaves after a stipulated date.[50] With this gradualism, there were persons who legally were slaves in the North until the generation before the Civil War.

Gradualism perpetuated the northern black codes, the special laws that gov-erned both slaves and those becoming free. Except in several New England states, these racial laws continued to spell out unequal rights throughout the antebellum years. Some of these ongoing colonial laws trained whites to be slave hounds. A New Jersey law authorized whites to check the passes of blacks, to administer lashes if papers were not in order, and to receive a reward for return-ing an escaped slave. For helping an escaped slave one was liable to a fine equal to the value of the slave.[51]

The freedom compromise, which left emancipation in the hands of masters, also left the door open to much legal evasion. Especially in New York, New Jersey, and Pennsylvania, owners

> employed an endless variety of schemes to avoid their slaves' manumission and sales restriction laws, including taking pregnant women across state lines so that their children would not be born free, manumitting their slaves under long indentures and then selling them to out-of-state buyers, "renting" their slaves to southerners on long term leases, selling slave children as "apprentices" to interstate buyers, and prosecuting their slaves for spurious reasons so that they could get permission from a judge to sell them south.[52]

Also it was becoming more expensive for slaves to buy their freedom. Josiah Henson's master, for example, was asking three hundred dollars for his free-dom. When the slave produced the money, his master accepted it but told him that his price had gone up to a thousand dollars.[53]

Few slaves in the North were freed by law. Most were freed by the voluntary actions of their owners. Emancipation from above, "without expense or inconvenience to ourselves," created not free men and women, but a caste of pariahs. Masters were responding to contrary pressures. On the one hand, they needed money. So they sold slaves to the Deep South where they were bringing ever better prices. At the same time, they were under religious and political pressures to emancipate.

Different kinds of slaves met these different kinds of demands.[54] On the secret altar of Mammon one could sacrifice a healthy young slave who would bring a top price as a prime field hand for a Deep South plantation.[55] A worn-out slave would bring a poor price, and misrepresenting the soundness of one with a less obvious disability could bring a buyer's lawsuit.[56] Yet the emancipation of such slaves could answer the demands of public piety and patriotism.

So often did masters emancipate elderly or unemployable slaves, and so often did these freed people become dependent upon charities or public poor relief, that virtually all states passed laws setting an upper limit on the age at which a slave might be emancipated. Such laws, however, did not solve the problem of destitute and dependent freed people. The marginality of these former slaves, a majority of them women, gave rise to a stereotype much like that of the "welfare queen" of later times, and, with it, to a vicious white backlash.[57]

State laws setting an age limit at which slaves might be emancipated often actually increased the marginality of freed people. If emancipation was to be without expense to masters, slaves had to earn their freedom. Masters normally set the conditions for emancipation during a slave's productive years. By the time those conditions were fulfilled, however, the slave had often passed the legal age limit for emancipation but was emancipated just the same.[58] So, in addition to being retired without a pension, the freed person still had a legal status that was less than free: emancipated by one's master, but still a slave under state law.

One way such laws contributed to the creation of a population drained of productivity and deprived of civil rights may be seen in the career of a Maryland carpenter known as "Old Basil." While many white carpenters had been using the earnings of their most productive years to set up their own business, Basil had been performing service toward his emancipation. His master indeed emancipated him, but only after he had passed the legal age limit in Maryland. This "emancipated" carpenter, who still had only the legal rights of a slave, continued to be productive. But his daughter was still a slave. He now applied his earnings to free *her*.[59]

A freed person who was dependent or barely productive might be looked upon with pity or contempt by many whites, regarded as a member of a sub-merged caste but otherwise left in peace. Not so a vigorous youth of seventeen. He had a market value too high for his own safety. He might be kidnapped.[60] Or, as in the case of James Cragg, somebody might see an opportunity to profit from the often cloudy legal status of a freed person in order to gain lawful possession of him. In 1823, a Maryland judge invalidated Cragg's manumission. The court found that when he and his mother were freed he had been less than two years old. At that time, he had been incapable of supporting himself as required by Maryland emancipation law.[61] Cragg as a nonproductive two-year-old had been emancipated. Now, as a very marketable prime hand, the court had restored him to slavery.[62] Conservative emancipation was master friendly.

The First Emancipation reconciled the interests of slaveholders with the ideals of their political constituents and their fellow church members. This compromise enabled masters to exploit slaves or ex-slaves often for another full generation. This gradualism also provided masters with the opportunity to sell south those slaves who had skills or youthful good health. In general, it was those lacking these qualities who were emancipated into the Darwinian competition of the capitalist labor market.

Gradualism, or voluntary emancipation, like the influx of immigrants from Europe, was a selective process. Each of these processes, emancipation and immigration, selected certain individuals for the American free-labor market and excluded others. Most immigrants were males in the prime of their lives who had sufficient money, or family backing, to cross the Atlantic and establish themselves in America.[63] With conservative emancipation, on the contrary, masters could sell south males in the prime of their lives, thus excluding from the northern free labor market the same kind of workers that the immigration process admitted: those who were most productive.

Master-friendly emancipation was also employer friendly. It provided employers with a reservoir of workers stripped of civil rights by the black codes. Underpaid and underemployed, these workers often could not survive without the "protection" of some important person. These were frequently employers who marshaled them to break strikes and debase the living stan-dards of white workers.

The post-slavery legacy in the North produced a planter-friendly ideol-ogy. The freed people in disproportionate numbers overwhelmed the poor relief and filled the jails. African American representation among the prison population of the antebellum North was about eight times their representation among the general population.[64] Top-down emancipation presented whites with a caricature of black freedom. The "common man" was easily convinced that free blacks were miserable and dangerous while plantation slaves were happy and harmless. The way was now open for a political alliance between the planter and the northern white "wage slave," an alliance that we shall examine later.

Yet the legacy of the Revolution was two-sided. It had ended the legal importation of slaves. It had created geographical space in which the free-labor system could grow. And grow it did. The free-labor system outstripped the spread of slavery and hastened the day when, as Lincoln predicted in his "house divided" speech, the nation had to "become all one thing or all the other."

Part 2
The Antebellum Republic

Chapter 5

The Old South's Triumph

The War for Independence created the United States. But by 1820 it was apparent that it had actually created the disunited states. A line that two surveyors drew separating Maryland and Pennsylvania, the Mason-Dixon Line, was now looming ever larger as the boundary between two societies. But the Mason-Dixon Line also separated a prosperous South that was enjoying a vigorous resurgence of its plantation export economy of colonial days from a North that, since the Revolution, had been suffering a troubled transition from a colonial economy to a national economy.

The South had recovered quickly from the Revolution. The war had resulted in defeats for the Indians and the opening up of vast stretches of the southern backcountry to southern pioneers. Their open-range livestock production was flourishing as never before. In long drives, they delivered thousands of cattle for slaughter in the ports of Charleston and Savannah, and the export of salted or smoked meat and tanned hides greatly expanded.

Events in Europe were driving a demand for southern exports. In Great Britain, industry and population were growing rapidly. Also, the British were involved in the wars of the French Revolution and Napoleon. They were supplying both their own wartime needs and the armies of their European allies, eagerly buying southern naval stores, animal products, rice, tobacco, and, especially and increasingly, cotton. Even better, the Southerners were selling to both sides. For shippers, these wars brought high profits but also the risk of having their ships destroyed or confiscated. For Southerners, since the European rivals carried away the exports in their own vessels, the wars were all profit and no risk.

Even the Chesapeake South was now prospering. In the 1770s the surplus of slaves had been for Chesapeake planters a liability. But now the economic boom in the Deep South had given rise to a thriving domestic slave trade and spiraling prices. Onetime surpluses had turned into tidy fortunes. To be sure, soil exhaustion had forced many planters and farmers to convert from tobacco to wheat. Yet, with the European wars, never had wheat brought such prices. Even the wheat of central and western Pennsylvania was being marketed, not in Philadelphia, but in the more convenient Chesapeake port of Baltimore.

The North's Slow Recovery

The adjustment of the North to independence, on the other hand, was slow and painful.[1] It was not easy for northern shippers and exporters to reenter the British-controlled Atlantic commerce. While the British eagerly bought southern commodities, they now favored their still loyal colonies in Canada for their lumber and salt cod. The British also regarded northern shipbuilders and shippers as competition to their own industries, and these were not welcomed back into the British commercial network. Indeed, Americans were largely excluded from the lucrative imperial carrying trade, and they were charged discriminatory duties in the many Atlantic ports the British controlled. The tiny navy of the young republic could offer little protection to American ships from seizure either by the British or their European rivals or by pirates.[2]

The difficulties of independence were giving rise to a new northern economy, but slowly. With the languishing of the Atlantic-oriented businesses of colonial days, some northern investors began to transfer their capital to textile manufacturing and other enterprises, which, because they produced for the home market, could operate independently of the British imperial economy.[3] But the road to economic independence was difficult. The home market was restricted by a primitive transportation system. American manufacturers did not have technical experts comparable to those in Britain.[4] Also, only in New

England was there a labor surplus sufficient to stimulate industrialization since elsewhere, land was cheap and the labor force was busy on family farms.

At times, during the wars of the French Revolution, the British needed American shippers and relaxed their restrictions. A precarious war boom came to the northern ports. But in 1805, the British, after their great naval victory at Trafalgar, once again tightened their restraints. Britain now "ruled the waves." And its government did so in ways that threatened not only the North's maritime prosperity but the nation's sovereignty as well.[5]

From the earliest days of the republic, southern leaders turned their strong economic position to political advantage. One issue was the location of the nation's capital. The logical choice was Philadelphia, the largest city, and the place where the constitutional convention and Congress had met. But Philadelphia was in a state where slavery was disappearing. Even more, it was a stronghold of the Quakers.

But the southern states also possessed an advantage on the issue of state debts. The northern states had come out of the Revolution heavily indebted and with a sluggish economy, while many southern states were becoming debt free. In 1790 Thomas Jefferson and James Madison brokered a deal with the northern leader Alexander Hamilton for the federal government to take over the state debts. In exchange, the southerners would pick the location of the nation's capital. The capital was thus located, not in a city, but on the marshy banks of the Potomac, nestled among the family fiefdoms of the Lees, the Washingtons, and the Carrolls.

The power of the South became even more apparent with the presidential election victory of Jefferson and his Democratic-Republican Party. The federal government had passed under the control of the "Virginia dynasty." For a full generation the White House would be occupied by Jefferson or his friends James Madison and James Monroe.

Great Britain Threatens America's Newly Won Independence

To accommodate or resist? Since the Revolution, the paramount issue in national politics had been foreign policy. British policies irritated Americans. They had taken years to withdraw their troops from American territory in the Northwest, and even after they withdrew they continued arming the Indians. And the Royal Navy stopped American ships and impressed American sailors. In the European wars both sides seized American ships; but the British, as the dominant maritime power, seized the most.

The struggle with Great Britain had continued since the 1760s. The conflict had been at times political, at times military, but always costly. Some in the Federalist Party were ready to make concessions to Britain or even become their ally in the European wars.[6] This idea was especially popular among northeastern shippers who wanted to gain the protection of the British fleet and cash in on the profits of the wartime trade. In 1798–1800, pro-British Federalists managed to involve the nation in an undeclared naval war against France. This war was highly unpopular, as many Americans remembered the decisive help that France had given during the independence struggle. It split the Federalist Party and, in 1800, brought victory to the Democratic-Republicans, whose feisty nationalism opposed any violations of American sovereignty.

If the Democratic-Republicans were angered by British violations of American sovereignty, they were even more angered by British aid to Indians. In the Mississippi Valley, the Shawnee chief Tecumseh and his brother, the Prophet, were organizing a movement that showed prospect of uniting Indian nations from the Great Lakes to the Gulf. Weapons were reaching these peoples from Canada and from Florida, a colony of Spain, a British ally. Responding to this threat to the advancing American frontier, a group of leaders from the South and West, the "war hawks," called for the conquest of Canada and Florida.

Despite the popularity of the war hawks in the South and West, the national leaders, the Virginia dynasty, recognized that a war with Britain would divide the nation. Pro-British Federalists were strong in the northeastern port cities. So the administrations of both Jefferson and Madison tried to steer a middle course between the war hawks in their own party and the Federalists. But British attacks and war hawk pressure finally in 1812 forced them to declare war.

For two years the war went badly. A bungled invasion of Canada was defeated by the Canadians and Indians, who then captured Detroit. Far from rallying to the defense of the nation, the Federalists expressed their spirit of accommodation to the British when on June 15, 1814, official Boston celebrated the triumph of Great Britain and its allies over Napoleon. A procession organized by the Federalists marched to King's Chapel. There they heard speakers, among them the Massachusetts senator and former governor Christopher Gore. Gore spoke of the "late wonderful events which have delivered a great portion of Europe from the most iron-handed despotism." That evening, 2,600 candles illuminated the State House, and fireworks lit up the sky over Boston.[7]

The British navy was at that moment blockading Boston's harbor. It had captured Nantucket and attacked small port towns near the city, burning ships in their harbors. Towns on the Cape Cod peninsula had escaped the torch by paying the British a thousand-dollar "contribution." The week before the

Federalist celebration, rumors had circulated of a proclamation by Admiral Sir George Cockburn, promising protection to all who would not resist a British occupation.[8]

In this city of finance and commerce, there were men for whom the War of 1812 had not been a disaster. Indeed, they had compensated themselves for their war losses with treason, doing business with the British. Some had contracted to supply beef and flour to Britain's armies preparing to invade from Canada, and to its warships offshore.[9] Many moneylenders had favored British securities because the Federalist Party had discouraged its members from making investments that aided "Mr. Madison's war."

The British were preparing to reassert their dominance in North America. From veterans of Britain's wars against Napoleon, the Duke of Wellington had put together the most formidable military force ever sent to the New World. In the face of this unprecedented threat, the government sued for peace. But for much of 1814, British terms were harsh. They refused even to discuss freedom of the seas or their impressments of American seamen, or American fishing rights on the Grand Banks. They wanted territorial concessions in Maine, and they wanted the western part of the United States divided into two Indian confederations under British protection. They underscored these demands in August 1814 when they raided Washington and burned the nation's capital.[10]

Seven months after the Federalists in Boston had rejoiced in the triumph of British arms, another victory jubilee, in New Orleans, celebrated the triumph of *American* arms. It would have mattered little to the happy throngs that flooded the streets of New Orleans had they known that two weeks before the battle the British, now confronted with diplomatic complications in Europe, and at home with war weariness and a soaring war debt, had softened their terms and offered the Americans a return to the "status quo ante bellum," terms the United States negotiators had eagerly accepted.

The multitude filled the Place d'Armes as the hero of the day, General Andrew Jackson, proceeded through a deluge of admirers to take his seat of honor in St. Louis Cathedral. Salvos of artillery thundered and the tightly packed spectators cheered as he proceeded through the arch of triumph erected for the celebration. Young ladies, each costumed to represent a state or territory of the Union and forming a corridor to the steps of the cathedral, threw flowers in his path. At the door he was welcomed by Abbé du Bourge, in full robes of office, flanked by a college of priests. The choir began to intone the Te Deum. This ancient hymn of thanksgiving was taken up by the joyous crowd that overflowed the cathedral and packed the Place d'Armes outside.[11]

The victory celebrations in Boston on June 15, 1814, and in New Orleans on

January 21, 1815, seem to define in a peculiar way the shape of the antebellum republic. In Boston, Federalist moneylenders and war contractors had thrust the emblem of the republic into the dust. In New Orleans, Jackson, a planter and slaveholder, had snatched up the national colors and carried them on to victory. For a century and more, folk singers would celebrate the exploits of "Old Hickory" and his yeoman followers.[12] The Federalist period lay in the past.

America Enters the Age of Jackson

Jackson, with his steady focus on military success and his disregard for legal niceties, was the Old South's archetypal leader. His rise from common man to great slaveholder was a route that thousands of hog drivers and cow herders were eager to follow. His aggressive methods won for the Old South plantation bottomlands and livestock range.

Previous southern leaders had been more cautious. President Jefferson had negotiated with France for the Louisiana Purchase, doubling the nation's territory. President Madison had negotiated with Spain for Florida, his diplomacy backed by "unofficial" American raids into the territory.[13] These efforts failed when Spain formed an alliance with the British.

Jackson succeeded where Madison failed. One of the reasons for his success at New Orleans was that, before the British could land significant forces on the Gulf Coast, he and his army of frontiersmen had crushed a large band of Creeks allied to Great Britain. In the treaty that he imposed on the whole Creek Nation in August 1814, he confiscated half of the lands of the pro-British Creeks. He also confiscated half of the lands of the pro-American Creeks.

Next he turned to Florida. Despite the Anglo-Spanish alliance against Napoleon, Spain was not officially at war with the United States. Jackson nevertheless had occupied Pensacola, in Spanish Florida, to prevent the British from using the port to supply their Creek allies and for their attack on New Orleans. He had ruled New Orleans by martial law. Trials had been swift, punishments harsh.

After the war, Jackson again brushed aside Spanish Florida's legal boundaries like cobwebs. Some slaves, taking advantage of the disruptions of the war, had escaped and fled across the border. Likewise, many Creeks, whose lands in Alabama and Georgia Jackson had confiscated, had also crossed over into Florida where they were joined by Choctaws and others. Black and brown refugees thus settled in the bottomlands along the Apalachicola River from the Georgia line to the Gulf, where, like the white pioneers in Alabama and Georgia, they engaged in small-scale farming and large-scale livestock raising. Jackson's confiscation of a broad band of Creek territory across southern Georgia and Alabama, and peace with Great Britain, had touched off a feeding frenzy of real estate speculators. Some were already turning their eyes to south of the border, to those rich bottomlands and livestock ranges along the Apalachicola.

But the refugee Creeks and escaped slaves occupied a well-stocked former British fort on the river. The whites now called it "Negro Fort." Jackson instructed General George Strather Gaines:

> If they are a Banditti assembled on the Territory of Spain or claim to be the subjects of any other power and are stealing and enticing away our negroes, they ought to be viewed as a band of outlaws—land pirates, and ought to be destroyed. Notify the Governor of Pensacola of your advance into his Territory and for the express purpose of destroying these lawless Banditti[.]
>
> I have very little doubt . . . that this fort has been established by some villains for the purpose of murder rapine and plunder and that it ought to be blown up regardless of the ground it stands on, and . . . if your mind should have formed the same conclusion, destroy it and restore the stolen negroes and property to their rightful owners.[14]

Gunboats dispatched from New Orleans met troops marched down the river from Georgia.

Meanwhile several hundred women and children had taken refuge in the fort, which was defended by about a hundred warriors. In the siege, a cannonball heated red hot, known as a "hot shot," was fired into the fort's magazine, exploding seven hundred barrels of gunpowder. Two hundred seventy men, women, and children were killed in the blast. Most of the sixty who survived the explosion died a short time later. The commander of the fort, Choctaw Chief Garçon, was captured alive and executed. Other survivors were taken across the American border as slaves. As the invaders devastated the cornfields and melon patches along the Apalachicola, those who had escaped the onslaught fled with their livestock herds into the wilderness of central Florida.[15] Meanwhile, the Spaniards, with "not enough Gunpowder to fire a salute,"[16] soon opened negotiations to sell their colony.

Not the least impressed by the destruction of the Negro Fort were the real estate promoters. Although the feverish buying and selling of Creek lands was still in full swing in Georgia and Alabama, the speculators did not wait for the Spaniards to leave before launching the first real estate boom in Florida. The drive for plantation bottomlands, livestock range, and real estate profits helped to make northern Florida a part of the Old South and to make Andrew Jackson president of the United States.

Southern Expansion into Texas and the Old South's War

The Old South's expansion into Texas, then a Mexican territory, was in many ways like that which had just occurred in Florida. First came the military adventurers, who tested the power or, perhaps, demonstrated the weakness of the existing government. Next came those whose deeds are not always celebrated in frontier legend, the land speculators and real estate promoters. Then came the pioneer herdsmen who brought in a few slaves. Last to arrive were the substantial planters, who assumed control over the military, the courts, and the political and religious institutions.[17]

From the beginning, many leaders of newly independent Mexico had recognized the danger posed by unregulated immigration. Finally, in 1830, laws were passed to restrict the settlement of Texas to Mexicans or to foreigners whose presence would not be disruptive to Mexican society: slavery was prohibited. Immigrants must be Catholics, and their settlements were generally to be away from coastal and border areas. But for more than a decade, the insolvent government of a severely divided people made little attempt to enforce its immigration laws. When it finally undertook to police the border, it was already too late. With the connivance of land speculators, many of them Mexicans, the Americans were by then concentrated in the coastal low country and in the river bottomlands along the border with American Louisiana. They were practicing slavery. Few were Catholics. Fewer spoke Spanish.[18]

Thus began a period of American-Mexican conflict that ended only in 1848 after the United States had conquered the northern half of Mexico. In the Mexican War, unlike the War of 1812, Americans suffered no humiliating defeats. Instead, newspapers glowed with tales of brilliant victories and shining heroes, southern heroes. This was a conflict that greatly inflated southern expectations about what might be accomplished by military valor and war. Much of the glory was divided between General Winfield Scott of Virginia and General Zachary Taylor of Louisiana, future president and one of the nation's largest slaveholders.

But no returning heroes were given a more ecstatic welcome than Jefferson Davis and his Mississippi Rifles when they landed in New Orleans. The city already knew the story of the "V of Buena Vista," a tale that had lost nothing in the telling. Everyone had heard how the Indiana volunteers had panicked and fled. But Jefferson Davis, though shot through the foot, had remained on his horse and had rallied the remnants and placed them together with his own steadfast Mississippi Rifles into a defensive wedge-shaped formation. Into the deadly jaws of this open "V" had ridden Mexico's finest troops, the mounted lancers, only to be cut down by the accurate crossfire of American rifles.[19]

At Buena Vista the Americans had been outnumbered four to one. Yet Jefferson Davis and southern valor had carried the day. To many of Davis' admirers it appeared that, as in the War of 1812, once again gun-shy Yankees had dishonored the nation. But, as Andrew Jackson had done then, another great slaveholder and brave gentleman had once again turned defeat into victory, humiliation into glory.[20]

Climax of the Cotton Bonanza

American slaveholders never enjoyed more prosperity than during the twelve years that followed the Mexican War. During these years there was a global rise in the demand for cotton and hence in cotton prices. Happily for many growers these climbing prices occurred at the same time that the Mexican War had made vast stretches of prime cotton land safe for slavery.[21] Even in the long-cultivated regions to the east, despite declining yields, planters were enjoying the high prices.

Some of the bounty, furthermore, trickled down to the yeomanry. Cotton was a high-risk, high-return crop grown mainly by planters and prosperous farmers, those who could afford an occasional bad year.[22] Thriving cotton plantations, moreover, especially in the Southwest, provided a good market for the livestock and food crops of the plain whites. The rising prices and the bountiful harvest of cotton on the Old South's most recent frontier kindled anew the hope of some farmers and cow herders that they too might become gentlemen. Slaveholders, even in the tobacco-growing border states and the Upper South, where little cotton could be grown, also felt the exhilarating effects of the southwestern bonanza. They were sellers of slaves, and never had slaves brought such prices. After 1850, slave prices climbed even faster than the price of cotton.

Plantation Prosperity and Northern Profits

From the Mason-Dixon Line to the Gulf, the confidence of southern leaders soared with the fortunes of the "land of cotton." But the success of the planters and their commodity export economy did not end at the Mason-Dixon Line. It reached the great port cities of the Northeast, the nation's main centers of maritime commerce and banking. Here during the early decades of the nineteenth century, shippers and bankers did not find the North a particularly attractive place for business: The products of free labor accounted for scarcely one-third of American exports.[23] Most people lived on family farms and had little collateral to secure a bank loan and little need for one. Until the eve of the Civil War, American industry was still in its infancy. The typical "industrialist" ran a small shop and, like a family farmer, had little collateral or need for credit.

But planters had valuable bottomland and slaves for collateral and they needed credit to buy more bottomlands and slaves for their sons. Indeed, northeastern capital fueled much of the wildfire spread of the plantation economy, which in one generation swept beyond the Carolinas and Georgia to Texas.[24]

Also sharing in the cotton bonanza were the northeastern export houses, shippers, and insurance companies. Some Southerners advanced the "forty bales" theory that of every hundred bales of cotton that planters produced, forty went to compensate these northeastern businessmen for their services.[25]

Some of the plantation wealth reached the Old Northwest, today's Midwest. Until the opening of the east-west canals and railroads in the late antebellum years, the Mississippi was the main avenue of trade. Planters specialized in commodity exports. Northwestern farmers specialized in food crops and livestock production. Much of their corn and salt pork floated down the Mississippi to plantation markets.

Northern Politics and the Cotton Connection

The triumph of the Old South was also political. If some planters resented sharing their bounty with their northeastern business partners, they nevertheless gained political advantages for doing so. The same labor system and federal policies that made planters prosper also made bankers and commodity exporters prosper. This gave rise to "the Slave Power," a political alliance that protected the wealth of planters and their northeastern partners. In commercial cities from Cincinnati to Boston, planter prosperity meant profits and jobs. In these cities, especially, mobs burned down black neighborhoods and pelted abolitionists with rotten fruit. Even in Utica, New York, a mob led by the "dough-faced" congressman Samuel Beardsley broke up a convention of the New York State Anti-Slavery Society, and the same day in Boston a mob dragged the abolitionist William Lloyd Garrison through the streets with a rope around his neck.[26]

"No, you dare not make war on cotton," Senator James H. Hammond of South Carolina warned his northern colleagues in 1858. "No power on earth dares to make war on it. Cotton *is* king."[27]

Chapter 6

The Old South's Crisis and the Emergence of the White Solidarity Myth

At first, the worried voices had been infrequent. Many planters were of a pragmatic mind, concerned with personal fortunes and family dynasties. For them the compelling reality was that cotton grew high in the South's virgin western lands and sold high in Liverpool. The intoxicating effects of this bonanza were being felt from the valley of the Rio Brazos to the valley of the Delaware, and beyond.

In a society where the most articulate people are prospering prodigiously, it is not easy for its spokesmen to see a coming crisis. But in the Old South, there were such persons. Besides the present-minded there were also ideologues, individuals who thought in three tenses: past, present, and future. For them there was *history;* and in important ways history had been unkind to the Old South in recent decades.

The South's Declining Position in Washington

This decline first became evident in the House of Representatives. The lower house was based on population; and four out of five immigrants were settling in the North. As early as 1820, the white population of the North was greater than that of the South.[1] This difference was not immediately reflected in Congress because the Constitution provided that a slave be counted as three-fifths of a person. Yet, with every federal census, the North had gained, the South had lost representation.

The South, it is true, had held its own for a time in the Senate, which was based on territory. The southern frontier had moved rapidly, and every time a free territory had applied to enter the union as a state there had also been a slave territory ready to enter. Thus southern parity in the Senate had been maintained. But then, somewhere toward the 98th meridian west, the frontier of plantation agriculture appeared to be approaching a final halt, a point where the Old South met the Old West.[2] So, in 1850, when California applied for admission as a free state, there was no corresponding slave state that could be admitted to maintain the North-South balance of power in the Senate. It was alarmingly apparent to many Southerners, furthermore, that California was only the first of a series of free states that would be admitted without any counterbalancing slave state.[3] Southern influence in the Senate would slip as surely as it had done previously in the House of Representatives.

By midcentury, southern control of the White House also seemed threatened. Until then, there had been only twelve years when it had not been occupied by a slaveholder. But now a growing majority of voters were in the North. These had become less enthusiastic about planter presidents than they had been during the days of Washington and Jefferson.

Leaders of the Old South often expressed concern over the decline of their influence in Washington. But, like some historians since, they regarded planter society as stable, internally sound. They thought the threats came from the outside. Yet there were always individuals who noticed that the Old South had problems that could not be attributed to antislavery sermons of New England preachers or to hostile articles in distant and small-circulation newspapers.[4]

The South's Internal Decay

The South's leading economist, J. D. B. DeBow, in 1854, warned: "It is not to be disguised, nor can it be successfully controverted that a degree . . . of poverty and destitution exists in the southern states, . . . , almost unknown in the manufacturing districts of the North."[5] In the South's older states, along the Atlantic seaboard, the North-South differences had become especially striking. In the Northeast, the passing of the frontier had left a landscape thickly sown with cities, many of them large. As immigrants poured in and farms reoriented toward urban markets, small-scale agriculture had taken on new vigor.[6] But in Virginia and the Carolinas, "signs of senility and decay" were "apparent," and by 1855, this "senility" had reached Clement C. Clay's native Alabama County, where wealthy planters had bought up the lands of yeomen: "Numerous farm houses, once the abode of industrious and intelligent freemen, now occupied by slaves, or tenantless, deserted and dilapidated; . . . , fields, once fertile, now unfenced, abandoned, and covered with those evil harbingers, fox-tail and broomsedge."[7] In the Southeast there were few immigrants but many signs of out-migration. By 1850, 25 percent of the people born in Georgia had left the state. In North Carolina, the figure was 30 percent and in South Carolina 40 percent.[8]

Those who have regarded the Old South as internally stable have noted the vast tracts of unimproved land even in the oldest states. Of what importance was it then that the ultimate western limits of plantation agriculture had been reached? How could poverty arise in an area where there was so much un-cultivated land? But much of the hill country had been eroded by destructive farming techniques and abandoned for fresh fields farther west. In places, even rich alluvial valleys had been abandoned because runoff from rains in the gullied upland was causing crop-destroying floods.

Certainly much good uncultivated acreage in the long-settled southern states could have been put into immediate production had these lands been for sale at prices that land-poor or landless families could afford. But such was not the case. Especially in counties in the Black Belt—an area extending with some interruptions from southeastern Virginia to Texas—the process that was actually taking place was the consolidation of land holdings. Large landowners were buying up the farms of their poorer neighbors.[9] And many were also buying up large tracts elsewhere to hold for speculation or for their descendants.[10] Simply population growth was evermore ruling out the prosperous open-range herding that the yeomanry had enjoyed in the 1700s. The wilderness had vanished, and with it the gigantic herds and long drives. Many plain whites, if they had the resources to make the journey and set up anew, were trying their luck farther west.

The frontier country, the land of the second chance, was no longer just beyond the horizon. It was now in distant Texas. Those who made the journey passed already wasted lands and joined the competition with other families for fresh fields and pastures on the Old South's last frontier.[11]

In the 1700s, when cheap or free land had been close by, it had been the poorest of the poor who had been most prone to move west. Now it was this class, without the resources to move, who had to remain behind. The Old South was thus still exporting many of its people, but no longer its poorest.[12]

For all the misery the Civil War created, the creation of the white poor began before the war. The late antebellum cotton boom enjoyed by planters and an upper crust of farmers hid another reality in southern society: for a generation before the Civil War a new frontier had been moving from east to west across the Old South, a frontier of poverty.[13]

The Failure of Agricultural Reform

Not all of the planter South reacted to the region's difficulties with xenophobic rage against abolitionists and Yankees. Indeed there was a movement led by scientific-minded planters and editors of agricultural journals to combat the destructive exploitation of land and to crusade for sustainable farming. The most distinguished of these reformers was Edmund Ruffin. Ruffin owned three plantations in tidewater Virginia, the oldest cultivated region in Anglo America. There he experimented with techniques for restoring fertility to worn-out land and made his findings known through his journal, the Petersburg *Farmer's Register.*

His model was Europe, especially England, where agriculture had been maintained for more than a millennium and, during the past century, production had been dramatically increased. Ruffin and his fellow reformers demonstrated that yields could be increased substantially if the soil was treated with marl, particles of shell found in many local deposits along the Atlantic coast. Similar results could be obtained from lime, also available in many places. Dramatic increase came as well from the use of imported guano fertilizer.

Yet, after a ten-year crusade, Ruffin closed down the *Farmer's Register* and turned from agricultural reform to "southern rights" politics. As a staunch defender of the Old South, even his success brought frustration. His methods had been accepted enthusiastically *north* of the Mason-Dixon Line.[14] The farmers of New Jersey answered his call to enrich the soil with marl. They had the capital as well as a well-developed system of canals to transport the bulky mineral from pit to field. In 1850, New Jersey had 142 miles of canals while Georgia, seven times as large, had only 28 miles.[15] In Georgia, the necessary capital was being invested in slaves and virgin bottomlands on the southwestern cotton frontier.

To be sure, the reforms Ruffin urged were adopted in the border slave states along the Mason-Dixon Line, though less extensively than in the North. Yet even here the results were not entirely gratifying to Ruffin.[16] Much of the capital for marling, liming, drainage, and other improvements came from the sale of slaves; and, once landlords in Delaware and Maryland had sold them and converted to free labor, they began to behave like northern landlords: their principal wealth now consisted of land, not slaves. Hence they lost interest in southern efforts to extend the western frontier of slavery and thus increase the value of slaves. Instead, like northerners, they became keenly interested in developments closer to home that would increase the value of their property in land: soil improvement, certainly, but also projects for the construction of canals and railroads. For the same reason they began to promote immigration and urban development. And, all along the Mason-Dixon Line, landholders continued to convert to free or half-free labor. In 1860, as the now "southern rights" firebrand Edmund Ruffin saw it, "The vacancy of population thus made near the border [by the sale of slaves to the Deep South] will, in time be filled by immigrants and hirelings from the North; . . . This end has already been reached in Delaware, is fast approaching in Maryland, and next, Missouri, Virginia and Kentucky, under the existing circumstances, must successively be subjected to the same course."[17] The planter South was shrinking. Its border states were rapidly being lost to plantation society. They were becoming northernized.[18]

The Northernization of Southern Cities

The process of northernization did not end in the border states. It was also taking place in towns and cities throughout the South. "Our whole commerce except a small fraction is in the hands of Northern men," a Mobile judge wrote to John C. Calhoun in 1847. "Take Mobile as an example—⅞ of our Bank Stock is owned by Northern men—as is a large part of the Insurance Stock . . . half our real estate is owned by non-residents, of the same section. Our wholesale and retail business—everything in short worth mentioning is in the hands of men who invest their profits at the North."[19]

Until about 1850 southern urban development was sluggish. Then came the cotton boom and with it an upsurge in railroad construction. But the lines built to export cotton brought further changes. Previously the only true cities in the South had been either seaports or those along its northern border. Now interior towns began to grow vigorously. Furthermore, industrialization began in southern cities, even if not so rapidly as that in the North. By 1860, half the industry in the South had been constructed within the past ten years.[20]

Southern leaders looked on these developments with mixed feelings. On the one hand, the War of 1812 had demonstrated the disadvantage of an agricultural nation involved in a struggle with an industrial one. Some industry could strengthen the South in its dealings with Great Britain and with the North. But, on the other hand, leaders of the Old South often took an unfriendly view of cities.[21] A correspondent of John C. Calhoun wrote to him in 1849 that Georgia and Alabama were loyal to southern interests, except for the cities of Savannah, Augusta, and Mobile. "However, I fear for Louisiana. New Orleans is almost Free Soil in their opinions. . . . The cities all of them are becoming daily more and more unsound and uncertain and all for the same reason. The infusion of Northerners and Foreigners amongst them and their influence is being felt in the interior." He feared that "the issue of the Free laborer against Slave labour will soon be made at the South."[22] His distrust of New Orleans was on target. On the eve of the Civil War, the Secessionists carried the city by only 2 percent, and the New Orleans recruits sent to Fort Jackson to defend the mouth of the Mississippi mutinied when the Union fleet approached.[23]

Planter society had little cause to worry about cities until about 1850. But then came the upturn in urbanization. Society in southern cities then became more and more like that in the North and radically different from that in the plantation South. Like northeastern cities had developed a century earlier, southern cities, as they grew larger, as they acquired more industries, became whiter and freer. As had happened in the North, the black proportion of the urban South was declining; and, of those blacks who remained in the cities, many were freed people.[24] As in the North of the 1700s, urban masters in the South found it difficult to control slaves.[25] And often, especially before slave prices became too high, those masters struck emancipation bargains with slaves in exchange for years of payments or services. More often, especially with the cotton boom, urban owners sold off their chief troublemakers, generally young men, to southwestern plantations, creating a "whitening process" in southern cities.[26] Also, the blacks remaining in cities were disproportionately women, many of them emancipated. Black workers were being removed from southern cities even as urban labor requirements increased.

While planters clamored for more slaves even as slave prices spiraled ever higher, urban employers clamored for white labor as the cities grew. Surrounding these cities were poor whites. They worked only sporadically. One reason for this was that planters treated wage labor as a temporary makeshift. But also, poor whites did not adapt easily to wage labor. They believed that many of the jobs that planters or prosperous farmers offered them were slave jobs. As J. D. B. Debow noted, "[A poor white man] will endure the evils of pinching poverty rather than engage in servile labor under the existing state of things [slavery], even were employment offered to him, which is not general."[27] And it was humiliating to take orders from a person no whiter than they were. As one employer complained, "It appears to me that they are the gentleman & I am the workman. . . . tomorrow morning I may have 7 or 8 at work or I may have only one."[28] Not surprisingly, employers in southern cities filled their grow-ing labor needs not from the underemployed white poor in the surrounding countryside but with northerners and immigrants, who also more likely had the urban skills that rural southerners lacked.[29]

Urban demography may have been one reason why many dignitaries of the plantation South did not like cities. It was a population that included a surplus of unattached black women, many of whom were no longer slaves. Now coming into these centers were immigrants, overwhelmingly unattached young men, many of whom were poorly instructed in caste behavior. Evangelical Christian-ity thrived on saving sinners. But except for police reports we would scarcely know that in the shadowy recesses of the cities, in the hidden sanctuaries of Satan, a kind of racial integration was threatening the moral foundations of the social order.[30]

This hidden scandal also threatened the stability of the labor system. South-ern law defined status in simple terms of black and white. But in the urban South, it was sometimes hard to tell who was "black."[31] While census takers may have been prone to underestimate embarrassing evidence of racial mix-ing, their findings are significant. They found that while the overall southern nonwhite population was 12 percent racially mixed ("mulatto"), in St. Louis, Baltimore, New Orleans, and other southern cities, the figure approached 50 percent. The "problem" of racial blending, furthermore, appeared to be in-creasing. During the last antebellum decade, the overall urban and rural slave population increased 22 percent. But the "mulatto" population increased 67 percent.[32] The Old South faced a situation in which many "blacks" were no longer black. Even worse, some white "blacks" ended up on the wrong side of the racial divide. In South Carolina, this problem was sufficient to cause the legislature to refuse to establish a legal definition of blackness.[33]

The Free-Soil Movement

What kind of ideology prevailed in these cities as they became more and more like northern cities? In the North of the era of the American Revolution, espe-cially in areas such as upper New England, where the influence of slavehold-ers was weak,[34] free laborers sometimes had taken the radical position of the abolitionists: the way to end the conflict between two labor systems was to abolish the coercive one. They thus attacked slavery itself, although less often attacked the racial defenses of slavery. An attitude that became more common in the North, and virtually universal in southern cities,[35] was not abolitionism but the more cautious and pragmatic view of the "Free-Soilers."[36]

Free Soil, originally a movement to exclude slavery from free states and territories, became by extension a demand to exclude unfree labor from cities and from occupations. While the movement at times included radical opponents of slavery, most Free-Soilers demanded not abolition but containment of slavery. Most also ignored the sometimes uncertain distinction between slaves and quasi-freed people.

Indeed quasi-free workers were a more immediate threat than slaves. They could be used as strikebreakers North and South. The financial loss to an employer was great if a white mob killed one of his slaves, but not if they killed a free person. And mobs could justify such violence by the North-South racial consensus. Also, Free-Soilers tried to exclude free blacks from work such as barbers in Baltimore, carters in Richmond, and longshoremen in New Orleans. To be antislavery was to invite violent retribution. To be antiblack was merely to repeat what the nation's leaders were saying.

The basic view of the Free-Soilers was: keep your slaves and semi-slaves where they cause me no problems and I will raise no fuss. Such views were typical of immigrants, a sizable minority in southern cities. They had crossed the ocean to improve their personal and family situations, not to improve society. They wanted to become good Americans, not to change America. The last thing they wanted to do was to challenge the ideas that dominated their new homeland.

The Hegemonic Racial Defense of Slavery

For more than two thousand years the defense of slavery had been the deflection of the hostility of free people from slaveholder to slave. Slaveholding societies had always conceded that free non-slaveholders had legitimate grievances. But they had always insisted that the cause of these problems was not the intrusion on their lives of a coercive labor system but rather the debased character of whatever ethnic, religious, or racial group had been reduced to slavery. Viewed in this light, slavery appeared to be good. It disciplined, controlled, and civilized a depraved population.

The form this argument assumed in the United States was that the grievances of free people were to be explained not by slavery but by race. This idea became hegemonic in the United States, internalized by upstanding citizens, the mainstream of society. It was an idea critical to the defense of slavery. To be sure, where there was slavery, manual labor was often held in low esteem. And certain occupations associated with slaves were tainted with a caste-like stigma. Wages were depressed.[37] But there was only one explanation: race—not the slaveholders and their labor system, using both slaves and "free" blacks to the detriment of free labor and free society, but blacks, their very presence.

For more than a decade before the Civil War this belief was no ordinary political doctrine. It was the "sound" or orthodox view, expressed by the leaders of all mainstream political parties, North and South.[38] Everywhere, it separated the upright citizen from the abandoned agitator. To deny this doctrine, to argue, as the abolitionists did, that the problem was not race but slavery, was, in the North, to put oneself beyond the pale of respectable society.

Although Huckleberry Finn and Jim are fictional characters, Mark Twain knew well the upper Mississippi borderland between slavery and freedom. The fourteen-year-old Huck's claims to respectability are tenuous indeed: a vagabond who often slept in a barrel, son of the town drunkard. Jim is an escaped slave whom Huck likes. Huck does not want to betray Jim, but "people would call me a low down abolitionist and despise me for keeping mum." In the story, friendship triumphs over rectitude.[39]

In the South, for a person to express racial views that were "unsound" was often to put oneself beyond the protection of law altogether.[40] Even in the North, abolitionists were sometimes attacked by mobs. In the South, federal mails were searched for "incendiary" materials. There were state censorship laws and public burnings of books. In North Carolina the Reverend Daniel Worth, a Wesleyan minister, was sentenced in 1860 to a year in prison for circulating copies of Hinton Rowan Helper's *Impending Crisis*.[41] The Free-Soilers internalized the racial doctrine that stood behind this legal repression and extralegal violence. They manipulated the beliefs of mainstream society to defend their livelihood from unfree labor, or opportunistically to displace free blacks from jobs or trades such as longshoremen or carters.[42] As had happened earlier in the cities of the North, white urban laborers became ever more assertive as they became more numerous.[43] A visitor to New Orleans, in 1853, reported hearing an immigrant mechanic say that white "working men were rapidly displacing the slaves in all sorts of work, and he hoped and believed it would not be many years before every negro would be driven out of town."[44] By the 1850s, slaves had become too expensive to be exposed to such hostility. And white solidarity was too critical to the fragile national power structure. So New Orleans, which in 1805 had had a black majority, was 86 percent white by 1860; and of the blacks still remaining in the city, 44 percent were free.

The Urban Middle Class and the "Traffic"

Despite the sharp upturn in urban growth at the end of the antebellum period, town-dwelling Southerners remained a small minority. Urban folk, except in the region's most northernized centers along the Mason-Dixon Line, still generally acquiesced to the leadership of planters.[45] Probably the most old-fashioned city in the South was Charleston, where northernization was slight. In 1850, Charleston was largely what it had been a century earlier, an outlet for low-country commodities. Its growth was sluggish. The population was still almost half black, and there was little industry.

The middle class was small. Indeed a Scottish visitor to Charleston in 1857 saw no middle class at all: "There are many large imposing houses with pillars and verandahs, no doubt the residences of the aristocratic Southerners; the rest of the habitations are small and poor-looking. There seems to be no middle class; only rich and poor."[46] Businessmen mainly subsisted by supplying the commercial needs of the plantation gentry, who did not always treat them with respect but to whom they were generally subservient. "What should I do in Charleston, for heaven's sake?" Hugh Legaré sniffed in a letter to his sister. "The town *bourgeoisie* is *so* odious!"[47]

Yet even in conservative Charleston, although the business community enjoyed little power and prestige, it was able to defend its interests at times against the planter-controlled legislature. Like other southern states, South Carolina passed laws against trafficking with slaves. In this informal business, slaves exchanged plantation products for store-bought goods, especially liquor.[48] Since slaves were closely supervised, the plantation-city link in the "traffic" was often provided by freed people or underemployed poor whites, who had become a sizable group by the 1850s.[49]

Most whites, particularly merchants who supplied the gentry, expressed disapproval of this trade. In the words of the *Savannah Republican,* it was "an inducement to theft and intoxication" and was "a grievance of great and growing magnitude."[50] Proprietors of small groceries and grog shops, on the other hand, often took a tolerant view of the traffic.[51] This lively trade in the streets and small shops brought money into the city. The spin-off effects were felt by much of the middle class.

Trafficking became increasingly widespread with the upsurge of urbanization. State authorities often received little cooperation in the very communities where the traffic was rampant.[52] And they were hampered by the larger political situation: after 1820, the North-South conflict was never far from view. The last thing the southern leaders needed was a fundamental split among whites. So the traffic persisted. The "odious bourgeoisie" prospered and became ever more influential.

Much larger than the commerce between shopkeepers and slaves were the economic ties being formed between the urban centers and the rural, non-slaveholding whites, the fastest growing population in the South. They were more numerous than the blacks, even in most parts of the Black Belt, and had a far greater buying power. Villages and towns rather than plantations were now becoming the focal points of exchange. By the 1850s many southern plain whites had less need for the patronage of a gentleman to market their crops, obtain supplies, or for credit, nor did they depend upon the services of his plantation blacksmith or shoemaker. They now came to the crossroads merchant, the Yankee shopkeeper, or the immigrant craftsman.

Deference to the gentry was still ingrained. But a growing non-slaveholding population in town and country was now creating its own network of exchange. It was conducting business in ways that resembled the way it was done in the North. In short, one of the strongest foundations of planter hegemony—control over the economic infrastructure of southern society—was being rapidly eroded during the 1850s by the growth of towns, where merchants and free craftsmen were now providing the goods and services that had once been provided by planters and their slave craftsmen.[53]

The Appearance of the Poor Whites

The westward expansion of plantation agriculture was giving way to its internal expansion, within the South. In the Black Belt, cotton plantations were expanding and sustaining a high demand for slaves. There, slave labor plantations were displacing the yeomanry.[54]

This expansion of the plantation economy in the Black Belt during the 1850s accentuated the division of the South into a predominantly free-labor white South and a more and more slave-labor Black Belt South.[55] This geographical separation was weakening the traditional economic, military, religious, and social ties between the planters and many of their yeoman constituents, as more and more plain whites moved out of the Black Belt. Ultimately it was the yeomanry who watched the slaves and maintained social stability. Without them the Old South would suffer the fate of Santo Domingo.

Now the yeomen were moving out, the poorer ones to the marginal lands, to the wiregrass country, the piney woods, the Appalachian highlands, where in growing numbers they competed for scant farm and range land.[56] Their pioneer prosperity was fading. Already some were indeed "poor whites." Their political support for planter society was now less sure.[57] Indeed, by 1850 several predominantly white counties in North Carolina had laws that made service in the slave patrols solely the duty of slaveholders and overseers.[58]

Support for the leaders of the Old South was less certain in a growing number of white counties. Even more problematical was the support that they could expect from the now half-northernized border states, where the cotton bonanza in the Black Belt was draining off slaves and thus contributing to the conversion to free labor. What would be the attitude of these states once the last slave had been sold south or emancipated?

The Irrational "Ultras"

Despite all these developments, the master class of the Old South enjoyed considerable prosperity, if little security, during the last antebellum decade. After 1850, slave prices spiraled out of reach of even prosperous farmers, dashing their hopes of entering the charmed circle of planter society. A wave of anxiety swept the South.[59]

Southern politics took on an explosive character. Southern "Ultras" sometimes took extreme positions that seemed to many people unreasonable. Although abolitionists in the North were politically marginalized, and most people there looked on them as eccentric and inconsequential, the Montgomery *Advertiser* charged that the abolitionists "control both the great parties of the country, and have most effectively given direction to federal policy." David Hubbard, an Alabama congressman, argued that it would be unconstitutional for Delaware, a state whose slave population had now fallen to less than 1 percent, to abolish slavery. To do so "would reduce the remaining slave states to a minority in the Senate, and thus violate the spirit of equality."[60] Furthermore, some of the positions taken by southern leaders seemed to many people to be more symbolic than practical; for example, the *right* to bring slaves into federal territories in the northern plains, an area where few masters would have thought of actually bringing slaves or trying to grow plantation crops.[61]

Who and what stood behind these positions, which seem irrational and emotional and which were certainly confrontational? The most respected voices of the Old South were, either as individuals or by family connection, members of the planter elite; that is, a class owning roughly twenty or more slaves. This group occupied the most important positions of power in the South and not a few in the federal government. But as a class, capable of amplifying an ideology, their numbers were slender indeed. In 1860, this elite amounted only to 46,274 persons. Even with the addition of their families, they still constituted only about 4 percent of the white South.

The planter elite, however, had a substantial and enthusiastic constituency made up chiefly of prosperous, slaveholding farmers. Although their numbers were declining as plantations expanded, still, even in 1860, these almost-planters comprised about one-quarter of southern whites. Certainly, slave-holders had been a shrinking proportion of the white population for at least a generation, as slave prices rose and as livestock herds now seldom provided the capital to make one a planter.[62] Yet on the eve of the Civil War, slavehold-ers, large and small, still constituted 25 percent of the white South. And in the Black Belt, half of the whites were members of families who owned at least one or two slaves. Slaveholders, furthermore, were not only a sizable group, numbering almost two million in a nation of thirty million; but also, nowhere in the United States was there a class of comparable numbers as rich as they. Slaveholders as a group had five times the wealth of the average northerner and more than ten times that of the remaining three-quarters of white southern farmers who owned no slaves.[63] This was a constituency whose interests could not be ignored by leaders of national stature. Political leaders who spoke to and for slaveholders were not wasting their words.

But why their politics of confrontation, escalation, threats to dissolve the Union, and hints of military preparedness? "With so much to conserve," Gavin Wright has asked, "why were they not more conservative?"[64] Some planters, especially large and established ones, were indeed conservative, opposing ag-gressive and confrontational politics. As Whigs, they had opposed the Mexican War, anticipating the North-South crisis that it precipitated. In 1860, as Con-stitutional Unionists, they opposed such "Ultra" demands as the annexation of Cuba. Was the Old South's predicament so severe as to require desperate measures? Indeed the slave South was shrinking. Perhaps it would be reduced eventually to the Deep South Black Belt. While the South's internal stresses were becoming apparent and in the North there was a small but steady current of Radical criticism, did these gradual developments constitute a crisis for the slaveholders of the 1850s or for their grandchildren?

It was hard to find a mainstream political leader in the North who did not take pains to distance himself from the abolitionists. The much-feared Re-publican Party, it is true, tolerated a small Radical faction, but many of these individuals internalized a belief in white superiority, which debilitated their criticism of slavery. As for the threat from within, the continuing ruin of the bulk of the yeomanry was a process that was hardly complete at the end of the nineteenth century. Also unfolding slowly was an urban-oriented, over-whelmingly white, industrializing South founded on free or half-free labor. Yet southern leaders of the 1850s saw a crisis, their crisis, not that of their grandchildren.

Were they overreacting when they responded violently to what others con-sidered faint and distant signals? Behind their apparent irrationality, however, were some sober economic realities of cotton and slaves. After a slight drop in the early fifties, cotton prices resumed their upward movement. But the price of slaves was rising even faster than that of cotton. Slaves were the most expensive component in the production of cotton, and they normally sold at prices that were influenced by the anticipated higher price of cotton.

But slaves became transformed from an ordinary commodity to one that was also speculative, "subjective," or "detached from earnings."[65] The ideas of southern leaders seemed to reflect the speculative character of their most valuable property, their slaves. The price a person was willing to pay for a slave was affected by the way one read the future: Would cotton prices in Liverpool continue to rise? But also would the geographical area in which slaves could be sold expand or would it contract? What did the growing strength of the free states in Congress foretell about the future of slavery? Were the street throngs pelting the abolitionist speakers with rotten fruit or were they listening to them? For almost two million slaveholders, such considerations influenced the way they counted their wealth.

Despite many uncertainties, slaveholders were nervously optimistic in the 1850s. The ongoing cotton bonanza in the South's western lands, the continuing expansion of the cotton Black Belt within the South, and the rising cotton prices all combined to drive upward the price of slaves and to brighten slaveholders' mood. A master who owned just two slaves and nothing else was as rich as the average northerner. A family owning a single individual was likely to count their slave as their most valuable possession. Visions of self-worth had soared on the wings of the imagination when the Southwest had been made safe for slavery. But the flight was precarious, for wealth in slaves was speculative. Good news made the slaveholders richer; bad news made them poorer.

The slaveholders' nervous optimism may provide insights into the ideology of the late antebellum South. To attribute the beliefs of an individual to economic self-interest is hazardous. To attribute the shared beliefs of a social class, of a large group of people who function in a similar way in society, to their economic interest is in this case possible. From John C. Calhoun and Jefferson Davis down, southern leaders were slaveholders, large and small; and despite their talk of states' rights, the Constitution, and race, their underlying consuming passion was a defense of the property that made them the richest class of comparable size anywhere in the nation.

The "emotionalism" that marked their politics, moreover, may well reflect the inflated "subjective equity" in slaves whereby they calculated their self-worth.[66] Their personal fortunes floated upon ideology, upon what others might say or imagine. And perhaps this explains why the Old South placed a higher value on "honor" than upon "conscience."[67]

But at the same time, the southern leaders were not like some Wall Street banker who, due to a loan default, ended up owner of a plantation in Mississippi.[68] They lived and breathed in a slaveholder's culture. They met slaves face to face daily. They saw the resentment, the tension that was built up by the coercion of labor. They were experts in reading the degree of "insolence" in the glance or the degree of subordination in the shuffling gait of a slave. They were the ultimate beneficiaries of a hair-trigger society that wavered between confidence and fear.

This most stable of plantation societies was disoriented periodically by successive waves of panic, touched off at times by some flare-up of black anger, or, at other times, apparently only by fear itself. During these times of hysteria, whites who tried to hide or protect a favorite or valuable slave sometimes suffered the same fate as the black victims. Such episodes often ended in grisly scenes of torture, bodies swinging from trees, or crowds watching victims being burned alive,[69] after which the Old South could return to the belief that slaves loved their masters.

The fortunes, and the safety, of slaveholders depended on the undivided support of non-slaveholding whites. By the 1850s, white solidarity, that jugular vein of planter society, was threatened by several developments. But the most immediate threat did not come from the growing numbers of the white poor, as these were largely marginalized and politically inactive; nor did it come from the urban business class, nor even from urban Free-Soil workers. The numbers and influence of both were not yet great. It came rather from that still sizable part of the yeomen who were still prosperous.

The Movement to Make Every White Man a Master

Many substantial farmers and stock raisers owned a few slaves, perhaps their most valuable possessions. But it would take more than a few slaves to justify an overseer and to be freed from work in the fields, to give one's family the leisure to improve their education, to make it possible for one's children to marry advantageously, to be active in the politics of the state and of one's church, and to have the wealth to form one's own militia company. In a word, with enough slaves, a farmer/cow herder became a planter. But the high and rising cost of slaves shattered these visions.

Prosperous yeomen were the backbone of the Old South. In the Jacksonian tradition, they were assertive and articulate. But their hands were "cotton-picking hands." They were not "quality people" like the gentlemen they elected to office. And in the 1850s, they were listening to political agendas that were dangerous to planter society. Increasing numbers demanded the reopening of the Atlantic slave trade. Thousands of almost-planters were listening eagerly to speakers who explained that by importing more Africans, slave prices would be rolled back and missing rungs restored to the ladder of upward mobility.[70]

Out of the blighted hopes of these would-be gentlemen, the partisans of the Atlantic slave trade whipped up a desperate challenge to the established planter class and to the stability of the Old South itself. The every-white-man-a-master movement threatened the equity that established planters held in slaves. Furthermore, if these upstarts glutted the cotton market and caused prices to collapse, they also threatened the planter's income. They were, likewise, confronting the slave-selling elite of the Upper South.[71] "What right has Congress," one Mississippi editor asked, "to force a planter to pay a negro breeder of Virginia $1,400 for a negro man, when the same can be purchased in Ludamas [in Africa] for $150?"[72]

And the issue was a godsend to the abolitionists.[73] On no other question could they have hoped for such a broad and sympathetic hearing. On this issue of importing more slaves they could mobilize even the most pragmatic, shortsighted, and antiblack of the Free-Soilers.

The movement to reopen the Atlantic slave trade threatened white solidarity in the South, threatened the delicate ties southern leaders had with their northern allies, threatened to pit the Deep South against the Upper South, against the North, and against Great Britain, which was now combating the slave trade. Perhaps most of all, the movement threatened to bring the abolitionists out of the shadows into the political mainstream. Southern leaders were unable to quiet this seemingly suicidal clamor, which grew louder and louder until it was finally drowned out by the guns of war.

Southern leaders held that race in the South, and in the nation, had replaced class. But it is likely that their confrontational "southern rights" politics were driven by class tensions, especially by signs of disaffection from the constituency of plain whites upon which planter hegemony rested. In politics there are few things so effective in managing a split within one's ranks than the discovery of a menace from without. Faced with this dire threat from within the South, southern leaders sounded the alarm about sermons preached in distant New England and editorials in small-circulation newspapers. They talked about war and the need for preparedness.

The "Filibuster" Campaigns for More Slave States

Past wars had solved problems for southern whites. Since the days of Bacon's Rebellion, each time the planter-yeoman society had been caught in an impasse, the bold deeds of armed men had given it a fresh start. These adventurers, with or without the help of the government, had shot Native Americans and Mexicans, conquered lush bottomlands and abundant pastures. They had brought into the Union new slave states that sent planters to the Senate and to the White House. And it was to these tried and true methods that some southern leaders turned in the 1850s: "I want Cuba," Senator Albert G. Brown shouted to a Mississippi "multitude" in 1859, "and I know sooner or later we must have it. . . . I want Tamaulipas, Potosi, and one or two other Mexican States; and I want them all for the same reason—for the planting or spreading of slavery. And a footing in Central America will powerfully aid us in acquiring those other states."[74] Private armies of "filibusters" invaded Cuba twice during the last antebellum decade, Mexico at least four times, and Honduras once. Nicaragua was occupied from 1855 to 1857 by the followers of William Walker who, reenacting the Texas scenario of an earlier generation, legalized slavery and invited in American immigrants.[75] In 1856, a proslavery paramilitary band rode into Lawrence, Kansas, put the Free-Soil settlers to flight, and sacked and burned the town.[76]

The southern press followed these adventures with avid interest. But times had changed. The Manifest Destiny crusade to the lands below the Rio Grande was reported with less enthusiasm in the North, where some people had concluded that one Texas, at the very most, was sufficient. The federal government, now under greater free-state influence, showed more caution in aiding the intrigues and military expeditions of the filibusters. All told, after ten years of conspiracies and heroic bloodshed, all that these soldiers of fortune could show for their efforts was the Gadsden strip, a band of desert in southern Arizona. The western boundary of plantation agriculture had not budged. "Kansas, Cuba, South America," lamented a leader of the "southern rights" movement in 1858, "all loomed up as inviting to Southern expansionism, outlet & development. The dream has been sadly dissipated."[77] The efforts of the Old South's filibusters to open a new frontier had been even less effective than the earlier efforts of Edmund Ruffin to reform an agricultural system that wore out land at a devastating 3 percent per year.

Agricultural reform had failed. Territorial expansion had failed. The number of poor whites was growing.[78] It had always been the plain whites, their prosperity and optimism sustained by an advancing frontier, who made planters more secure in the Old South than were those in Jamaica and Santo Domingo. But expanding cotton production was encroaching more and more on the plain whites, who "constitute our militia and our police."[79] Increasing white poverty was widening the gap between planters and the plain whites, upon whom they depended for safety.

The Emergence of the White Solidarity Myth

And it was this most critical social fissure that the Old South shrouded with its most compelling myth. In 1848 John C. Calhoun told the Senate that in the South, "the two great divisions of society are not the rich and the poor but white and black, and all of the former, the poor as well as the rich, belong to the upper classes."[80]

Race only now, more than two hundred years after the arrival of the first Africans in the Chesapeake original South, had become an important subject of political discourse, indeed an obsession. Since that first frontier on the Chesapeake, it had been lands and slaves that had made a white person upper class. Now it was simply white skin. As the Vicksburg *Daily Evening Citizen* cultivated the myth on the eve of the Civil War, "Instead of an aristocracy of wealth, we have an aristocracy of race which elevates all white men with the true spirit of freedom, and a chivalry to maintain it at every sacrifice."[81] The pioneer economy of the plain whites and the more market-oriented economy of the planters for almost two centuries had marched westward side by side. The line that separated planter from yeoman had been fluid. Many born in the log cabin had ended their lives in the plantation "big house." But when plantation agriculture reached its western limits in Texas, it continued to spread, but within the South, hardening class lines, turning evermore plain whites into poor whites.

From the days of Bacon's Rebellion to the Mexican War, white men had stood together against Native Americans, rebellious blacks, and "foreigners." Their conquest of plantation bottomlands and livestock range had nurtured white solidarity. But with the weakening of the planter-yeoman symbiosis, the Old South faced an internal impending crisis. What united whites now was no longer the old reality of shared opportunity, but the new myth of shared equality.

Chapter 7

Emancipated but Black
Freedom in the Free States

Paradoxically, as slavery disappeared in the North, the expressions of racial animosity there grew more strident. In the North, the southern slaveholders and their northern allies were vulnerable. They more and more needed northern support to maintain their dominant influence in the federal government. Never before had American leaders pressed the racial defenses of slavery more vigorously. Prejudice in the North reached its zenith during the 1850s. Indeed, in the Dred Scott decision of 1857, the Supreme Court ruled that free blacks were not citizens, and, in the words of Chief Justice Roger B. Taney, "had no rights which the white man was bound to respect."

The North for whites, even for those in distant Europe, was truly the land of the free. No place on earth did whites enjoy more opportunity than in the free states. For them, this society, despite its class differences, was the most democratic in the world. White Americans were an optimistic people, placing the highest value on upward mobility. Passionately opposed to aristocracy, they were also passionately committed to a doctrine that fixed forever a person's status at birth, by the color of one's skin. The "common man" inflicted bloody retribution on anyone, black or white, who challenged the rules of caste.

In 1859, during the fury that swept the slave states following John Brown's raid on Harper's Ferry, a small group of abolitionist families from Kentucky, led by the Reverend John Fee, crossed the Ohio River and settled in the outskirts of Cincinnati.[1] In Kentucky, Fee and his followers had founded Berea College and adopted as its motto "God hath made of one blood all nations of men." This "meant the co-education of the (so-called) races." For they knew that Christ "would not turn away anyone who came seeking knowledge, even if 'carved in ebony.'" For such a faith the Blue Grass country of central Kentucky had exacted a fearful price. Fee's father had disowned him. Twenty-two times he had been "mobbed," and twice left for dead.[2]

Yet when Fee and his followers had been forced to abandon Berea College and to seek refuge in the North, they could have had few illusions about the free soil beyond the Ohio. If they could expect greater safety in Cincinnati than in Kentucky, they could scarcely have expected a friendly welcome. In Cincinnati there had been major outbreaks of antiblack rioting in 1829, 1836, 1839, and 1841. In 1834, both the *Cincinnati Whig* and the *Daily Post* had called upon their readers to lynch abolitionists.

No city in the slave states had such a record of antiblack pogroms. But some in the free states did. Philadelphia had major riots in 1829, 1834, 1835, 1838, 1842, and 1849. There were few northern cities with black minorities where there were no such attacks. The riots in New York in 1834 destroyed sixty houses and six churches.[3]

Why So Much Animosity against So Few?

Abuse of the freed people defied arithmetic. Although they were more numerous in cities, their overall numbers never reached 2 percent in the antebellum North.[4] In the South, free blacks were slightly more numerous but outnumbered by slaves ten to one. The nation was the land of room enough, its doors wide open to immigrants. And there was room enough for slaves. For a half century, slave prices rose virtually without pause, and in the South a movement erupted in the 1850s to import more from Africa.[5] But in the land of room enough there was no room for freed people. Most states had laws prohibiting their migration from other states. Southern states passed laws making it more difficult to manumit slaves. In the "land of the free," few whites could tolerate the idea of freeing blacks unless it was coupled with a plan to deport them "back" to Africa or to virtually any place.

The treatment of the freed people defied the normal requirements of social stability. Most societies did not treat a people in such a slavish way if they did not have the control over them that they had over actual slaves. In Russia, the Cossacks were the freed people, many descended from escaped serfs. Yet the government made concessions to them. Cossacks became the staunchest defenders of the empire and its labor system. In Jamaica, planters struck bargains with "maroon" communities of escaped slaves: they would allow them to live in peace if they returned any additional escaped slaves to their owners. In Brazil, emancipated Afro-Portuguese yeomen, like the white yeomen of the South, formed a symbiotic relationship with the planters, furnishing them with livestock and other products. They also helped planters hunt down escaped slaves.

In the United States there was no such accommodation. From the very outset of the Industrial Revolution, about 1800, northern employers, even where labor was scarce, discriminated against black workers. They forced them into less-steady construction work or low-paid service jobs. Yet as the labor surplus grew, even these jobs were no longer safe. During an economic downturn, white workers often needed the less-desirable jobs that were ordinarily left to blacks. At such times there were mob attacks on black neighborhoods, which received little protection from the authorities.

A Philadelphia citizens' committee, investigating the causes of the 1834 riots, concluded, "An opinion prevails, especially among white laborers, that certain portions of our community, prefer to employ colored people . . . to the employment of white people; and that . . . many whites . . . are left without employment, while colored people are provided with work."[6] Here was a scandalous paradox: employers favoring people who had no customary rights over those who did.

These rioters did not invent the labor system that privileged white skin. It went back to the 1500s, when planters hired Europeans to control their black slaves.[7] But once colonial society had defined freedom and slavery by color, it followed that no black worker, even if emancipated, was truly free. Slavery had disappeared from the North but had left behind the idea that a black worker really belonged in the slave South, that if he had a job, a house, or virtually anything that a white worker wanted, he was "out of his place."

Employers in northeastern cities had learned that this two-tiered, racially defined labor system was useful. In the same way that planters could use a few privileged whites to control many blacks, employers could use a few underprivileged blacks to control many whites. By the 1840s, refugees from the Irish famine were enlarging the employers' labor surplus. Whenever workers organized, they negotiated with employers in the shadow of the black strikebreaker, whose condition was more wretched than their own.

The First Emancipation was not an event but a process. The American Revolution had opened a window of opportunity for the opponents of slavery. But with the cotton bonanza and the ascendancy of the Slave Power, the planters and their northern business partners, that window of freedom had all but shut. In most of the North, the gradual emancipation preferred by masters had prevailed, and the process also ended with the freed people still hobbled by the black codes, laws originally written to control slaves.

The New England Paradox

In most of New England, the freedom process had been completed. In Boston, blacks were equal to whites before the law. Yet, ironically, here, where black legal rights were greatest, their job opportunities were fewest. Here the competition for employment was most intense. While in much of America, labor was still scarce, in some eastern cities, especially in New England, employers enjoyed a labor surplus. New England was the first part of the nation to reach a labor surplus sufficient to stimulate industrialization. The region's exceptionally high birth rate, coupled with its limited potential for agriculture, resulted in rural workers' seeking jobs in the towns. Moreover, the cheapest fares available to immigrants were those offered by British ships bound for Canada to pick up lumber cargoes. These newcomers found themselves in a land with many trees but few opportunities. So by the thousands they flooded across the border into New England, where the Industrial Revolution was under way.[8]

There, no one had to buy them or indenture them. Under no form of coercion more serious than starvation, they freely offered themselves at low wages. Industrialists continued, however, the centuries-old Atlantic world's custom of privileging white labor. A newly arrived immigrant could usually claim a "white man's job" while a native black worker was the last hired if hired at all. White workers arriving in the city thus found an operating racial system already in place. Their responsibility for this system consisted in their accepting the racially privileged access to a job, defending it violently against anyone who tried to take it away, and having a vision of the world that extended little beyond personal and family advancement.[9]

Labor Becomes a Commodity

The Industrial Revolution was intensifying labor competition in the northeastern cities by undermining the skilled trades. Back in the 1700s, artisans had enjoyed a high degree of security and independence. Labor was scarce then, and they were further protected by their hard-to-acquire skills. Many of these artisans were antislavery.[10] But the Industrial Revolution was eroding the skilled crafts and bringing about a different way of looking at one's labor. For an increasing part of the workforce, especially for those in factories, it was no longer the *product* of labor that one sold. The artisan shoemaker had sold the shoes he made in his own shop. But the worker in a shoe factory now sold, not shoes, but his working hours to his employer. In this ever more industrialized labor market, one's labor itself was a commodity.

As the urban labor market became more crowded, competition sharpened between individuals and ethnic groups to sell their labor. An employer could choose among native born, Catholic, black, German, or other labels, each with its own claim. Most workers became participants in this invidious rivalry. A mean spirit of competition became even meaner as party activists organized this competition into politically motivated ethnic and religious hostility. A native-born worker thus, by becoming a Whig or a Know-Nothing, could show what he thought of immigrants and papists, or, by becoming a Democrat, show what he thought of blacks.[11]

These workers had come from farm and village cultures where important values derived from the mutual dependence and cooperation within the family and community. But in the city, where labor was being bought and sold like potatoes, and rivalry for jobs was growing, conflict increased not only between ethnic groups but also between individuals. In the city, a new, more individualistic culture pitted one against the other.

Some advocates of organized labor recognized that this spirit of ethnic, racial, and individualistic competition made workers more vulnerable, and urged, instead, broad class-based cooperation.[12] But labor unity did not flourish. Some ethnic constituencies did enjoy upward mobility, their situation being improved by winning influence at city hall. But free blacks, cut out of the political system in most places, could expect none of the protection and opportunity that city bosses provided for party-loyal ethnic street gangs, such as the Skinners, the Bleeders, the Deathfetchers, and the Killers. It was they who rallied the voters, the white males of the neighborhood, and organized the street violence that decided who voted.[13] The police more or less refereed conflicts among white gangs and fire companies but looked the other way when blacks were attacked. The racial status system in the North was being dramatized in the streets.

The racially and ethnically fragmented urban job market drove what would later be called American exceptionalism, with its weak tradition of trade unionism, and the rejection of class as the basis for political bonding. The Irish washerwoman did not reach out to her black sister, nor did the Irish hod carrier to the native Protestant who worked beside him. They reached not *out* but *up*, to an Irish labor contractor, a political boss, or a Catholic bishop. And so it was with other ethnic contingents.[14]

Threats to the Land of Opportunity

New job opportunities in the free states attracted young villagers from both sides of the Atlantic who were willing to leave family, friends, and traditions and try their luck in the city. But the land of the free upon which they pinned their dreams was in trouble. During the winter of 1819/20, the Missouri crisis, like a flash of lightning in the night, had revealed the new political landscape.[15] The North-South agreements that an earlier generation had reached, when both sections had practiced slavery, were no longer politically negotiable. Now, many saw that compromises between the free-labor North and the slave-labor South of the cotton bonanza would no longer be happy bargains but makeshift efforts to maintain a precarious truce.

In this troubled political climate, the blacks and their abolitionist friends seemed to be the troublemakers. To raise issues that the republic could no longer solve, to say what must not be said, was to attempt by subversion what British generals had failed to accomplish on the battlefield.[16] A Calvinist sense of destiny permeated Jacksonian nationalism: the Almighty had guided Americans through their severest trials, from the tribulations of the Pilgrims to Jackson's great victory over the British at New Orleans. The republic seemed the fulfillment of a divine plan.[17] But sectional tensions had put this national faith at risk. Without a faith, without a unifying ideology, a society collapses into chaos. The abolitionists preached that "the land of the free" was the land of the slave, that "the republic of virtue" was the republic of sin. Righteous patriotism charged the backlash against the abolitionists with terrible energy.

As the cotton establishment gained ascendancy over the nation's economy, politics, and culture, a white solidarity myth became hegemonic, accepted by all classes of whites: whites were all equal, and superior to nonwhites. As class differences increased, in the North as in the South, the doctrine of the shared superiority of whites masked the growing gap between rich and poor. It gave shantytown immigrants something in common with the carriage class. It also explained how a free republic could practice slavery, explained how black people, as closely supervised slaves, committed few crimes, contributed much to the nation's prosperity, and were happy. Blacks who were free were idle, miserable, dependent on charity, and prone to crime. This consensus about race hamstrung the abolitionists' criticism of slavery.

What Kept Slaves on the Plantations?

The opportunities enjoyed by northern whites created an extraordinarily curious pattern of population movements. The free states were the world's most powerful magnet attracting immigrants. In the 1850s, this magnet drew more than three million Europeans across the Atlantic but less than one-twentieth as many black Americans across the Mason-Dixon Line. Was this because of slave patrols and bloodhounds? Southern freed people rarely moved to the North, where they often faced vagabondage and persecution or, worse, prison. They were held in northern prisons at a rate about eight times greater than that of the general population.[18]

In 1860 there were still more freed people in the South than in the North. Baltimore, just thirty miles south of the Mason-Dixon Line, had more freed people than any city in the nation. Even escaped slaves usually returned to places in the South where they had family or friends. Few tried to reach the North.[19] The free-state magnet of opportunity, such a powerful force in distant Europe, failed at the Mason-Dixon Line.

The North was the promised land only for whites. Pennsylvania industrialists hired workers from Central Europe while there were equally qualified black Americans in neighboring Maryland and Virginia. This can hardly be explained by the effectiveness of southern slave patrols. Present-day border patrols with all their surveillance aircraft, razor-wire barriers, night vision devices, and the like have little success in stopping workers from moving to places where jobs are available. The King Cotton republic, however, was able to sharply reduce the loss of its plantation labor supply by virtually eliminating opportunity for blacks in the North. This required a racial ideology and culture that entirely mobilized mainstream northern whites.

How were the nation's leaders able to gain broad popular support for measures that kept blacks "in their place"? A frequent answer is that northern workers were afraid that blacks coming north would take their jobs. Yet despite the efforts of the Know-Nothings, northern society adopted no such effective methods to stop immigrants from taking their jobs. How could workers be mobilized against the trickle of blacks but not against the flood of immigrants?

Immigrants might be taking the jobs of native-born workers, but for the nation's leaders they were making northern labor cheaper. Slaves, on the other had, when they left the plantation, were abandoning the engine that drove the economic growth of the antebellum nation, North and South. Until the eve of the Civil War, the cotton, tobacco, naval stores, rice, and sugar that slaves produced furnished about two-thirds of the nation's exports.[20] The "foreign exchange" that these slave-produced exports earned made their masters the richest class in the country. But much of this wealth went to businessmen in the northern commercial and financial centers. Some Southerners claimed that in the cotton trade, 40 percent of the returns went to these men. Black slaves thus made these northern businessmen second in wealth only to the planters.[21]

The share that big-city businessmen received was in payment for their services in "freighting, brokering, selling, banking, insuring, etc., that grow out of Southern products," as well as from the rich Southerners who "come north in the summer to enjoy and spend their share of the profits." Until well after the Industrial Revolution had reached a takeoff point during the 1840s, such activities were the main business of financiers.[22] Opportunities were limited for investment in early industries, still largely family-run shops. In this agricultural nation, investors mainly "moved the crops." They mostly moved plantation crops, since family farmers, North or South, were only marginally involved in the market economy and had neither the need nor the collateral for much credit.

Planters, on the other hand, using land and slaves as collateral, borrowed in order to buy more land and slaves for their sons.[23] It was this credit that fueled the spread of the plantation system, which, during a single lifetime, swept from the Carolinas to Texas. Borrowers sometimes defaulted and the bank or export-import house foreclosed. So some northeastern businessmen found themselves transformed into absentee planters. Indeed, the outbreak of the Civil War revealed that several of the largest slaveholders in the United States were gentlemen who had rarely ventured south of Wall Street.[24]

The Freed People Subverted King Cotton

The racial system kept slaves on the plantations, and plantations drove the economic growth of the nation, North and South. But this racial system had other results. As surely as the mistreatment of the freed people kept slaves on the plantations, it also made them the brothers and sisters of the slaves, the unrelenting enemies of slavery. And they were strategically located. In almost equal numbers, they lived in the northern promised land of the whites and the southern "Egypt land" of the blacks. They would become the link between the slaves and certain northern whites who took issue with the cotton politics of Washington.

It was for good reasons that southern authorities regarded freed people as troublesome and subversive. Their destabilizing presence is particularly evident just south of the Mason-Dixon Line, in northern Virginia and Maryland, where they were concentrated in large numbers.[25] Here their numbers gave protective coloring to escaped slaves, many of whom, rather than fleeing north, chose to "pass for free" in this region where there were still job opportunities for half-free workers.

As mixed farming in northern Virginia and Maryland replaced tobacco monoculture, slaveholding had declined. Yet fully free labor was still scarce and expensive. Here freed people were mostly landless. Yet they and escaped slaves could make a scant living by offering their labor to farmers during planting and harvest seasons. They thus were working in competition with the slaves being offered for hire by the remaining planters of the region, who could no longer keep their hands fully employed. Slaves were now harder to control in a region where many blacks were free or passing for free, and their competition reduced the value of a planter's remaining slaves. This situation pressured planters to sell off their most valuable slaves to the cotton states and strike emancipation bargains with the rest.[26] The presence of freed people was thus contributing to the decline of slavery in Virginia and Maryland.

Their presence also weakened planter control over the local economy. Since the 1700s, yeomen had come to the plantation storehouse to buy and sell. But with the rise of towns, urban classes were taking over this function. The freed people's mobility enabled them to serve as a link in the "traffic," the mostly illegal commerce whereby plantation products surreptitiously found their way to town markets. Almost nobody defended the traffic. Planters denounced it as organized theft, and southern legislatures passed laws to suppress it.[27] But this shadow economy brought plantation products to town markets, and their sale brought money into town. Local authorities were often lax in their efforts to suppress this shady but economically stimulating business. An officer of the watch in Charleston, whose duty it was to suppress the traffic, was himself indicted for taking part in it.[28]

The traffic not only made the planter poorer but had other disagreeable implications. For pork that fattened in his acorn forest to reach the consumer, it might pass through the hands of a slave, a freed person, a poor white, and a shopkeeper. In two North Carolina counties, three-quarters of those who were tried for trafficking were free blacks or landless whites.[29] In Georgetown, South Carolina, the slave patrol was warned of "that dangerous intercourse between blacks and designing white men."[30] This kind of interracial negotiation not only threatened the planter's control over the local economy but also threatened white solidarity, the bedrock of planter hegemony.[31]

Freed people also weakened the planter's control over the local culture.

They set up their own schools, teaching who-could-say what kind of mischief. They also formed their own churches. Now, if there were still churches where one learned of a God who was an ever-vigilant overseer from whom no malingering, no insolence could be concealed, there were also other churches praising a liberator God who broke the bonds of the Hebrew children and let the oppressed go free.[32]

It was often said that the presence of freed people demoralized slaves.[33] The horizons of the slave quarter were as narrow as bondage could fashion. But all the tranquility, the stability that was born of rural isolation and illiteracy, could be blown away by the appearance in the neighborhood of a few manumitted people. These were people whose roots, whose ties of kinship and friendship, stretched from the constricted, unlettered world of the slaves to the cities where one-third of the South's freed people lived.[34] For slaves, emancipated black people were a window, at times a bridge, to the relatively free environment of the city.[35] Though despised and treated as outcasts, the freed people were the link between slaves and all the exciting and liberating ideas that rippled through the world of the nineteenth century.

By the 1850s, the Old South seemed to be headed for a crisis. The westward spread of plantation society apparently had come to a final halt in Texas. And along the Mason-Dixon Line, landholders continued to convert to free or half-free labor. By 1860, some 90 percent of the black population in Delaware had been manumitted and in Maryland about half. The South passed laws to make it more difficult to free slaves. Both the North and the South passed laws to make life more difficult for freed people. Still the unraveling of slavery continued, especially in Delaware, Maryland, and Virginia.[36] And much of the unraveling was done by freed people.

From the point of view of slaveholders, however, no freed people were capable of as much mischief as those in the North. Whenever the quiet recovery of a fugitive slave exploded into a noisy scandal and a civil disturbance, freed people were most often the leading fomenters.[37] These rescue riots, furthermore, increasingly gained white support, and thus demonstrated the fragility of King Cotton's influence in the North. On the one hand, few whites challenged the racial consensus. But, on the other, many did not like raids by slave catchers, who were sometimes federal marshals, sometimes members of criminal organizations, such as the Cannon-Johnson gang.[38] Neither federal marshals nor kidnappers looked for people who were old and nonproductive. They wanted prime workers who would fetch a high price on the slave block. They took away breadwinners, broke up families, and left behind helpless dependents, overburdening community charities.

Whites sometimes joined blacks in rescue riots to fight kidnappers, federal marshals, or police. They also joined interracial vigilance committees, who kept an eye out for spies, informers, and agents who posed as labor contractors, luring victims to "job sites" where press gangs seized them and sold them as slaves.

The Rise of Radical Abolition

Free blacks played an important role in the radicalization of the antislavery movement. Throughout the First Emancipation, during the era of the Revolution, many slaves had pinned their hopes for liberty on benevolent masters. But these had most often exacted a fearful schedule of payments, and the "freedom" that they had handed down little resembled that of the whites. As a result, by the 1820s, many blacks and a few whites had become impatient with this owner-friendly approach to emancipation as represented, for example, by the American Colonization Society.[39] Fewer and fewer slaves were being set free, and, more and more, their "freedom" no longer appeared genuine.[40]

In 1829, this dissatisfaction erupted with the *Appeal*, a pamphlet written by David Walker, a freedman in Boston who evoked the worst fears of the southern leaders. The legislatures of Virginia and North Carolina actually met in closed sessions to consider a response. With such literature in circulation, legislatures throughout the South tightened black codes and tightened prohibitions against teaching black people to read.[41]

Walker's *Appeal* was not the usual plea aimed at some aging planter with regrets about his abandoned concubines and mulatto children, and who could be persuaded that emancipating his slaves would provide him with fire insurance for the hereafter. Rather, Walker denounced slavery as despotism worse than the one against which the colonists had taken up arms in 1775.[42] He roasted as hypocrites those who mouthed words about liberty and Christianity yet condoned slavery.

Walker's *Appeal* was directed toward blacks, but he stirred some whites as well. Following Walker's death in 1830, William Lloyd Garrison, also in Boston, began the publication of the *Liberator*.[43] Garrison was a pacifist and wanted to steer abolitionists away from the violence implied by Walker.[44] In time Garrison would build a substantial following among whites. But, during the critical early years of the *Liberator,* it was the freed people who nurtured his "root and branch" attack on slavery. In 1832, *Liberator* representatives in seven cities were black, and even after the third year of publication, 75 percent of the subscribers were black.[45]

In the conservative emancipation movement of the late 1700s, black Americans had often found white patrons and even benefactors. But beginning in the 1830s, they found in radical white abolitionists, for the first time, genuine allies. Yet this black-white alliance had its problems. For one thing, while some abolitionists, including William Lloyd Garrison and Benjamin Lundy, came from poor families, most were from professional or other comfortably situated families. They also were a product of the society that had nurtured them. Few were able to divest themselves of a residue of white supremacist habits and ideas. Tensions of this kind still persisted between white and black allies and friends.

Abolitionists found it hard to promote antislavery among white working folk. Usually upper class, white abolitionists were typically little concerned with the problems of immigrants and of organized labor. Many were hostile toward strikes and labor militancy. They often disliked Catholics and favored a stricter observance of the Sabbath and stricter controls on alcohol. These other concerns of white abolitionists did not help black abolitionists make common cause with such exploited groups as unionized workers and immigrants. Nevertheless, an alliance with white abolitionists was their best option. They were not the same "better class" as the gentlemen who had dozed through the meetings of the American Colonization Society. In antebellum America, they, like no one else, were forthright in their condemnation of slavery, although often less so in their condemnation of the racial ideas sustaining slavery.[46] Many were animated by what would later be called liberation theology.

At the beginning of the 1830s, three men, David Walker, William Lloyd Garrison, and Nat Turner, had brought into focus an unrelenting current of opposition to the King Cotton republic. Walker was a black used-clothing dealer who had written a pamphlet; Garrison, a white maverick printer who had begun publishing a newspaper for several hundred mostly black subscribers; Turner, a slave and a prophet who, with a handful of believers, had carried out a bloody rampage that expressed what many a silent slave must have felt. The leaders of the Old South reacted with fear and fury.

But in reality, could publications as slender as those of Walker and Garrison, or a revolt as unpromising as that led by Turner, actually pose a threat to planter society? Planters clearly thought that they were threatened. Reports or rumors of revolts or conspiracies increased, resulting in tightening of the black codes, making slavery more burdensome. Slaveholders were often required to hold regular roll calls of their slaves and to write passes for them when they sent them on errands. Increased patrols could mean increased taxes upon all whites while only about one in four belonged to a slaveholding family. Slave patrols were reinforced by less-disciplined vigilante groups, who sometimes turned night rides into drunken frolics. Vigilance was sometimes hysterical, and even whites fell under suspicion. They might return home to find that their houses had been searched.[47]

Turner's bloody revolt, and its even bloodier suppression, was a direct blow to one of the sustaining pillars of the antebellum republic, the generally accepted belief among whites that slaves were happy and masters kind. Turner and his followers gave relevance and urgency to the message that came from minuscule abolitionist newspapers. Yet, at this time, only a small number of people in the North, and virtually nobody in the South, actually heard an abolitionist. Rather they heard *about* abolitionists, and heard less often that abolitionists opposed slavery than that they were "amalgamationists." They wanted to "mix the races."

Northerners, it is true, maintained a certain openness about slavery itself, despite their fears that debating it threatened the Union. Discussion was hard to discourage because slavery constantly gave rise to immediate problems that were not easily ignored: a northern community sometimes faced the tragic breakup of a family when a fugitive slave was arrested,[48] or a shocking murder might call attention in the community to a gang who kidnapped free blacks and sold them south.[49] Northern political leaders at times were embarrassed when their southern colleagues insisted that they suppress all antislavery agitation, if necessary by means that their constituents regarded as unconstitutional and unjustified. Also, as new federal territories were formed, disputes arose about whether they were to have legalized slavery.

With so many slavery-related issues to be settled, slavery continued to be a legitimate if touchy subject in the North. Even abolitionists were tolerated within uncertain limits, albeit mostly outside of mainstream respectability. Yet, if northern society maintained a cautious openness about slavery, or at least slavery-related issues, there was no such openness about the racial ideas justifying slavery. Thus, while a broad community audience might hear a lecture critical of slavery, the speaker typically felt constrained to concede some of the racial arguments used in the defense of slavery. If an antislavery speaker wanted to be heard, it was important to state at the outset a firm support for the separation of the races.[50] Yet, if the need for segregation was conceded, one had to admit that slavery was certainly an effective way to achieve it.

The Critical Issue of Segregation

In the North, a largely customary but rigorously enforced segregation was widespread, especially in those cities where blacks were concentrated. Segregation was a highly visible, ongoing celebration of subordination, with rituals that inculcated visceral racial attitudes. Since these rituals were performed in conspicuous places such as public transportation and theaters, or at Sunday worship, participation was virtually unavoidable.[51] In these daily public dramas, each individual, white or black, acted out the hegemonic racial message.

Northern society showed a certain pluralism in airing the issues that had to be settled between the free and slave states. But the segregation rituals were critical to the wealth and power of those who governed the republic; and anyone who violated them could expect no such liberality. The Presbyterian congregation of the Reverend Samuel Cox in New York City, for example, had shown a degree of tolerance for his criticism of slavery. But "amalgamation" was a different matter. In 1834, another Presbyterian minister, the Reverend Samuel Cornish, a very light-skinned black, came to hear him preach. But Cornish, instead of taking his place in the pews designated for blacks, accepted an invitation to sit with a white friend.

Had the roof of the church come crashing down on their heads, many in the congregation would scarcely have been more displeased. Excitement erupted into an angry protest rally. In a later sermon, Cox, apparently trying to conciliate, explained that "Christ himself was not of our complexion; that he was of the dark Syrian hue, probably darker than brother Cornish." A "merchant," speaking with "clinched fists," exploded, "He's against slavery, and the South, and the Union! And would you believe it? He called *my Savior* a nigger! G-d d—n him!"[52]

Racial ideas helped manage a growing number of threatening tensions in the republic. In the South, for example, if there was now a new class of landless white sharecroppers who had been left behind in the westward march of the cotton bonanza; or in the North, if there were now volatile immigrants living in shantytowns, these poor, by virtue of their color, were "upper class." Above all, "race" justified Southern slavery.

The Irrepressible Conflict

The republic was nevertheless approaching a crisis. By the 1850s, some of the conditions bringing on the Second American Revolution were already apparent. There was the mounting frustration of Whiggish businessmen who, despite no tariff protection for infant industries or subsidies for their canals and railroads, had greatly expanded their enterprises. Yet the Mexican War had divided and destroyed the Whig party. Never had they enjoyed so much economic power, and never so little influence in King Cotton Washington.

Equally frustrated was a small group of ideologues, the abolitionists. For a full generation they had looked on with anguish as slavery grew like a cancer.

Yet never had they been more isolated from mainstream America than at the beginning of the 1850s. Never had the wall of ideas protecting slavery been more formidable. A white person protesting the torching of a black neighborhood was likely to be met with the retort, "How would you like for your daughter to marry one?"

Yet, as John Ashworth reminds us, the tremors that brought down the antebellum republic began neither in the frustrations of businessmen nor in the moral torment of abolitionists but in the nation's human mudsills, the four million slaves at the bottom, who produced the commodities that drove capital accumulation and economic growth.[53] The Old South never suffered the massive servile upheavals that shook Russia, the West Indies, and Latin America. It had sufficient popular support and military muscle to contain slave revolts. Armed men seized suspects, exacted testimony by torture, held often irregular trials, burned some at the stake and hanged others, including an occasional white who tried to protect some valuable or favorite slave. Postmasters censored the mails. Mobs burned books. People were jailed for possessing prohibited publications or for teaching blacks to read. Professors with "unsound" views were fired.[54] Thus the Old South contained slave unrest.

But this containment was achieved, as a northern visitor to Charleston noted, by despotic police methods

> such as you never find under free government: citadels, sentries, passports, grape-shotted cannon, and daily whippings for accidental infractions of police ceremonies. I happened myself to see more direct expression of tyranny in a single day and night at Charleston, than at Naples [under the repressive Bomba regime] in a week; and I found that more than half the population of this town are subject to arrest, imprisonment, and barbarous punishment, if found in the streets without a passport after evening "gun-fire." Similar precautions and similar customs may be discovered in every large town in the South.[55]

The Old South had the methods to contain slave unrest, but these methods had consequences that they could not contain. The means used to dominate blacks sent shock waves through American society from bottom to top. "Muzzles were made for dogs, not for men," growled a maverick white Virginian.[56] Although Stephen Colwell thought that slavery could be justified on "humane and Christian considerations," he did not like the "savage and watchful despotism enforced for some years past in parts of the Southern States."[57] Neither did thousands of settlers on the frontier, farmers in the free states, and citizens everywhere. Although these might believe every detail of the racial consensus, when they looked at slave-based society, they did not like what they saw. They did not want that "savage and watchful despotism" extended to Illinois, Kansas, or anywhere else.

While American whites in the 1850s agreed about race, they nevertheless disagreed about these other matters. According to Senator James H. Hammond, in both houses of Congress, "the only persons who do not have a revolver and knife are those who have two revolvers."[58] In 1860, a near-riot erupted in the House of Representatives when both sides leaped to their feet and confronted each other in the well of the House. A Georgia representative later recorded, "I . . . cocked my Revolver in my pocket and took my position in the midst of the mob. . . . I had made up my mind to sell my blood at the highest price possible."[59]

It was by complex routes that the suppressed rage of the slave quarter ultimately found this expression in Congress. But one important route was the freed people: Sojourner Truth, Harriet Tubman, David Walker, Frederick Douglass, and the countless organizers of vigilance committees and rescue riots.

In the world of ideology, the story that came down to the American citizen from virtually every vehicle of culture was that slaves were useful and happy, masters were kind, and free blacks were miserable and dangerous. But the free blacks told a different story, one that was based on personal experience and from sources in the slave pens and cotton fields. Now their story was being heard by white people who had their own reasons for disliking the cotton establishment.

As surely as defining Americans as "whites" created white solidarity, it also created black solidarity. If it made the southern piney woods cow herder and the northern shantytown hod carrier the equal of the planter, it likewise made the half-free black pariah the brother or sister of the slave. They were a "troublesome people" whom the antebellum republic had neither co-opted, neutralized, nor deported. And despite all restrictive laws, they had remained mobile. Their ties stretched from the four million slaves at the bottom of American society to a small but growing band of white Radicals. They were a vital link in a movement that would change the nation.

Chapter 8

The Planter and the "Wage Slave"
A Reactionary Alliance

In "the South they hunt slaves with dogs—in the North with Democrats," Thaddeus Stevens exploded in 1860.[1] Was Stevens exaggerating? In a democratic republic, could slaveholders have such control over the dominant political party in the North? The nation's population was thirty million. Only two million of these belonged to slaveholding families, virtually none of whom lived in the North. Yet Stevens was right. In the North, federal marshals, with the help of party-loyal Democrats, hunted down escaped slaves.

In the 1850s, there were two apparently contradictory but actually interconnected developments. On the one hand, the Slave Power in Washington was growing ever more fragile. In 1850, the last planter president, Zachary Taylor, died in office. And the southern minority in Congress was shrinking further year by year. But on the other hand, it was during these years that the racial system reached its zenith. Never before had racial discrimination been so widely sanctioned, or had ordinary citizens more fervently embraced the racial myths that actually disempowered them and validated the agenda of those in control. For the full decade of the 1850s, southern planters and their northern business partners managed an impending crisis by the strident promotion of racial ideas.

The extension of the cotton establishment's power over the federal government and thus over the free states had begun in the early days of the republic. And still in the 1850s, whenever a measure came before Congress that divided the free states from the slave states, the Southerners carried the day.[2]

The Missouri Crisis

So it had been in 1819–20. Northern congressmen tried to block the extension of slavery into the Missouri territory, whereupon southern leaders threatened the breakup of the Union. At the decisive vote, some Northerners were reported to have blanched at the southern threat and changed their vote. John Randolph of Virginia mocked the retreat of these "doughfaces," an epithet that, until the Civil War, stuck to Northerners who supported the planter agenda.[3] Thus the Missouri crisis was resolved by a "compromise": slavery would be extended into Missouri and other territory where the climate was suitable for plantation agriculture, but would be excluded from territory where the climate was not suitable.[4]

The Nullification Crisis

Issues not directly related to slavery could precipitate a crisis if they threatened the interests of planters. The "American System," an agenda for modernizing the national economy, led to such a crisis in 1832. In the War of 1812, the British invasion had revealed the republic's vulnerabilities: its primitive transportation network, its chaotic system of banking and public finance, and its continuing colonial economy, with its exportation of plantation commodities and importation of manufactured goods, both hostages to the British fleet.

After the war, in the euphoria following the victory at New Orleans, a nationalistic congress launched the American System: a federally funded network of roads and canals to bind together a fragile union and open up an internal market; also a federally chartered national bank to end financial chaos; and a protective tariff to stimulate manufacturing.

Yet much of the funding for this costly program came from the protective tariff, which depressed the prices that planters could get for their commodities overseas and raised the prices they had to pay for manufactured goods. Slaveholders, moreover, had a political reason to oppose federally funded projects.

Planter control over the slave states was secure. But, since the free states were equally numerous and growing faster in population, planter control of the federal government was less certain.

Anything that increased the power of the federal government was therefore a threat. "We have abolition, colonizing, bible and peace societies," wrote Nathaniel Macon of North Carolina in 1818, "and if the general government shall continue to stretch their powers, these societies will undoubtedly push them to try the question of emancipation." And later he wrote to the same correspondent, "If Congress can make canals, they can with more propriety emancipate."[5] Because of such economic and political concerns, most planters soon repented their nationalism. Reacting to the passage of the Tariff of 1832, anti-tariff planters in South Carolina "nullified" the tariff law within the state, precipitating a crisis, which would leave the American System in shambles. In this crisis, President Andrew Jackson, the old hero of the battle of New Orleans, bruised the ears of his nullifying fellow planters with threats and patriotic lectures, while playing Santa Claus to their wishes:[6] a return to a tariff low enough to afford no protection; a return to laissez-faire banking and to the system of chaotic public finance that, although it had brought the nation to the brink of defeat during the War of 1812, now assured southern leaders of a weak federal government. Moreover, he gave the planters a free hand with Indian tribal lands in the South, even though these lands were secured by federal treaties that he was constitutionally bound to uphold.[7] Following Jackson's recommendation, furthermore, southern postmasters began removing antislavery literature from the federal mails, and this continued throughout the antebellum years. In such a Union, who needed nullification or secession?

Historians disagree whether it was more Jackson's threats or his enticements that persuaded the nullifiers to accept the authority of the federal government. But none of his threats was carried out while all of his enticements were. The legacy of these planter-oriented policies continued until the antebellum republic dissolved in civil war twenty-eight years later. Though the American System continued to enjoy support, gaining support in the North,[8] no subsequent antebellum administration would promote it. When business leaders, especially in the North, pressed for federal aid in the development of the transportation system and measures that would boost economic growth, their proposals were rejected by a government committed to "laissez-faire." But when planters noticed some valuable and poorly defended bottomlands and livestock range beyond the national borders, laissez-faire quickly gave way to the nation's Manifest Destiny.[9]

Whigs versus Democrats

To the cotton politics of the federal government and the Democratic Party, the Whig Party continued to offer an alternative vision, that of a modern industrial society. Before the rise of the Republican Party in the mid-1850s, the abolitionist Thaddeus Stevens had found an uneasy place for himself in the Whig Party. But were the Whigs any different from the Democrats on the question of slavery? Leaders of *both* parties attempted to remove any discussion of slavery from mainstream politics.

Until the 1850s, abolitionists such as Stevens could say little about slavery if they wanted to work within the established political system. Eventually the Whig Party split into "conscience Whigs," who were willing to incur the wrath of slaveholders in order to promote their increasingly popular American System, and the "cotton Whigs," who realized that to push ahead with this program would precipitate another crisis and perhaps break up the Union.[10] Many have been fascinated by the lively political debates of these years, by the choices that voters were offered. But in the give-and-take of this two-party system, voter choices were all limited to measures acceptable to the planter class.

We have seen how planters were able to assert hegemony over southern society. But society in the North differed greatly from that in the South. In the North, slavery had never been critical to the economy and was now disappearing altogether. The North had a greater population and a steeper rate of population growth. As the Industrial Revolution spread throughout the region, these states were now attracting seven out of eight immigrants. Still the antebellum political system continued, and Southern leaders continued to control the federal government.

Slavery and Capital Growth

One source of the influence of the Slave Power in the North was economic. Until the eve of the Civil War the products of free labor accounted for only about one-third of American exports. The high rate of capital growth that the northeastern business elite enjoyed came mainly from financing the expansion of plantation production and from brokering and shipping southern commodities. For at least a generation, the cotton trade alone contributed more to the growth of the port of New York than all the commerce passing through the Erie Canal. Even as late as 1860, the South's leading economist, J. D. B. DeBow, could boast that, due to the cotton trade, New York was "almost as dependent on Southern slavery as Charleston itself."[11]

Since the crops were sold mostly in Europe, the plantation trade put European money into the hands of American businessmen. With this "foreign exchange" these men could buy items that were either scarce or not yet available in the United States, often British rails for American railroads or machinery for factories. The commodities that slaves produced thus drove capital accumulation and industrial growth.

Southern leaders, in contrast to Northerners, showed little enthusiasm for industrialization. It was taking place largely in the North, gradually shifting the balance of power from the South to the North. And, as planters saw it, it was from their own pockets that these northern "middlemen" were exacting the necessary means. Southern leaders thus did not always rejoice in the relationship they had with their northern partners.

Yet, like it or not, they were deriving some solid benefits from their none-too-happy marriage to northern finance. The most affluent and influential men in the free states wanted to see hardworking slaves and an uninterrupted flow of commodities. New York's mayor, Fernando Wood, during the secession crisis of 1861 proposed that, since the Union was breaking up, New York should be made a "free city." In his reelection campaign of 1859, he had declared that the city's "profits, luxuries, the necessities, nay even the physical existence, depend upon the products only to be obtained by the continuance of slave labor and the prosperity of the slave master."[12]

The abolitionist Samuel J. May recalled a New York merchant's threat: "There are millions upon millions of dollars due from Southerners to the merchants and mechanics of this city alone, the payment of which would be jeopardized by any rupture between the North and the South. We cannot afford, sir, to let you and your associates endeavor to overthrow slavery. It is not a matter of principles with us. It is a matter of business necessity. . . . We mean, sir, to put you abolitionists down—by fair means if we can, by foul means if we must."[13]

The richest families in America, North and South, owed much of their prosperity to the labor of slaves. It was thus no accident that the free states produced "doughface" leaders, northern men subservient to the South, or that the racial ideas sustaining slavery were the beliefs of both the Democratic and Whig parties.[14]

Popularity of Planter Power

The plantation–Wall Street connection goes far toward explaining the southern orientation of most of the nation's leaders. But it scarcely explains their popularity. Throughout the 1850s, and into the Civil War, the Democrats, the most pro-southern party, in places like "shantytown" and "little Dublin," continued to harvest the votes of thousands of poor workingmen. Rarely do citizens have an opportunity to vote directly for their bread-and-butter interests. Most often they vote for political rhetoric that seems in an uncertain way to express their interests, and for visions of the world held out to them by leaders. How had this political ideology evolved since the foundation of the republic?

Politics Moves from Liberty to Race

During the long struggle with Great Britain, especially during the two wars, American leaders held out a promising picture of the benefits that victory would bring. They saw their struggle as a revolution; and they showed that inclination of revolutionists to promise more than they could deliver. They created a crisis of expectations: patriots sang of their "sweet land of liberty," of "the land of the free," dedicated to the proposition that "all men are created equal." These ideas had radical implications, the potential for far-reaching applications. Once the stirring words of the Patriots were on everybody's lips, it was only a question of time before someone would ask, "What about the rich and the poor?" "What about women?" "What about slaves?" The War for Independence had uncorked a revolutionary genie in the land.[15]

But by the 1840s, except for a handful of radicals, the revolutionary genie had been put back into the bottle. Though people were still singing the same songs about liberty, intoning the same sacred texts about equality, they were marching to the polls under banners that celebrated their native birth, their religion, or their skin color.[16] Sometimes they simply voted for the funniest clown who performed for them on the political stage.

What had arrived by 1840 was a particular political style, a particular way of thinking about politics, that later would be called "American exceptionalism."[17] According to this view, in the Old World, social classes were relatively inflexible. And, therefore, they were important in shaping people's political outlook. But not in America. To be sure, in America a certain *idea* of class played a role in political rhetoric. It was fashionable, for example, for a successful man to have been born in a log cabin. But, except in political campaign pageantry, no honors were conferred on those who still lived in log cabins. What was really being celebrated was success. For whites at least, it was said that there was so much opportunity in America that its social classes were too fluid to form the basis for political organization.[18] What shaped politics in America, on the contrary, was religion, place of birth, the ability of a candidate to perform in the political comedy. But, increasingly, it was race.[19]

Race was the key idea, and the Democratic Party was the key vehicle, whereby the retainers of King Cotton established a large and loyal constituency in the free states. No feature of American exceptionalism was more extraordinary than this alliance between the richest people in the republic and many of the poorest. If party policies suggested that some Democrats were planters and commodity brokers, party majorities proved that many more Democrats were southern non-slaveholders, the urban poor, and immigrants.[20]

The racially and ethnically fragmented job market drove the politics of American exceptionalism, with its weak tradition of trade unionism, and the rejection of class as the basis for political bonding. As some Irish miners in Pottsville, Pennsylvania, saw it, "We do not form a distinct class of the community, but consider ourselves in every respect as CITIZENS of this great and glorious republic."[21] The "common man" reached not *out* but *up*, to an employer who was a compatriot or to a successful member of his church. The Jacksonian movement had broadened suffrage to include all white men. But these voted for successful men, who if born in log cabins had long since moved to more comfortable quarters. Jacksonian democracy had made little impact on the nation's leadership. Both before and after the common man got the vote, the republic was led by great planters and their business partners.

But if the broadening of suffrage did not change power relationships, it changed the political style. It gave rise to what would later be called the politics of negativism. Political coalitions, be they of "papists" or of nativist patriots, could agree on few practical bread-and-butter issues. So political leaders offered their followers an opportunity to vote not for what they were *for*, but *whom* they were against. The Whigs, and even more the Know-Nothings, thus harvested the votes of those most easily incited against immigrants and Catholics. The Democrats harvested the votes of those most easily incited against blacks.

Yet, political leaders did more than promote malice toward people living in the "other neighborhood." They also held out a vision of the world, but not an attainable agenda for the future. Rather it was a reactionary vision, a vanishing world of the past. With opportunities in America fewer, the memory of the pioneer past was pure political magic. Stories of great men born in log cabins evoked a time when a rich and thinly peopled land lay before the white settlers, a land in which, if you were white, the most precious of all resources was the labor of your own hands.[22]

Wage Slavery / White Slavery

By the 1850s, the white solidarity myth of Jacksonian days was beginning to wear thin. Of course, given the outcast condition of the freed people, white superiority was generally assumed without argument. But, with the widening class differences, with the growing squalor of the immigrant "shantytowns," the idea of the equality of all whites was sometimes viewed as a happy notion not to be confused with reality.

In this new situation, some Democratic Party ideologues advanced a second racial theory, inconsistent with the first. They still held that southern whites, rich and poor, were all "upper class." Sometimes they said the same of northern whites. But at other times urban workers were called "wage slaves," or "white slaves."[23]

The Aristocratic Critique of Capitalism

The northern labor market, in the words of George Fitzhugh, was the "White Slave Trade." It was a "free labor system" not for workers but for capitalists. The northern capitalist paid for a laborer's working hours but was otherwise free of all responsibility for his workers: for the nonproductive years of their childhood, their old age, or when they were incapacitated by an accident or illness. Planters, on the other hand, assumed responsibility for the total life of the worker.[24]

The theory of wage slavery, or white slavery, had important implications as to where northern workers might find reliable allies against the local industrialists who exploited them. According to the New York publisher John H. Van Evrie, surplus profits in the North became "capital," which was invested in enterprises that exploited white workers. Not so in the South: there, surplus profits were invested in more land and slaves; and no white person was therefore exploited.[25] The planter, for this reason, was the natural ally of the white slave.

White slaves, unlike black ones, voted; and sometimes they even reached positions of influence in the government. Michael Walsh rose from leader of a band of toughs on the streets of New York to popular labor orator and publisher. He widely publicized the idea of the two kinds of slavery and the common interests of planters and workers.[26] Despite his passionate language about the exploitation of white labor, or perhaps because of the political following it won for him, Walsh enjoyed the patronage of men such as George Steers, a New York shipbuilder, and President John Tyler, a Virginia planter.

With the patronage of such wealthy men and the votes of shantytown and little Dublin, Walsh was elected to Congress. There he defended the Old South and amplified John C. Calhoun's aristocratic critique of capitalism, at one point arguing that the only difference between a black slave and a wage slave was "the one has a master without asking for him, the other has to beg for the privilege of becoming a slave."[27]

The doctrine that some poor whites were wage slaves or white slaves was not compatible with the other racial position that all whites, certainly all southern whites, were upper class.[28] Yet each of these theories appealed to large constituencies and served the Democratic Party well on election day.

Zenith of the Racial System

By the 1850s the North-South racial consensus was virtually without challenge. In the great northern cities segregation was enforced less by law than by public demand. Never before had the freed people been so driven into the most debased margins of American society or so persecuted. Yet it was during these years that the westward spread of planter society had stalled, while that of free labor society had continued with increased vigor. Also, the Slave Power could no longer elect a planter president, and southern representation in Congress declined year by year.

In the North there was a growing opposition to the cotton politics of Washington. In vain, northern congressmen demanded federal aid for canals, railroads, or other projects within their districts. But their opposition was pragmatic, narrowly focused on particular issues. Virtually no one questioned the hegemonic racial ideas that justified the Slave Power.

Shrinking Benefits of the Southern Connection

Bankers and great merchants had derived much of their original capital from financing the spread of the plantation economy and from the exports that slaves produced. But the investments that they had made in the North were now producing new financial opportunities in transportation, commercial agriculture, and meat production in the Midwest. Also, mining and manufacturing were less and less small family operations, but increasingly larger enterprises needing loans. For workers, too, it was the growing northern economy, not slave-produced exports, that now provided most job opportunities.

The antebellum regime by the 1850s was sustained as never before by ideology. The street gangs who attacked abolitionists and blacks were doing little to promote their own self-interest. When they burned black neighborhoods they made housing scarcer and rents higher. When they drove out black workers, they never drove them far and thus did little to raise the "wages of whiteness." White wage negotiations were still conducted in the shadow of the black strikebreaker. Whites were still haunted by those they had made their enemies. If, for the thousands in shantytown, race was a claim in the hands of the white worker, it was a club in the hands of his boss.

The common man's racial animosity grew as the nation's impending crisis drew near. Mobs were defending the status quo. Antebellum leaders were "their" leaders. Free blacks and abolitionists were "their" enemies.[29] They were defending the world that they knew, and they envisioned no other.

Americans, North and South, had once been mobilized by the idea of liberty. But now liberty was a destabilizing concept, suggesting the radical Liberty Party or the machinations of the Free-Soilers. Race was now what held the fragile republic together. So long as the white North and the white South stood together against blacks and "race mixers," the nation would remain together as one.

King Cotton's challengers were thus few, and fewer still were Radicals who saw racial ideas as a major obstacle to the nation's well-being. Even the sharpest critics of slavery, especially in their public statements, expressed ideas that sustained the Slave Power. The Radical Free-Soiler Salmon Chase conceded, for example, that if "both races were free they would naturally separate."[30] The antislavery novelist Harriet Beecher Stowe repeated most of the popular stereotypes of blacks and also put into the mouth of a friendly character the theory of wage slavery: "The slave-owner can whip his refractory slave to death,—the capitalist can starve him to death."[31] These critics certainly believed the wage-labor system was incomparably superior to slavery. Even workers who elected the proslavery zealot Fernando Wood as mayor of New York and sent Mike Walsh to Congress did not show the slightest inclination to trade their capitalist masters for plantation overseers. How indeed did racial ideas, of such doubtful benefit to most, come to saturate white society?

People learned racial ideas from segregation, from its daily rituals of dominance and deference. They also learned racial ideas from leaders, role models, who commanded listeners because of their prominence in the government or in business, such as the planter Senator John C. Calhoun, or the financial writer Thomas Prentice Kettell. A citizen learned about race from a local newspaper, a preacher,[32] a teacher, a stump speaker running for some office, a performer on the stage, indeed from virtually any professional who shaped ideas.

There were, of course, those bold dissident voices that we remember and celebrate. But most of those who molded mainstream culture were like prudent rabbits, their ears tuned to those who could endanger or advance their careers. Certainly they had to engage their readers, their congregations, or audiences. But they found ways to do so without upsetting influential patrons.

Those who tilled the fields of culture knew that it was not they who owned the fields. They could be replaced. They created a culture that mirrored the distribution of power in the antebellum republic.

What was acted out in the daily segregation drama, what was taught in the school, printed in the newspaper, proclaimed at the political rally, preached and prayed in church, upheld slavery and all the wealth and power that slavery upheld: all whites were equal and were superior to all nonwhites. And inconsistently: sympathy should go to the "white slaves" of the North, not to those pampered clowns on southern plantations. This racial ideology saturated virtually every vehicle of American culture. But most vividly it found expression in the minstrel show, which, as the irrepressible conflict neared, became America's most popular entertainment.

Chapter 9

King Cotton's Jesters
The Minstrel Show Interprets Race for the White Working Class

For white workers the most exciting entertainment by far was the minstrel show. No other type of theater captivated such massive audiences or was more influential. More than from newspapers, books, or sermons, it was from the minstrel show that white workers formed opinions about the South, about plantations, slavery, and how black people responded to freedom. The performers

> burst on stage in makeup which gave the impression of huge eyes and gaping mouths. They dressed in ill-fitting, patchwork clothes, and spoke in heavy "nigger" dialects. Once on stage, they could not stay still for an instant. Even while sitting, they contorted their bodies, cocked their heads, rolled their eyes, and twisted their outstretched legs. When the music began, they exploded in a frenzy of grotesque and eccentric movements. Whether singing, dancing or joking, whether in a featured role, accompanying a comrade, or just listening, their wild hollering and their bobbing, seemingly compulsive movements charged their entire performance with excitement.[1]

In 1843 a troupe of northern big-city white actors calling themselves the Virginia Minstrels launched this new form of entertainment, which became a national sensation. The representation of slaves and servants as buffoons or clowns was no invention of American theater. In ancient times, there had been such characters on the stages of Greece and Rome. At a time when many slaves were coming from Thrace, for example, and when audiences thought of Thracians as people with red hair, a Roman comedian wore a red wig when playing a slave.[2] In early modern times, when most slaves brought to Western Europe came from West Africa, blackface comedians appeared in England and in other countries. At least one comic slave had turned up on the American stage by 1769.[3] By the early 1800s, such blackface characters were familiar features of entertainment in theaters and circuses and on showboats.[4]

Jim Crow

In 1829, toward the end of a decade when antebellum society was feeling the tremors of the Denmark Vesey conspiracy and of David Walker's *Appeal,* theatergoers were provided with a comic relief from these disconcerting events by a new stage personality, Jim Crow, who brought nationwide renown to his creator, T. D. Rice.[5]

A fellow actor recalled that Rice, who did "little negro bits" between acts, hit upon the idea when he was performing at a theater in Louisville. Behind the theater was a livery stable that employed "an old decrepit" slave named Jim Crow.

> He was very much deformed, the right shoulder being drawn higher up, the left stiff and crooked at the knee, giving him a painful and at the same time laughable limp. He used to croon a queer old tune,
>
>> Wheel about, turn about,
>>   Do jis so,
>> An' ebery time I wheel about,
>>   I jump JimCrow.
>
> Rice watched him closely and saw that here was a character unknown to the stage. He wrote several verses, changed the air somewhat, quickened it a good deal, made up exactly like [Jim Crow], and sang it to a Louisville audience. They were wild with delight, and on the first night he was recalled twenty times.[6]

His fame spread nationwide. Soon he would be performing in New York, where the Bowery Theatre announced that "Mr. Rice, whose celebrated song of 'Jim Crow' has drawn crowded houses in Baltimore, Philadelphia, etc. is daily expected."[7]

Rice was the superstar of the 1830s, and everywhere he had imitators. During this decade, the conflict over slavery was radically intensifying: The *Liberator* and other abolitionist publications emerged. The American Antislavery Society was formed. Nat Turner's insurrection panicked the slave states and they drastically strengthened their black codes. In the free states, mobs attacked abolitionists and blacks, sometimes burning black neighborhoods. Congress adopted the "gag rule" against antislavery petitions. Abolitionists mass-mailed antislavery tracts. Southern postmasters intercepted them. The Underground Railroad expanded throughout the North. At the end of this decade, in 1840, the Liberty Party held its first convention. And the New York *Knickerbocker* found the Bowery Theatre "crammed from pit to dome, and the best representative of our American negro that we ever saw was stretching every mouth in the house to its utmost tension. Such a natural gait—such a laugh!—and such a twitching up of the arm and shoulder! It was the negro par excellence. Long live James Crow Esquire!"[8]

Rice and his imitators expanded their Jim Crow acts into "Ethiopian operas." These were skits that provided a comic addition to the theater program whose centerpiece was traditionally a major play.[9] Yet, despite the immense popularity of Rice, who became known later as "the father of minstrelsy," his blackface performances, and those of his many imitators, remained throughout the 1830s and into the '40s only a part of the main program. Finally, in 1843, the fully evolved minstrel show, an entire program devoted to blackface entertainment, sprang into popularity.

The Primary Minstrel Audience

The rise of blackface minstrelsy paralleled the national stirrings over slavery. But it was also responding to a rapid and far-reaching change in American society. During the 1830s and '40s, especially in the North, country towns were bursting into cities. Their streets teemed with what to most Americans was a new class. These were mostly young males, native-born and immigrants. They were footloose, having often left their families behind on farms and in villages on both sides of the Atlantic. Torn from many of their ties with women, and from the constraints of a rural community, they were fired with the hope of achieving success in the city. Yet most were poor, and with the Panic of 1837, which began an economic slump unrivaled until the Great Depression of the 1930s, their poverty sometimes sank into the misery of scant food and rooms unheated in winter.[10]

Yet, thanks in great part to the Jacksonian movement, these frustrated young men had the right to vote. This was scary for old-fashioned citizens. But even scarier was that they also had the inclination to riot. Owning no property themselves, they sometimes burned down whole neighborhoods belonging to others. Which way, against whom, were their votes, their violence, to be directed?

With the economic collapse after 1837, the nation's leaders scrambled to stay on their political feet. There were not many traditionally sanctioned ways that men in government could deal with urban misery. They might protect some urban business and its jobs by a tariff. They might promote publicly funded "internal improvements." They might revitalize the economy by involving the country in a war to advance the nation's Manifest Destiny. But any of these remedies was certain to unleash again the monster of North-South conflict and perhaps break up the republic. What could the nation's leaders do when the solutions were too volatile for public discussion?

By the midpoint of this great depression, in the election of 1840, they had found the answer: an election campaign as show business, in which the most substantive questions were barely mentioned. The Whigs led the way with their "log cabin" campaign. Their successful candidate for president, the aristocrat William Henry Harrison, was passed off to the voters as a frontier rustic.[11] His campaign workers would pull a log cabin on wheels through the streets to an election rally enlivened with fireworks. The Democrats were not slow learners. More and more they were calling on urban voters at their own flamboyant rallies to defend the white race, defend the Irish Americans and the rights of Catholics. The young men of the streets battered each other in election riots, then voted for their skin color, their national origin, their religion, or often just for the funniest comedian who had performed for them at the political rally. The modern American political system had been born.

It was in an America in which politics was taking on the features of show business that the evermore political minstrel show became a national sensation. The meteoric rise of the Virginia Minstrels in New York City inspired countless competitors.[12] Companies with a national reputation packed the big-city playhouses while those aspiring to fame filled village theaters or, traveling in show wagons, carried their performances to the rural countryside. Showboats, such as the *Banjo,* spread the minstrel craze to remote villages and steamboat landings along what were called "the western waters." Everywhere, amateur groups sprang up.

By 1847, the blackface furor had reached California, where American soldiers were staging minstrel performances. During the 1850s, the state had "a total of nearly thirty regular minstrel troupes," including five professional companies in San Francisco. New York had ten major minstrel theaters. As early as 1844, the Ethiopian Serenaders performed at the White House.[13]

The minstrel stage engaged the talents of America's most gifted composers.

Stephen Foster, whose songs achieved worldwide fame, began his career at age nine as a blackface performer, and it was through minstrel theater that his music reached millions.[14] Daniel Decatur Emmett, one of the original Virginia Minstrels and composer of "Dixie," is regarded as one of the best American composers of the nineteenth century. His music, especially his banjo tunes, enlivened the most isolated hamlets and mining camps.[15]

Despite the minstrels' blackface makeup and their songs about plantations, much of what they had to say had little to do with slavery or the South. To appreciate the full range of topics that they addressed, consider their primary audience. Although almost everybody enjoyed minstrel shows, these performances had their original and primary audience. That audience was largely the northern and urban "common man," more specifically, young men, recently from the farm, often separated from their families, and who spent their evenings in the streets. It was clearly workingmen, not the carriage class, whom Charley was addressing from the stage when he bragged that the new place that he had rented "does not have a single bug. All of them are married and have large families."[16] It was primarily for a northern working-class audience that the equally northern and big-city minstrels created their blackface fantasy world. Minstrel theater was thus part of urban "low culture." While upper-class people often attended minstrel shows, no one confused these productions with the "high culture" of the carriage class.[17]

Why entertain in blackface these working-class men, both native born and immigrant, with songs and skits about plantations? Minstrel performers sometimes borrowed from African American music, dance, and folklore; but, otherwise, as big-city professionals, they knew almost as little about black people and the South as did their primary audience.[18] But they were not concerned with realism. Their burnt-cork faces did not resemble the faces of African Americans, nor was their "'nigger' dialect" like black speech, nor were the plantations of their songs like those in the South. What they had created was a dramatic convention, a fantasy world.[19]

Such fantasy worlds have always been an important feature of folklore and popular culture, often representing animals doing what people do. Such were the goat and horse characters of ancient Greek satyr plays, and so are the animals of African American folklore. Since the audience recognizes instantly that the situation is pure fantasy, they give the storyteller a freedom that they would not tolerate if the setting were realistic. No one is likely to become upset by something said by a character as unlikely as Mickey Mouse.[20] The storyteller is allowed to touch on sources of anxiety that would otherwise be painful. But in a world of make-believe everybody laughs and feels better.

The Issues Addressed by Minstrel Artists

The enthusiasm that greeted minstrel theater suggests that these comic performers successfully touched on important sources of anxiety. One was the tension between men and women. On the farm, much of what was produced had come from the work of women and children. But in the city, for those who had brought their families, income now likely came only from the breadwinner. Unless the wife could take in work, the tradition that a woman's place is in the home, an ideal still viable enough among the upper classes, simply did not work in shantytown. A poor woman had to find a job, and the more she did "men's work," the more she expected men to do "women's work" at home. But conservative men could appeal to the authority of tradition, to the customs of the rural and upper classes, to resist such humiliation.

The minds of these onetime or would-be rural patriarchs were as overcrowded with old-fashioned phalliocratic ideals as their households were overcrowded with nonproductive dependents. Often for them, women were either a burden or, if they had a job, they no longer showed their husbands proper respect.[21] While the upper-class male, wearied by his day in the counting house, may have looked forward to returning to his sanctuary of comfort and peace, his working-class counterpart at the end of his day may have felt his footsteps being drawn not to that overflowing cauldron of conflict and confusion he called home, but to the saloon, the brothel, or just to friends on the street corner.

But there was also the minstrel show. There, blackface artists sang to an overwhelmingly male audience about a plantation never-land where men and women still knew what was expected of each other, and where romantic love still had a chance. But then, in a sudden shift, they could also speak to the bitterness of their listeners. "Wench characters," men dressed as women, acted out caricatures of unorthodox women.[22] Their favorite targets were the women who were trying to find a more workable role for themselves in a changing world.

Especially after the women's rights convention in Seneca Falls, New York, in 1848, a standard feature of the minstrel show became a "stump speech" on women's rights, a high-flown harangue undermined by mispronunciations, blunders, and malapropisms. In San Francisco "there was no bigger hit than Elph Horn." When he appeared "wearing a Quaker bonnet and umbrella to deliver his 'Lecture on Women's Rights,' he started a laugh that kept his audience aching to the end." And there was the popular minstrel skit *The Female Forty Thieves,* as well as that other "laugh-raiser," *Female Firemen or Women's Rights and Men's Wrongs.*[23] No one could miss the point. Women, like blacks, had their place and should stay in it.

Minstrel performers also made effective use of the tension between the low culture of the big-city poor and the high culture of the upper classes. Most of the audience was a part of that low culture, and the condescension that many of them had suffered in real life was a source of humiliation. But at the minstrel show they had their revenge. In real life, few things were less likely than an upper-class black snob. But in the fantasy world of minstrelsy, such characters strutted nightly on the stage, and their class pretensions were brought crashing to earth with a devastating punch line.[24]

In the antebellum North, class conflict surrounded the debate about liquor. The upper classes were troubled by the disorder released by the mushrooming growth of cities, a disorder made worse by the unregulated use of alcohol. But for workingmen, drinking was an escape from the stress of that disorder and from the boredom of endlessly repetitive work. So in the theater, they enjoyed seeing liquor upheld and temperance laid low.[25]

Social classes had different sexual problems. Among the well-to-do, traditional courtship and marriage had suffered little disruption. Yet among the uprooted population of the streets there was a disproportionate number of unattached young males. They observed family values well enough in theory, but their failures were frequent enough to make the upper galleries of theaters notorious as rendezvous of prostitution.[26] Of the possible ways of managing sexual tensions, these young men may have found their ideals of romantic love and traditional courtship among their least accessible options. The compromises they made, the makeshift expediencies that they adopted, undoubtedly shamed them. But in the minstrel theater, sinners enjoyed the needling that Victorian morality suffered on the stage; and they roared at the broad sexual innuendoes.[27]

Minstrel theater also captivated urban America because these theatergoers were united in a belief that made each the rival of the other, the gospel of success. Some were winners, some losers, but all knew what it took to succeed in America, to succeed in the city. Village friends and kin had to be left behind. One had to grapple in an unfamiliar world of strange faces. It meant hard work, doing without, and saving. Marriage had to be delayed and, when married, family size severely limited. Even sexual moderation was not enough. Total abstinence worked better. To be able to seize the big opportunity when it came, one had to give up so much that was pleasurable and natural. "Could the fantasies of such men have been other," Nathan Irvin Huggins has asked, "than the loose and undisciplined creatures of appetite—Sambo, Jim Crow, Jim Dandy?"

> What would be more likely and more natural for men who were tied up in the knots of an achievement ethic—depending almost wholly on self-sacrifice and self-restraint—than to create a *persona* which would be completely

self-indulgent and irresponsible . . . one which was loose of limb, innocent of obligation to anything outside itself, indifferent to success (for whom success was impossible by racial definition), and thus a creature totally devoid of tension and deep anxiety.[28]

The Politics of Minstrel Theater

Minstrel theater thus offered comic relief for a wide range of tensions. The tensions that were becoming ever more disturbing to antebellum America, however, were political. The land of the free had drawn in people from near and far, and it had drawn in those most eager to improve their lives. Yet the republic upon which they had pinned their hopes seemed headed for a breakup. Each North-South confrontation had been more threatening than the one before: the Missouri crisis of 1819–21, the Nullification crisis of 1832–33, and then the crisis of 1850.

As the free-labor system spread, moreover, into the western territories and into the South's northern border states, the planters, commodity brokers, and bankers who held sway over the Union needed more and more to win votes in free states. They were able to accomplish this, at least until the end of the 1850s, through the Democratic Party and mainly in the great commercial centers, with their rapidly growing electorate and where they received nightly help from minstrel spellbinders. These performances were not only immensely popular but also consistently partial to the Democratic Party.[29]

There was much in minstrel theater that appealed to the largest immigrant group, the Irish. The Irish were undoubtedly relieved to find that while in the popular theater of Great Britain, they had been the chief butt of stage jokes,[30] in the United States it was African Americans who were the targets.[31] A number of leading minstrel artists were themselves Irish Americans, men who understood the sadness of the immigrant experience, what it was like to have one's village and family an ocean away. In their songs these artists knew how to draw from that river of pathos that flowed in the tradition of Ireland, as well as in the tradition of black America.[32]

They also knew how to touch the resentment that their audience felt for Ireland's traditional oppressors. For real-life black people, twisting the tail of the British lion was not a top concern, but it was otherwise for the burnt-cork celebrities of the stage. If the patrons of the Democratic Party were receiving handsome profits from the commodity export trade with Great Britain, voters in shantytown were receiving their psychic reward in minstrel theater, as the longtime enemy of Ireland and the United States was trounced nightly on the stage. Already in the 1830s, blackface actors had taken a keen interest in the disputed boundary between Canada and Maine. Some called for a war of retribution against Britain and offered to fight.[33]

But there were no bottomlands for new plantations in Canada. The King Cotton republic, for all its twisting the lion's tail, was not inflexible in negotiating territorial disputes with its onetime enemy, now chief purchaser of plantation commodities. Not so with the lands to the south. The United States supported to the point of war the most dubious territorial claims of Texas, conquered the northern half of Mexico, and gave covert aid to private armies of filibusters to invade Cuba, Central America, and Mexico. Manifest Destiny, ostensibly a national policy, had a distinctly southern accent. So it was also on the minstrel stage. The feats of the filibusters were celebrated nightly.[34]

The men of power in the antebellum republic were concerned about Manifest Destiny, the conquest of virgin land for plantation agriculture. They were also concerned about the "place" of blacks in American society. Blacks were in their place wherever they were creating fortunes in plantation exports. But they were very much out of their place wherever they had become free and become the chief troublemakers against the King Cotton establishment.

The Racial Message

The concern about where African Americans belonged in society was one of the consistent themes of the minstrel stage. Take, for example, the most roundly ridiculed character of minstrel theater, in one typical representation, named Caesar Mars Napoleon Sinclair Brown, more often called Zip Coon. This pompous clown came on stage wearing white gloves and an eye piece and aped the great aristocrat. On the one hand, he gave the cast an opportunity to ridicule the high culture of the carriage class. But he also represented a northern free black, who, in real life, was the target of savage abuse. His clownish posturing and affectation showed that he was definitely out of his place, both by being free and by being in the North.[35] The tycoons of minstrel theater popularized support for slavery by ridiculing black freedom.

The dramatic foil to the ostentation of this northern free black was the jovial southern slave, who presumably did plantation work when he found time from his singing and dancing. From the stage, burnt-cork performers sang:

> Old Massa to us darkies am good
>   Tra la, tra la
> For he gibs us our clothes
> and he gibs us our food.[36]

A theater in California announced that "the most attractive Ethiopian songs will be introduced, delineating the high life among the Southern Negroes."[37]

This convention of a happy slave on an idyllic southern plantation was a contribution of the minstrel show to previous blackface entertainment. He was rarely referred to as a slave. Issues were more and more presented as racial, almost never as concerning the labor system. This character loved his plantation home, was totally devoted to his master, and accepted without reservation his humble place in the world. If one can believe the beautiful songs of Stephen C. Foster, it was not violence and fear that kept plantations running. It was loyalty and love.[38]

The racial ideas that saturated American culture—and were so clearly expressed in the minstrel show—help explain why the progress of abolition in Great Britain was more than a generation ahead of that in the United States. English workers gave broad support to the abolitionists. The Irish, too, in their own country, often linked their own oppression to that of black slaves. But when the Irish came to the United States, they frequently joined mobs that pelted abolitionists with rotten fruit, burned down black neighborhoods, and voted for proslavery Democrats. The Irish reformer Daniel O'Connell thought that there was something in the "atmosphere" of America that changed the racial attitudes of immigrants.[39]

What changed them, however, was King Cotton's power and the hegemonic culture and ideology it nurtured. Some scholars have concluded that the working-class audience shaped the culture of the minstrel stage.[40] But workers were the *consumers* of minstrel culture. Theater tycoons and the artists they employed produced it. The producers, of course, had to engage their audiences sufficiently to bring them back for more. Yet they had some choice in the entertainment they offered. The small audiences that the abolitionists reached were fascinated by the stories of escaped slaves and the adventures of activists in the Underground Railroad. But these exciting tales were not offered to the throngs crowding into minstrel shows. The entertainment offered to white workers was a defense of the plantation system that drove the economic growth of the antebellum republic.

The minstrels interpreted race, slavery, and the South primarily for the white working class. Their burnt-cork makeup and plantation settings were not purely formal devices, dramatic conventions for telling stories. The form was the content. The actor's grotesque face and his "'nigger' dialect" conveyed a message that was critical to the wealth and power of planter and commodity broker alike: Opportunity in America was for whites. Slavery was the "place" of blacks.

Chapter 10

The War of the Cabins
The Struggle for the Soul
of the "Common Man"

In the 1850s, no president, no general, no public figure was more controversial than Harriet Beecher Stowe. The southern poet William Gilmore Simms charged that she projected "a malignity so remarkable that the petticoat lifts of itself, and we see the hoof of the beast under the table."[1] But a correspondent for an abolitionist newspaper, watching a theatrical performance of *Uncle Tom's Cabin,* exclaimed, "O, it was a sight worth seeing, those ragged, coatless men and boys (the very *material* of which mobs are made) cheering the strongest and sublimist anti-slavery sentiment."[2] More than anyone else, Stowe brought the antislavery message out of the shadows into the cultural mainstream.

Stowe has always presented a problem to her biographers: a housewife with seven children who wrote one of the most popular and influential works in history. As she described in a letter to her sister-in-law, Sarah Beecher, "I have been called off at least a dozen times; once for the fish man to buy a catfish; once to see a man who had brought me some barrels of apples; once to see a book man; then to Mrs. Upham to see about a drawing I promised to make for her; then to nurse the baby . . . ; then to the kitchen to make chowder for dinner; and now I am at it again, for nothing but deadly determination enables me to write."[3] But Stowe presents an even harder problem for anyone trying to understand the relationship between culture and power. At the time her novel appeared, the antislavery message in the North had rarely reached mass audiences.[4] The respectable norm of the day was that the disputes disrupting the republic were "sectional," North versus South; or "constitutional," states' rights versus federal authority; or "racial," white versus black.

But to say that the root cause of all these disputes was *slavery*, and that it was cruel and un-Christian, was to be branded an abolitionist, a "race-mixer," and to become a solitary voice crying in the wilderness. Despite the draconian Fugitive Slave Act of 1850, what ordinary Americans most often heard was that the plantation was a place of romance, certainly an improvement over northern factories and mines; and that blacks were banjo-strumming clowns who would scarcely feel the weight of oppression if indeed they had ever experienced any.[5] In a matter of months, Stowe moved the antislavery message from church bulletins to the saloons, the street corners, and the parlors of America.[6]

To understand this sudden widening of the slavery debate, one needs to consider how hegemonic belief systems evolve. Commonly, only people with great resources can popularize their views and displace or marginalize the views of others. Governing classes possess the resources for shaping the prevailing outlook of a society.[7] They can define orthodoxy and heresy, and determine which are proper topics of conversation in polite society and which are considered irrelevant or bizarre. They can define even the language, the phraseology, that a person must use to be understood or even heard. Class hegemony is achieved when most people do not perceive the limitations imposed by the prevailing belief system of their society, either its restrictions on subject matter or the biases inherent in the words that they use. Instead, one normally assumes that the discussion of everyday issues is framed by self-evident truths.

The Hegemony of the Racial Defense

By the 1850s, the racial doctrines that sustained planters and their northern partners had become hegemonic. Many people in antebellum America did not like all or much of the cotton establishment's agenda, but they could not challenge what appeared to be the irrefutable arguments that sustained it. So they piggybacked—endorsed the national racial consensus—but tried to bend it to their own purposes. Thus, in 1847, when the United States was poised to take over a large part of Mexico, Representative David Wilmot advanced what became known as the Wilmot Proviso, which would have prohibited the extension of slavery into territory where it had been illegal under Mexican law. It was a free-soil amendment wrapped in the language of racial orthodoxy: "I have no squeamish sensitivity upon the subject of slavery, no morbid sympathy for the slave. I plead the cause and the rights of white freemen. I would preserve to free white labor a fair country, a rich inheritance, where the sons of toil, of my own race and own color, can live without the disgrace which association with negro slavery brings upon free labor."[8]

Wilmot's logic, his appeals to white solidarity, to the self-evident truths that sustained planter power, did not fool John C. Calhoun, who blocked Wilmot's proviso in the Senate. A much more successful piggybacking occurred five years later when Harriet Beecher Stowe published her "Wilmot Proviso" of popular fiction. Just as the Free-Soilers attempted to manipulate to their own purpose the hegemonic racial beliefs, she conceded rather than challenged this prevailing racial justification of slavery. But she bent it to her antislavery purpose.[9]

The City Where All the Issues Collided

For eighteen years Stowe had lived in Cincinnati, on the North-South border, a cockpit of conflict like no other in the nation, where the issues of slavery, race, and free speech were subjects of frequent debates and sometimes violent confrontations. There, she joined the liberal Semi-Colon Club, where the controversies of the day were aired and where she got to know a future Radical member of Lincoln's cabinet, Salmon P. Chase. It was in Cincinnati also where she became friends with Gamaliel Bailey, the antislavery editor, who was to publish *Uncle Tom's Cabin*.

She was no detached observer in the debates that divided the city and engulfed her own family, radicalizing perhaps three of her brothers. Her father, Lyman Beecher, as president of Lane Theological Seminary, and her husband, Calvin Stowe, as a professor at Lane, were caught in the middle of a conflict that almost destroyed the seminary, between the radical idealism of the students and the dollars-and-cents conservatism of the trustees. Then, in 1837, when James G. Birney brought the antislavery *Philanthropist* to Cincinnati, and a wave of anti-abolitionist, antiblack hysteria swept the city, she published, under the pen name "Franklin," a letter defending the right of abolitionists to free speech.

In the antagonistic environment of this border city also, she had had personal contact with African Americans, albeit supervising their labor at such times when the Stowes could afford a servant. Yet even here "the irrepressible conflict" erupted: The Stowes learned that their cook was a fugitive. Her master had come to Cincinnati looking for her. Whereupon, Stowe's husband, Calvin, and her brother Henry armed themselves and drove the woman twelve miles to the farm of John Van Zandt, a station on the Underground Railroad. It was also while living in Cincinnati that she had gotten to know the Reverend John Rankin, an activist in the Underground Railroad, who told her about helping a slave mother who had fled with her child across the ice of the frozen Ohio River.[10]

Stowe's life experiences come to the surface from time to time in her novel, giving it a captivating vitality. But if the characters in *Uncle Tom's Cabin* had been drawn entirely from real life, her book might have reached only the small circle who had read *Narrative of the Life of Frederick Douglass* or had heard the protest songs of the Hutchinson family.[11] Stowe knew only too well from her life in Cincinnati that to speak in realistic terms about slavery, as Douglass was doing, was no way to reach a mass audience. Indeed, in Cincinnati, James G. Birney, Salmon P. Chase, and others had put their lives at risk with such talk.

Bypassing the Racial Defenses of Slavery

By at least beginning by telling people what they already believed, Stowe could get a hearing.[12] So the characters on her "Shelby plantation" came less from life than from the minstrel show fantasies of mainstream America. The aged, loyal, pious, black "uncle," who loved his master and his own servitude, was already a standard fixture of popular fiction and theater.[13] Her "Uncle Tom" became the definitive representation of the character, and even became a word in the English language. Ever since, black men who have internalized the point of view of their oppressors, who behaved obsequiously toward whites, have been derisively called Uncle Toms.[14] And no old plantation of minstrel theater or popular fiction was more idyllic than her Shelby plantation or had a master more kind.[15]

She thus began her story with what was to her readers a familiar southern landscape, peopled with characters that they had encountered many times before in popular fiction and theater. There was nothing here to disturb what most antebellum Americans accepted as self-evident truth. But the men of the King Cotton establishment were no more fooled by her romantic plantations and dancing "darkies" than they had been by the Free-Soiler Wilmot's appeal to white solidarity. They saw that her real story was a thrust at slavery's heart.

Who could deny, for example, that a happy plantation could be overwhelmed by financial disaster, and that property was then put up for sale? When this happened, what was to prevent the property, pious old Uncle Tom, from falling into the hands of a whiskey-swigging psychopath such as Simon Legree? The cruelty, the evil, that she presented, therefore, came from slavery, from holding as property members of the human family.

The Scandal of the White Slave

In pages overflowing with racial stereotypes, Stowe made another thrust at slavery. She presented the scandal of the white, or nearly white, slave. The defenders of antebellum society lost few battles so long as they were able to mount their defense behind a barricade of racial ideas. These ideas derived from a hegemonic color equation: black equals slave, white equals free. Anything that violated or distorted this color equation subverted the defense of slaveholding society and threatened the Union itself.

There were, therefore, two situations that were especially disturbing to antebellum society. One was a fully free African American, such as Frederick Douglass, who could brush aside this social equation, stand tall, and address the world as an equal. Anybody who could do this caused an instant scandal. The other situation was equally shocking: the white, or, more often, "apparently" white, slave.

The slavery of Jordan Chambers, for example, was not the white slavery of Yankee factories. Born in 1813, Chambers appears to have been the illegitimate son of a North Carolina planter, Colonel Andrew Caldwell, and an Irish immigrant mother, probably an indentured servant. Upon the death of the colonel in 1824, Chambers lost not only his father but also his protection. The eleven-year-old was playing with some black children when he was seized by strangers, probably at the instigation of an older, legitimate half brother, and turned over to a speculator, who took him to Charleston for sale. A mob, scandalized by the boy's wrong color, prevented his being sold but failed to secure his freedom. Chambers remained in slavery until the end of the Civil War, but subsequently he was prudently referred to as a "mulatto," or "nearly white."[16]

In 1850, Dennis Framell arrived in New Albany, Indiana, with a warrant to arrest as fugitive slaves three residents who were apparently white: a woman, her daughter, and her grandson, who was attending the local school. An aroused public opposed the action. But Framell convinced the special federal commissioners appointed under the Fugitive Slave Law of 1850 that they were his property. Federal marshals delivered the three to him in Kentucky. But there a scandalized mob of slaveholders rescued them and took them before a local court, which released them as white persons. In the South, more important than the recovery of three slaves was the ideology of white solidarity, without which slavery could not survive.

Meanwhile back in Indiana, incensed citizens of New Albany, to prevent further humiliation of these apparently white people, collected the six hundred dollars asked by Framell for a bill of sale, and returned them to freedom in Indiana. Here, in 1850, if the escapees had been black, their capture would have offended few of these good citizens. For, if the people of Indiana no longer practiced slavery, they shared in a racial consensus that was national, a consensus that normally served well southern masters in recovering slaves.[17]

In *Uncle Tom's Cabin,* Stowe knew how to use the scandal of the white, or "nearly" white, slave to aim a thrust at slavery's heart.[18] Racial beliefs had anesthetized the conscience of most people to the suffering of black Americans. But, in the novel, the beautiful Eliza, her husband, George, and their infant son, Harry, were not black, or were not black enough. In respect to them the prevailing ideology faltered.[19] Readers could not trivialize their anguish or smile at their discomfort as if they were minstrel-show clowns. What this family experienced was fully human suffering. Stowe had thus not attacked but outflanked the racial defense of slavery.

Because of this, despite the phenomenal success of *Uncle Tom's Cabin,* she had scarcely made a dent in the primary defense of slavery, which was racial. If anything, her stereotypes had further popularized and reinforced this ideology. Her achievement was that she had successfully piggybacked. She had attached an antislavery message to people's well-established prejudices.

A Vibrant North, a Revolutionary Idea

Her story of Uncle Tom's martyrdom and Eliza's desperate escape came to countless readers like a revelation: slavery is wrong. By 1852, the North was ready for new ideas.[20] No other place on earth was surging with such energy. During the 1850s, the United States built more railroads than the rest of the world put together, two-thirds of them in the free states. Three million immigrants entered the country, 87 percent of them settling in the free states. All across the Upper North, along the line of the Erie Canal and the Great Lakes, where the economic influence of King Cotton was almost nonexistent, towns were forming and cities were rising: Rochester, Buffalo, Cleveland, Detroit, Milwaukee, and Chicago.

By the end of the 1850s, canals and railroads were bringing an ever-increasing volume of wheat, corn, and salt pork from the Midwest to the eastern ports. These exports were overtaking in value those from the South. Now free workers as much as slaves were generating the capital that drove the growth of industry and transportation and created new jobs.[21] It was in a North surging with strength where more and more people were feeling the irrepressible urge to challenge King Cotton's rule of the federal government.

Stowe's publisher had feared that his business might suffer for publishing an antislavery book. But during the months after it appeared, eight power presses running night and day could not keep up with the demand. Boys were hawking the book in the streets like newspapers.[22] Dramatic renditions of the story appeared that played to packed theaters from Boston to San Francisco.[23] Traveling troupes carried the drama to villages and country crossroads in the North, and showboats brought it to remote steamboat landings in the American heartland.[24]

In the rural and village North, especially the upper North, the tycoons of minstrel theater had less influence than in the large cities. People were more tolerant of antislavery ideas. When a traveling troupe arrived in town, they would often treat the community to a parade, giving them a foretaste of the drama. Local boys would be given the privilege of leading down the main street, one by one, a column of "bloodhounds," often in reality larger and uglier mastiffs; and everybody knew that these fierce-looking beasts would soon be at the heels of poor Eliza and little Harry. Then hisses would arise from the throng as the cart bearing the arch villain appeared—Simon Legree in full costume. Unintimidated by their hatred, he would crack his terrible whip at the crowd and shout, "I'm looking for a likely-looking yaller gal named Eliza. . . . She belongs t'me an' I want her."[25] Not much new was being said in Washington by the dignitaries in the administrations of Franklin Pierce or of James Buchanan. But something new was happening in the villages and towns of the free states.[26]

The Conservative Counterattack

In a sense, *Uncle Tom's Cabin* was not so much the Wilmot Proviso of popular culture as it was the Fort Sumter. For in the world of the imagination, a civil war had already begun. The retainers of King Cotton struck back. The editor of the *Southern Literary Messenger* wrote to a trustworthy reviewer that he wanted a piece on the novel that would be "as hot as hell-fire, blasting and searing the reputation of the vile wretch in petticoats who could write such a volume."[27]

The review began with a question on which Stowe could expect little support, even in the North: the right of women to speak out on political issues.

Many abolitionists themselves thought that a woman's proper sphere was her own home and family. The reviewer thus spoke with hegemonic authority when he wrote that he did not subscribe to that novel doctrine "which would place woman on a footing of political equality with man, and causing her to look beyond the office for which she was created—the high and holy office of maternity—would engage her in the administration of public affairs; thus handing over the State to the perilous protection of diaper diplomatists, and wet-nurse politicians."[28] Stowe was besieged with hate mail, which she and her husband dutifully opened and read. One letter enclosed the severed ear of an African American.[29]

In the South, heavy-handed censorship was applied. Daniel R. Goodloe, a civil servant in Washington, was fired after he made favorable comments about the best seller.[30] Samuel Green, a freedman in Maryland, was sentenced to a ten-year term in the state prison after constables searching his home found a copy of the novel and two other "incriminating" documents. A bookseller was hounded out of Mobile for selling it.[31] It is unclear how effective these methods were. Frederick Law Olmsted, traveling by steamboat on the Mississippi, heard that passengers were reading the book and that it was available in New Orleans.[32] Even in Charleston, a traveler, seeing one of the many anti-Stowe novels being displayed at a hotel bookstand, asked the vendor if he also sold *Uncle Tom's Cabin*. "I can get it for you," the man replied. "[I] don't sell it openly."[33]

Initially, publishers had refused Stowe's manuscript on grounds that publishing a "nigger book" might injure their business. But Dr. Gamaliel Bailey, whom Stowe had known in Cincinnati, agreed to publish it serially in his moderately antislavery *National Era,* a paper that had already suffered a mob attack. It was the lively interest created by this newspaper series that prompted a book publisher to risk an edition. The first dramatic adaptation of the story, in 1852, at Welch's National Amphitheatre in Philadelphia, was broken up on opening night by a mob.[34] Yet suppression of the story was never an actual possibility in the North.

There, the battle was on over the morality of slavery. The defenders of the antebellum Union were well armed. In addition to the many anti-Stowe book reviews, editorials, and pamphlets, at least twenty-seven "literary works" appeared in opposition to *Uncle Tom's Cabin.*[35] In general, these were novels that retold the popular tale, or a similar one, and addressed the issues that Stowe raised from a "southern" point of view. Since suppression had been only dubiously successful in the South and a failure in the North, conservatives adopted the tactic of co-option. They, too, knew how to piggyback, to attach their own message to a popular idea.

Co-option of the Uncle Tom Story

There were also opportunities for scriptwriters and producers of conservative dramatic adaptations of the story. Alexander Saxton has shown that there were important ties between show business, especially minstrel theater, and some of the more important political actors of the Democratic Party.[36] The leading tycoon of West Coast minstrel theater was Tom McGuire, a former Tammany stalwart. The famous minstrel composer Stephen Foster was connected by marriage to the family of President James Buchanan, for whom he composed a campaign song.[37]

The tie between King Cotton politics and popular culture was particular evident in New York City, especially through the Wood brothers. The theatrical promoter Henry Wood was a partner in the trend-setting Christy and Wood's Minstrels, as well as the owner of Broadway Theater and Marble Hall. Benjamin Wood published the New York *Daily News* and was a multi-term pro-southern congressman. Fernando Wood, a millionaire, served several terms both in Congress and as mayor of New York.[38] As mayor during the secession crisis of 1861, Wood, with the support of his brother's *Daily News,* proposed the city also secede so as to maintain its friendly commercial relations with the South.[39]

The conservative orientation of show business may be seen in the novel's adaptations for the stage. One appeared on the Baltimore stage early in 1852, even before serialization of the novel in the *National Era* had ended. According to the playwright, he had written it "to counteract a vital danger." He had therefore retold the story "from the slavery viewpoint, an answer to Mrs. Stowe's libel." His Uncle Tom at one point is made to say, "Sha! I was born a slave, I have lived a slave, and bress de Lord, I hope to die a slave!"[40]

Like the minstrel show, these "southern" Uncle Tom plays were primarily aimed at a northern audience. Their way of adapting the novel to the stage was what Bruce McConachie has called the "normalization" of *Uncle Tom's Cabin,* playing down Stowe's antislavery message, but stressing her conventional racial stereotypes.[41] The adaptation by Henry J. Conway opened at P. T. Barnum's theater in New York. His production, Barnum claimed, while showing the cruelties of slavery, did not "foolishly and unjustly elevate the negro above the white man in intellect or morals." It gave a "true picture of negro life in the South."[42] The Conway version reduced Topsy to a standard minstrel show "wench," even giving her a conventional "stump speech" on "de necessity ob doin' somethin' for dere coloured brethen in bondage." Slave sales, which in Stowe's novel were a horror, in the hands of Conway became the solution to Uncle Tom's problems: In a dramatic last-moment rescue from Simon Legree, a white benefactor appeared with money enough to buy not only Uncle Tom but his entire family, thus completing the transformation of an antislavery tragedy into a minstrel-type comedy.[43]

The Bowery Theatre, a leading competitor of Barnum's establishment, engaged the most famous of all minstrel clowns, T. D. Rice, the creator of Jim Crow, to play Uncle Tom.[44] Christy and Wood's Minstrels carried the normalization even further. In their *Happy Uncle Tom,* which "set the tone for many of the minstrel versions of the play that followed it," they removed not only the villain, Simon Legree, from the story but anything else suggesting cruelty and suffering. They ended their play with plantation slaves singing and dancing at a Christmas Eve feast.[45] The normalization, or minstrelization, was now complete.

A version of *Happy Uncle Tom* played in Philadelphia from 1853 until the outbreak of the Civil War. From the stage these minstrels sang:

> Oh, white folks, we'll have you to know
> Dis am not de version of Mrs. Stowe;
> Wid her de Darks am all unlucky
> But we am de boys from Old Kentucky.
> Den hand de Banjo down to play
> We'll make it ring both night and day
> And we care not what de white folks say,
> Dey can't get us to run away.[46]

John Owen, a Baltimore producer and comedian, explained his preparations for playing Uncle Tom. "I've raked up all sorts of situations from old farces, and so on—anything to cover up the real drift of the play."[47] Thus, on the stage, conservatives had largely taken over the story, stripped it of its antislavery message, and reinforced its conventional racial features.

The Antislavery Uncle Tom

Yet they were never able to displace totally Stowe's antislavery tragedy with a proslavery comedy. In the religious and antislavery environment of the upper North, the Howard-Fox troupe produced a drama that not only remained true to the antislavery spirit of her novel but also fared well in competition with the "southern" versions. The playwright, George L. Aiken, spoke to the piety and idealism of small-town America. Aiken dramatized to the fullest Eliza's heroic dash to freedom with little Harry in her arms, across the breaking ice of the Ohio. The orchestra furiously heightened the excitement of the chase.[48]

Also Aiken's treatment of Uncle Tom was different from that in the southern renditions of the story. Stowe's Uncle Tom had been drawn less from life than from the celebrated "uncle" of the minstrel stage. As an ideological construct, this character was ambiguous and thus open to differing interpretations. Just as the big-city theaters were playing Uncle Tom as a dancing plantation clown, Aiken stressed his unresisting, Christ-like humility. At one point, although Uncle Tom knows that he is going to be sold, he refuses his opportunity to escape with Eliza. To do so would be to betray his master's trust, and his own faith:

> Him dat save Daniel in the den
> o' Lions an' bring de chillun outer
> de fiery furnace—Him dat walk
> on de sea an' tell dem winds
> dey got to be still—He's alive![49]

Overtrustful, perhaps, but this Uncle Tom was no minstrel clown.

Uncle Tom pours out his pathos in song, including Stephen Foster's "Old Folks at Home" (or "Swanee Ribber"); and at the moment of his final martyrdom, each measured, undeserved lash, laid on by Simon Legree, is reinforced with a crashing chord by the orchestra.[50]

Unlike New York City, the atmosphere in upstate New York was antislavery. During an unprecedented ten-week run in Troy, New York, a city of 30,000, perhaps 25,000 people attended the play. After another successful run in Albany, the troupe decided to storm the bastions of King Cotton, the great commercial cities. They broke up into several groups, each of which, joined by other players, took their production to a different city, including to the National Theater in New York, the scene of earlier anti-abolitionist, antiblack riots; and to the Chestnut Street Theatre in Philadelphia, a city where a mob had broken up an earlier version of the play on opening night.[51] In these cities, they certainly found enemies, but they also found friends—church members, for example. Protestants, who traditionally had shunned the theater as the very sump hole of debauchery, made an exception for Aiken's *Uncle Tom's Cabin*. Although a smaller part of the population in the great cities, they were the same kind of people who had made the Aiken play a prodigious success in the upper North. They came in droves, sometimes accompanied by their pastors.[52] And these were organized citizens, active in the affairs of their communities. In a friendly gesture to this new, upstanding, audience, the National Theater announced, "Females of improper character are not admitted in any part of the house." Also it opened "a neat and comfortable parquette" near the pit for "colored" patrons, segregated but nevertheless admitted.[53]

The "War of the Cabins"

Uncle Tom's Cabin was also bringing out the audience that had long enjoyed theater, their curiosity piqued by the runaway popularity of the novel and the Aiken play: the carriage class, the working class, the devotees of high culture, of low culture, firehouse gangs, and the unchurched, footloose sinners of the saloons and streets.[54]

Audiences were as varied as the city itself, and now, for the first time, they were being offered different points of view. In New York, a patron might select Christy and Wood's "Happy Uncle Tom," or Barnum's "just and sensible" Uncle Tom, or they could see a funny one sung and danced by "Jim Crow" Rice at the Bowery, or Aiken's tragic Christ-like figure at the National.

There was such a rush of theatergoers downtown that the Second and Third Avenue horse railroad companies prospered, and the price of their shares rose on the stock market.[55] Each night, when the final curtain came down on the play, the drama had not ended. Debates broke out in the lobby or in the street outside, often continuing far into the night. There were street fights between the partisans of northern or southern renditions of the story. From Sweeny's working-class saloon to the sumptuous Prescott House on Broadway one heard one topic only: *Uncle Tom's Cabin.*[56]

Immigrants became involved, especially the Germans. An *Onkel Tom's Hütte* opened at the Deutches Theatre in New York. German-speaking Philadelphians could choose between two versions of the play. It was said to be the talk of every *Verein,* or club. Traditionally Democrats, German loyalty to the party of King Cotton was now wavering.

In the world of the popular imagination, the battle lines had already been drawn in what one author has called the "War of the Cabins."[57] The entire nation was obsessed with a tale written by a woman seated at her kitchen table or on her back steps. Yet this was a story that encompassed the tensions that drew the country inexorably toward a dimly seen day of reckoning.

As in the politics of our own day, much depended upon the attitude of those who were uncommitted, those who were often the most weakly politicized and most poorly informed about public affairs. Many who knew little about politics were forming opinions about poor Eliza, or Simon Legree, or had been touched by the heartrending songs of Uncle Tom. Theatergoers attending the Aiken renditions noted that the cheaper seats, in the "pit," were occupied by the kind of spectators who had traditionally been reliable supporters of King Cotton. A Philadelphia abolitionist was elated to see an audience of three thousand "unconsciously accepting anti-slavery truth—hundreds of boys—

incipient rowdies, growing up to become the mobocracy of another generation." He predicted that "in Philadelphia, abolitionists may have to intercede to save slaveholders and planters from the fury of the mob, so long directed against us."[58]

The battle was on for the loyalty of the working class. As a result of the Uncle Tom phenomenon, antislavery artists had gained a toehold in mainstream theater, a slender access to the working class. But far more typical of the experience of dissenters trying to make themselves heard was that of the singing Hutchinson family. They performed before small antislavery groups throughout the free states and even traveled to England. During their concert tours in the winter months, they earned enough to cover their traveling expenses, but not a living. When time came for spring planting, they were back at work in the fields of their farm in New Hampshire.[59]

It was the tycoons of professional theater, the retainers of King Cotton, who spoke most often to mass audiences. Their control over the minstrel stage, the entertainment in which the working class was most sharply targeted, continued. Every night before packed houses they wove a tale of a plantation never-never land without the woes of industrial society. With increasing frequency this country was called the "land of Dixie."

In one rendition, "Jonny Roach," by Daniel Decatur Emmett, the protagonist had made his way, by means of the "railroad underground," to Canada. But there his disillusionment was complete:

> Gib me de place called "Dixie Land,"
> Wid hoe and shubble in my hand;
> Whar fiddles ring an' banjos play,
> I'll dance all night an' work all day.[60]

Later, Emmett returned to the same theme:

> There is a land where cotton grows
> A land where milk and honey flows
> I'm going home to Dixie.
> I've wander'd far both to and fro'
> But Dixie's heaven here below
> I'm going home
>   . . . .
>
> O list to what I've got to say
> Freedom to me will never pay!
> I'm going home
>   . . . .

A shadow and a phantom frail,
The mighty truth it must prevail!
I'm going home

. . . .

In Dixie Land the fields do bloom
And color'd men have welcome room
I'm going home

. . . .

I will proclaim it loud and long
I love old Dixie right or wrong
I'm going home.[61]

By the eve of the Civil War the popularity of the minstrels could hardly have been greater. They had met Harriet Beecher Stowe and had parried her attack. In most theaters they had "normalized" Uncle Tom. They had torn the bleeding martyr down from his cross and had recycled him to the public as some version of Jumping Jim Crow. The minstrels had outstripped by far every other form of popular entertainment. Their songs were on everybody's lips. Their vision of the South, of slavery, of African Americans, was for many people, perhaps most, more real than reality itself.

During these days of unprecedented glory for minstrel theater, Emmett, while mining that rich vein, African American folk music,[62] produced a "Dixie" that was one of the most stirring and distinctly American compositions of the century.[63] It was released in New York in 1859, first as a "Cornshucking Dance," then as a "Walk Around," or grand finale of a production by Bryant's Minstrels and interpreted by the entire cast of dancers and musicians. It was an instant sensation. Songs of "Dixie" were typically sad, contemplative outpourings of nostalgic yearning for a lost homeland. But this "Dixie," bursting with energy, burning with excitement, electrified audiences from Boston to San Francisco.

Abraham Lincoln, attending Rumsey and Newcomb's Minstrels in Chicago, according to a friend, was "perfectly 'taken' by their rendition of 'Dixie.'" He "clapped his great hands, demanding an *encore,* louder than anyone. I never saw him so enthusiastic."[64] Another rising president also liked the song. It was played in Montgomery, Alabama, at the inauguration of the Confederate president Jefferson Davis.[65]

On the level of ideology, apparently nothing much had happened in America. Some favored secession, some the Union; but, in either case, one appealed to a common cluster of ideas about freedom and equal rights. The North-South racial consensus also seemed little disturbed. Even Harriet Beecher Stowe had had to adapt her protest against slavery to this all-pervasive view.

But something, indeed, had happened. In a republic where people thought that race should count for everything and classes for nothing, there had been, at least for the moment, a realignment of social classes. Stowe had planted a seed of revolution. Part of the working class, most notably among German immigrants, had abandoned their reactionary alliance with the planter. They had joined the Republicans.

The cradle of the Republican Party was the upper North, rural New England, upstate New York, and the Great Lakes country. This was a land where villages exploded into towns and towns into cities, a land that owed nothing to slavery. In this world there were "manufacturers" who still worked with their hands and railroad operators whose tracks barely reached the next village, but whose ambitions spanned a continent. Many had heard the protest songs of the Hutchinson family, or on stage had seen the heroism of Eliza and the martyrdom of Uncle Tom. Nowhere did King Cotton have more disloyal subjects than among this almost bourgeoisie.

They were restless, feeling new political strength. They had discovered "free labor" allies among the urban working class, even in the biggest eastern cities. Now in the elections of 1860 they had challenged the planter-"doughface" regime with an economic program that looked like a reincarnation of Henry Clay's American System. But, unlike Henry Clay's Whigs, the Republicans tolerated within their ranks a band of antislavery Radicals. Yet from the streets of Montgomery to the sidewalks of New York, bands were still playing and people were still humming, "I wish I was in de lann ob cotton."

Part 3

The Racial System
Challenged and
Revised

Chapter 11

The Republican Revolution and the Struggle for a "New Birth of Freedom"

Like a moth to the flame, John Brown was drawn by an ancient Christian vision of liberation. His 1859 raid on Harper's Ferry had rocked the nation.[1] This was not because adventures by private armies were unusual in the 1850s. Nor was Brown's raid bloodier than those of Narciso Lopez into Cuba, or William Walker's takeover of Nicaragua, or the "border ruffians" raids into Kansas. Rather it was because while these had attempted to carry the power of the southern slaveholders into Latin America and into the American West, Brown's band had struck a blow at slavery, and in Virginia, in its home territory.[2]

Also the raid unleashed panic across the South, because it involved both whites and blacks. White solidarity was the jugular vein of the Old South. Now whites were under more scrutiny. In the low country of eastern North Carolina, there was alarm at reports of a "swamper" who, when asked what kind of a man he was, replied, "I am a John Brown man, and damb my sole if I dont carry out John Brown law." Even a large slaveholder did not escape suspicion. Charles Pettigrew returned to his Bonava plantation to find that the place had been searched by the slave patrol.[3] The hanging of John Brown, therefore, was no routine execution.

Among the multitude that crowded around the gallows were important actors in the drama that was beginning to unfold: Edmund Ruffin, who would be credited with touching off the first cannon fired on Fort Sumter; Robert E. Lee; the future "Stonewall" Jackson; J. E. B. Stuart; and John Wilkes Booth.[4] Of the thousands who attended the execution, or the millions who followed it from afar, there were few citizens indeed who shared Brown's view of slavery and racial equality. Yet three years later, a new federal government would begin doing what these spectators in 1859 considered criminal or insane, the freeing and arming of the slaves.

As he was being led from his cell, Brown handed a note to one of the guards: "I John Brown am now quite *certain* that the crimes of this *guilty land, will* never be purged *away;* but with Blood."[5] Four months later, his prophecy began unfolding at the Democratic national convention in Charleston.

Breakup of the Democratic Party

Because of Harper's Ferry more than any other event, the conflict that had been mounting for generations was now indeed "irrepressible." Delegates from the Deep South were now demanding greater protection for slavery than even the most pro-southern Congress or president had ever before provided them. They would have to have Cuba as a future slave state. They would have to have black codes for the federal territories so that planters could safely continue their westward migration. If these assurances were not forthcoming, they warned, the South would have to seek safety outside the Union.

Even as these delegates were demanding more, those from the North were constrained to concede less. On the day of Brown's execution, church bells tolled in mourning from New England to Kansas. Banners were strung across the streets of Cleveland reading, "I cannot better serve the cause I love than to die for it."[6] Brown had evoked an age-old source of authority that resided not in the government nor in the courts, but in the conscience. Out of the shadows into broad daylight he had brought the ancient vision: in Christ there was neither "Greek nor Jew, . . . Barbarian, Scythian, bond nor free" (Colossians 3:11).[7]

Now it did no good to warn those people troubled about the morality of slavery that the Union was coming apart, that already the major religious denominations of the land were split into northern and southern branches, that the Republicans had only a regionally based organization, and that the Democratic Party was the only institution based broadly enough to hold the country together. For them, slavery was a sin. Such people of moral commitment influenced both society and the coming elections beyond their numbers.

In the North, candidates who supported black codes for the federal territories were facing defeat.

At the 1860 Democratic national convention in Charleston, northern and southern delegates for the first time were unable to reach a compromise.[8] Their convention, and their party, broke up in anger.[9] A northern president and a northern party won the national election. The republic was torn by secession. It now appeared that the old prophet had died on the scaffold like the blinded Samson had died at Gaza, by pulling down the palace of his enemies on their heads.

The Second American Revolution

Brown had foretold the bloodletting that would be required to atone for America's sins. And, indeed, slavery was so embedded in the antebellum economy, the power structure, and ideology that it was dislodged only by a revolution of fearful proportions. But the Republicans, who gathered in Washington in 1861 to form the new administration, contemplated no such fundamental changes. Their vision of the future was the rapidly expanding society of the free states, but they had no intention of abolishing slavery in any state where it existed legally. Despite the faults American society might have, these men were thoroughly committed to the Constitution and to the Union as they understood it. The Republicans were thus anything but revolutionists. Yet, under their leadership, the nation was on the road to revolution.

Perhaps the leaders of the new party took the first step along this course when they decided that the legitimacy of the new administration came from their having won the 1860 elections, not from having won the consent of those whom they had defeated. They thus rejected the Crittenden compromise, which would have extended westward the legal boundaries of slavery, and other efforts to reconcile the secessionists by leaving the door open for the admission of future slave states. Such a concession threatened the very existence of the Republican Party, which brought together diverse factions who agreed on a single issue, their shared opposition to the further extension of slavery: "We have just carried an election on principles fairly stated to the people," Lincoln wrote. "Now we are told in advance, the government shall be broken up, unless we surrender to those we have beaten. . . . if we surrender, it is the end of us. . . . A year will not pass, till we shall have to take Cuba as a condition upon which they will stay in the Union."[10]

The Republicans made a second decision closely related to the first, which also had fearful consequences. Since the voters had indeed sent a legitimate government to Washington, the authority of that government would be asserted in every state, North and South, the secession movement notwithstanding. This was a bold stand. It united in defiance Southerners of every stripe, both those who favored secession and those who had opposed it. On the other hand, it united under Republican leadership nationalists of every stripe, including Jacksonian Democrats who had made many concessions to save the Union but for whom the Union itself was not negotiable.

Lincoln's decision to "provision" Fort Sumter, in the Charleston harbor, provoked a Confederate attack on the fort, and thus dramatically transformed the political landscape. There was a patriotic rallying around the flag and president in the North, a similar rallying to the Confederate standard and president in the South.[11] Republican insistence on the legitimacy and authority of their administration precipitated war.

They had precipitated a war of a special kind, a revolution. A revolution is a war that results not simply in changing the policies of a government or even changing the government itself, but in changing the character of a society. The movement for independence from England had split the planter/merchant elite, opening for a generation political space for the opponents of slavery. But both the rebellious Patriots and the accommodationist Loyalists had planters and slave traders within their ranks. Antislavery thus remained subordinate to the dominant issues of accommodation or rebellion. The change in the racial system was confined to the North, where slavery was a minor labor system and where few African Americans lived. Yet the struggle for independence had been no ordinary war. It had created the free states, space where an economy based on free labor had grown prodigiously.

In 1861 an African American newspaper, the New York *National Principia*, recognized that the conflict unleashed by the attack on Fort Sumter was no ordinary war. It would not leave American society unchanged. In an article entitled "Second American Revolution," the editors concluded "that this Revolution has begun, and is in progress. We say so, because the *Nation* has come into direct physical conflict with the slaveholders! Slowly, unintentionally, the present Federal Administration has done so. *The war is an accomplished fact. . . .* Therefore the Revolution is going forward."[12]

Ironically, the secessionist leaders themselves helped turn their slaveholder's rebellion into a revolution. Their way of life rested on slaves and land. The wealth produced by this property, shared with northern bankers and shippers, won them allies among some of the most powerful men in the United States. While many people in the North disliked slavery, many, probably most, regarded slaves as property, and property was sacred.

But in the South, while the election of Lincoln was still being debated and not a shot had been fired, secessionist mobs and militia bands began making property less sacred. They seized federal arsenals, army and navy installations, federal mints and post offices. The *Mobile Advertiser* called on the newly formed Confederate government to issue letters of mark for the capture of northern ships: "There is no sea upon which the ships of New England and New York do not cluster thickly, and such is a rich prize for a daring navigator. Let the note of war be sounded, and soon hundreds of crafts, bearing letters of mark of the Confederacy, would be scouring the oceans to prey upon the defenseless commerce of Lincoln's people." And indeed, on April 17, 1861, in the euphoria following the Confederate capture of Fort Sumter, President Jefferson Davis issued a proclamation deputizing armed vessels for the capture of Union ships.[13]

Confederate leaders had declared war on their best friends in the North, the shippers and bankers. They had converted "doughfaces" on Wall Street into Union men. They had increased the influence of their Radical enemies in Congress. Now many in the North believed that perhaps not all property was sacred. Indeed slaves might not be property at all, but people.

Few Republicans were revolutionists by choice. Even in December 1861, after eight months of war, Lincoln in his annual address said that he had been "anxious and careful" that the conflict "not degenerate into a violent and remorseless revolutionary struggle."[14] Republican war objectives could have been totally satisfied had the Confederate leaders just renounced secession and accepted the outcome of the 1860 elections. Ostensibly the Republicans were fighting a war not for change but for restoration. For most of them this was a white man's war, fought by white men who were trying to keep the slave states in the Union against white men who were trying to take them out.[15]

The War to Restore the Old Union

For more than a year the Union's conservative war to restore the antebellum republic moved slowly toward success.[16] With a loyal navy, backed by superior industrial resources, the North tightened a blockade around the Confederacy, occupying key positions along the south Atlantic and Gulf coast, a campaign that culminated in the capture of the lower Mississippi and the largest Confederate city, New Orleans.

During this time, the federal government built on the upper Mississippi and Ohio rivers a formidable freshwater navy. This fleet steamed up the Cumberland and the Tennessee rivers, capturing most of Kentucky and Tennessee; and down the Mississippi, as the saltwater fleet pushed northward, all but cutting the Confederacy in two.[17] By May 1862, the eastern and the western parts of the Confederacy were held together only by the fortress city of Vicksburg.

Meanwhile the Union had mounted a land and water offensive along the rivers and peninsulas of eastern Virginia, aimed at Richmond, the Confederate capital and principal industrial center.[18] By June 1862, Union soldiers had drawn so close to this key objective that they could hear the church bells tolling inside the city. So confident was the Union of victory that on April 3, 1862, the War Department suspended enlistments and shut down the recruiting depots.[19]

It was a colossal mistake. With the end of the spring freshet and the falling water level in the Mississippi, the Union's deep-water fleet was forced to retreat down the river to below Baton Rouge. With the onset of the southern "season of the fevers," three-quarters of the Union soldiers and half the sailors who were besieging Vicksburg fell sick.[20]

The Confederate Counteroffensive

The Confederates, meanwhile, stung by earlier defeats, moved toward total war, bolstering their armies with the first draft act ever passed in North America, which provided for the conscription of white men ages eighteen to thirty-five. This unprecedented measure was possible because the Union occupation of wide areas of the South had precipitated a strong popular reaction. For many thousands the occupation had turned a rich man's war into a poor man's fight. Thus energized, the Confederates opened an offensive in the spring of 1862 led by the most able generals in North America, and assisted by pro-Confederate "Copperheads," or "Peace Democrats," behind the Union lines.

The Confederates struck at the overextended Union forces, seizing control of a two-hundred-mile segment of the Mississippi. They then opened an offensive in Tennessee and Kentucky, capturing Lexington and the Kentucky capital, Frankfort, where they inaugurated a Confederate state government.[21] This advance also threatened Union control of the Ohio River, a strategic east-west communication link, as well as the important industrial and ship-building centers Louisville and Cincinnati.[22]

At the same time in the East, Robert E. Lee's Army of Northern Virginia broke the siege of Richmond and inflicted a stinging defeat on the Union Army at Second Bull Run. The Confederates were now poised to invade Maryland and were threatening the nation's capital, Washington.

Behind the Union lines, the antiwar Democrats, called Copperheads by their enemies, had been relatively quiet so long as the Union appeared to be winning. But as the news spread of the federal retreat from Richmond, they became more vocal. Congressman Clement L. Vallandigham, in whose honor a Confederate military training camp had been named, addressing the Democratic State Convention of Ohio, asked the delegates "if there is not already a spirit in the land which is about to speak in thunder-tones" to the Lincoln administration, which he called "the strong arm of despotic power." He reminded his listeners of the "broken and shattered columns of McClellan," the Union commander in Virginia.[23]

Bad news for the Union was also coming from abroad. Since the outbreak of war, millions of ordinary Europeans had been stirred by the Union cause, which they associated with a land of opportunity, with antislavery and democracy. But factions within the British, French, and Spanish governments saw the conflict differently. For years, the Monroe Doctrine, backed by the United States' growing power, had threatened their influence in the New World. Now the Confederate challenge offered an opportunity to recover some imperial power.

Spain annexed the Dominican Republic. The French emperor, Napoleon III, initially backed by Britain and Spain, landed troops in Mexico and set out to convert it into a French protectorate. With the Confederate offensive, the prospects for a quick northern victory faded, and friends of the Union on both sides of the Atlantic became more disheartened. The imperial strategists became bolder. Both the British and French governments appeared on the verge of extending full diplomatic recognition to the Confederacy, placing their industrial might squarely behind the advancing Confederate armies.

In December 1862, following another Union defeat at Fredericksburg, the influential editor of the New York *Tribune,* the usually Radical but unpredictable Horace Greeley, corresponded with the Clement L. Vallandigham, a Copperhead. Together they drew up a plan for ending the war through the mediation of Napoleon III, whose ambitions in Mexico could not be achieved without a permanently divided United States. The emperor responded favorably, but Lincoln ignored the plan.[24]

The Crisis of the Union

By the summer of 1862, military reverses and political events at home and abroad had thrown the Union into a crisis. At first, its leaders responded, as leaders of the republic had always done in wartime, by organizing rallies and calling for more volunteers. But the enthusiasm that came in reaction to the Confederate attack on Fort Sumter was now gone. The casualties of Shiloh and in Virginia were more devastating than in any war in the nation's history. Also the booming war economy offered opportunities to men who might otherwise have enlisted. As Union desertion rates soared, the call for enlistments failed.[25]

Next, Union leaders, following the example of the Confederacy, passed the Militia Act, making all able-bodied white men between the ages of eighteen and forty-five members of their state militias and empowering the president to call them out. But the response to the draft in the North was not the same as it had been in the South. Thousands of young men left for the western territories or Canada. The paramilitary Knights of the Golden Circle, which had promoted proslavery filibuster raids into Mexico before the war, now promoted the Confederate cause in the Midwest. Copperhead groups organized antidraft riots and killed recruiting officers.[26]

The Union had the material resources to win. But it seemed to lack the political will. One problem was the Republican Party. In 1860 the Republicans had taken thousands of voters away from the other parties when they had demanded "land for the landless" and federal aid for a railroad to the Pacific. Alone among the four parties they had declared that "all men are born free and equal" and that the "natural condition" of the federal territories was freedom.[27]

But once in the government, most Republicans had toned down their language. The issues that excited voters would never lure slave states back into the Union. So, in an abrupt switch, they passed resolutions declaring that they would never abolish slavery. Army officers were ordered to respect Rebel property, and some even returned escaped slaves to Rebel masters. Yet, after more than a year of this "white man's war" to restore the Union "as it was," the Confederates were marching northward and the Copperheads and the European imperialists had never been bolder. It was becoming clear even to conservative Democrats that the negotiated peace they were demanding would result not in the restoration of the "old Union" that they loved, but the permanent division of that Union.

The War Becomes a Revolution

In the summer of 1862, as the crisis deepened, more and more people were listening to a small band of Radical Republicans.[28] As if the voice of John Brown were thundering from the grave, Representative Thaddeus Stevens cried out, "free every slave—slay every traitor—burn every rebel mansion, if these things be necessary to preserve this temple of freedom. . . . [We must] treat this [war] as a radical revolution . . . and remodel our institutions."[29]

Lincoln, despite his matchless political talent, could not forever reconcile the conservative agenda with the Radical one. He could not forever harmonize respect for private property with freeing slaves and burning Rebel mansions. More and more, as hope for restoring the old Union faded, Republicans became united by the Radical vision of a new and freer nation. Observing the crisis from Europe, Karl Marx noted, "So far we have only witnessed the first act of the Civil War—*the constitutional* waging of war. The second act, the revolutionary waging of war, is now at hand."[30]

Even before this crisis, the war itself had forced the Republicans to make several sharp breaks with the past. In early 1861, the secession of the South resulted in the loss of the lucrative plantation commodity trade causing a financial panic and a drop in the government's credit rating. To find operating funds, congress passed the first tariff increase in more than a generation. Later, as the Radicals gained political ground, there were further tariff increases, giving American industrialists "encouragement" that was beyond Henry Clay's wildest dreams.

Henceforth rails for American railroads would be supplied not by British but by American iron mills. Now if Americans needed steel they would have to make it themselves; and the first steel would be poured in 1864. If European capitalists still wanted to profit from the American bonanza they could continue doing so, not by exporting goods to America but by investing in its industry.[31]

The Republicans now both financed the war and strengthened the central government at the expense of the "sovereign" states, with the nation's first national currency, the "greenback," and the first federal income tax; and they bolstered the ability of the national government to borrow by creating a more centralized banking system. Wall Street bankers, who had once financed the expansion of the plantation economy, now bought Union war bonds, on which the interest was payable in gold. Bankers could use these bonds as collateral for issuing and lending paper money. But the value of their bonds depended on a Union victory. Also, bankers and merchants had lost their southern business and now British-built Confederate warships were destroying their vessels. Copperhead sentiment on Wall Street sank. Enthusiasm for the Union soared.[32]

Land for the Landless

As Britain controlled an ocean, so American capitalists with tariff protection would now control a continent. But in half of that continent there were few settlers. The Republicans passed the Homestead Act. To ordinary people, North and South, no issue was more exciting than land for the landless. Such measures had been attempted in antebellum days only to be defeated by the planter-doughface coalition. Now for the first time, a family, for a small fee and a period of settlement, could acquire a farm in the West. The law created a surge of hope that rippled from Kansas across the North, indeed across the Atlantic as far as central Europe. Three hundred thousand people migrated westward during the war years. Almost eight hundred thousand immigrants landed in northern ports, more than all who died in the war on both sides.[33]

Higher Education for the Common Man

The Homestead Act sent covered wagons rolling westward and inspired Germans and Swedes with the vision of a farm in Minnesota or the Dakotas. But in other ways, the Republicans made America more a land of opportunity and tied the Union cause to the hopes of the common man. They passed the College Land Grant Act, an education measure without parallel in the world of the nineteenth century, and possibly the most important law ever passed by Congress. It appropriated federal land to fund the creation or expansion of colleges and universities teaching agriculture and engineering.[34]

The College Land Grant Act was a reversal of the attitude of the federal government toward education. In 1825, President John Quincy Adams had proposed a federally funded national university, as well as federally funded scientific research. But a planter-dominated Congress greeted his proposal with laughter and ridicule.[35] Now in the midst of the crisis of 1862, the Republicans passed a law that eventually funded more than sixty institutions of higher learning.

The College Land Grant Act constituted a change in the direction of American education. Antebellum colleges had mainly taught Greek and Latin to young gentlemen, and were beyond the means of most people. The new institutions would be affordable. They inspired a vision of experts who would modernize agriculture, of engineers who would enable American industry to overtake its British rivals, of a nation that one day would be distinguished by its advanced technology and science. For thousands these projected colleges and universities offered the hope that, if the Union prevailed over the slave masters and the Copperheads, they too might succeed.

Federal Aid to Railroads

For businessmen, the American continent beckoned as a potential market unlike any other on earth. But, unlike Britain's oceans, much of the continent, despite vigorous railroad construction in the 1850s had no modern transportation at all. In 1862, the Republicans thus passed the Pacific Railroad Act, the first of a series of laws appropriating public land to finance the construction of railroads. Before the war, such measures had been regularly introduced and regularly defeated.

Railroad legislation fired the imaginations not only of businessmen but also of nationalist-minded citizens who had been troubled by the narrowly regional or local outlook of the old Union. Leaders of the old Union had stressed the rights of the "sovereign" states. Secession had been a recurring threat: the lower Mississippi in the 1790s, New England in 1814, South Carolina in 1833, the South in 1850 and 1861. Now, if the Union prevailed, the republic upon which they staked their future would be bound together with bands of steel.

The John Brown Idea

The defenders of the Union made their most fundamental break with the past during the Confederacy's 1862 offensive. To meet this crisis the Radicals pressed their most revolutionary demand, to free and arm the slaves. Yet Lincoln held back. Certainly such an explosive measure would reinvigorate the Union cause. But it would also unleash a more fearful white backlash behind the Union lines, as the Copperheads claimed that a war to free the blacks would be a war to enslave the whites.

A look ahead indicates that Lincoln did not exaggerate the fury that emancipation would bring. During the days after the Battle of Gettysburg, for example, antidraft demonstrations in New York exploded into an insurrection that dwarfed all the previous antiblack/anti-abolitionist riots in the nation's history. Crowds ripped up railroads, destroyed telegraph lines, and burned houses of blacks and Republicans. One mob lynched a crippled black coachman, while raising cheers for Jefferson Davis, longtime hero of the North's "white slaves." At Gettysburg, three regiments, poised to pursue the retreating Confederates, had to be dispatched to New York.[36]

Even as late as 1864, Congressman Benjamin Wood, publisher of the New York *Daily News,* traveled to St. Catherine's, Ontario, where he received twenty thousand dollars from the Confederate commissioner to Canada. The money was to be used to foment another uprising in New York that would draw Union troops away from a larger operation that the Peace Democrats were planning for the Midwest.[37]

In the crisis of 1862, Lincoln thus moved with caution. On the one hand Southern armies were still advancing, and behind the Union lines Copperheads were helping Confederate prisoners to escape and were smuggling arms to enemy forces.[38] So he wanted to revitalize the energy of Unionists by raising the cause of black freedom. But he wanted to do so in a way that would minimize the fury of the white backlash. Thus on July 13 he held a White House conference for the senators and representatives from the four "loyal" slave states. Lincoln proposed that in exchange for freeing their slaves, masters in these states would receive interest-bearing government bonds. But two-thirds of these congressmen, perhaps with an eye on current Confederate military successes, rejected the plan.[39] Now there was no way left to reconcile respect for private property with freedom for slaves.

Four days later, Congress, led by the Radicals, made a leap into the unknown. They passed the Second Confiscation Act, declaring that slaves in the Rebel states "shall be forever free," and the same day, they passed the Militia Act, empowering the president to enroll "persons of African descent," a move that eventually provided the Union with almost two hundred thousand troops, many from the South. In another four days Lincoln announced to his cabinet his Preliminary Emancipation Proclamation. In just eight July days, at the moment of the Union's greatest crisis, the government had transformed the character of the Civil War: a limited war to pressure the slaveholders to return to the Union had become an all-out war to free the slaves.[40] Within a year, this policy had undermined slavery so completely that it would have been impossible to restore slavery regardless of who won the war.[41] The offense for which only three years earlier John Brown had been hanged—his attempt to free and arm slaves—had now become law.

The Confederate advance on Washington and the menacing actions of the Copperheads and the European imperialists had precipitated the Union's crisis of 1862. Yet this crisis was but the catalyst, the culminating event in a chain of episodes that turned the planter rebellion into the Republican revolution. In the words of one Radical, the rebellion of the slaveholders had revealed "the new heavens and new earth."[42]

Slaves from the outset had played a part in transforming the war from an effort to win back the loyalty of slaveholders into a revolution against slavery. Since the day the first fugitive slave appeared before the Union lines, some officer had to decide whether to return him to his master or to accept his services for the Union. Ideology is a very conservative feature of society, as it derives primarily from historical rather than current experience. The racial consensus of the antebellum republic lay heavily upon the land. The hegemonic ideas that upheld slavery appeared to most defenders of the Union as "self-evident truths." Yet, despite these beliefs, many came to recognize in the summer of 1862 that the fate of the Republican revolution, with its vision of land, education, and opportunity in a growing economy, was bound up with the fate of four million slaves.

Old ideas and new challenges clashed in the mind of a Union officer with a command on the Tennessee River. As late as April 1862, General O. M. Mitchel had ordered escaped slaves arrested so that their masters might reclaim them. But a month later he wrote the secretary of war of the "absolute necessity of protecting slaves who furnish us valuable information. . . . My River front is 120 miles long and if the Government disapprove what I have done I must receive heavy re-enforcements or abandon my position. With the assistance of the Negroes in watching the River I feel myself sufficiently strong to defy the enemy."[43]

The same conflict between conservative ideology and efforts to save the Union arose in the disputes among the defenders of Cincinnati when the city was threatened with capture by the Confederates in early September 1862. After the fall of Lexington, Kentucky, the main Union force retreated to Frankfort in an effort to save the state capital and Louisville. But this move left Cincinnati exposed to attack; and, on September 4, Confederate forces were reported only sixteen miles from this industrial and shipbuilding center, throwing the city into "great excitement," with all businesses shut down except "butchers, provisions dealers and bakeries."[44]

To prepare the defenses of the city, the mayor appealed to "[e]very man of every age, be he citizen or alien." Yet, when black volunteers reported to the provost, he told them: "you know d—m well he doesn't mean you. Niggers ain't citizens." And it did no good for the volunteers to remind the provost that the mayor had called upon both "citizens" and "aliens," and of these they had to be either one or the other.[45]

But the Union general, Lewis Wallace, overruled the provost; and during the next three weeks, between seven hundred and a thousand members of the Black Brigade of Cincinnati applied themselves in ways that must have pleased all but the Copperheads. Working at times nearly a mile in advance of the Union lines, where they risked capture and reenslavement, the Black Brigade cut down hundreds of acres of trees to obstruct the Confederate advance and give the defenders a clear field of fire; they dug miles of rifle pits, and built military roads and powder magazines.[46]

Union soldiers had no trouble seeing the advantages of the earthen breastworks constructed by black laborers, nor of the information brought to them by black scouts and spies. They knew the value of a strategic strong point such as Fort Pillow, which in the pestilent low country along the Mississippi was defended by a black garrison. Especially after the assault on Fort Wagner in 1863, they began to appreciate the desperate valor that black Americans often showed in battle.[47]

Yet, since the end of the 1600s, black Americans had been the mudsill of American society. Even older were the myths engraved on the American mind. The strange new things that one saw black people doing, were these normal activities for them, or were these just a part of the topsy-turvy nightmare of war? Conservative friends of the Union often viewed the wartime contributions of the former slaves not as earning for them a new place in American society but rather as one more of the aberrations of war, like the heretofore unheard-of sales tax and income tax, the wartime wages that were paid in debased paper money, the draft, the tyranny of military discipline, or the insane cruelty of combat.

Nevertheless, the defeats the North suffered in the summer of 1862 disposed many Unionists, whose Radicalization was slight, to look to the blacks for help. A member of the Third Iowa Cavalry may have spoken for many a young recruit when he told a reporter that when he had enlisted he had been an "ardent Democrat [from a] bitterly anti-abolitionist family. [But] I am anxious to see my mother. And if the 'niggers' will help me get home sooner, I am willing for them to lend a helping hand."[48] This soldier, like many another, could welcome a change in government policy that promised to bring him home sooner, but still adhere to the racial doctrines that had integrated the prewar North and South.

Yet from the outset, even as Union leaders had clung to their original objective of bringing back the slave states, this had been a war of a different kind. Confederate leaders with few exceptions were slaveholders and the most strident defenders of the interests of their class. James H. Hammond, a large slaveholder and once South Carolina governor, complained in 1863 that Confederate president Jefferson Davis, in his efforts to bolster the Southern military, was making "demagogical" concessions to the white poor. Hammond minced no words: "this war is based on the principle & *fact* of the inequality of mankind—for policy, we say *race*, in reality as all history shows it, the truth is classes."[49]

The war experiences caused some in the North as well as in the South to recognize that words about race often obscured reality. From the beginning, therefore, the war had created new space not only for opposition to slavery but also for opposition to the racial ideas that sustained slavery.

The Vision of Equality

The spread of Radicalism perhaps can be detected in the growing popularity of a song. Shortly after the fall of Fort Sumter, members of the Fourth Massachusetts Volunteer Infantry were reported to be singing, "May Heaven's rays look kindly down / Upon the grave of Old John Brown!"[50] Like many army ballads, the verses were sometimes ribald or satirical, as when a battalion of the Boston Light Infantry used it to poke fun at a sergeant whose name happened to be John Brown.[51]

Yet as the song spread and gathered new verses it continued to celebrate the old guerrilla fighter of Kansas and Harper's Ferry. By the summer of 1861 it had reached the Midwest, where the *Chicago Tribune* of August 9 reported the "curious" fact that "the favorite song of the new volunteers is a negro doggerel in which John Brown is glorified as living in spirit in this campaign. Even the Webster regiment, the pet corps of Boston conservatism, sung it, in their march through State Street, the other day. . . . It is a queer medly, but the soldiers like it, and sing it with great energy to an old camp meeting melody."

The growing popularity of the song reflected the changing meaning of the Union cause. For many, "the Union" was coming to mean not simply a combination of states but a principle: freedom. Whatever their individual beliefs, the soldiers now sang of a hero who fought slavery and stood up for racial equality.

The antislavery author Lydia Maria Child noted the change: "the tune is an exciting, spirit-stirring thing. . . . the air is full of it, just as France was of the Marseillaise."[52] A message as old as Christendom, once whispered in the shadows of American society, now poured from the throats of marching soldiers. Civilians also were beginning to sing it. Early in 1862, a New York lawyer, who had cultivated musical taste, noted that a "queer rude song" about John Brown "seems to be growing popular."[53]

Indeed, a poet had already added some verses. During much of 1861, Julia Ward Howe had been in Washington, virtually a frontline city with its constant troop movements and military hospitals. At night she could see the "watch-fires of a hundred circling camps." Howe, her pastor, and some Boston friends were provided with a carriage for a trip out into northern Virginia to witness a military review. But a Confederate raid required a withdrawal to Washington. During their retreat, the weary soldiers took up the John Brown song, and Howe and her friends joined in. In Washington the next morning, she arose before dawn and composed some verses of her own,[54] lines that glowed with apocalyptic mysticism:

> Mine eyes have seen the glory
>   of the coming of the Lord:
> He is trampling out the vintage
>   where the grapes of wrath are stored;
> He hath loosed the fateful lightning
>   of His terrible swift sword:

His truth is marching on.[55]

By the end of the war, Radical views about race and equality had by no means become predominant. The old beliefs of the antebellum republic still retained much of their authority. But Radicalism had entered the mainstream. A senator, noting this change, commented acidly on the ideological climate in Washington before the war: "In ancient times, the Apostle Paul proclaimed a God who 'made of one blood all nations of men. . . .' Had he ventured such a statement in Washington six years ago . . . , he would have been driven out of the city."[56] The senator did not have to remind his listeners that there was now a small bloc of congressmen, and some of their supporters, who believed that the human family was one.

Chapter 12

Reconstruction
The Radical Challenge, 1865–77

The Confederate surrender left open two intertwined political questions: What kind of society would now prevail in the South? And what rights would the emancipated blacks enjoy? If they returned to work for planters, often the same ones who had held them as slaves, would the South have a free-labor society? Would not the old North-South conflict continue? Some Radical congressmen thought that for the Union victory to be complete, and real national unity established, the type of society that prevailed in the North had to be extended southward to the Gulf: "The South shall cease to be a section and become part of the nation, . . . the church and schoolhouse will appear and the light of knowledge will illumine her dark corners; freedom of speech, of opinion and the press will be as much secured in South Carolina as in Maine; all men shall be citizens . . . ; the whole land will revive under the magic touch of free labor."[1]

But the military threat of the Confederacy was gone; and, in the months following the war, the Radical vision of a democratic South stirred little enthusiasm in a war-weary North. The attention of most Northerners was on the new opportunities closer to home that had come with victory.

The Economic Revolution

The greatest opportunities were for the capitalists. The Republican revolution had broken the constraints that King Cotton had put on them. Unprecedented land grants subsidized their railroads. They controlled a growing continental market that tariffs now protected from foreign competition. New government-subsidized colleges and universities were training their engineers. Experts from these institutions were turning family farms into market-oriented enterprises that required loans from their banks, bought barbed wire and irrigation piping from their steel mills, or provided freights for their railroads and raw materials to their processing plants.

If the captains of industry and finance received a lion's share of the new opportunities, there was also some for others. For the working class, native-born and immigrant, new jobs opened up in the expanding industrial and transportation system. Land was now more accessible. Education was more accessible. For most people in the North the long struggle was over. They could return to the ways of peace, get on with life, and leave to others worries about the status of black Americans and the social order of the South. Radicals continued to sound the alarm over these issues, but few people listened.[2]

When Northerners shifted their attention from the Radical vision to practical concerns, the "freedom" of black Americans became uncertain. And their prospects for the future shrank further when, after Lincoln's assassination, the policies of the new president, Andrew Johnson, unfolded. Like other conservative Unionists, Johnson considered most of the Radical laws passed during the war to be revolutionary and unconstitutional acts that had no place in peacetime society.[3] So he quickly demobilized the army and reduced Union presence in the South to a token force. He pardoned the Confederates for treason, allowing them to re-enter the political arena on an equal basis with those who had supported the Union.[4]

Counterrevolution in the South

Soon Rebel officers, commanding battle-hardened bands of Confederate veterans, were carrying out a reign of terror against freed people who refused to behave like slaves, against white Unionists, and against squatters of both races.[5] These postwar terrorist bands often grew out of the guerrilla tactics that many

Confederate units had adopted late in the war.[6] General Nathan Bedford Forrest, for example, whose men had massacred black prisoners at Fort Pillow, founded the Ku Klux Klan. By planting time in 1866 they had gained control over the land, livestock, and food in a region where famine was widespread. This allowed them to begin the new crop year with the unfree or half-free labor of peons, "convicts," "apprentices," sharecroppers, and contract workers.[7] Johnson's "Presidential Reconstruction" was virtually Confederate Reconstruction.

For Republicans, reports from the South were disturbing: massacres, which the press called "race riots," and slave-like labor practices.[8] Encouraging, however, was the prospect that restored plantation production would allow planters to resume shipping cotton to northern mills, and to resume payments on prewar loans from northern banks.

If most Republicans could tolerate "race riots" and unfree labor in the South, the outcome of Southern congressional elections was a different matter. In 1865–66, returning Southern congressmen, now calling themselves Unionists, included Rebel generals, Confederate senators, and the Confederate vice president himself.[9] Worse still, the South was now entitled to more congressmen than before the war, when its representation had been based on the constitutional stipulation counting a slave as three-fifths of a person. With emancipation, a freedman, still not allowed to vote, now counted as a whole person, entitling the South to substantially more representatives than before. For Republicans, Confederate forces had again crossed the Potomac. Joining with their Copperhead friends in the North, they could take back the control of Congress that they had before the war.

If King Cotton were thus restored in Washington, what would happen to the towering war debt? Wall Street had lent most of this money. If honored, this debt was capital. It would finance railroads and steel mills. Would vengeful Confederates and discredited Copperheads now win back their old popularity in a tax-weary North with a "soft money" solution to the debt? They could pay it off not by taxation but by the printing press. If the debt were thus dishonored, if this great mass of capital vanished, many economic empire-builders might be reduced to what they had been before the war: port city bankers who "moved the crops."

It was not only the debt and the capital it stood for that were threatened. If the old regime were reestablished in Washington, the entire revolutionary program of the Lincoln administration could be repealed. In 1866, the fruits of the Republican revolution consisted mainly of some laws on paper and a dream on the distant horizon: the first of the transcontinental railroads had not been completed. The steel industry was just beginning. Few of the new colleges and universities had opened their doors. Confederates with their artillery, Copperheads with their subversion, had failed to take Washington in 1862. Now in 1866, using time-honored political methods, would these same men succeed?

The Republicans Rally: the Radical Experiment

It was not for this that 350,000 Union soldiers had died. Republican congressmen, as they had done when Lee's army had crossed the Potomac, were once again united in their wartime sense of mission. They refused to seat the ex-Confederate congressmen. They once again closed ranks behind the Radicals in a crusade to carry their revolution to King Cotton's homeland.

If the benefits of free-state society were to extend southward to the Gulf, there was indeed much reconstructing to do. For this the South needed a political leadership that would welcome the revolutionary agenda. And the way to bring forward such leaders was to mobilize Southern blacks. Blacks could turn the Rebel South into the Republican South.

In April 1866, the Republicans, overriding the president's veto, passed the Civil Rights Act, extending unprecedented power to the federal government. This act overrode every state black code in the land, North and South. Repudiating the Supreme Court's racial definition of citizenship in its Dred Scott decision of 1857, Republicans defined an American citizen as anyone, white or black, who had been born in the United States, except for the children of tribal Indians and foreign visitors. All these were entitled to equal rights in court and the security of their persons and property. Anyone attempting to enforce a state or local law that violated any of these basic rights would be subject to criminal prosecution in the federal courts. It required the president to use the armed forces to guarantee compliance.[10]

No mention was made of the right of blacks to vote. Democrats had often made their opposition to black voting the "main issue"; and the white racial consensus was still so strong that to favor black voting was to court defeat. Also, many conservative Republicans were recycled Whigs who thought that voting was not a right but a privilege that should be extended only to worthy groups. Indeed, they believed Jacksonians had debased American politics by extending this privilege to economically dependent and poorly informed whites.[11]

The Republicans feared that it was only a matter of time before the antebellum judges still on the Supreme Court would strike down the Civil Rights Act. So to prevent the Court from restoring a racial definition of citizenship, they proposed the Fourteenth Amendment, incorporating the citizenship principle of the Civil Rights Act into the Constitution. And they went one crucial step further. The amendment, stopping short of declaring voting to be a right, stipulated that any state barring blacks from voting would have its representation in Congress reduced. Only its white population would be counted.

If Ohio continued to withhold the ballot from blacks, its loss of representation would be only about 2 percent, but if South Carolina did so, its loss would be perhaps 60 percent. The amendment also contained a provision important above all to Unionists who had gotten rich financing the war: it declared the Union debt valid and "shall not be questioned," while the Confederate debt was void, as were any claims for compensation for the loss of slaves or other Rebel property. With a stroke of the pen the Republicans had wiped out property in slaves, the chief wealth of what had once been the richest class in the nation.[12]

The Fourteenth Amendment thus brought together the concerns of Radical Republicans about the civil rights of black Americans with the worries of conservative Republicans about the security of loyal financiers. This effort, within the space of a few sentences, to link the interests of the poorest people in the land with the interests of the richest surely reveals the internal tensions of the Republican revolution.

But how were three-fourths of the states ever to be persuaded to ratify a revolutionary amendment that sharply subordinated their power to that of the federal government, and made blacks citizens? Again the South, especially the black South, was key. The atrocities of the Ku Klux Klan and the paramilitary bands had to be made the concern of every voter who pinned his hopes to the Republican vision of the future. Congress investigated politically motivated massacres, the so-called riots. Their investigations provided party activists with explosive evidence: in the Memphis "riots" of May 1–3, 1866, 46 blacks, mostly Union Army veterans, had been killed; 75 wounded; 5 black women raped; 91 homes, 12 schools, and 4 churches burned.[13] The conclusion of an investigation into the July "riot" in New Orleans was similar. A mob led by police had attacked a Radical political convention with a resulting victim list much like that in Memphis.[14]

Bloodletting in the South changed minds in the North. Northerners were especially incensed by reports that recent Rebels were terrorizing white Unionists and black veterans; and that southern hotels, restaurants, and other public accommodations were discriminating against northern travelers. Searching for an appropriate reply to such outrages, many in the North now endorsed the idea of giving southern blacks the right to vote, giving them the means to strike back at these enemies of the Union.

But what about northern blacks? The Radicals brought out of the closet their idea of universal manhood suffrage. It was an idea whose time had not yet come: outside those northeastern states whose few blacks had traditionally voted, the Radicals won their right to vote in only two new states, Minnesota and Iowa.[15] Although more white citizens were now voting for black suffrage than before the war, in order to gain a solid Republican vote for ratification, the Radicals dropped the black suffrage requirement from the Fourteenth Amendment.

Meanwhile Congress had passed the Reconstruction Acts of 1867.[16] Accordingly, the Union Army organized elections for state constitutional conventions in the former Confederacy. In these elections, blacks were enfranchised while the leading Rebels, whom Johnson had identified and then pardoned, were once again excluded. As a result, slightly more than half of the Southern voters were black.

By 1869, interracial conventions had written constitutions for the former Confederate states. These documents resembled northern state constitutions. They also reflected some of the reform thought being debated among Radicals.[17] They often began with the language of the Declaration of Independence, "All men are created equal." They established the democratic election of county governments. In the Old South, the governor had appointed justices of the peace, or squires, to county courts that both conducted trials and governed. These offices were often considered the hereditary right of a prominent family.

In criminal law, the new constitutions often replaced the "vengeance of society" with the newer idea of the reform of the offender. The number of capital crimes was reduced and flogging and branding were replaced by terms in penitentiaries where criminals were to be rehabilitated. Married women could hold property in their own right. Dueling was prohibited. They introduced into the South the concept of free, state-funded public-school education.[18] Democratic newspapers, North and South, using images from the minstrel show, attacked these conventions with a scurrility rarely equaled even in that age of unrestrained journalism.

The Revolution That Came Too Late

But the Republicans carried their revolutionary program to the South only after the historical moment favorable to fundamental change had come and gone. While northern Radicals had been fighting for the Civil Rights Act, for the Fourteenth Amendment and the Reconstruction Acts, southern conservatives, commanding mounted men armed with pistols and sabers, had driven black as well as white producers of turpentine and tar from the pine forests, had driven informal farmers from plantation fields, and restored these resources to their prewar owners.[19]

While Radicals won elections, bands of Confederate veterans won control over fields where corn grew, forests where cattle and hogs fattened and where firewood was gathered. Radical legislators passed laws, but basic power remained in the hands of those who controlled the resources that sustained life. Blacks and whites might now be equal before the law, might legally have the equal right to vote; but it was still to a commander of the county militia, or to a cyclops of the Ku Klux Klan, that the voter went for his cornmeal and salt pork.[20]

Yet even as late as 1868, the national Republican Party still had the means for completing its revolution in the South. Certainly the interracial state and local governments that Republicans had created in the South could not survive so long as their opponents commanded formidable bands of night riders and controlled the rural economy. But the Union Army, although greatly reduced by President Johnson, could have disarmed these Rebels, who, if they took up arms against legally constituted authorities, would provoke major federal intervention and indictments for treason.

At least one Radical leader, Thaddeus Stevens, understood the difficulty of establishing political equality in a land where there was equality in nothing else. He had advanced a project for land reform that would have sharply reduced the economic power of the former Confederates and increased the economic independence of both freed people and white Unionists. Stevens's plan called for confiscating 400 million acres of land belonging to the richest 10 percent of Southerners. Forty million acres would be distributed in homesteads of 40 acres to each of the South's one million black families. The remaining 360 million acres would be sold in plots, not exceeding 500 acres, and the proceeds used to compensate the southern Unionists, who during the war had been pillaged by both sides, and to pay benefits to Union veterans as well as to pay down the Union war debt.[21] Ninety percent of white Southerners would be unhurt by the plan. Indeed many would benefit.

At the beginning of 1868, the Republicans appeared to still have a fist raised against their remaining enemies in the South. But they never delivered the knockout blow. Stevens's plan for breaking up plantations into family farms met with a frigid reception in Washington, opposed even by some of his fellow Radicals.[22] For certain powerful Republicans, plantations were once again profitable. Before the war, northern financiers had accumulated much of their capital from the profits of plantation loans and from the plantation export trade. Now the war had starved Europe and the North for plantation commodities, and they were bringing unprecedented prices.

New Source of Cheap Labor

The reconstructed plantation economy showed an unprecedented potential for growth, no longer limited by a relatively fixed number of slaves. For in addition to the available labor of millions of landless blacks, a large and growing number of whites, ruined by the war, were eager to find work as tenants or sharecroppers. The war had sharply accelerated the prewar transformation of plain whites into poor whites. Armies had lived off the land. Livestock herds, the yeomen's chief wealth, had often vanished, along with their crops and draft animals, sometimes paid for with Confederate money, sometimes seized outright by one army or the other.[23] A returning veteran often found his farm in ruins. He was often forced to sell out to a large landholder who had the resources to survive the crisis.[24]

Stripped of his old backwoods prosperity and independence, many a plain white farmer was for the first time dependent on credit.[25] Often he was left with but one treasured resource, his white skin. White politicians evaluated this asset highly. But when he appeared at the plantation commissary or the country store and requested credit for provisions that he needed to raise a crop, planter and merchant alike demanded material collateral. For credit, these "furnishing men," planter or merchant, demanded the security of a lien on a cash crop, in most regions, cotton.

Their new dependency on credit changed the lives of plain whites. Cotton was a high-risk, high-return crop, and before the war, they had grown little, favoring instead food crops. But as their debt grew, they had to plant cotton all the way to their cabin door, and the furnishing man marketed their crop. Cotton exports soared. But the garden disappeared. Pellagra, a disease of malnutrition, appeared for the first time.

Both revolutions and counterrevolutions recruit from the poor. The Republican revolution drew strength from blacks, and indeed from a substantial number of whites who had glimpsed a better tomorrow. The "New South" counterrevolution drew strength from whites dreaming of a golden pioneer past when whites had been independent and prosperous. These white poor, like the upper classes, had their lost cause. By the thousands they rallied to leaders who, like themselves, looked backward to better days. They often supported the very men who exploited them.

The New National Power Structure

By 1868, it was obvious that the power of the Old South elite in Washington and on Wall Street had been permanently reduced.[26] The planter might command a formidable band of nightriders and lord it over his white and black tenants. But before the Yankee banker, he waited his turn in line.

Northern Republicans, especially conservatives, increasingly were turning a blind eye to terror in the South. Nightriders posed no threat to corporate America, nor did the Democratic Party, either in the South or in Washington. It had once been the chief vehicle of planter power. But now, unable to combat the Republican entrepreneurial revolution, the Democrats had joined it. Indeed the party's primary patronage now came from northern businessmen, including many who also funded the Republican Party.

This new political system would henceforth be in full swing as the Democrats became converts to the Republican economic agenda and the Republicans more and more confined their civil rights concerns to the speeches they made on Lincoln's birthday. The captains of finance and industry now controlled not simply a party but a party system and a political culture. Fundamentally, they no longer had to worry about what happened in the South or even about what happened on Election Day. Since they funded both the "ins" and the "outs," they could live with the election results whether the day was carried by the forces of Tweedledee or by those of Tweedledum.

The South's Industrial Evolution

Ironically, defeat created conditions in the South more favorable to industrialization. The growth of industry in the South took an upward turn after the Civil War. This did not occur because of the influx of outside capital. While the war-ruined South created fire sales for northern and European investors, they bought railroads, mines, timberland, and other natural resources. They did not build factories that would compete with those they had at home.

Rather, indigenous capital drove industrialization in the South. The image of the planter returning from the war to his ruined plantation obscures a less common reality: If the war cost Paul Carrington Cameron his 1,900 slaves, it still left him with a fiefdom stretching across three North Carolina counties.[27] Defeat did not make the richest class in antebellum America suddenly poor. Also if the South had lost a war, a very few Southerners had won a fortune. Many of these winners among the losers were planters or merchants who, during the Union blockade and world cotton famine, amassed vast quantities of cotton. At the end of the war they sold it at unprecedented prices.

Before the war, planters had invested some of their profits in railroads that moved their crops or in cotton mills that garnered profits that would have otherwise gone to a Yankee manufacturer. But these had been their minor investments. More lucrative were their investments in the cotton bonanza: buying slaves and virgin cotton lands on the southwestern frontier. The war closed this option and thus changed the direction of planter investments.

The Prussian Road

The South had thus taken the road to industrialization, although slowly, lagging far behind the North. Contrary to some predictions, industrialization brought little convergence of the political culture of the North and the South. In the North, as in England, industrial capitalism arose from a liberal middle class. In the South, as in Prussia and Japan, it arose from a landed gentry. The traditions and frequently the families of the New South industrial leaders were rooted in slavery. Their future prospects lay in the exploitation of cheap and often half-free labor.

Travelers sometimes noted that southern textile establishments resembled plantations. Often located in isolated rural areas, they had their "big house" and row of dwellings for mill hands. Also, little of the ideology of the New South was new. If some leaders now had factories instead of plantations, their mentality was much like that of the Old South. They still celebrated, for example, its cult of militarism. As late as 1955, Georgia was reported to have 2,500 lawyers who claimed the title of "colonel."[28]

Northern Republicans Repent Radicalism

By the late 1860s some Republicans already were taking a more benign view of the conservative New South. True, nightriders in the South were still killing white and black Republicans. But the Ku Klux Klan posed no threat to the corporate agenda, nor did the growing political strength of the New South leaders. Conservative Republicans had had enough of Reconstruction, enough of the blacks and especially of the Radicals. As Henry Cooke complained to his brother, the Civil War financier Jay Cooke: "These reckless demagogues have had their day and the time has come for wise counsels. Wade uttering agrarian doctrines in Kansas . . . , trying to array labor against capital . . . ; with Butler urging wholesale conscription [proscription?] throughout the South and wholesale repudiation throughout the North . . . ; with Stevens advocating a flood of irredeemable paper money . . . ; with Pomoroy and Wade and Sprague . . . calling for the unsexing of woman and putting the ballot in her hand."[29] Agitation for civil rights and against atrocities in the South was disrupting a promising and expanding area of investment and a source of cheap raw materials. Over the next decade the ex-Confederate terrorists would overthrow the interracial governments in the South. In the final analysis, this was because northern financiers and the New South elite had parallel goals: the revival and expansion of a southern economy based on the export of raw materials produced with cheap labor.

Collapse of the Radical Bloc

Meanwhile, in the summer of 1868, the Radical bloc in Congress was having internal problems. The cement that had maintained their solidarity had been their shared commitment to antislavery and to saving the Union. Now that slavery was gone and the Union saved, what should come next? For some it was the civil rights of blacks. For others it was the rights of labor, or the rights of women, or debtor relief. In 1868, after twenty-five months of ascendancy, the Radical bloc disintegrated into feuding factions.[30] More pragmatic leaders took charge.

Yet despite a more conservative leadership after 1868, the Republican Party supported one more item from the Radical agenda, the Fifteenth Amendment, which incorporated into the Constitution the right of black Americans to vote. Much of the credit must go to a new Republican faction, the Stalwarts, whose interest in the amendment was inspired less by their egalitarian ideals than by their ability to count votes.

In the election of 1868, Grant had received a majority of only 300,000. Yet 450,000 black Southerners had voted for him, despite the Ku Klux Klan and similar groups who had carried out a campaign of murder, torture, and arson to keep Republicans away from the polls, while President Johnson scarcely lifted a finger to mitigate this horror.[31]

These election numbers interested even those Republicans whose Radical ideals had disappeared with the Confederacy. What if the northern states also got rid of their black codes and tried universal manhood suffrage? It was, perhaps, such practical-minded Republicans whom the embattled Radical Charles Sumner was addressing when he told the Senate: "You need votes in Connecticut, do you not? There are three thousand fellow-citizens in that state ready at the call of Congress to take their place at the ballot box. You need them also in Pennsylvania, do you not? There are at least fifteen thousand in that great state waiting for your summons. Wherever you most need them, there they are; and be assured they will all vote for those who stand by them in the assertion of Equal Rights."[32] From right to left, Republicans were convinced and put the full strength of their party behind the Fifteenth Amendment, planting the right of black Americans to vote into the Constitution and beyond the reach of the antebellum judges still on the Supreme Court.[33]

Even as early as 1868, the shape of the new national regime was becoming clear. Yet, the Republican leaders appeared to be in no hurry to impose final peace terms on their erstwhile enemies. So the halfhearted tug-of-war of Reconstruction continued. As New South terrorists toppled, one by one, the interracial state governments, Republican congressmen, from lack of power or lack of will, did little to help their southern colleagues. By passing the Ku Klux Act, they forced the terrorists to change their costumes from white sheets to militia uniforms.[34] They also passed another civil rights act that, predictably, the courts threw out.[35]

The Wormley Bargain

In the winter of 1876–77, a crisis arose that gave the New South elite political leverage at the national level. In the 1876 elections both parties had committed fraud and both claimed the presidency. According to the Constitution, the dispute had to be settled by Congress, where the terror campaigns of southern Democrats had gained them a deciding bloc of seats.

The negotiations between the two sides were finalized in the Wormley Hotel in Washington. The highest bidder for the votes of the southern bloc was the Republican candidate, Rutherford B. Hayes, who indicated that he would not use federal troops to support southern Republican governments. Hayes became president. Abandoned and without adequate military establishments of their own, the last Republican state governments soon capitulated.[36]

In the gun smoke before Fort Wagner, black soldiers had died for their freedom and their rights as citizens. Now in the cigar smoke of a Washington hotel, Republican politicians had struck a bargain that placed the rights of blacks as citizens at the mercy of hooded night riders and paramilitary bands. For the national Republicans, the effort to bring democracy to the South had served its political purpose. They were ready to move on with their entrepreneurial revolution.

Chapter 13

Between Slavery and Freedom
The Conservative Quest for a Halfway House

The Wormley Bargain was a sort of peace treaty between the Republicans and the former Confederates. Conventionally it has also served as a marker ending Reconstruction. Yet the New South elite would have to struggle until the end of the nineteenth century to consolidate their control of the South. If the bargain they had struck in Washington secured them against federal military intervention, their power still remained fragile.

Before the New South leaders could consolidate their halfway house between slavery and freedom, they had to overcome the resistance of African Americans, who still could vote and were organized and mobilized. And the white solidarity of antebellum days was in disrepair. Although most whites retained their traditional loyalty to the Democrats, which conservatives now dubbed the "white man's party," some defected to the Republicans, and at times others would defect as Independents, Readjusters, Greenbackers and, finally, as Populists.

The Republican revolution had politicized African Americans and fired them with a vision of liberation. They now had organized a network of their own churches, schools, lodges, benefit societies, and the Union League. There were still black elected officials at various levels so that any substantial defection of Democrats could bring about more interracial governments. The national Republicans also sometimes caused problems for the Democrats. When they needed an extra seat in Congress, they sometimes helped their southern Republican colleagues.

Yet when Democratic leaders tried to restore antebellum laws to prevent these setbacks, they were hobbled by the Radical state constitutions. These contained features popular with their own Democratic rank-and-file. Many voters liked electing their own local officials and having public schools, and they balked at the return of the whipping post and branding iron. So, in rewriting state constitutions, Democratic leaders had to include some Radical features in order to maintain white solidarity.

But the greatest obstacle to creating the New South was a deepening agrarian crisis. Merchants providing credit demanded as collateral a lien on the farmer's crop. And this meant a cash crop, usually cotton. In their desperation for credit, farmers were forced to convert from food crops to cotton, thus glutting the market. Cotton prices were dropping and would continue to decline until the end of the century. Debts to the "furnishing man" were growing. Farmers were now squeezed by the falling price of cotton, the high cost of credit, and the high prices of most things that they bought, which were fixed by merchants and the corporate trusts.

Falling prices affected cotton producers, both rich and poor. But since most planters and merchant-landlords were also creditors, their high credit charges shifted some of the burden to their tenants and sharecroppers. And as creditors they were getting help from the federal government, which kept the greenback dollar tied to the limited supply of gold. So as the economy grew, greenbacks became scarcer and more valuable. Tight money, therefore, enabled creditors to collect dollars more valuable than those they lent, increasing the distress of debtors. The cost of credit (special "credit prices" plus interest) for sharecroppers in Georgia, for example, reached an average of 59.4 percent.[1] Some farmers were being reduced to peonage, or debt servitude; many others lived in its shadow.

The farmers' crisis was embarrassing to the Democrats. They claimed to be the spokesmen for the agricultural South. They were nothing of the kind. Indeed, a number of the party's state chairmen were presidents of northern-owned railroads. To the extent the Democrats really spoke for the rural South, it was for the planters and the merchant landlords.

White solidarity was as much the jugular vein of the New South as it had been of the Old. The hegemony of the antebellum planters derived in part from the restraint and respect they had long shown toward their plain white followers. Did the Democrats still appear to be the "party of the fathers," the "white man's party," when more and more often a planter/merchant, the local leader of the party, foreclosed and evicted a once-proud yeoman who had ridden with the planter's slave patrol, had fought the war against the planter's Yankee enemies and then loyally fought the planter's Radical Reconstruction enemies? The anger of many white farmers irrupted in protest rallies against leaders of the Democratic Party.

The Readjuster Revolt

The most successful challenge to the New South regimes irrupted in Virginia, a state burdened by debts contracted before the war for railroad construction. Three-quarters of this debt was now held by northern or European investors. The Conservative Party (later Democrats) was dominated by the "funders," who were eager to attract outside investors by "honoring" state debts, keeping corporate taxes low and privatizing the remaining state-owned railroads.[2] To achieve repayment, the legislature hiked real estate taxes, angering farmers, large and small. It also cut public services, especially in education. Teachers went unpaid, and some schools closed.[3]

These measures gave rise to the Readjusters, who proposed scaling down the debt. In 1879 they captured the legislature, aided by a large number of black voters. The Readjusters increased taxes on railroads and corporations, repudiated one-third of the state debt, and reduced the interest rate on the rest. They reduced the property tax, abolished the poll tax, and outlawed the whipping post. Within four years they had nearly tripled the number of black schools, prohibited racial discrimination in teachers pay, and created a black college.

Virginia Democrats sounded the alarm over "black domination." In their 1883 campaign, they followed the scenario that Democrats had used all over the South: first a withering barrage of racial animosity. Next, in a city targeted for a takeover, came murders or a massacre, which the dominant press dutifully called a riot. Finally, Democrat-led militias or rifle clubs moved in to "restore order" and take control. In 1883, the centerpiece of the Democrats' election campaign was Danville, where white and black Readjusters held a majority on the city council and occupied some other public offices. Just before the election, four of Danville's black citizens were killed in a "riot," whereupon armed Democrats invaded to restore order. In the following election, the black vote remained solid, despite warnings that any who voted would be "shot down like dogs." But with these murders and the military takeover of Danville, the racial hysteria remained high. "The 'Nigger Cry' was kept up so incessantly and howled so fiercely that many of our people became really frightened, and some men who have been true Republicans since the war voted against us." The Democrats carried the election by a slim margin.[4]

The Challenge of the Farmers' Alliance

During the 1880s and '90s, the agrarian crisis converged with unrest throughout the nation: strikes, demonstrations of unemployed in Washington, the Knights of Labor organizing nationwide, even in the South, where black cotton pickers and sugar cane workers struck. In a nation largely of farmers, and with the ever worsening agrarian crisis, the Farmers' Alliance movement arose throughout rural America.

The farmers' plight was most severe in the semicolonial society of the South, and it was here that the farmers' movement had its greatest strength. White Alliance farmers gathered in mass meetings of thousands. The Colored Farmers' Alliance, faced with uncertain white allies and certain terror, organized in secret.[5]

The Alliance movement created farmers' cooperatives, an alternative to the furnishing merchants. And it fought the corporate trusts. In a clear-cut victory, it forced the "Jute Trust" to back down from a huge price increase for bagging. It provided a way for farmers to escape the squeeze between the depressed prices they received for their crops and the rigged prices of things they bought. And credit cooperatives avoided the credit exactions of the furnishing merchants, which had been reducing some farmers to peonage.

Farmers joined the Alliance first for the liberating advantages of its cooperatives. But then, once in the Alliance, they also gained an economic and political education. The movement had its own press, amplified by hundreds of country newspapers. It fielded a nationwide army of "lecturers" to organize and educate farmers. In opposition to the acquisitive values of the market, they promoted a movement culture, stressing generosity and cooperation.[6] Yet, despite this elaborate educational program, they failed to tackle the racial ideology that had debilitated every political revolt since 1865.

Corporations threatened by the farmers' movement opened a counteroffensive with their financial and market powers: they owned the railroads, the grain storage elevators, the commodity exchanges. All of these charged cooperatives discriminatory rates or boycotted them. But the Alliance's main problem was a credit boycott. Thousands of farming poor, pooling their scant savings, or more often having only debt, could not raise enough capital to sustain the co-operatives for long. The cooperatives were the heart of the movement and they began to fail.[7]

Initially, the Alliance had avoided politics, which divided farmers. Outside the South, most were Republicans, as were black farmers everywhere, while most white southern farmers were Democrats. Now the farmers' movement was forced to turn to political solutions, to gain help from the government to regulate the hostile market world. Indeed from the outset, many of the reforms that the Alliance favored were political, such as the revision of the crop lien laws. Making common cause with labor, the Alliance called for the abolition of the convict lease system, of the vagrancy laws used against unemployed or striking workers, and the use of child labor.

Mainly, however, the Alliance focused on federal "goldbug" monetary policy. Based on a limited gold supply, this policy was forcing down crop prices while corporations, which were often organized as trusts, maintained their high prices. And with the increasing value of the greenback dollar, creditors lent cheap dollars and collected more valuable ones.[8] To combat this practice, the Alliance demanded a "flexible money supply" that would rise and fall with the economy.

The Populists

So the Alliance movement reluctantly entered party politics, and indeed party politics divided it. Moderates wanted to convert the Democrats to some of the Alliance reforms. The radicals wanted to form an independent party that would carry the entire Alliance platform to the huge farming majority of that era and defeat the corporate minority at the polls. These, in 1892, organized the Peoples Party, or Populists.

In the South, while the Populists could win only with a white-black alliance, they were imbued with the hegemonic culture of the centuries-old racial system. Here and there, haltingly, inconsistently, white Populists made overtures toward political collaboration with blacks but were usually unwilling to share power in the party with them. In Texas, however, where the farmers' movement was strongest, black Populists participated even in the leadership.

As the Democrats saw the farm crisis worsen, they saw increase the fearful possibility of a white-black alliance of the poor against them. They sounded the alarm of "black domination." They promoted lynchings, which increased in frequency and ferocity as the agrarian crisis deepened, reaching an all-time high in the 1890s. More and more elections were decided by violence and fraud.

At the same time, the corporate economic counteroffensive was breaking the Alliance's cooperatives, the backbone of the agrarian movement.

For the Populist party the showdown at the national level came with the 1896 elections. The Democratic presidential candidate, William Jennings Bryan, adopted one plank from the ten-plank Populist program, the free coinage of silver at sixteen to one. But since he failed to adopt its prolabor planks, the Republicans won the city labor vote by representing this mildly inflationary measure as amounting to a wage cut.[9] Most Populist supporters, deciding that part of a loaf was better than none, voted for Bryan.[10] Many did not vote. The poorly funded Populist Party received few votes. Most blacks stuck with the Republicans. The election was thus a stunning defeat for Bryan, for the Populists, and for reformers within both the Democratic and Republican parties. The Alliance movement was finished nationally.[11]

The Fusion Challenge

The election had a very different outcome in North Carolina, where it gave rise to the last challenge to the New South elite. While southern Populists often struck election bargains with white supremacist Democrats, those in North Carolina formed an alliance, or "fusion," with Republicans, led by Daniel L. Russell.

A Populist-Republican fusion was possible here because Russell held political views that were rare indeed for a Republican leader in the late 1800s. A former Confederate, Radicalized by war, he became a Republican judge. He bolted the party, however, after its leaders betrayed the blacks and Radicals in the Wormley Bargain. He was then elected to Congress by the Greenback Labor Party, whose monetary reform ideas were adopted by the Farmers' Alliance and the Populists. With the demise of the Greenback insurgency, he returned to the Republican Party, but grumbled that "Vanderbilt and Gould are our masters," that power was now held by "eastern millionaires and southern Bourbons"; and he called for the public ownership of railroads. Such a Republican the Populists could support.[12] Russell's main political support came from North Carolina's largest city, predominantly black Wilmington, and from the heavily black eastern counties. He also enjoyed support in the traditionally Republican white counties in the Appalachian West.

In 1896 the Republican/Populist Fusionists elected Russell governor and captured control of the legislature. The Democratic legislature, like Democrats had done in other states, had replaced elected officials with appointed ones in black majority counties and towns. The Fusionists restored local self-government. While the Democrats had starved public services, the Fusionists increased appropriations for schools and set up teacher training institutes, programs funded by raising taxes on railroads and businesses.

But the Fusionists fought their greatest battle with the northern railroad tycoon J. P. Morgan and his white southern allies. Morgan already owned the Southern Railroad. In a move that would have enabled him to charge higher freight rates, he had struck a secret bargain of doubtful legality with the Democratic governor for a ninety-nine-year lease on the state-owned North Carolina railroad.[13]

In the battle with Morgan, Russell learned the extent of corporate penetration of his own party. Not only did the Democrats vote with the railroad interests but so did two-thirds of the Republicans. The Fusionists defeated the Morgan lease in a close vote due to the solid Populist part of the coalition, to the minority contingent of Republicans, and to a few voter-intimidated Democrats.

By the 1890s, industrialists had become important in North Carolina politics, and they joined the Morgan forces in the campaign. They were alarmed by the prolabor language of the Fusionists. As one textile manufacturer protested, "We have the most contented labor and the time will soon come when no child under twelve will be working in the mills and none that cannot read and write."[14]

The Fusionists suffered the same liabilities that had debilitated every insurgency movement since 1865: Many Republican activists were poor and vulnerable to campaign contributions from lobbyists or to patronage by national leaders. Populist leaders were often substantial farmers who exploited black labor and were reluctant to share power with black allies. But it was not so much internal weaknesses as racial ideas and paramilitary politics that brought down the Fusionist regime.[15]

The Coup d'Etat

The fragile Fusionist movement could not long prevail against white supremacy zealots and their corporate backers. In the election of 1898, the Democrats launched perhaps the most violent campaign in Southern history. After thirty years of violence and ballot box stuffing, the power of the New South elite was not yet secure. But by the 1890s, they knew that they had nothing to fear from any national administration, Democrat or Republican. With the Wormley Bargain, national leaders had given them a wink that they would have no more trouble from the army. Other signals followed. There was the failure of the Lodge bill, the so-called force bill, which would have increased federal power to monitor elections. Then Congress abolished election monitors altogether. Finally, the Republicans dropped from their platform their long-standing plank "a free election and a fair count."

Such signals made the New South elite ever bolder. Months before the 1898 elections they were targeting Wilmington, the heart of Fusionist power.[16] Colonel A. M. Waddell, chief architect of this "riot," declared that the Democrats would take Wilmington "if we have to choke the current of the Cape Fear with negro carcasses."[17]

But there was a problem. In nearby Fort Macon was stationed a black regiment, the Third North Carolina Volunteers, led by black officers and commanded by a staunch ally of Governor Russell. With the Spanish-American War, however, this regiment had been mustered into federal service. At the beginning of the election campaign, President McKinley's War Department ordered the Third North Carolina to leave Fort Macon, not to fight in Cuba but to do hard labor in Tennessee.[18] Indeed the hostilities with Spain had been over for more than two months. Massive voter intimidation gave the Democrats a narrow victory.[19]

But ever since the Civil War, such Democratic victories had been temporary. What they wanted now was not simply to regain control of the legislature but to destroy the popular Republican base in Wilmington and in the state. Two days after the election, the long-planned "race riot" began. Militia units and paramilitary groups moved in to support the white mob. They burned the nation's only African American daily newspaper, put the Fusionist board of aldermen to flight, and killed a large number of the city's black citizens.[20]

Fusion governments "resigned" or were overthrown in Greenville, New Bern, and other eastern towns and counties. Governor Russell was traveling by train when he learned of an assassination plot. He concealed himself in the baggage car before the Red Shirts boarded the train.[21] After these days of terror, Wilmington, once predominantly a black city, now had a white majority.[22] Governor Russell now faced a legislature controlled by the Democrats. Lacking enough votes to sustain a veto, the governor and his allies had to watch the entire Fusionist program overturned.

For thirty years the Democrats had been putting down an insurgency in one place only to see one appear elsewhere. And never had the resistance to their counterrevolution been greater than in the 1890s. But now they knew what was required to consolidate their power. In this land of so much misery, there were too many voters, too many parties, and too much collaboration between whites and blacks. In Mississippi, South Carolina, and elsewhere, Democrats had already shown that the solution was disfranchisement. As a Mississippi congressman boasted, they had "disfranchised not only the ignorant and vicious black, but the ignorant and vicious white as well." Take away the votes of African Americans and those of the poorest whites, and no insurgency could succeed, no opposition party could survive.[23]

Soon after North Carolina's election, the state's leading newspaper declared: "The victory won last November will be short-lived and almost barren unless it is garnered. To leave on the registration books every ignorant Negro . . . , would be to invite a repetition of the disgraceful rule of 1895–1899 whenever there is ever any considerable division among the white voters."[24] The Democrats set out to garner their election victory, with a campaign for a disfranchisement amendment to the state constitution.[25] In the spirit of the campaign, Colonel Waddell, the commander of the Wilmington "race riot," rhetorically ordered a pro-amendment rally: "Go to the polls tomorrow and if you find the negro out voting tell him to leave the polls. If he refuses kill him, shoot him down in his tracks."[26] The next day North Carolina became a part of the "solid South." The Populist Party was dead. The North Carolina Republican Party, which for thirty years had won roughly half the votes, no longer functioned as a state party. It had been reduced to a circle of federal patronage officeholders.

How was it that after a thirty-five-year struggle, the New South elite were finally able to consolidate their power with a one-party segregated South? They had won, of course, by racial ideology and ultimately by paramilitary force. But they had been "winning" by such methods since their Memphis and New Orleans massacres of 1866. A better explanation is the defeat of the agrarian movement. Corporate power had strangled the Alliance cooperatives, the movement's main attraction for farmers. And despite its extensive educational efforts, it had failed to challenge the racial ideas that undermined every insurgency.

The agrarian movement did not rebound after its political defeat in 1896. The farm crisis was becoming less severe in the late 1890s. And while national leaders had not repented "gold bug" politics, gold had become more plentiful from new discoveries and from the new cyanide process for extracting gold from leaner ore. Cheaper gold eased the downward pressure on farm prices and made debts easier to pay. Also farm prices rose as the world geared for war. The Spanish-American War was the first of a half dozen small wars preliminary to the Great War of 1914. The profits of large producers and exporters rose. But in the South, little of this wealth filtered down to the people at the bottom.

The Disfranchised, One-Party, Segregated South

With disfranchisement, voters, even white ones, were few. And those who still voted were often dependent upon landlords and employers. One "reform" at the time was the "white primary," allowing for contested elections within one-party states. It was, in fact, the final step that consolidated the solid South. In nineteenth-century contests, a voter might know little about the individual candidates but he knew their parties. Voter turnouts had been large. Not so now when serious candidates all wore the same party label. An office seeker gained attention not by presenting his party's well-known agenda, but by becoming a showman who could attract apathetic and uninformed voters. If he succeeded as a performer, he attracted wealthy patrons. The South now produced a new type of politician, one who would have been strange in the South of Thomas Jefferson or even of Jefferson Davis: the demagogue, the man with a populist style and a corporate agenda.[27]

Meanwhile the Supreme Court had been chipping away at the Fourteenth Amendment, which Radical congressmen had written to make blacks citizens. In a series of decisions, the now Republican Court seemed to have decided that a purpose of the amendment was to protect corporations. Their judicial counterrevolution culminated with *Plessy v. Ferguson* (1896), giving legal sanction to segregation with the fiction of "separate but equal."

The High Court thus conferred constitutional authority on a wave of the most draconian segregation laws in American history.[28] These laws consolidated the conservative halfway house between slavery and freedom. They restricted the biracial gatherings and individual contacts that had made possible every insurgency since the Civil War. But more important, segregation rituals were educational: a daily drama about white domination and black subordination. Everyone, white or black, was required by law to act out one's designated place in the world.

The Legacy of Reconstruction

The Radical vision of a democratic South was now in shambles. Did anything of value survive? Peonage and convict labor fell far short of a free-labor society.[29] But peons were not slaves. Their families were not broken up and sold.[30] Despite the efforts of landlords to tie down labor by debt, law, and violence, most black southerners maintained their mobility. A cropper who could move might negotiate a better crop share or find a better job working on the railroad. The ability of the worker to move tempered harsh treatment.

Also, even as political oppression increased, black culture flourished. While, with political defeat, funding for black schools was drastically cut, most schools survived. Black churches organized others. Literacy spread.[31] By the end of the century, there was an explosive growth, even in small towns, of black newspapers with a largely rural circulation. Black churches became the backbone of a relatively independent community life.[32]

But otherwise by 1900, the New South counterrevolution had succeeded. The conservative constitutions eliminated almost all blacks and many poor whites as voters. The loss of political influence by the people at the bottom, black or white, exacerbated their growing poverty.[33] For blacks, the new legal doctrine, "separate but equal," meant scandalously unequal schools and denial of many public spaces that they had once enjoyed.

African Americans had thus begun their nadir, the low point in their history between Reconstruction and the black freedom movement a half-century later. By 1900, it appeared that whatever the Civil War and the Republican revolution had accomplished, the "new birth of freedom" meant little to black Americans and to the South. The Fifteenth Amendment appeared dead, since so few black Southerners could still vote. The Fourteenth Amendment, written to define the civil rights of all Americans, was now reinterpreted by a Republican Supreme Court as a protection for corporations. The Thirteenth Amendment had abolished slavery and involuntary servitude, yet several forms of involuntary servitude were practiced in the South.

Disfranchisement, segregation, and conservative control over the telling of history never wiped from the memory of black Americans what they had done. They had taken up arms and fought for their freedom. In the face of terror, their votes had made the Reconstruction amendments part of the nation's highest law. And these amendments were more than lifeless monuments upon which were carved the dreams of long-departed Radicals. They were sleeping giants waiting for another heroic generation to awaken them.

Part 4
The Racial System
in a Rising
Superpower

Chapter 14

The Age of Segregation at Its Zenith

The Racial System in a World of Colonialism

Black history since the defeat of the Radicals, despite hard-fought battles, had been a downward spiral of declining political influence, declining economic opportunity, and increasing violence. The Philadelphia *Christian Recorder,* on March 24, 1892, reported that in Arkansas during "the last 30 days there have been not less then eight colored persons lynched."[1] African Americans had reached the low point of their post-Emancipation history.

But the horrors of lynching and racial oppression were far from the concerns of the nation's leaders. Indeed, Senator Albert Beveridge thought that the United States provided a model for the world: "Our institutions will follow our flag on the wings of our commerce. And American law, American civilization, and the American flag will plant themselves on shores hitherto bloody and benighted, but by these agencies of God henceforth to be made beautiful and bright."[2] For most American leaders the "Negro problem" had been solved by disfranchisement and segregation, and it was now time to move on to a dazzling future.

In the second half of the nineteenth century, the nation had been turned upside down. The once-dominant South had been devastated by war and its four million slaves freed. In the West, a land of tribal hunters had been conquered and transformed into a land that produced commodities for the world market. In the North, a world of farmers and villagers was becoming oriented to rapidly growing and industrializing cities. Yet by the century's end, whatever else might happen in American society, the "place" of black Americans seemed forever the same.

The Emerging Corporate Hegemony

The victory of the Union had released the brakes that the Old South had put on the North's industrial machine. Now, entering the new century, it was racing past all rivals. Much of the nation's industrial success was due to its post-Reconstruction political system: two parties, funded largely by the same institutions and individuals. The new system began to operate when most Democrats adopted the Republican economic agenda, and Republicans acquiesced to southern white views on civil rights.

The location of political power in the nation had shifted from the plantation big house to the corporate board room. Yet the one-party South still influenced national politics. In Washington, the South was represented by what came to be called the Jim Crow bloc. Since southern election laws discouraged voting, these congressmen were elected with few votes and sometimes elected unopposed. Nominally Democrats, they crossed over freely to vote with the Republicans on conservative issues, a practice that discouraged reform-minded factions in both parties. Corporate lobbies could count on the support of the Jim Crow bloc for measures that voter-intimidated congressmen of either party dared not endorse.

If southern Democrats represented few voters, southern Republicans represented none at all. Their party in the South had been reduced to a circle of appointed federal officeholders who no longer took part in state elections. Yet they turned up at Republican national conventions, where they gave their support to the GOP national machine upon which they depended for their jobs. The "rotten boroughs" of the South provided conservative Republican national leaders with a bloc of captive delegates to combat the delegates from the upper North where, since the days of Lincoln, Republicans had had a strong grassroots constituency.

A prophecy of John C. Calhoun was coming true. "It is impossible with us" in the South, he had told the Senate in 1838, "that the conflict can take place between labor and capital. . . . The blessing of this state of things extends beyond the limits of the South. It makes that section the balance of the system;

the great conservative power, which prevents other portions, less fortunately constituted, from rushing into conflict."[3] The South did indeed function as the "great conservative power." The failure of the Radical vision in the South had helped to make the two national parties the right arm and the left arm of corporate power.

The Cultural Legacy of the Conservative Victory

The position of the South as the bulwark of conservative power in national politics also influenced American culture. It shaped a memory of the Civil War that was different from the memory of any other American war. As wars require the sacrifice of life, humankind's highest value, they are ordinarily justified by other high values. Even the shabbiest military adventure, carried out for whatever reason, is often explained by some version of "these died that the nation might live free." But in the reconstituted nation, the war over slavery and freedom was reinterpreted as a tragic misunderstanding between the "North" and the "South."[4]

The Civil War was also the only American war about which the losers were allowed to tell the story. The Confederates' story dominated literature.[5] And then in motion pictures, from *The Birth of a Nation* to *Gone with the Wind*, those who fought for the "lost cause" were given the last word.[6] It was less awkward to allow the defeated Rebels to tell about the cause they lost than for the victorious Republicans to tell about the one they betrayed.

As great as the war's impact was in determining who ruled America, its impact on racial ideology was slight. The minstrels continued to sing of a plantation never-never land where masters were kind and "darkies" danced. As the minstrel show finally declined in the early decades of the twentieth century, its stereotypes were picked up by vaudeville theater, by Hollywood, and by Madison Avenue.[7]

Imperialism and "Scientific Racism"

American leaders thought that the nation, having solved its internal differences, was now in a position to assert its position as a world power. The American racial system was thus developing in tandem with global events and global ideas. Many American whites were reassured to learn that the leaders of much of the "civilized world" now shared racial ideas much like their own.

In Europe, the revolutions of 1848 had given rise to an elaboration of political thought about the part that class and race play in social change. Reacting to revolutions that shook some dozen European countries, Karl Marx had projected a theory that class conflict drives fundamental social change, and that it leads to revolutions which throughout history have enabled societies to advance from lower to higher stages.

But a very different European political theory influenced many leading Americans. Like Marx, Count Arthur de Gobineau had written in reaction to the revolutions of 1848, but arrived at different conclusions: it was not class but race that explains fundamental historical change. He held that there were three pure races. In descending order of intelligence, they were the white, the yellow, and the black. From these derived a myriad of mixed races. He further identified ten great civilizations, all of which had been founded by people who were "pure white." Each of these civilizations declined when their talented founders allowed their "blood" to become mixed with that of the lower races.[8]

This racial theory came to be considerably elaborated in the following decades as "scientific racism." Adapting Charles Darwin's theory of evolution, its advocates claimed that different races have levels of intelligence that derived from thousands of years of evolution. Scientific racism was also elaborated by the theory of eugenics, the notion that human beings, like livestock, can be improved by selective breeding.

After World War I, the eugenicist-biologist Charles Benedict Davenport and the president of the New York Zoological Society, Madison Grant, and others, founded the Galton Society for the study of race and eugenics. It was to be "very limited in members, and also confined to native Americans, who are anthropologically, socially and politically sound, no Bolsheviki need apply."[9] Grant argued that race improvement can be accomplished by

> the elimination of the least desirable elements in the nation by depriving them of the power to contribute to future generations. . . . [I]t would not be a matter of great difficulty to secure a general consensus of public opinion as to the least desirable, let us say ten percent, of the community. When this unemployed and unemployable human residuum has been eliminated, along with the great mass of crime, poverty, alcoholism, and feeblemindedness associated with it, it would be easy to consider the advisability of further restricting the perpetuation of the then remaining least valuable types.[10]

Perhaps the most influential member of the Galton circle was Theodore Lothrop Stoddard, a lawyer and the author of fifteen books that had received many favorable reviews and won him the praise of President Warren G. Harding and invitations to testify at congressional hearings on immigration policy. Stoddard was alarmed by the Russian Revolution. But he thought that such a disruption could be prevented by the application of biology to society: "The elimination of neurotic, irrational, vicious personalities, weak-brained and weak-willed, would render social cataclysms impossible."[11]

The new racial theories gave a scientific gloss to discrimination against the "dark and swarthy" immigrants from southern and eastern Europe arriving in the great industrial centers. As the poet Thomas Bailey Aldrich saw it,

> Wide open and unguarded stand our gates,
> And through them press a wild and motley throng—
> Men from the Volga and the Tartar steppes,
> Featureless figures from the Huang Ho,
> Malayan, Scythian, Teuton, Kelt, and Slav.[12]

Scientific racism thus justified prejudice against the "new immigrants" as well as against blacks.

Dreams of empire popularized scientific racism. They also popularized the idea that white people had a civilizing or Christianizing mission on shores "hitherto bloody and benighted."[13] It was a time when almost everybody of prominence in the North, the South, or in Europe seemed to agree about white superiority. Scientists and scholars imbued these views with special authority.[14]

The Frozen River

The racial system appeared to be completely stable, like a frozen river. Yet underneath its motionless surface, a current of change was sweeping along like a spring freshet. The imperialist agendas greatly reinforced racial ideas, but imperialist agendas had other consequences. The "pure white" nations of northwestern Europe were falling out about territory, control of the seas, and markets. The Aryan Germans went to war with the Anglo-Saxon English.

World War I created a dilemma for American industrialists: their sales orders soared off the top of the chart, but war severely restricted their supply of immigrant labor.[15] They were trapped between their bias in favor of white labor and their bias in favor of profits. Their resolution of the dilemma had far-reaching results for African Americans. Employers continued to discriminate. Whites got the best jobs. But blacks got jobs. Before, when black workers found industrial jobs, it was often as strikebreakers, jobs that lasted only as long as the strike: short-term jobs, long-term antipathy against black workers.[16] Now, for the first time in American history, they were entering the mainstream of the industrial working class in substantial numbers. This threatened the historic "divide and rule" practices that marginalized black workers to low-paid service jobs and undermined trade unions.

The war had other consequences. For the first time, significant numbers of black Southerners began to move to the North.[17] Even in the South, they were moving into cities, into industry. Restless urban crowds were not so easily controlled as scattered rural families. In the cities there was a flourishing of black advocacy organizations, including the National Association for the Advancement of Colored People (NAACP) and the Urban League. In northern cities, blacks were becoming too numerous for urban bosses to ignore. In the North they reentered politics.

Also, the armed forces recruited more than 300,000 black soldiers to fight a stridently advertised "war to make the world safe for democracy." At the same time, the Woodrow Wilson administration was making democracy unsafe at home. It shut down newspapers, jailed dissidents, segregated the civil service, and revised the totem pole of scientific racism by demoting America's largest ethnic minority, the once "pure white" Germans, to "Huns."[18]

Official myth clashed with reality. In 1918, the *New York Tribune* fired its managing editor, Ernest Gruening, after he juxtaposed two pictures, one of black soldiers marching from combat in France, the other of a lynching in the South.[19] Never had African Americans been so aware of the larger world of empire and color. Cracks were appearing on the frozen river even as the spring freshet underneath flowed faster.

Urbanization affected black culture. While ghetto schools were poor, ghetto populations could read. They read black newspapers. For the first time, a sophisticated urban black culture emerged: journalists, educators, sociologists, historians, playwrights, and poets. Black musicians collaborated with white musicians to create a new type of music, one that excited the entire nation, indeed the world. Jazz formed a bridge across the racial chasm. World War I and urbanization gave rise to the more globally aware and sophisticated "new Negro."[20] These were the voices of the Harlem Renaissance.

And some whites were now listening, including scholars, novelists, and playwrights, especially those who were immigrants and those antagonized by wartime hypocrisies. As World War I widened the space between reality and mainstream racial myths, a revolt was brewing among a band of anthropologists at Columbia University, just a few blocks from Harlem, the center of the renaissance of black culture. At their head stood the immigrant scholar Franz Boaz, a "Hun" during the war years. Many of his students and disciples were also from the immigrant communities and shared his wrath against the racial theories of the Anglo-Saxons who dominated most scientific institutions.[21]

The Backlash

With World War I, the threat to the racial system had spread from coast to coast. And so had the backlash. In 1915, Hollywood weighed in with its unprecedented extravaganza, *The Birth of a Nation,* celebrating the Ku Klux Klan. President Woodrow Wilson, at a special White House showing, pronounced the film "writing history with lightning," according to the president's college classmate Thomas Dixon, author of *The Clansman,* the novel upon which the film was based. Dixon also arranged advance showings for members of the Supreme Court and Congress.[22] According to Dixon, when he invited Edward White, Chief Justice of the Supreme Court, to the showing, White "leaned toward me and said in low tense tones: 'I was a member of the Klan, sir.'"[23]

Hooded horsemen, whom a subtitle identified as "defenders of Aryan purity," were wildly cheered as they galloped across the screen. In the famous "rape scene," the "black brute," Gus, pursues the angelic adolescent, Flora, through a forest. Finally, to save herself from a fate worse than death, she throws herself over a cliff and is killed. One southern audience was so carried away that some whipped out pistols and shot up the screen.[24]

The Klan itself revived, no longer confined to the South. Now it was organized throughout the United States. More blood flowed in the Red Summer of 1919 than in civic violence of any year in the nation's history.[25] But as the Klan widened its scope to target Catholics, Jews, Japanese, and "new immigrants," it inadvertently created new allies for African Americans. The backlash was now nationwide. But it was no longer containing the threat.

Impact of the Russian Revolution

Out of World War I came another challenge to the American racial system, and indeed to white supremacy regimes around the world. The war resulted in the collapse of the Czarist empire and in the Russian Revolution. The revolution had arisen out of a war between empires, empires that had subjugated many peoples. Earlier revolutionists had appealed to the workers in industrial countries. But the Communists linked the struggle of industrial workers with those of colonial liberation movements.

As Communist revolutions failed in Germany and in other industrial countries, the leaders of the Communist International, the Comintern, made their historic "turn to the East."[26] The immediate future for revolution, they decided, lay not in the industrial West but in the colonial East and among oppressed people of color everywhere. In few places in the world was the oppression of people of color more evident than in the United States, especially during the summer of 1919.

Wartime repression and the Russian Revolution had given rise to an American Communist movement. But at first, Communist attitudes toward black workers were like those of the Socialists and other radical groups. For a half century the writings of Karl Marx had circulated among American radicals. But his view that racial prejudice was a critical obstacle to the American labor movement had made no impact.[27] American radicals thought that the plight of blacks was because they were workers or because they were a minority like the white ethnic minorities. Also, like other labor militants, they saw black workers as potential strikebreakers. Yet Communists at first mounted no concerted challenge to the practices in the labor movement that produced black strikebreakers: their unequal treatment or exclusion from unions. Few blacks joined white radical movements.[28]

The urban New Negro, however, was reacting to the Russian Revolution as well as to the bloodletting of 1919.[29] More than white radicals, the New Negro movement noted the Comintern leaders' claim that in addition to oppressed classes, there were also oppressed nationalities, and their claim that the Soviet Union had abolished inequality between ethnic groups. They also noted that the Soviet government had taken vigorous action against pogroms, mob attacks against Jews and other minorities, while the American government had done virtually nothing against mob attacks against blacks.

A small stream of black Americans made pilgrimages to the Soviet Union. One reported that before the Revolution there had been "Jim Crow street cars in Uzbekistan. The old partitions that once separated natives from Europeans, colored from white, were still there. . . . But now anyone sat anywhere."[30]

Some of these pilgrims were invited to speak before the Comintern. In 1922, the dining-car waiter, lyric poet, and novelist Claude McKay, best known for his sonnet "If We Must Die," told the delegates from dozens of countries, "There is a great element of prejudice among Socialists and Communists of America. They are not willing to face the negro question. In associating with the comrades of America, I have found demonstrations of prejudice on various occasions when the white and black comrades had to get together; and this is the greatest difficulty that the Communists of America have got to overcome."[31] In Moscow some black Americans enrolled in the Communist University of Toilers of the East, created to train organizers for work in colonial countries. Teachers there stressed the revolutionary potential of "oppressed nations."

The importance that Comintern spokesmen attached to the "national ques-tion" was elevating the political fortunes of Joseph Stalin, the Commissar of Nationalities, who dealt with the affairs of the non-Russian peoples of the Soviet Union, about 46 percent of its total population. The Bolshevik revolu-tion had been largely a "Russian revolution." In the non-Russian borderlands, the Bolsheviks had been outnumbered by rival parties, mostly nationalists.

But at the center of the Soviet Union's vast non-Russian arc from Finland to the border of China, there was one notable exception: Bolshevism had taken root in the Caspian oil fields. There, a group of Bolshevik labor leaders headed by a divinity student turned organizer, Stalin, had created what Soviet leaders called their "indomitable fortress of Baku." How was it possible for Bolsheviks, who preached class consciousness, to establish a strong base in this land where class consciousness was overshadowed by the conflict between Christians and Muslims, by rivalries between ethnic groups, by aspirations for national independence, and especially by hatred for the Russian conquerors?[32]

In 1913, Stalin had written *Marxism and the National Question.* His beginning point was that in a world of imperial and subject nations, there were oppressed nations as well as oppressed classes.[33] Some Communists thought the book had relevance to the United States, where class conflict and class consciousness had often been overshadowed by ethnic rivalry and racial prejudice.

Stalin had said nothing about black Americans. Indeed some argued that in terms of his analysis these did not have all of the attributes of a "nation." But V. I. Lenin in 1917, following the Easter Week uprising of the Irish against Brit-ish rule, and again following the fierce resistance of black Americans against the racial attacks during the Red Summer of 1919, compared the situations of the American blacks and the Irish. He suggested that in the parts of the South where blacks were the majority, they were a subject nation.[34]

Most American delegates to the Comintern, both blacks and whites, dis-agreed. They held that blacks had a firm American identity and that the orga-nizing idea should be not self-determination as in Ireland, but full equality. Nevertheless, American Communists were now debating the "national ques-tion," and members of the radical African Blood Brotherhood, formed during the Red Summer, were now moving into the Communist Party.

The national question was settled in 1928 at the eighteen-nation Sixth Con-gress of the Comintern in Moscow: black Americans were defined as an "op-pressed nation."[35] The Congress further decided that American Communists had neglected "Negro work" and, like other Americans, were infected with "white chauvinism."[36] Some American delegates had supported the oppressed nation formulation; most had opposed it; but, as soldiers of a "world revolu-tion," all were committed to carrying out the decision of the Congress. Yet none knew how it could be applied at home.[37] This debate about the "national question" and the South had taken place within a small political organization. But it was the first time since the days of the abolitionists that a band of radicals had made the "Negro question" and the South the center of their agenda.

Chapter 15

Radical Challenge, Liberal Reform
African Americans Gain New Allies

The solid South was vulnerable to a new wave of radicalism. War prosperity had collapsed soon after the war. The prices of cotton and tobacco had dropped precipitously. More than half of the farmers, whites and blacks, no longer owned their land. The company-owned white cotton mill villages often resembled plantation slave quarters. Child labor was widespread. Wages were so low that many workers were afflicted with malnutrition.[1]

If the Communists were devils to the many, they were avenging angels to some. Desperate whites, as their parents and grandparents had done in the farmers' movement of the 1880s and '90s, put on hold enough of their racial feelings to rally to the cry, "Don't Starve, Organize!"[2] They joined Communist-led interracial unemployment councils, labor unions, and the International Labor Defense. They marched in Communist-led demonstrations that demanded the suspension of rent payments for the unemployed and free lunches and textbooks for their children.

In 1928 in Gastonia, North Carolina, the Communists organized a union that shut down for several weeks the overwhelmingly white Loray Mill, the largest textile operation in the South. One organizer, years after he broke with the Communist Party, remembered that when the North Carolina governor called out three militia companies to break the Gastonia strike, he inadvertently "advertised our strike throughout the country, especially in the South. Workers came from every southern state. By foot, horse, ramshackle car, they came to join the union."[3] A southern editor lamented, "How our good mill people can be led by these people, who are not our kind, who defy God, flaunt religion, denounce our government, and who are working for social equality among white and black is a mystery."[4]

"These people" also organized share croppers. A black cropper, Nate Shaw, remembered the coming of the union to Tukabachee County, Alabama. One organizer whom Shaw called "this teacher" was "a colored fella . . . don't know where his home was; he had a different way of talkin than we did. . . . [He] would send out literatures. . . . I couldn't definitely say what them literatures said—I ain't a readin man. [But] the people was advertisin this union: they were tired of the rich man getting richer and the poor man getting poorer. . . . That's the way I looked into it and the rest of them . . . too. [The teacher was] helpin us and we had to look out for him."[5]

The Communists focused a glaring light on the southern justice system, most prominently on the Scottsboro case in which nine black hoboes, on the flimsiest of evidence, were charged with the rape of two white women hoboes. The lynching of blacks, and trials that were travesties, had once been little more than local news. With the Communist campaign around the Scottsboro case, they became an international scandal.[6] Later, the NAACP and the American Civil Liberties Union joined with the Communist-led International Labor Defense in the fight.[7]

After the Communists organized the Share Croppers' Union (SCU) in Alabama, a group of left-Socialists organized the Southern Tenant Farmers' Union (STFU) in Arkansas. In the older tradition of the American left, they were more circumspect on the question of race. Nevertheless, their largely white STFU and the Communist-led largely black SCU sometimes cooperated.[8] The Socialists also founded Highlander Folk School in East Tennessee for training labor organizers. At first it was open only to whites. In 1940, following the biracialism of the Communists, they opened Highlander also to blacks.[9] Charges of "communism" followed, along with vigilante attacks.[10]

The failures of the Communists have often been noted. The Gastonia strike was lost. Strikers who had been evicted from company houses set up a tent city and defended it against vigilante attacks. In a shootout, one striker and the chief of police were killed. Two union leaders escaped to the Soviet Union.[11]

Another leader, Ella May Wiggins, was assassinated.[12] Elsewhere the results were similar. In Greenville, South Carolina, the Communist organizer Clara Holden, in the spring of 1931, organized an interracial marched of 2,000 unemployed. Then came a summer of terror in which she herself was kidnapped and beaten by the Klan. In the fall she reported only 500 members of the Unemployment Council. The 46 party members she reported in the spring were now down to just 18, 10 whites and 8 blacks.[13]

Besides the Klan, the Black Shirts now appeared on the streets of Atlanta, Charlotte, Gastonia, and elsewhere. They included the future Georgia governor, Eugene Talmadge. One of their leaflets appealed to the "HE white man" who wanted to have "all the fun we please." Like the Communists, they recruited from the desperately poor. But unlike the Communists they attracted people who wanted, not to change the racial status quo, but to benefit from it. Although they were inspired by the Italian Fascist Movement, their agenda was deeply rooted in American history: to solve the unemployment of the whites by driving blacks from their jobs. In 1930 they claimed 27,000 members in Georgia and declared: "Before Christmas there will not be a black bell boy or a black truck driver in Atlanta."[14]

Once again the backlash appeared to be working. Several members of the Gastonia strike committee recanted and even joined forces with the segregationist Charlotte General Labor Council of the American Federation of Labor (AFL) to send "Major" Alfred Lee Bullwinkle to Congress.[15] As the Populist Thomas Watson had done a generation earlier, many returned to the ideas they had once challenged, sinking back into the racial culture from which they had come.

New Dealers Marginalize the Communists

By the mid-1930s the Communist challenge was beginning to recede. This resulted from the reforms of the New Deal. The New Deal movement had its origins in the stock market crash of 1929, which had opened the first major split in the American elite since the Civil War. One faction wanted to wait for the "invisible hand of the market" to solve the Great Depression as it had done in previous economic downturns. But the New Dealers, led by Franklin D. Roosevelt, were afraid to leave unprecedented poverty to the operation of the market. Years later an associate remembered Roosevelt's saying, "I was convinced that we'd have a revolution in [the] US and I decided to be its leader and prevent it. I'm a rich man and I have run with your kind of people. I decided that a half a loaf is better than none—a half a loaf for me and a half a loaf for you and no revolution."[16] Drawing on the experiments of progressive city governments, the New Dealers called for recycling some of the surplus wealth of the rich into economic and social programs for the poor.[17] In 1932, with this agenda, Roosevelt was elected president.

The economic crisis had become also a political crisis, threatening a shakeup of the post-Reconstruction party system. The Democratic Party was an increasingly unlikely combination of progressive reformers, Wall Street bankers, and Jim Crow conservatives. Once organized labor, the ethnic communities and the blacks became New Dealers, there could be no more papering over North-South differences such as the South's semicolonial wages, disfranchisement, peonage, and lynching.[18] The New Deal unleashed a "soak the rich" genie in the land that even a man with the matchless political skills of Roosevelt would have a hard time putting back into the bottle. Even the solid South appeared less solid when in Birmingham, the most terrorized city in the nation, the Communists organized demonstrations and marches demanding freedom for the Scottsboro Boys. And surely something was amiss in Dixie when in Atlanta, Angelo Herndon, a nineteen-year-old black coal miner and Communist firebrand, could lead a thousand unemployed workers, two-thirds of them white, to the city hall to demand relief.[19] He was arrested, and the prosecutor demanded the death penalty, asking the all-white jury, "must the State of Georgia sit idly by while he . . . is organizing an army to march into the state to murder, kill and assassinate all white people, take away their property and set up a nigger kingdom?"[20] So long as the government allowed the miseries of the Great Depression to continue unchecked, the police, the FBI, the Klan, and the Black Shirts had more success dealing with insurgents than with insurgency. Driven from one community, Communists or other dissidents, sometimes changing their names, often resurfaced in another.[21] The New Dealers, however, using the carrot rather than the stick, seized the initiative and marginalized the Communists. The Communists made demands, but the New Dealers passed out government food.

The Communist challenge to the racial system weakened not only because of things happening in the United States but also because of events in the Soviet Union. As a man of power, Stalin attracted a different following than he had as a harassed labor leader in the Caspian oil fields. Men seeking power warned him about the conspiracies of their rivals. He no longer had to defend his opinions, which were now echoed by a clamor of voices. His words came to be regarded, not as the ideas of an individual, but as the consensus of millions. Like other political strong men, he became increasingly isolated from information that flows from society's grass roots. Famines and purge trials followed. Stalin gave Communism an uglier face at a time when Roosevelt was giving capitalism a kindlier one.

Legacy of the Flying Squadrons

One of the early New Deal measures touched off a moment of unprecedented but short-lived labor militancy in the South. The National Recovery Act (NRA) promised the right to organize, and required a wage increase.[22] Textile employers indeed raised wages but then fired many workers and increased the workloads of the rest, outraging both those fired and those retained. They thus triggered the second-largest strike in American history, the general textile strike of 1934, with its "flying squadrons."[23]

It began in the Charlotte-Gastonia center of Communist activity. In Gastonia one citizen reported, "Several times daily hundreds of men, women and children parade though town yelling, screaming, threatening and intimidating citizens of the town, stating that they intended confiscating automobiles and other personal property as their needs demand."[24] The flying squadrons were really caravans of cars and trucks loaded with strikers who entered mills, knocked off transmission belts, and called on the workers to join their caravan. From Alabama to Maine they virtually shut down the textile industry.

But Communists did not lead the strike. Even their participation was not always welcomed.[25] When the workers had their leader in the White House, who needed one like the assassinated Ella May Wiggins or the fugitive, later convict, "Red" Hendricks, or the black coal miner Angelo Herndon, now on trial for his life?[26] In Spindale, North Carolina, women stormed four mills, shutting them down with the cry, "They can't do anything to us. Uncle Sam is with us."[27]

But Roosevelt disappointed the strikers. Since the mill owners had evaded the intent of the NRA, workers urged him to shut down the mills by executive order until their grievances were settled. His reply came in a radio address, expressing "my sincere hope that all employees now on strike will return to work and that all textile manufacturers will aid the government in carrying out the steps outlined" to address workers' grievances.[28] The strikers trustingly returned to work, but their grievances were not addressed. Indeed the owners refused to take back some twenty thousand strikers, and they blacklisted "ring leaders."[29]

Yet workers did not blame Roosevelt for their defeat. His policies fed the hungry. Many concluded, instead, that unions and strikes were a bad idea and that salvation came from the man whose "fireside chats" they heard on the radio. Roosevelt fed the hungry and disempowered labor in the South.

The Progressive Challenge

In contrast to the defeat of the flying squadron strikes in the South, organized workers in the North and in the West won the most important victories in American labor history. Such success was possible because in the early 1930s a broad popular movement for political reform was gathering strength. The upsurge in labor militancy, together with the reform movement, had far-reaching results for the two million African Americans who now lived outside of the South. Historically, they had encountered some of their bitterest enemies in trade unions and in the immigrant communities. But by the mid-thirties, black and white working folk, including white ethnic groups with different political persuasions, were drawing closer together.

One source of this unity was the threat of fascism. Many, especially labor people and those on the left, were alarmed by recent developments in Germany. With the economic crisis, the Nazi Party had absorbed a number of likeminded groups, becoming a major political force. The United States also had such groups, including the Black Shirts, the Black Legion, the Klan, the German American Bund, and others.

The fascist threat became more menacing in 1937 when Germany, Italy, and Japan formed an Anti-Comintern Pact, placing themselves at the head of a world crusade against Communism. They violently eliminated political opponents and "solved" the Great Depression by converting to a wartime economy, mobilizing large armies that absorbed the unemployed. They had embarked on a campaign of territorial expansion that threatened world peace.

As the first threatened by these governments, Communists sounded the alarm about the fascist danger and radically changed their tactics. For the moment, they put revolution on hold and called for a united front against fascism, which, by including the Soviet Union, would confront the Axis Powers with the prospect of a two-front war. But the liberal governments of Western Europe were unwilling to form a united front that included the Soviet Union. So the Nazis were able to overcome Germany's dread of a two-front war by playing off the Communist East against the liberal West, a diplomatic game ending in global war.

But if the united front movement failed at the international level, it was critical to the achievements of the New Deal. A coalition of Communists, leftists, liberals, and progressives brought about the most far-reaching program of social reform since the Civil War. Crucial to this achievement was the unprecedented growth of unions. The success of labor would not have been possible without a sea change in the attitude of trade union leaders toward black workers, two million of whom were now in the North. Union leaders had blamed black strike breakers for the defeat of the Homestead strike of 1892 and the steel strike of 1919.[30] But now many unionists were seeing black workers not as a threat to organized labor but as a critical resource.

The central importance of the "Negro question" was no longer the exclusive soapbox of the Communists, but had begun to spread through left, liberal, and progressive circles. Greater cooperation between different political and ethnic groups was creating a cross fertilization of ideas. The new spirit of tolerance was evident when the black Communist Angelo Herndon released on bond by a more liberal lower court, appeared at a rally in New York. He was greeted by Rabbi Stephen Wise and by leaders of the black mainstream NAACP, the white liberal American Civil Liberties Union, and the Dressmakers' Union.[31] These groups were not only cooperating with the International Labor Defense in Herndon's case but also in defense of the Scottsboro Boys.

The qualified acceptance of Communists within the labor movement was pivotal to the extraordinary growth of unions during these years. Many of the unions in the newly formed Congress of Industrial Organizations (CIO) utilized Communist organizers in their drives to unionize coal miners, steel, auto, and packinghouse workers, among others.[32] All of these unions, officially at least, admitted black workers and promoted civil rights. When Communist organizers created new unions or gained leadership ("domination") of existing ones, these unions adopted more inclusive admission practices. Unions often had had an ethnic composition and had functioned as vehicles of ethnic combat. But now, with Communist leadership, both the mainly Jewish Fur and Leather Workers and the traditionally Irish Catholic Transport Workers opened their ranks to other ethnic groups, including blacks. Other Communists-led unions followed the same policy, including the Maritime Workers, the Office and Professional Workers, and the Radio and Telegraph Workers. As a result of the "united front" idea, workers, historically divided by race and national origin, were now empowered by membership in the same unions.

The dramatic growth of unions in the North and West, and their increasing militancy and unity, bore fruit in the unprecedented Second, or Progressive, New Deal of 1935, a mass of legislation and social programs that would be a battleground between progressives and conservatives into the twenty-first century. Experimental or token social programs of the First New Deal were now heavily funded.[33]

The Second, or Progressive, New Deal had an immediate political consequence. The united front became more united when African Americans en masse deserted the party of Lincoln for the party of Roosevelt.[34] For the first time in American history they were finding political allies, not among the well-intentioned "better class of whites," but among working folk with interests much like their own. The political result of this grassroots drawing together of minorities and labor was the stunning popular endorsement of the New Deal in the election of 1936. Roosevelt carried all states except Maine and Vermont and gained control of both houses of Congress.[35]

The Nation's Number-One Problem

Against this surging movement for change in the North and West, the solid South stood as the conservative force that John C. Calhoun predicted that it would be. In the early thirties, more black Southerners were being held as peons than had migrated elsewhere. For many New Dealers, the South, with wage levels half those in other areas, was a threat to their progressive gains. They saw the South as the nation's number-one problem.

By 1936 Roosevelt held unprecedented power. The public adored him as the embodiment of the New Deal. But his power came more from his position as head of the Democratic Party. He stood as arbitrator between the New Dealers, the most progressive people in the country, and the Jim Crow bloc, the most reactionary. He was no Thaddeus Stevens. From the outset, his agenda had been recovery, not revolution. He sought to conciliate, not overthrow, the New South elite.

The power of the southern Democrats came from their insulation from democracy. They were elected by virtually no black votes and few white ones, and some of them were elected without opposition. They served so many consecutive terms in Congress that, with its seniority rule, they held more than half the committee chairmanships.[36] So Congress wrote New Deal laws with prudent loopholes that especially benefited its Jim Crow bloc. The Social Security Act, for example, was amended to exclude from coverage agricultural and service workers. This denied benefits to 65 percent of African Americans.[37] The National Recovery Act (NRA) had a similar provision: while requiring employers to boost wages, it allowed them to fire some workers while increasing the workloads of the rest. Blacks were the first fired. Some said that NRA stood for "Negro Removal Act."[38]

Thousands of black southerners also lost jobs as a result of the Agricultural Adjustment Act (AAA). This measure offered parity payments to "farmers" if they reduced production of cotton or other cash crops. But the AAA made these payments not to tenants and sharecroppers but to their landlords, who used these payments to buy machinery, mechanize production, downsize their workforces, and evict thousands of tenants and sharecroppers, including peons. They then hired wage laborers who had no legal claim to a share of the "parity payments."[39] The AAA thus had a far-reaching impact on the South, stimulating the modernization of agriculture, the decline of peonage, and the growth of cities containing large numbers of underemployed rebellious black economic refugees.

The Southern elite regarded New Deal poverty relief and work projects with the same hostility as they had once regarded the post–Civil War Freedmen's Bureau programs, and for the same reason. Poverty relief gave the poor bargaining power in negotiating better terms with landlords and employers.[40] To conciliate the Jim Crow bloc, the administration had originally set southern relief payments at about half those in the North and West.[41] Yet the misery was so severe in the South that even these small payments had a remarkable impact. They derailed the militancy of the Communists, the flying squadrons of textile strikers, and even the Black Shirts. Yet some southern leaders still saw poverty relief as a threat to cheap labor. Indeed, certain New Deal work projects paid twelve dollars a week while planters paid only six.[42]

Especially hostile to poor relief was the Georgia governor, Eugene Talmadge, a former Black Shirt who had used the National Guard to put flying squadron strikers behind barbed wire at Fort McPherson.[43] A New York journalist asked him:

> "What would you do for the millions of unemployed? In New York we have about a million and a quarter people who are on relief or [Work Projects Administration] work. Without either they would literally starve."
>
> "Let 'em starve," [Talmadge replied.] "What you need in New York is not [Mayor] La Guardia but Mussolini."[44]

New Threats to White Solidarity

Cracks were beginning to form on the surface of the solid South. The New Deal divided whites along class lines. The poor were delighted by measures that the rich abhorred. Middle-class whites also defected. When the Great Depression caused customers to vanish, many small merchants were devastated. The spinoff effects from federal programs helped hard-pressed small-business people and professionals. Now many such families tuned their radios to Roosevelt's fireside chats.

Southern New Dealers found themselves in a position much like that of the white Unionists after Reconstruction. They were vulnerable to a political and legal system controlled by their enemies. Labor activists and liberals thus began to study ways to unravel the South's tangle of legal and bureaucratic devices that disfranchised millions. Like post-Reconstruction white insurgents, they had to reach out to blacks.

In 1938, New Dealers organized the Southern Conference for Human Welfare (SCHW) at a convention in Birmingham, Alabama. Twenty percent of the delegates were black and they were not segregated in conformity with the state's law. The speakers included the First Lady, Eleanor Roosevelt; a number of southern white intellectuals; and the black educator Mary McLeod Bethune. They wrote an agenda calling for an end to lynching, peonage, the poll tax, and other restrictions on voting. On the second day of the conference, the police of Birmingham's Eugene "Bull" Connor intervened. They divided the hall, forcing blacks to sit on one side and whites on the other. Eleanor Roosevelt placed her chair on the dividing line and sat there until the police forced her to move.[45]

The Southern Conference for Human Welfare opened a campaign against the poll tax as well as against "literacy" tests and long residency requirements, which were unconstitutional laws that eliminated voters. They registered blue-collar whites and some black city dwellers as well. Especially in the Upper South, these were now voting in substantial numbers for the first time in a half century.[46]

Change was in the air. By the late 1930s, it appeared that the racial system was approaching another crisis. A redefinition of the position of black Americans seemed imminent. This was evident in the nation's capital on Easter Sunday 1939. Washington was a southern city—segregated. Recently the local chapter of the Daughters of the American Revolution (DAR) had denied the use of their Constitutional Hall for a concert by the great contralto Marian Anderson because she was black. Eleanor Roosevelt had resigned from the DAR in protest. She and other progressives arranged an alternate performance in the open air before the Lincoln Memorial.

This Easter concert was "controversial." Official Washington was poorly represented. Yet seventy-five thousand of their constituents, black and white together, massed before the statue of the Great Emancipator. Anderson began with a song that had stirred Americans since the days of the Revolution, "America." It had snowed the night before, and the cold still hung on. But now the sun had come out. Winter was giving way to spring.[47] The political climate was also changing. White solidarity was faltering. The breakup of America's racial system did not seem far distant.

But an extraordinary change had occurred in the national agenda. By the late 1930s, the split that the stock market crash had opened in the American elite was now being healed by the growing prospects for war. War seemed certain to end the Great Depression and mitigate the bitter debates over social programs that the economic crisis had engendered. The new global agenda required refocusing the nation's attention away from such divisive questions as disfranchisement and lynching to unifying national ideals.

Chapter 16

The American Century, the American Dilemma

At the beginning of the 1940s the Great Depression still hung on. Newspapers were full of reports about wars in Europe and Asia, but most people were less concerned about foreign affairs than about the social programs of the New Deal that were now under attack. To a nation absorbed with such homebound concerns, the media giant Henry R. Luce, in his *Life* magazine, America's most widely read periodical, sounded a wakeup call. The nation must rise to its global mission, to its duty and opportunity to make the twentieth century "the American Century." "The fundamental trouble with America . . . is that whereas their nation became in the 20th Century the most powerful and the most vital nation in the world, Americans were unable to accommodate themselves . . . to that fact. . . . And the cure is this: to accept wholeheartedly our duty and our opportunity . . . to exert upon the world the full impact of our influence, for such purposes as we see fit, and by such means as we see fit."[1]

It was an idea whose time had not yet come. The press gave wide publicity to Luce's "American Century" article. Yet the public response to this clarion call was not enthusiastic. Citizens favored aid to the democracies, if this could be done without involving the nation in their wars. But they still showed more interest in solving problems at home than in assuming world leadership.

African Americans were especially cool to the new shift by the nation's leaders from domestic problems to foreign policy. Perhaps they remembered more keenly than others President Woodrow Wilson's crusade to "make the world safe for democracy," which had brought them the worst orgy of racial bloodletting in American history. As a black journalist put it, "Our war is not against Hitler in Europe, but against Hitlers in America. Our war is not to defend democracy, but to get a democracy we never had."[2]

The "American Century" plays out like Stanislaw Moniuszko's opera *Halka*. The curtain rises on a sparkling party: a young nobleman is celebrating his betrothal to a lady of his own class. But at the height of the festivities, his conspicuously pregnant peasant girlfriend turns up. The nineteenth-century Republican economic empire–builders, in their rush to fame and fortune, had come to an understanding with their Civil War enemies at the expense of black Americans, who had played a critical role in the Union's victory.[3] Yet by the end of the century the nation's leaders had forgotten them and had virtually excluded them from politics. Now by the 1940s, as these leaders contemplated a dazzling global future, the forgotten ones had reappeared on the political scene.

The New Deal had reached its high-water mark in 1935 when Congress passed a far-reaching program of reform.[4] In the following election, Roosevelt had swept every state except Maine and Vermont. So great was his mandate that he did not need a single Republican vote or a single southern vote to carry forward the New Deal.[5]

But he did not do so. Instead he immediately began to use his political capital to heal the split in the corporate elite. He began to dismantle the controversial social programs that the voters had so enthusiastically endorsed, leading to the so-called Roosevelt Depression, or economic downturn of 1937. Whereupon he reversed course and once again increased federal spending. But now economic "pump priming" took a new turn with the passage of the Naval Expansion Act of 1938.[6] Also Congress passed the nation's first peacetime draft. At last, the administration had turned to a way of managing unemployment that certain other governments around the world had been adopting since the stock market crash.

Since the dawn of the Industrial Revolution, business people and governments had found that an economic crisis could be solved by expanding their markets and their control over sources of raw materials. But acquiring new markets, or even defending old ones, often required the use of military force.

All over the world the Great Depression had given rise to military governments that jailed dissenters and put the unemployed in uniform. Italy, Japan, and Germany had advanced aggressive agendas of expansion threatening the peace that the victorious nations had agreed upon after World War I.

By the late 1930s the issue that divided American leaders had become not the New Deal but war. In this split, Roosevelt—cautiously at first, but then more openly—established himself as the leader of the stronger of the two factions. These controlled most of the media and thus defined the terms of the debate. They called themselves "internationalists" and their opponents "isolationists."

The internationalists pushed successfully for expanding trade with countries that were at war or were stockpiling for war. At first they showed little inclination to discriminate among customers, whether fascist, Nazi, or democratic. But as the global war economy expanded, they settled on a campaign to make America "the arsenal of democracy."[7]

The "arsenal of democracy" idea attracted New Deal liberals and leftists, who brought to the internationalist campaign a crusading zeal. Some saw it as part of a worldwide united front against fascism, others as an effort to save the "democratic" empires of Britain and France, and a few saw it as a way to save the Soviet Union, the world's only socialist state. But this campaign alienated them from old friends, who remembered Wilson's crusade to make the world safe for democracy, which at home had destroyed a progressive reform movement and had unleashed a backlash of racial and anti-union bloodletting. The internationalist orientation of many New Dealers also forced them to temper their wrath against some old enemies, such as the Jim Crow bloc, who had become their new foreign-policy allies.

Roosevelt himself, after failing to reduce the power of the Jim Crow bloc, compromised with it. He announced a new racial policy for the military, at this time dominated at the top by southern conservatives.[8] He expanded racial stratification: while the three existing black regiments would be left with black officers, all formed in the future would be commanded by whites.[9] New Deal internationalists now had a foretaste of the kind of compromises they would need to make if they were to carry out their global mission of saving democracy.

The war was the most divisive question of the day. The internationalists did not enjoy unqualified popular support until after the nation was in a shooting war. They were hindered by debilitating political burdens: the unpopularity of war itself, the memory of Wilson's crusade, and their exposure to the charge of favoring the interests of Britain, China, or the Soviet Union over those of the United States. Ten months before Pearl Harbor, however, Luce's widely reprinted and discussed "American Century" article was not only a rallying cry to internationalists but also suggested a way to manage some of their political liabilities. It was not for Britain, not for China, that Luce called upon Americans to act. It was in the nation's national interests to bring about the American Century.

The most hotly debated issue in the press was whether measures to aid the democracies would bring the country into war. But for Luce this was no issue at all: America was already "for a fact in the war," he announced ten months before the Japanese attack on Pearl Harbor.[10] But this was not to be regretted. Because once the war was accepted it would bring to the nation the same political unity and sense of national purpose that it had brought to Britain. That and much more:

> The vision of America as the principal guarantor of freedom of the seas, the vision of America as the dynamic leader of world trade, has within it the possibilities of such enormous human progress as to stagger the imagination. . . . Our thinking of world trade is on ridiculously small terms. For example, we think of Asia as being worth only a few hundred million to us. Actually in the decades to come Asia will be worth to us exactly zero [if Japan prevails]—or else it will be worth to us five or ten billions a year.[11]

Black Challenge to the Global Agenda

Black Americans, however, were rallying to a clarion call very different from Luce's "American Century" idea that was being so widely echoed in the media. A. Philip Randolph, trade unionist and the most influential black leader of the day, was organizing what promised to become the first massive black march on Washington. The demonstration would culminate on July 1, 1941, in time for all the patriotic Independence Day speeches about the freedom and equality set forth in the Declaration of Independence.[12] It would focus world attention on segregation in the armed forces and the exclusion of black Americans from jobs in the arsenal of democracy.[13]

Despite the growth of war industry, the Great Depression still hung on. Millions were still unemployed. But as was their custom, employers were hiring whites and leaving blacks on the street.[14] Billions were being poured into war industries from which blacks were excluded. Also, among those who had jobs were the most exploited workers in the nation, some two million domestic servants, nearly half of whom were African American women.[15]

As the March on Washington movement (MOWM) won the support of the black press and was endorsed by such middle-class organizations as the National Association for the Advancement of Colored People (NAACP) and the Urban League, President Roosevelt became alarmed.[16] To manage the threat he turned to New Dealers with long-standing commitments to civil rights but who were firm supporters of his foreign policy. He called in Aubrey Williams:

> "Go to New York," he ordered, "and try and talk Randolph and [Walter] White [secretary of the NAACP] out of this march. Get the missus and [Mayor] Fiorello [La Guardia] and Anna [Rosenberg] and get it stopped."[17]

On June 13, 1941, at the New York City Hall, black leaders met with President Roosevelt's liberal contingent. "You know where I stand," said Eleanor Roosevelt,

> "but the attitude of the Washington police, most of them Southerners, and the general feeling of Washington itself are such that I fear that there may be trouble if the march occurs."[18]

She thought the march would do no good. Randolph interrupted,

> "I'm certain it will do some good. In fact, it has already done some good; for if you were not concerned you would not be here now."[19]

To the contention of the black leaders that their requests to see the president had not been granted, Mrs. Roosevelt replied, "I will get in touch with my husband immediately because I think you are right."[20]

On June 24, 1941, the White House meeting took place. The MOWM spokesmen held fast to their demand that the president issue an executive order prohibiting racial discrimination in the government service, the armed forces, and industries holding government contracts. White was considered more moderate than Randolph.[21] According to White, Roosevelt turned to him and asked:

> "Walter, how many people will really march?" I told him no less than one hundred thousand. The President looked me full in the eye for a long time in an obvious effort to find out if I were bluffing or exaggerating. Eventually he appeared to believe that I meant what I said. "What do you want me to do?" he asked.[22]

On June 25, 1941, less than a week before the projected march, Roosevelt made a major concession: if they would call off their march and drop their demand to integrate the armed forces, he would issue an executive order for black job opportunities "with teeth in it." The black leaders accepted this compromise. The president then issued Executive Order 8802: "there shall be no discrimination in the employment of workers in defense industries or Government because of race, creed, color, or national origin." The order stipulated that all defense contracts were to have a clause prohibiting discrimination, and a Fair Employment Practices Committee (FEPC) would be appointed to hear complaints.[23]

Victory! Executive Order 8802 was hailed by the African American leadership and press as the most important presidential document since the Emancipation Proclamation. But the victory was short lived. Six months later came Pearl Harbor. In a matter of hours, Japanese bombers achieved for Roosevelt a political objective that had eluded him for four years: The public rallied around the flag. Isolationism vanished. The nation acquiesced as silently to FDR's Executive Order 9066 for the internment of citizens of Japanese descent as Germans had acquiesced to the deportation of the Jews.[24] Moderate black leaders began to distance themselves from the March on Washington movement.[25]

After Pearl Harbor, the FEPC, the watchdog against discrimination, turned out to be a watchdog with rubber teeth. Even before Japanese bombers turned around the political situation, Roosevelt's appointments to this body seemed to show more political prudence than intent to carry out the purposes of the FEPC. For chairperson he bypassed all nationally prominent civil rights leaders, black or white, to pick Mark Ethridge, a southern moderate who was anxious not to put too much distance between himself and the immoderates who dominated the South.[26]

Although there was no shortage of lily-white industries with government contracts, nor shortage of complaints by victims of discrimination, the committee, with "pitifully small staff and a minute budget,"[27] was not provided with the means to investigate and document what everyone with eyes to see already knew, the factual existence of discrimination. They canceled the El Paso hearings because the State Department was afraid they would call attention to discrimination against Hispanics.[28] Also the Democratic Party retreated from its pre–Pearl Harbor position on civil rights.[29]

From Working-Class to Middle-Class Black Leaders

World War II changed the class orientation of African American leadership. At the outbreak of the conflict, their hopes were focused on the March on Washington movement. At the heart of the MOWM was A. Philip Randolph and his Brotherhood of Sleeping Car Porters (BSCP).[30] All across the country, even in towns too small for a train stop, porters threw out to black bystanders bundles of newspapers to let them know "what was happening."[31] Wherever Pullman cars rolled, the influence of the Brotherhood was felt. But mainly,

Randolph and the MOWM spoke to a restless, inner-city black proletariat. They did not call for "meetings" or for "negotiations," but for "mobilizations" and "marches," and their "demands" were focused on the inner city's hunger for jobs and better jobs.

But Pearl Harbor transformed the political landscape. It was no longer a political secret that "Dr. New Deal" had been displaced by "Dr. Win the War." Official commitment to racial justice faded and black American grievances took a poor second place for the duration. Even though the political space for dissent had shrunk sharply, the MOWM still managed to organize huge rallies in New York, Chicago, and St. Louis.[32] But then the NAACP, which had adopted the slogan "Victory Is Vital to Minorities," dropped away from the movement. The Urban League also defected.

Meanwhile Roosevelt had downgraded the FEPC from his own responsibility to that of the War Manpower Commission. The chairman of this agency, in a move that seemed aimed directly at Randolph and his Brotherhood, ordered the "postponement" of public hearings on racial discrimination by the railroads.[33] At the same time, the "extreme pressure" on the president's time prevented him from having further meetings with movement leaders.[34]

The message that filled the press and crowded the airwaves was that freedom and equality marched forward with the victorious American armies. Reality limped far behind. The frustrations of the inner city exploded in the 1943 riots of Detroit, Harlem, and elsewhere.[35] But in time, as unemployed white workers became absorbed into the booming wartime economy, employers, as in World War I, began to hire black workers.[36] Even for the MOWM's core constituency, the inner-city poor, the urgency was gone. As the movement shrank, the black press began to call attention to its weakness, to the demands that it could not enforce, to the march that would not take place, while the white press hinted at treason.[37]

Although the MOWM declined, discredited by failure, African Americans continued to organize. They joined the NAACP. While its leadership had not changed, this once small, mainly northern and middle-class organization now during the war years increased its membership eightfold.[38] It was reaching into virtually every African American community in the land, North and South.

Giant Changes in the South

During this time, while the war revived the nation's economy everywhere, it would transform it in the South. At an extraordinary tempo, the region that

President Roosevelt declared the nation's number-one economic problem, with a backward economy dominated by agricultural interests, was on the road to becoming a modern one dominated by urban interests.

Important in this transformation was the Tennessee Valley Authority (TVA). To help manage the Great Depression, Congress authorized the construction of a system of dams, power stations, and projects that stimulated the overall development of the region of the Tennessee River and its tributaries. The war effort greatly accelerated the TVA program. The vast project attracted industry, even the industry that built the atomic bomb. The TVA would eventually reach into seven of the eleven ex-Confederate states, and its economic influence even farther.

In time, the TVA would help shape the political transformation of the South, for it developed population growth and economic power outside of the South's plantation, or "Black Belt," region where dominant political power had always resided. But in spite of economics, the old Black-Belt elite would long remain in control of southern politics.

The war effort also brought investment to the whole South. The construction of military camps, along with their payrolls, created boomtowns nearby. To feed the camps and the cities, War Planning Boards set food production guidelines and goals. The camps and the nearby boomtowns as well as the war-stimulated cities soon became insatiable markets for these food crops. The war was thus diversifying southern agriculture away from plantation monoculture. King Cotton was becoming just another crop.

The South's lack of skilled workers had always discouraged companies from locating there. Now the federal government ran an extensive program training southern workers for industry. Companies came south to take advantage of this cheap, skilled, and, above all, nonunion labor. In the war boom, as industrialists ran short of white workers, they hired black workers, at first in the North, later in the South. Southern black merchants often got their paychecks. The urban black small-business class grew in the South; and a growing "Negro market" would one day politically influence southern white merchants.

Urban black Southerners, increasing in number and wealth, could build stronger social institutions, the church at their center. This was creating the institutional basis for organizing a future freedom movement more radical than the NAACP, itself now rapidly gaining members.

At war's end, the attraction of trained, cheap, and nonunion labor brought even more industry to supply the growing southern market, and more and more to produce for export. Southern capital itself invested in the new opportunities.

An economy that had been semicolonial since the Civil War, largely rural and serving the North's economy with cheap-labor produced raw materials and as a captive market for its manufactured goods, was now becoming urban centered, at the point of the classical economic takeoff. In the 1950s and into the '60s, the economic growth rate of the South would be several times the national rate,[39] shifting economic power to the growing urban classes. But there was no change in the political system of Black-Belt rule, and no change in the racial system.

The Japanese attack on Pearl Harbor had given rise to a hegemonic idea: citizens must subordinate their individual grievances to the nation's goal of victory. Yet wages were frozen, and prices rose. Workers had more grievances than their employers, and blacks more than whites. But war made protest unpatriotic. Popular leaders who said "all for victory" were more successful than those who insisted on "some for us." As a result of the war, assertive labor-oriented leaders, such as A. Philip Randolph, were forced to yield the initiative to the more moderate leaders of the churches and the NAACP. But if the black leadership was now more patient and less demanding, black America was spring-loaded for change.

No black Americans found the racial status quo more restrictive than the million black war veterans. None had experienced the American dilemma more dramatically. Half of them had served in Europe or Asia. They had heard things that one did not hear in rural Mississippi.[40] They had won war veteran's benefits, and by the 1950s, 128,000 black students were attending college.[41] They aspired to middle-class jobs, not to the opportunities of a ghetto.

Despite the sweeping changes in the economy and sociology of the South, the political system had changed but little, the ideology of whites even less. Few whites now challenged the undemocratic political system or doubted the importance of their color. Indeed, war prosperity had mitigated many sources of their discontent, displacing much of the class conflict of the 1930s with traditional white solidarity. More than other Americans they idealized war, not just World War II with its invigorating economic impact, but every other war, including the disastrous Civil War, now enshrined in heroic mythology. The increasingly powerful southern entrepreneurs shared the ideology of the New South political class, whose racial politics contributed much to the region's low wages and anti-union climate. The sharpest ideological divide was one that separated southern whites from southern blacks, who were now becoming urbanized, organized, and more often college educated. These had arrived at different conclusions, not only about the meaning of World War II but also about their place in the postwar world.

The Cold War

The atom bombs that fell on Hiroshima and Nagasaki had turned World War II into the Cold War, a conflict that had a contradictory impact on the racial system.[42] Defeat of the Axis brought no peace dividend. But millions were enjoying a war dividend, a booming economy, an "American way of life" that was the envy of a war-devastated world. Most Americans did not idealize war to the same degree as white southerners, yet so much had World War II been the "good war" that it improved the reputation of war itself.[43] Thereafter a word that evoked horror in much of the world became, in the United States, a metaphor for serious collective effort, as a "war on poverty" or a "war on drugs."

From Pearl Harbor to Hiroshima and beyond, for millions of Americans war was the economic escalator that had lifted them out of the misery and humiliation of the Great Depression. Militant unionism and war had doubled the real wages of steel workers in one generation.[44] But wartime and Cold War hiring practices did not treat black and white alike. Whites were the big winners. Skilled and semiskilled workers moved to the suburbs, bought homes, and became "middle class"; in time, some would vote Republican.

By the 1950s, many Americans were losing sight of some bedrock sources of their success: the organizing of massive labor unions and progressive legislation. Instead, they were acquiring new concerns about real estate taxes and, in the North, about how blacks moving into white neighborhoods might affect their equity in their homes.[45] Concepts of "patriotism" were being reshaped as the government, increasingly the Pentagon, became the fount from which many blessings flowed. The New Deal alliance between blacks and white ethnics was now weakening.

The Cold War also had a corrosive effect on labor unions, and virtually destroyed the movement for black rights led by the Old Left. During the "united front" of the 1930s and '40s, most civil rights leaders had worked for the same objectives and often in the same organizations as Communists. But after Hiroshima, as the cold warriors became increasingly vocal, Communists became "the enemy," and united-front groups now became "Communist fronts." For a full decade the Cold War had a chilling effect on civil rights militancy.[46]

Gerald Horne provides a case study of how the Cold War and the crusade against Communism, spearheaded by Senator Joseph McCarthy, influenced working-class ideology. In the 1930s and '40s the Communists and their more numerous allies had gained influence in Los Angeles, in the International Longshoremen's and Warehousemen's Union (ILWU) and elsewhere. Leftist leaders downplayed race and ethnicity and emphasized the politics of class.[47] Thus the ILWU in 1945, when about a quarter of its members were black, suspended the charter of its Stockton local because a majority of its members refused to work with Japanese Americans just released from internment camps. As the ILWU president, Harry Bridges, put it, the union "would not compromise on it one moment, for to do so would be to pick up the banner of fascism where Hitler dropped it."[48]

But then came the crusade against Communism, which devastated the Left-led unions and opened more space in the inner city for such nationalist movements as the Nation of Islam. The result was a different way of interpreting social conflict. In the Watts uprising of 1965 the cry was no longer against the sharp practices of businessmen and landlords, but against whites or, sometimes, against Jews.[49]

The Cold War Crisis

The Cold War annihilated the Left-oriented movement for civil rights and brought the old militancy to a virtual halt. But it also cast worldwide a glaring light on the racial system, and thus gave rise to a new, liberal-led wave of revolt. The colonial empires were in shambles and their subject nations in revolt. More than two-thirds of the earth's inhabitants were people of color, and American racial practices had been widely known since the 1930s, ever since the Communists had made the Scottsboro case a global scandal.

In the colonial world, many rebels thought that their best option for the future was the Soviet model of a state-planned and -operated economy. For others, America gleamed like a vision of affluence and freedom. Perhaps the defining issue of the early Cold War was a question in the minds of millions in the colonial world: would America help them become free and prosperous? Through the North Atlantic Treaty Organization (NATO), Washington's chief Cold War allies were the European colonial powers. Would the nation therefore side with these powers against the hundreds of millions of people of color that they held in subjugation? For American Century strategists, the racial time bomb, ticking since the 1930s, was about to explode.

Chapter 17

The Black Freedom Movement

After World War II, American leaders positioned themselves not simply as heading a nation, but as the leaders of the "free world." They contrasted the freedom and the affluence of the United States with the lack of freedom and the misery of the war-devastated Soviet Union. But their Achilles' heel was the racial situation: every antilynching bill to appear before Congress had failed. A Jim Crow army, with segregated black soldiers commanded by white officers, had advertised American racial practices around the world.

True, on the home front, the chief critics of the racial system, the Communists and their allies, were nearly silenced and in full retreat. Grassroots pressure for change in the racial system was virtually paralyzed. But now the nation was moving out onto the global stage. Since the Scottsboro scandal, thoughtful American leaders had known that the time would come when people of color would ask embarrassing questions about American freedom. American global power required a change in racial practices.

Reform from Above: The Palace Revolution

The racial system was in crisis, but it was a crisis for which American leaders were not caught totally unprepared. Even in the 1930s, people concerned with the big picture had worried about the "ticking bomb." In an effort to defuse it, institutions of the federal government had begun what may be termed a palace revolution, reforms to reduce the tension between the nation's foreign policy and its racial practices, reforms handed down from above so quietly and gradually that they would not stir the wrath of the Jim Crow bloc.

When the approach of World War II had made national unity important, racial reforms by Congress were sure to threaten North-South harmony. But the global strategists got help from a nongovernmental agency. In 1937, the Carnegie Corporation commissioned the Swedish sociologist Gunnar Myrdal to carry out a study of "the Negro problem." In 1944 Myrdal and his research team completed their landmark *An American Dilemma: The Negro Problem and Modern Democracy,* which for reformers was a treasure trove of information.[1]

Meanwhile the Supreme Court, responding to cases brought by the NAACP, had been chipping away at the racially biased decisions of the late nineteenth-century Court that had all but nullified the Fourteenth and Fifteenth amendments in the South. In a series of decisions, the judges were gradually recanting the legal doctrines of their predecessors and had begun to restore the vitality of these post–Civil War amendments.[2] President Harry S. Truman was also feeling the pressure for change. To contain "Soviet expansionism" he had called for the reinstitution of the draft, whereupon Philip Randolph and his followers threatened a campaign of civil disobedience against segregation in the armed forces, much like their March on Washington movement of World War II.

This revolt posed a serious challenge to Truman's effort to lead a "free world" crusade with a Jim Crow army. The challenge became even more serious because of a change in electoral demographics. By 1948, there were some three million increasingly politicized African Americans living outside the South. They were the swing voters in perhaps sixteen states, thus in a position in 1948 to give the presidency to either a Democrat or a Republican. Faced with the threat of both black civil disobedience and black swing voters, Truman issued Executive Order 9981, desegregating the armed forces.[3] By the 1950s they would be successfully integrated.

But the armed forces to a great degree lived apart from American society. It was in civilian life where top-down racial reforms would be most troublesome. Truman and later presidents adopted a middle course, seeking Jim Crow votes in the South and black votes in the North. To manage this dilemma, they tried to satisfy northern blacks with rhetoric and southern whites with inaction, a tactic that ultimately angered both.[4]

As the anti-Communist crusade intensified and made the racial situation more embarrassing, the Supreme Court's decisions gained momentum and importance, and the cold warriors made the most of these reforms. By the 1950s they were presenting to the world their story of racial progress primarily through the United States Information Agency (USIA). This agency, drawing upon the talents of Madison Avenue, was employing 11,000 Americans plus some 1,300 locals in their worldwide installations. The USIA administered Voice of America broadcasts and distributed films, newspapers, magazines, and pamphlets.[5]

The official story of racial progress was vulnerable. True, presidents, Congress, and the Supreme Court had been drawing up documents that conceded rights to African Americans. But these contained few if any rights that had not been conceded on paper since Reconstruction. Indeed in 1776, the Declaration of Independence had proclaimed that "all men are created equal."

The most threatening challenge to the Cold-War racial narrative came from African Americans themselves. But the news media, both liberal and conservative, advanced a doctrine that largely confined this criticism to within the borders of the United States and subordinated it to the Cold War: Americans had different opinions about Jim Crow, but when traveling abroad, the responsible citizen did not discuss the nation's family differences before outsiders.

African American travelers might speak their minds freely if they agreed with the message of racial progress that the Voice of America broadcast around the world in thirty-five languages. Indeed, if they agreed, they were frequently offered Foreign Service jobs or funding for international lecture tours. And African American celebrities in the fields of music and athletics were sent on public-funded tours, giving visible proof of black progress.[6] But the nation's black spokesmen were required to stick to the official message.[7]

In 1947, the NAACP addressed to the United Nations an "Appeal to the World," protesting racial discrimination in the United States. Eleanor Roosevelt was an American delegate to the UN. She was also a member of the NAACP's board of directors. But she refused to introduce the NAACP "Appeal." President Truman had just pronounced the Truman Doctrine, dividing the world into the "free world" and the Communist "slave world."[8] The State Department lifted the passport of W. E. B. DuBois, the principal author of the NAACP "Appeal," as well as those of other outspoken black critics of the racial system.[9]

The State Department had trouble controlling the black actor and singer, Paul Robeson, the most celebrated African American at home and abroad. He was also a civil rights activist. Finally the House Un-American Activities Committee declared him a communist. As such, the Internal Security Act forbade him to use his passport, while he became virtually unemployable at home.

The State Department had more trouble controlling the criticism of Josephine Baker, an African American who had achieved acclaim in Europe as a musical comedy star and who had become a French citizen and had received the Legion of Honor for her part in the French Resistance during World War II. She followed closely civil rights issues in the United States and was an outspoken critic of Jim Crow. During a world tour, the State Department, informing governments that she was a "Communist," pressured them to cause her long delays in customs formalities or to deny her a visa altogether. In cities where she was to appear, the State Department provided the press with derogatory personal information about her failed marriages.[10]

Limits of the Palace Revolution

By the mid-1950s the limits of the palace revolution were becoming apparent. Congressional resolutions and court rulings often did little more than concede to African Americans rights on paper that they had possessed on paper for almost a hundred years. Yet such resolutions and rulings rarely failed to provoke a roar from southern dinosaurs that rattled television sets around the world. And stories in the world media often shattered the USIA's vision of peaceful progress.[11] One was the report of a UN representative seeking housing in New York for delegates. The spokesperson for an insurance company that owned suitable space informed him that they would accept "no persons other than the white race and few if any Jews."[12]

The judicial climax of the palace revolution was the 1954 Supreme Court decision *Brown v. Board of Education,* which restored to African Americans the legal rights they had been granted by the Fourteenth Amendment of 1868. Yet even this legally important ruling revealed the difficulties of reforms that were handed down from above. Within an hour of the Court's announcement, the Voice of America had broadcast the news around the world. But in the United States, Universal News Reels refused to carry the story on grounds that it was "too controversial."[13]

Except in the armed forces, effectively outside of the American mainstream, the government-sponsored racial reforms were not making much difference on the ground. President Roosevelt's 1941 Executive Order 8802, prohibiting racial discrimination in war plants, had been largely ignored by employers. Federal courts outlawed segregation. Segregation continued. Political parties composed civil right planks and Congress passed resolutions. Southern leaders disregarded them. In Washington, men who aspired to lead the world seemed unable to enforce federal laws in their own backyard.

Once the Supreme Court had made the *Brown* decision against school segregation, and once the State Department had made the maximum use of it in the global war of words, President Dwight D. Eisenhower gave clear signs that he had no intention of implementing it.[14] Black activists recognized, however, the vulnerability of the cold warriors: If the Cold War strategists could be forced to decide between honoring the North-South Wormley Bargain of 1877 and waging their present global war against Communism, there was little doubt about what would happen. The dilemma of American Century strategists was for African Americans the opportunity of the century. "Now is the time. Here is the place," said Chester Himes.[15]

The Palace Revolution Explodes into the Streets

What was now required to force American Century strategists to choose between their global agenda and the Jim Crow bloc was not more appeals to the palace, more legal cases brought before the High Court. The NAACP had been doing this for a generation. What was required was more action in the streets. In December 1955, on a city bus in Montgomery, Alabama, Rosa Parks refused to yield her seat to a white man. Her action ignited the Montgomery bus boycott, turning the palace revolution into a grassroots uprising.[16]

There had been boycotts before, and since 1940, many confrontations with police and vigilantes. These actions, however, had been local and isolated. The Montgomery boycott united all classes in the local black community and rallied African Americans nationwide. Funds poured in, some from whites. Montgomery began one of those rare historical moments when political initiative comes from below. It sent national leaders scurrying to their TV sets nightly to see where their followers were going to lead them next.

Because of the Montgomery boycott, the *Brown* decision was not going to be forgotten like yesterday's news. Now it was up to the government to say—and the world was listening—whether the Court's ruling was a propaganda ploy or a real commitment to democracy. After 381 days of black solidarity and sacrifice, the answer came. The High Court struck down the Alabama segregation law. Montgomery city leaders complied. Unlike the rural-based political leaders of the state, the prosperity of city business leaders required local peace, a need that tempered their racial bias.

If segregation was unconstitutional in Alabama, so it was from the Potomac to the Rio Grande. Fired by this victory, African Americans all across the South arose in full revolt. And the ringing words of a boycott leader, Martin Luther King Jr., were now circling the earth.

Massive Resistance and White Moderates

The backlash in the South had already begun. Following the 1954 *Brown* ruling, White Citizens Councils appeared. They quickly silenced talk by moderates of compliance with any desegregation rulings. Across the South they organized rallies, initiated legal assaults on the NAACP, and pressured employers to fire black activists. The Cold War gave them a devastating weapon. By associating civil rights activists with Communists, they posed as patriotic supporters of the nation's goals.[17] The Georgia attorney general, for example, charged NAACP officials with participation in Communist or Communist-front activities.

Conservative lawyers resurrected the pre–Civil War doctrine of "interposition" of state authority to prevent the implementation of federal court rulings. Almost the entire southern contingent in Congress united to issue the Southern Manifesto, declaring the *Brown* decision contrary to the Constitution and calling on the states to devise legal maneuvers to prevent its implementation.[18]

White Citizens Councils talked of legality but created an atmosphere of mob violence. Hate crimes increased, especially against black activists. Autherine Lucy was admitted to the University of Alabama by court order, but in the face of a mob, police simply removed her from the campus. Later, the university expelled her. On a Texas campus, mobs harassed black students while the police stood by.

The old political establishment had mobilized for "massive resistance" and had achieved, at least on the surface, a "solid South." But despite the power of their traditional ideology, they came more and more into conflict with the material interests of other southern whites. Most important among these were businessmen whose power base was in the larger cities. With the South's rapid urbanization during and since World War II, they now had more economic muscle than the more rural-based political establishment who still ran the state legislatures and occupied the seats in Congress.

These businessmen had, on the one hand, long benefited from a system that divided white workers from black workers. They also valued state governments based on rural "rotten borough" election districts. These traditional governments enforced an "anti-union climate" that provided them cheap labor and helped bring outside investment. On the other hand, the merchants among them, with their evermore important "Negro market," were vulnerable to black boycotts. And the growing number of businessmen with connections to national and international corporations feared that the racial crisis threatened corporate America's global objectives.[19] City businessmen were often "moderates." They thought they could manage the Court's *Brown* order, minimizing desegregation, and had spoken of "compliance." But with the massive resisters' drive for white solidarity, they had fallen silent.

As the civil rights movement created crisis after crisis in the cities, it drove a wedge into this crack in the solid South. Business needed stability. And the urban South, enjoying a rapidly expanding economy, could afford to be more economically inclusive. But urban whites, in this racial culture, supported their traditional leaders—until the political establishment ran out of other options for evading federal court orders and began closing schools. The middle class and even the working class needed education for upward mobility, and employers needed an educated workforce. When teachers started moving out of the state and new industry stopped coming, more and more white Southerners would reconsider the merits of a solid South. The moderates reentered the political arena. They did not challenge segregation per se but advanced goals that racial peace would make possible: open schools, economic growth, jobs. In bitter political struggles, the moderates, with more and more white support, would displace the massive resisters.[20]

As the World Watched

For most Americans, and indeed for the world, the Montgomery bus boycott was the first episode of a television drama. They saw democracy confront bigotry, and the words of Martin Luther King tapped into their deepest religious traditions. In later episodes, black students in Little Rock, Arkansas, walked resolutely to school through the gauntlet of a vicious mob. Viewers witnessed lunch-counter sit-ins where black students with disciplined serenity bore the harassment of bullies. They saw freedom riders, some of them white, and a burning bus. They saw Birmingham Police Commissioner "Bull" Connor's fire hoses and police dogs assaulting civil rights marchers. And when the jails were full with their elders, Birmingham's black children took to the streets.[21]

White solidarity faltered. Civil rights was a struggle for democracy, and many whites wanted to be a part of it. Some became activists. The fires of idealism, banked after Reconstruction, now blazed anew. Supporters around the world were singing "We shall overcome." Victims of discrimination in North Ireland and Quebec were taking note.

The climax of the civil rights movement began in 1963 with the Birmingham victory and the massive celebration on the Washington Mall, and ended with the Voting Rights Act two years later. During these climactic years, "Freedom Summer," a black voter-registration drive in Mississippi, faced a campaign of terror. The participation of students from other states, many of them white,[22] guaranteed media attention and more federal pressure on local authorities to reign in the terrorists.[23] Freedom Summer focused national attention on the racial system's denial of the right to vote, the basic right of democracy. It resulted in the formation of the Freedom Democratic Party of Mississippi, led by Fannie Lou Hamer, and eventually to the acceptance of black Mississippians into the state's "regular" Democratic Party, the most stubborn contingent of the Jim Crow bloc.[24]

Then, in 1965, television viewers witnessed "Bloody Sunday" in Selma, Alabama, as mounted police charged into voting-rights demonstrators at Edmund Pettus Bridge. They saw the democratic right to vote trampled. In response, fifty thousand demonstrators from all over the nation, many of them white, some celebrities, gathered for the protest march on Montgomery, the state capital. Even President Lyndon B. Johnson responded with the most famous speech of his career, ending with "We shall overcome."[25]

The Limits of the Liberal Movement

In 1965, the Voting Rights Act passed overwhelmingly and Martin Luther King received the Nobel Peace Prize. Yet even during these months of triumph, signs appeared of the demise of the liberal phase of the black struggle. Already the movement had achieved most of the objectives that were compatible, indeed beneficial, to the objectives of the cold warriors. The "white only" signs were down. African Americans had highly visible jobs in the Foreign Service, in the United Nations, and in the media. The race issue was no longer so embarrassing to the global agenda.

From 1955 to 1965, the civil rights movement, the liberal phase of the black freedom movement, had enjoyed its greatest popular support. During these years, however, the primary concern of the nation was not civil rights but the Cold War. Anti-Communism had become a hegemonic ideology, accepted as self-evident truth by all social classes.[26] Civil rights leaders, appealing to the nation's all-pervasive anti-Communism, had gained a wider hearing and thus had put pressure on the federal government to intervene on behalf of civil rights.[27]

Yet this was a tactic that both sides could use. Segregationists rightly charged that the demands of the civil rights protesters were the same ones Communists had been shouting for a generation. To give in to them was to appease Moscow. Indeed, in 1964, the Original Knights of the Ku Klux Klan chapter of Bogalusa, Louisiana, changed its name to the Anti-Communist Christian Association.[28]

For a decade, liberal anti-Communism had increased the political reach of civil rights activists. In the long run, however, civil rights leaders' use of the Cold War subordinated the aspirations of African Americans, particularly the poorest, to Cold War spending, which drained away resources that were needed to solve their problems. One New Deal type of proposal for addressing poverty, the guaranteed minimum wage, was estimated at a yearly cost equal to the annual budget of the current project of sending a man to the moon.[29] The cold warriors, however, were more interested in the space race than in poverty.

The gains that the civil rights movement had brought to African Americans were uneven. People with skills and education benefited greatly. Their principal problem had been job discrimination. Civil rights reforms and increasing black political power made possible their upward mobility in the vigorously modernizing economy of the urban South. The difference was less for urban blacks elsewhere. And rural black southerners suffered deepening poverty.

The mechanization of plantation agriculture that had begun in the late 1930s had now culminated in corporate "agribusiness." At a time when the attention of the world had been focused on the freedom riders and the Birmingham demonstrations, thousands of southern black families were being forced off the land. As big landowners bought tractors and cotton-picking machines, black agricultural workers and small farmers were retreating in quiet defeat to the city. But in the city, new technology was already eliminating many old entry-level jobs that country people could perform. And industries were moving to the suburbs, to smaller towns or offshore. The inner cities were more and more becoming industrial wastelands.[30]

Few people in the administration were interested in Roosevelt-era projects for managing poverty. Now that the most visible signs of discrimination had been removed, they were less supportive even of the legal reforms already in place. This waning of interest by people at the top was exacerbating tensions within the movement. Young black activists, especially, were noticing how indifference or sabotage by the white power structure could negate liberal laws, like those requiring school integration. This realization angered and radicalized a cadre of young activists and organizers.

By 1966 in Bogalusa, Louisiana, the limits of the nonviolent liberal civil rights movement in the South appear to have been reached. The junior high school had indeed been integrated according to the court order. But, as had happened elsewhere, the authorities were giving subtle encouragement to white students to pressure black students to "voluntarily" withdraw. The black students had been enduring this harassment in the spirit of "redemptive suffering" that the movement had taught.[31] Local activists, however, decided on a change of policy: "anybody hit you, hit back," a leader advised the students. "Anybody step on your feet, step back. Anybody spit on you, spit back."[32]

This defensive violence resulted in fights. Before school was out an armed contingent of the Ku Klux Klan had arrived. But a band of armed black Deacons for Defense and Justice also arrived. Then the police showed up and ordered the blacks to disperse. They refused. After a tense moment both sides put their guns away and left. But school authorities now required good behavior at Bogalusa Junior High.[33] "White power" was more in evidence than white friends. Frustrated by this reality, many blacks raised the slogan "black power," some even rejecting white support altogether.[34]

During the 1960s, the political landscape was transforming. The war on Communism was being escalated in Vietnam. Public attention was being directed to foreign affairs. Behind this change was a split that had occurred in the Kennedy administration. One faction, called the "doves" by the news media, was daunted by the growing cost of military and space programs, by the possibility of nuclear war, and by the rising black unrest and violence. They continued their public support for the Cold War but quietly sought some form of disengagement, or *détente*. The other faction, the "hawks," wanted to escalate the war on Communism.[35] This split, beginning as early as the Bay of Pigs invasion of Cuba in 1961, became wider after the missile crisis of 1962.[36] And, by the summer of 1963 the two sides were on a collision course.[37]

The immediate issue was Vietnam. Although supported by sixteen thousand military "advisors," the anti-Communist government of South Vietnam was collapsing. The choice was disengagement or massive intervention. President Kennedy ordered the withdrawal of a thousand of the "advisors."[38] Seven weeks later he was assassinated.

At first there appeared to be little difference between the new administration and the old. The new president, Lyndon B. Johnson, in his 1964 State of the Union address, projected a continuation of Kennedy's civil rights policies, and a redoubling of the War on Poverty. He thrilled much of the nation at the time of the Selma mobilization with his "We Shall Overcome" speech.[39] He also gave strong support to the Civil Rights Act of 1964 and the Voting Rights Act of 1965.

Even on foreign policy Johnson's public statements differed little from those of his predecessor. Indeed he was perceived as the peace candidate in the 1964 elections, his speeches contrasting sharply with the hawkish rhetoric of his rival, Barry M. Goldwater. But Johnson's secretary of defense, Robert S. McNamara, remembered that "behind the scenes, Johnson had made the goal in Vietnam crystal clear. 'Win the war!' he told Dean Rusk, Mac Bundy, and me in his first meeting with us as president."[40]

The new administration thus began covert naval operations against North Vietnam, which, however well known to millions at the scene, were a secret to most of the American media. But in August 1964 came the Tonkin Gulf incident: McNamara announced an unprovoked attack on an American destroyer while on routine patrol in international waters. The nation rallied around the flag. The president's approval rating jumped 30 percent. And having begun his presidency with sixteen thousand "advisors," within eighteen months he escalated the number to more than a half million combat troops.[41]

The Movement Turns Left

The war brought an end to the liberal symbiosis between justice for African Americans and the war on Communism. The massive diversion of the nation's resources to Southeast Asia reduced the War on Poverty to little more than words, redoubling inner-city desperation and violence. Beginning in Los Angeles with the Watts uprising of 1965, riots rocked cities from coast to coast.[42] Now when activists mentioned poverty, they mocked the president with his own words.[43]

The Vietnam War was not like World War II, the "good war," a benevolent tide that raised all boats. For a worker with entry-level skills the war job most readily available was now the military. Thousands of blacks enlisted or were drafted, and relative to their numbers in the general American population they were dying at twice the rate of whites.[44] The war eviscerated social programs and exacerbated desperation and violence in the inner city. And something new appeared on the fringes of American cities, the white trailer-park poor.

Civil rights victories had been mainly in the South. Black revolt now was mainly in the cities of the North and West, and people in these industrial wastelands were concerned not with legal rights but with poverty. Some civil rights leaders were still piggybacking on anti-Communism, explaining how justice for black Americans would help American foreign policy. Yet that policy was killing disproportionate numbers of black men in Vietnam and deepening the poverty of their families at home.

There was, to be sure, already some organized response to urban black misery, most notably by the Nation of Islam, which by the early 1970s claimed a disciplined corps of a hundred thousand and enjoyed the support of a much larger constituency of sympathizers.[45] Also, secular black power activists won support in the inner city. Like the Muslims, they gave African Americans, especially males, a more positive self-image and a greater awareness of the resources of their own community.[46] "Anything done for us," Malcolm X told his listeners, "has to be done by us."[47] But the inward vision of both religious and secular nationalists limited their impact on the larger society.

Yet even among black nationalists there was a response to a world transformed by the Vietnam War. The most charismatic voice of the inner city, Malcolm X, arriving at more inclusive religious views, broke with the Nation of Islam and founded a new movement.[48] In time even the Nation itself would change its name to World Community of Islam in the West and open its ranks to all races.[49]

The Black Panther Party followed a similar path. Under the banner of black power it organized social programs for the inner-city poor. But then, noting the far-reaching impact of war in Vietnam on American society, party members began to stress poverty more than color and to form ties with white Communists and other radicals.[50]

The Southern Christian Leadership Conference (SCLC), headed by Martin Luther King, was also shifting its emphasis, from civil rights to poverty, a shift it actually had begun in Birmingham, where the SCLC had demanded a "package deal": civil rights *and* jobs. These were moderate black leaders, the most reluctant to break with President Johnson, who had sponsored the strongest civil rights legislation and had spoken strong words about the plight of the poor. Yet they could not avoid the problem of the war.

Against the advice of many of his advisors,[51] King on April 4, 1967, broke with the president in an address at the Riverside Church in New York: "A few years ago there was a shining moment. . . . [T]here was a real promise of hope for the poor—both black and white—through the poverty program. There were experiments, hopes, new beginnings. Then came the buildup in Vietnam and I watched the program broken and eviscerated as if it were some idle political plaything."[52] This speech ignited a media firestorm. King was condemned by supporters of the war, and by supporters of the administration and by their allies within the civil rights movement.

The SCLC's stand against the war alienated its members from much of the elite, but placed them in a unique position to build grassroots support. They had a decade or more of experience organizing. They had nationwide connections through the black churches, and King, like no other black leader in the land, had access to the media. Opposition to the war was surging: from the restive millions of inner-city blacks to young whites threatened with the draft. No American leader had a greater reach than King across the barriers of race and class.

Like the civil rights movement, the war in Vietnam had a far-reaching impact both at home and abroad. As the death toll rose past two million, there were unprecedented antiwar demonstrations at home and around the world.[53] The hawks, with their massive intervention in Vietnam, had over-reached themselves. In time they would repent, not war, but the wrong war, in the wrong place at the wrong time. For the moment, however, they had created the conditions that produced the New Left.

The Path Blazed by the Black Freedom Movement

The Old Left had its origins in labor struggles that began in the late nineteenth century, in opposition to World War I and in reaction to the Russian Revolution. The New Left had its origins in the southern civil rights movement and the war in Vietnam.[54] In their civil rights struggle, African Americans had shown other disadvantaged groups how empowerment is won. In distant Northern Ireland, where opportunity was defined by religion, Catholics saw themselves as the blacks of Ireland. There, the words of Martin Luther King were on the lips of civil rights activists and demonstrators marching to the strains of "We Shall Overcome."[55] In eastern Canada, where opportunity was defined by language, French speakers saw themselves as "les nègres blancs du Canada."[56]

The black struggle reawakened women to new awareness of their own marginality, to assumptions of male superiority, and to employment discrimination in a world where women washed dishes and men designed bridges and composed symphonies. Women's liberation came out of hibernation and took to the streets. Gays and lesbians came out of the closet to protest the vilification and discrimination that they had suffered. People with physical handicaps demanded equal access to public places and to jobs that they could do. A movement of Native Americans and of Latinos followed the trail that African Americans had blazed.[57]

In 1968, a sharp threat to the global strategists appeared when the SCLC and Martin Luther King began to organize their Poor People's Campaign. Like the movement that A. Philip Randolph had led a quarter century earlier, their main focus was the black poor.[58] But their reach was far greater. They were organizing in the context of a different kind of war. Vietnam was no economic escalator for either blacks or whites. Unlike Randolph, King reached out to thousands of antiwar whites.

Also, unlike Randolph, King and the SCLC were planning not simply a march on Washington but the creation of an encampment of poor people on the Washington Mall, in a city that had a two-thirds black majority. Then too, 1968 was an election year. Robert F. Kennedy, campaigning for the Democratic presidential nomination, had endorsed the Poor People's Campaign. There appeared to be no way that the intertwined issues of war, poverty, and inner-city decay could be kept out of the campaign.[59]

The Decapitation of the Movement

On April 4, King was assassinated. In reaction, riots broke out in Washington and 124 other cities. Even with their leader struck down, the Poor People's Campaigners began the construction of what they now called, in his memory, Resurrection City. But then, upon winning the crucial California Democratic primary, Kennedy was also assassinated.

With the loss within two months of their most eloquent voice and their most important friend in government, the Poor People's Campaign was effectively decapitated. The Black Panthers and other militant groups suffered a similar fate. Many of their leaders were assassinated or driven into exile.[60] In Washington, protesters began taking down their dwellings and returning home. The police arrested the Reverend Fred Shuttlesworth, who had replaced King as head of the SCLC, and other stubborn ones who remained.

In the city where ninety-one years earlier, the Wormley negotiations had taken place, the official settling of the First Reconstruction, the dismantling of the Second Reconstruction had begun. Robert Finch, a conservative political strategist, caught the meaning of the moment. The 1968 elections, he predicted, would be won by the "unblack, unpoor and unyoung."[61] And so it came to pass. Richard M. Nixon was elected president. A counterrevolution, a season of reaction, had set in.

Thirteen years separated the arrest of Rosa Parks from the arrest of the Reverend Shuttlesworth. During these years African Americans blazed a trail followed by the victims of discrimination far and near. They had shown the nation, indeed the world, how the world is changed.

Chapter 18

The Racial System in the Age of Corporate Globalism, Technological Revolution, and Environmental Crisis

The 1960s had marked a turning point in the racial system: For the first time in three hundred years, class had become more important than race to African Americans. Now a black American with money could do virtually anything that a white American could and many things that a white without money could not do. But, paradoxically, class—being poor—was becoming an ever more formidable obstacle for any individual, black or white, to getting ahead. And for blacks, a history of slavery and discrimination had left a disproportionately large number on the bottom side of an increasingly polarized class society.

By the time of his assassination in 1968, Martin Luther King had already glimpsed one of the giant changes that would transform America in the late twentieth century: "One unfortunate thing about ['black power'] is that it gives priority to race precisely at a time when the impact of automation and other forces have made the economic question fundamental for blacks and whites alike. . . . [A] slogan 'Power for Poor People' would be much more appropriate than . . . 'Black Power.'"[1]

King was speaking when an epoch of social fluidity and upward mobility for ordinary citizens was ending. Having escaped the devastation of war, America for more than two decades had been the workshop of a war-devastated world. An entire generation, taking advantage of an economic escalator powered by World War II and the early Cold War, had moved up in the world out of the Great Depression. Also, millions were reaping the harvest of struggles that had begun during the 1930s: the building of giant labor unions, the winning of a New Deal that provided for the unemployed, the disabled, and the elderly; that had reforested eroded hills; and had brought electricity even to the rural poor.

African American Gains

The global ideological conflicts of the Cold War together with the colonial revolts had precipitated a crisis in a racial system that was already faltering. Black activists, seizing the moment, had first gained racial integration in the armed forces and then had overthrown the most salient features of the racial system: legal segregation and bars to black voting in the South. They also had breached southern employment discrimination and achieved effective federal employment laws.

African Americans had gained more political power, first in the North and finally in the South. They had used it, as ethnic groups had done before them, to win more employment as sanitation and transportation workers, as firefighters and police officers, as hospital workers and public schoolteachers. This power had also influenced corporations to hire them. Madison Avenue had welcomed these now more affluent newcomers to the consumer marketplace. In the media, gone were the old minstrel show stereotypes, replaced by the images of newly recognized black celebrities of entertainment and sports.

Also the change in the position of African Americans was conspicuous in the armed forces, especially the army. Here racial integration and equality of opportunity had most directly served foreign policy. Here the quiet palace revolution of the 1940s and '50s had achieved its greatest success. Blacks, attracted by military opportunities and driven by an unemployment rate double that of whites, filled recruitment quotas at a rate double that of whites. By 1998, while scarcely 13 percent of the population, they comprised 26.6 percent of enlisted soldiers, 12.7 percent of commissioned officers and 9 percent of generals.[2] Like the Cossacks of imperial Russia and the Scottish Highlanders of imperial Britain, they had become a disproportionate presence in the nation's globally expanding network of military bases.

Changes in the late twentieth century also had been blurring the historic color line. Racial blending had begun with the earliest colonial settlements and continued despite taboo and law. Black-white marriages, however, even in the 1960s were still rare, indeed illegal in most states. But they would increase sixfold by the end of the century.[3] Also a new wave of immigrants was arriving. But unlike the immigration surge a century earlier, these were mostly nonwhites from Latin America and Asia. America was becoming an ever browner land.

During the midcentury years of struggle and opportunity, perhaps half or more of African Americans had escaped from their historic place as the bottom layer of American society. In one segment of society then another, caste was giving way to class.

Those Left Behind

But all was not well. Ironically, as racial barriers were removed, the historical community of the racially oppressed had become less unified: In the cities, black families having the greatest resources and education, the traditional community leadership, were leaving the inner city. Black churches, historically the cohesive force for social and political action, were now weaker. Black small businesses, their market shrunken, were closing. Black newspapers were being replaced by the corporate media.

Class upward mobility was class polarization. Some African Americans had moved into middle America and a few had become affluent, reminded only occasionally of a grim past, perhaps by a racial-profiling policeman. But the less educated, those who still suffered the most from the legacy of slavery and segregation, often remained trapped in inner-city industrial wastelands, jobless ghettos, where sometimes the empty hulks of factories still stood, bearing the weathered signs of household-name companies that had moved away.

If color was now a less formidable barrier, blacks, especially the poor, still faced their old enemy, the racial system. Although reduced in scope and authority, it continued to function, now in less obvious ways.[4] People who opened and closed the doors of opportunity, for example, looked at apparently value-free numbers. But the graduates of well-funded suburban schools scored higher numbers than the graduates of underfunded and resegregated inner-city schools.[5] White salespersons, dealing with mostly white customers, scored higher sales records than those who were black. They got more commissions and more promotions. Discrimination based on numbers rather than color has given rise to the belief that America has become a color-blind society, that the civil rights movement leveled the racial playing field.[6]

Reformers continued to point out that most blacks were still handicapped by the legacy of slavery and segregation and, if there was to be a level playing field, there must first be affirmative action, measures that addressed the special disabilities of disadvantaged minorities. But the partisans of a growing conservative backlash made opposition to affirmative action their battle cry. They mobilized a large, "color-blind" constituency, people who had never felt a disempowering historical legacy and who could generally score hirer than blacks on tests. These were easily persuaded that the racial playing field was already level and that if it was not, it was somebody else's fault, and that if they lost out to a black for a job, a promotion, or a college scholarship, they were the victims of reverse racism.[7]

A New Divide between the Haves and the Have-Nots

In 1968, when King spoke of "automation and other forces [making] the economic question fundamental for blacks and whites alike," he had seen the beginnings of the most fundamental technological and social change since the Industrial Revolution of the 1700s. At the heart of this change is the informational revolution, which eliminates millions of jobs and facilitates the transfer of industries and services from high-wage to low-wage countries, and the transfer of political power from voter-intimidated governments to transnational corporations and supranational institutions under the General Agreement on Tariffs and Trade (GATT). Those who fared best through this upheaval were the rich and the "cognitive elite," people with a quality education that is out of the reach of most citizens.

Robert Reich, economist and secretary of labor in the Clinton administration, evoked the polarizing impact on society of this economic restructuring: "American cities . . . are starting to divide between 'people in glass towers' and everybody else. The glass tower people are highly skilled knowledge workers in sleek office buildings. They are . . . part of a global communications web. Cosmopolitan, they may have more in common with their counterparts in Germany and Japan than with their fellow Americans who work the assembly line across town."[8] More African Americans, as a result of the civil rights struggles, have "glass tower" educations. They enjoy employment opportunities not far below those of their white colleagues. But among the graduates of overcrowded and underfunded inner-city schools, these are few indeed.

The technological revolution has changed the meaning of "equal opportunity" in America. At the beginning of World War II, President Roosevelt, pressured by the March on Washington movement, issued Executive Order 8802, prohibiting racial discrimination in hiring for industries having government contracts. Despite weak compliance, it opened industrial jobs for many black workers, including those who were being displaced by the early stages of modernization in southern agriculture. Their mule-and-plow know-how was no obstacle to the many unskilled and semiskilled industrial jobs of that era.

Then, the obstacle to their upward mobility was the historical white-only hiring policy of industrialists. But the black freedom movement won laws requiring color-blind treatment of job applicants. Now, however, even with compliance in good faith, the impact of such laws has become more and more limited, since the resegregated schools that thousands of black children attend do not prepare them for the university education and advanced skills that glass tower jobs require.[9]

The poor face a widening technological divide. The millions who cannot cross it must seek employment in the low-paid sector of an increasingly service economy. With deindustrialization, the old reliable inner-city blue-collar job, that historic first rung on the ladder of upward mobility in the old industrial America, has been disappearing. In a globalizing economy, it often has been exported, stripped of its union wage and benefits, to a "developing country."[10]

At the same time, the new industries and services arising from the technological revolution have located not in the inner city but in the suburbs or in small cities, or near major universities. Opportunity for these jobs begins in an upscale high school geographically segregated from the black, Latino, and white poor, who are thus deprived of the quality education, the special training, and the social network of information and contacts that lead to high-opportunity positions. Available to the poor are "McJobs."[11]

The technological revolution and the global economy have produced enormous new wealth. But they have also produced something unknown to most Americans during the mid-twentieth century, the working poor. The level of employment remained relatively high. Yet as service jobs replaced industrial jobs, wages went down.

Family and the Working Poor

Lower wages have put a severe strain on the traditional American family. During the 1950s, a man with a good industrial job could support a family. His wife could be a "homemaker." For those employed in the low-paid service economy, however, homemakers have become rare. More than one income is required.[12] More and more, both parents have to work outside the home, and work longer hours. The forty-hour week has been disappearing as workers have tried to maintain their customary standard of living by holding two jobs or working more hours on one. Now economic crisis may result in no job at all.

The old industrial economy was mostly men's work. The new service-dominated economy employs more women, fewer men.[13] Downward mobility—unemployment—threatens the angry white male and the angry black male, who can not support a family, often leaving women with children. For these, welfare was the only solution.[14]

Traditionally, families have been mutual self-help teams who over the generations help each other to acquire the skills, education, and social ties for getting ahead. Functional families remember the struggles of their grandparents and dream of things their children might accomplish. They are the traditional institution through which ordinary people perceive history, acquire a sense of progress, and visualize the future. They provide incentives to resist momentary pressures and support plans for the future. But in the twenty-first century, the families of the poor are often shattered, their isolated members left in a chaotic "now" world where yesterday is shadow and tomorrow a black hole. The vision of a now world of consumer wealth shines from the television screen.

Welfare State under Attack

The 1960s had marked the end of an era. In the decades that followed, the poor, especially those who were black, suffered more and more from an unfriendly political climate. Reactionary leaders stepped up the campaign to demonize the welfare state and replace it with the national security state.

But at first they avoided directly challenging the immensely popular social programs that had begun with the New Deal. Indeed they treated cautiously such bread-and-butter benefits as Social Security. These programs were sacred cows or hot rails. Instead they built their political campaigns around cultural, or "wedge" issues, which turned many of the supporters of the New Deal legacy against each other. In the news media, they drowned out discussions of bread-and-butter questions with noisy debates about abortion, the right to bear arms, same-sex marriage, prayer in the schools, evolution, and the like. But whether these debates were won by the champions of the unborn fetus or those of the mother, by those who feared crime in the streets or those who were for defendants' rights, the coalition that created the New Deal legacy was in shambles. A movement drawn together by the shared needs of the common folk had been torn apart by conflicts promoted by the cultural politics of a conservative backlash.

The way was now open to the slaughter of the sacred cows. To accomplish this they seized a weapon that had maintained planter power in Washington until 1860, and that after Reconstruction had increased corporate control over both parties: race. To be sure, the black freedom movement had reduced the scope and authority of the racial system and had made "playing the race card" political bad manners. But George Wallace and others had already demonstrated how the rich and powerful could envelope the sources of their power in myth. Since blacks were still disproportionately represented among the poor, the traditional white-over-black shape of society made it possible to represent poverty as a racial issue. Aid to dependent children, for example, could be represented as aid to the "welfare queen."[15]

Crime and Color

Poverty can be racialized. So can crime: A recent visitor to a large city noted that the crowd on the sidewalks was overwhelmingly white. But here and there posted on a street corner was a neatly dressed young black man, greeting courteously those who passed. Someone remarked that periodically the police "discovered" what any thirteen-year-old on the street could have told them, that these young men retailed drugs. Once discovered, they were arrested, convicted, and jailed, whereupon other young men recruited from the same neighborhoods of extraordinarily high poverty and unemployment appeared on the same corners.[16] Many of these men were virtually unemployable in normal jobs because of their police records. Ironically, the periodic wars on drugs remove from the labor force the young and able-bodied, potential family breadwinners, who subsequently can survive only by the drug trade or a similar activity.[17]

Television depicts both ends of the narcotics trade: at one end, helicopters destroying the coca crops of Latin American peasants, at the other end, police rounding up street-level black retailers. But invisible in these dramas is the white face of a drug cartel executive or of the banker who laundered his profits.[18]

Beginning in the early 1970s, when the export of industry was accelerating, the "war on poverty" became the war on crime. The prison population increased fivefold, reaching two million by the end of the century. Americans who were caught up in the criminal justice system, awaiting trial, in jail, or on parole, had surpassed six million. This included one-third of black males between the ages twenty and twenty-nine. Of the 3,700 persons on death row in 2005, 43 percent were black. Some studies have found that the wars on crime have created a large population that is virtually unemployable because of their police records, thus further destabilizing the economic and social fabric of the inner city and causing crime rates actually to rise.[19] Meanwhile, police budgets have soared, judicial and prison budgets also. Many people have prospered from the criminal justice economy. The losers have been the people of the ghetto, the prisoners, and the taxpayers.

The Welfare State versus the Warfare State

The attacks on the social programs and the demonization of the "welfare state," which were so catastrophic for the nation's poor, were driven by the competing demands of the "national security state." The Constitution created three branches of government. World War II created a fourth, the Pentagon. Since then, what President Eisenhower called the military industrial complex has grown steadily. Also, while corporations have relocated many of their plants producing consumer goods to low-wage countries, they have generally kept at home those requiring government contracts. Thus the war economy has become relatively more important. Even before the end of the war in Vietnam, every congressional district in every state had at least one war plant or military installation. The Pentagon was at the center of a formidable patronage empire.[20]

The nation's new role as the world's policeman has provided opportunities for thousands of its poor. Military recruiters have had their greatest success in the postindustrial rust belt or in jobless small towns. Blacks have enlisted at twice the rate of whites.[21] The poor have learned skills while in military service and some have gained the opportunity to attend college. But if thousands have benefited from militarization, the lives of many thousands more have been harmed. Much of the rising costs of military and foreign policy commitments has been at the expense of public sector jobs, which have lifted many out of poverty, especially African Americans.[22]

The Judicial Backlash

The "conservative" counterrevolution has gained strength from the militarization of the economy. It has gained strength also from the changing composition of the Supreme Court. The conservative Court adopted a doctrine that made it more difficult for victims of discrimination to prove their cases. Under the liberal Warren Court, it had been sufficient for a plaintiff to show that a law or practice resulted in discrimination against blacks, women, or some other group. Now the judges demanded that the plaintiff prove that discrimination was the intention of those responsible for the law or practice. This new doctrine effectively denied many minorities and women a legal remedy to discrimination.[23]

The conservative Court also overturned laws that would have increased the representation in Congress of disadvantaged minorities. By 1990 there were enough black or Latino representatives in some state legislatures to influence the redistricting battles that follow each census. Both parties attempt to redraw district boundaries to their advantage. Redistricting fights generally ended with compromises that set up likely Democratic and likely Republican districts.

But after the 1990 census, the Democrats created several districts that had black or Latino majorities. "Color-blind" conservatives challenged these "racially motivated" districts in the courts, arguing that they violated the rights of white voters. Now, however, when it was "antiwhite" redistricting being alleged, the Court did not require that the challengers demonstrate that discrimination was the intent of the law. They simply overturned it. Antiblack redistricting had been practiced since the passage of the Fifteenth Amendment in 1870, but this practice had most often escaped the attention of the Court. What was new in 1990 was that the new districts would have increased the representation of disadvantaged minorities.[24]

Impact of the Immigrant Poor

During the 1950s and '60s, the mechanization of southern agriculture displaced a half million black farmers and sharecroppers. These economic refugees were arriving in the city with their hoe-and-plow skills as industrialists were beginning to relocate many entry-level jobs offshore, or the jobs were being eliminated altogether by the informational revolution.[25]

But the mechanization of agriculture was worldwide, displacing rural populations everywhere and bringing a flood of economic refugees from the poorest into the richest countries. In the increasingly overcrowded economic bottom rail, African Americans, by the twenty-first century, were outnumbered by poor immigrants who came from countries where wages were one-fourth or one-fifth those in the United States. Among these were some twelve million *alambristas* or "through the barbed-wire immigrants" from Latin America. The American labor force now included a growing number of workers who could be deported by one phone call, who were thus overwhelmingly nonunion and who could not vote. Their vulnerability drove down the labor costs of the rich and the wages of the native poor.

Even citizens sympathetic to immigrants worried about the growing number of disfranchised workers who were vulnerable to deportation. If a more disempowered workforce indeed made American industries more competitive with those in China and India, the cost might be to make American wages and living standards also more like those in China and India. Right-wing groups fanned this anxiety into a xenophobic rage aimed at the desperate "illegals."

An immigration reform often proposed was a guest worker program, giving legal sanction to a disfranchised part of the working class. The impact of a disfranchised immigrant working class on American politics is reminiscent of the impact of the disfranchisement of black southerners at the turn of the twentieth century. Laws then stripped millions of them of the right to vote and reduced grassroots influence in both parties. Now, in the twenty-first century, the nation's politicians, facing an electorate from which some twelve million workers are excluded, have dropped the phrase "working class" from their rhetoric.

Historically, immigration in the United States has created a fragmented working class, debilitated by ethnic and racial rivalries. The politics of porous borders has destroyed unions and widened the gap between rich and poor. According to a Los Angeles advocate of service workers interviewed in 2005, "Janitors in Century City and Beverly Hills, 10 years ago, were all making $11 an hour. All those companies got rid of the Americans, broke the union, brought in illegal aliens from Mexico and El Salvador, paid them 5 bucks an hour. You are going to tell me that those black janitors still don't want those $11 jobs? Sure they do. They would probably be $15 jobs now."[26]

The politics of "illegal" labor has also led to coerced labor. According to a State Department estimate, "as many as 50,000 women and children are smuggled into the United States each year to be forced into prostitution, domestic service or bonded labor in factories and sweat shops." Smaller numbers of men are also pressed into unfree labor.[27]

The Fate of the Middle Class?

Both Democratic and Republican leaders have made their appeals, not to those with a low income or to the working class, but to the middle class, people who by reason of their solid jobs, their education, their social connections, and property ownership have been affected less by the postindustrial economy. But in the new century, the well-being of even this middle class has become less secure.

As for "the cognitive elite" of the middle class, Asian educational institutions have been turning out large numbers of some of the world's most accomplished engineers. Many of these migrate to America or Europe, where salaries are many times those in their home countries.[28] But these immigrants, unlike those who slipped through the wire, were members of the "cognitive elite." They arrived at airports armed with special "L visas."[29] As a result of the informational revolution, furthermore, their physical presence is not always required. Often they have remained in their home countries and perform the same services for American corporations.

The tremors that began shaking the black inner city more than a generation ago were, by the new century, beginning to be felt by the cognitive elite, those who scored high on tests and worked in glass towers. Historically, African Americans, as the last hired and the first fired, have been the "miner's canary," the harbingers of a crisis. In the 1920s, when whites were still enjoying prosperity, blacks had already been struck by the Great Depression.[30] Is the crisis that has been developing for several decades in the black inner city likely to envelop the entire society?

The Road Ahead

Most of the nation's political leaders are concerned with immediate problems and generally do not look far down the road ahead. Military planners, on the other hand, often try to anticipate the nature of their future missions. According to Major Ralph Peters, writing for a publication of the Army War College, "The future of warfare lies in the streets, sewers, high-rise buildings, industrial parks, and the sprawl of houses, shacks, and shelters that form the broken cities of our world. . . . Our recent military history is punctuated with city names—Tuzlu, Mogadishu, Los Angeles, Beirut, Panama City, Hué, Saigon, Santo Domingo—but these encounters have been but a prologue, with the real drama to come."[31]

Neoliberal or libertarian writers, however, offer a less grim vision of the future. They see no looming crisis. Neoliberals, unlike traditional American liberals, have no faith in the kind of social programs that President Roosevelt employed to manage the Great Depression. They place their faith in the wisdom of the market, which, they hold, distributes resources in a way that rewards technological innovation, constantly expands production, and brings about a generally rising standard of living.

They note that since the dawn of the Industrial Revolution, some labor writers have predicted that labor-saving machines will bring about massive unemployment and a breakdown of capitalism. But such prophets were Luddites, enemies of technological progress. They did not understand the apparent paradox between inventions that eliminated jobs and the continuing high demand for labor. In reality, a growing population and an expanding market have over time reabsorbed displaced workers into new and better jobs.

Certain critics, particularly communists, predicted that the stock market crash of 1929 and the Great Depression would be the general or final crisis of capitalism. Yet the Great Depression gave way to the prosperity of World War II and the early Cold War. The Great Depression, like previous depressions, proved to be only a downward spike or momentary pause in a rising trend of growth. Neoliberals hold that a constantly growing economy and an expanding market will create a better life for all, even for those at the bottom. They see this process continuing indefinitely into the future.[32]

Critics have challenged the optimistic neoliberal scenario. Some concede that indeed for three hundred years workers displaced by new technology were in the long run generally displaced upward into better jobs and that the living standards of both rich and poor rose in roughly parallel curves. But, they argue, the informational revolution has changed all that. Since the 1970s most workers eliminated by new technology have not been upwardly displaced into more sophisticated jobs but downwardly displaced into low-paid service work. Their downward mobility widens the gap between rich and poor, and this growing disparity must at some point precipitate a crisis.[33]

The neoliberal vision of unending growth and rising social well-being has also been challenged by critics who predict that a crisis will result from the failure of a critical resource: cheap energy. They argue that since the 1600s, economic expansion has been driven by cheap fuels: wood, coal, oil, and natural gas. But cheaply recoverable reserves of oil and gas are now nearing depletion, while an expanded use of atomic energy and coal raises environmental and other problems for which no solution is on the horizon. With the end of cheap energy, the global economy will no longer work. It will no longer be feasible to fly fresh fish from Newfoundland to Japan or fresh fruits and vegetables from Chile to New York. Indeed the impact will be on our entire energy-driven way of life.[34]

The environmentalists, or "greens," also predict a crisis. But they take issue with those who ask how the world can find new sources of energy. This, they say, is asking the wrong question. The growing consumption of energy is pouring ever more pollutants into the atmosphere, the landfills, the water tables, and the oceans than the planet can absorb. The impending crisis results less from running out of energy than from running out of environment. According to Jared Diamond, the depletion of cheap energy is only part of the problem: "The prosperity that the First World enjoys at present is based on spending down the environmental capital in the bank (its capital of nonrenewable energy resources, fish stocks, top soils, forest, etc.). . . . [I]t is clear that we are on a non-sustainable course."[35] And global warming is leading to climate catastrophe. The earth itself has imposed limits on economic growth. The management of the crisis requires not only the consumption of less energy but also more efficient and renewable types of energy. Salvation requires restrictions on the economic expansion that laissez-faire capitalism must have.[36] Many citizens, of all persuasions, fear the more immediate future, having heard the rumblings in the financial system.

The Role of African Americans in a New Crisis

Many environmentalists and other critics predict a social collapse. Much of the misery and chaos that they foresee is already a reality in the racial world of the inner city. And a general breakdown of the larger society would certainly make conditions worse there. Yet the three major changes in the American racial system all took place because of crises in the larger society: the American Revolution, the Civil War, and the Cold War crisis of the 1950s and '60s. In each of these historical moments, African Americans took action and made the nation more aware of the contradiction between its ideals and its practices and affected the way the crisis was resolved.

In a new crisis, also, African Americans are likely to play a key role. No other group in America has a tradition—a historical memory extending over centuries—of viewing society from the bottom. Other groups have experienced analogous moments. A generation of Irish immigrants, beginning in the 1840s, lived in shantytowns and suffered job discrimination and ethnic stereotypes. But then, Irish political power opened doors, and the Irish blended into the great white majority. Anti-Irish stereotypes faded. A half-century later, the "dark and swarthy new immigrants" from southern and eastern Europe experienced life at the bottom. Yet this, too, would pass. With upward mobility and the "melting pot," each generation remembers more dimly, finally scarcely at all, the sweatshops where their ancestors worked and the discrimination they suffered.

But even when the racial barrier was most insurmountable, many whites had a fascination for black culture, with its memory of hard times over the centuries. The dominant media have always capitalized upon this interest and have promoted caricature interpretations of black culture, from the minstrel clowns of the nineteenth and early twentieth centuries to the "gangsta rappers" of the early twenty-first.[37] Yet African American religion, the spirituals, the blues and the gospel songs have flowed like a river of pathos across the centuries, carrying stories of injustice, survival, hope for renewal and liberation, themes that have always struck sympathetic chords in the wider world. Black writers have expressed, in novels, poetry, drama, and scholarship, their unique view from the bottom and have changed the intellectual debate in America.

To be sure, in every crisis of the past, whites who feared grassroots change have raised racial issues. In 1776 a British invasion demonstrated that slavery threatened both social stability and the moral claims of those who defended the "land of the free." Some tried to reconcile liberty and slavery with ideas about race and articulated early ideas of white superiority.

But Quakers and others responded differently: all the peoples of the earth shared an "inner light," even the Turk, the papist, the blackest African, the "wildest Indian." This tradition has been much admired but much ignored in a competitive and status-conscious world. Yet, politically, in times of crisis, when customary habits of thought no longer worked, it has been this ancient concept of the human family that gained the moral power for change.

During the Civil War, in the summer of 1862, Confederate forces crossed the Potomac. The survival of the American republic was at stake. Again the response was contradictory. Behind the Union lines, Copperhead mobs lynched blacks and killed Union Army recruiting officers. Yet the crisis created by the slaveholder's rebellion also, as a Radical Republican put it, revealed "the new heavens and new earth."[38] More people now listened to such abolitionists as John Fee, who preached a God who will break every yoke and let the bond go free. Before the summer of 1862 was out, the nation had changed its war objective from a limited war to bring rebellious slaveholders back into the Union to total war to let the bond go free.

In the middle of the twentieth century, American globalists called out a Jim Crow army and set out to become leaders of the "free world," a world seething with revolution and colonial revolt. African Americans saw their opportunity and seized it.

In this crisis, too, the response of whites was contradictory. Some raised Confederate battle flags, donned white hoods, burned houses, and bombed churches. But again there was an opposite response. Others heeded leaders like Martin Luther King, who evoked the ancient vision of a human family that included everybody.

The future is a secret. But in a new crisis, it is possible that, with the blurring of the color line and the widening gap between rich and poor, ideas about class will have impact. Yet, historically, it has been the "impractical" concept of a universal human family that has rallied the forces for democratic change.

For many, the bullets that struck down King struck down his dream as well. But the ideas that bridged the racial gulf, that rallied the forces for change, were neither born nor did they die with Thomas Paine, John Brown, John Fee, or Martin Luther King. In time of crisis, their age-old vision of human unity has risen like a "pillar of cloud by day and a pillar of fire by night" to point the way ahead.

Notes

Prologue: Race and the Human Race

1. *La esclava de su galan* (c. 1626), 2.3 (Real Academia Española, eds., *Obras de Lope de Vega*, nueva edición, 13 vols. [Madrid: Sucesores de Rivadeneyra, 1916–30], 12:147). The play employs the dramatic device of characters in disguise. Alberto represents himself as a sea captain.

2. For the story of this Caucasian slave in the nineteenth-century United States, see J. David Gillespie and Judi F. Gillespie, "Struggle for Identity: The Life of Jordan Chambers (A *Phylon* Document)," *Phylon* 40 (Summer 1979): 111. (I have standardized Chambers's spelling.) Much of the controversy about the reliability of slave narratives would disappear if more scholars would follow the lead set by the Gillespies in this article. They checked more than sixty names, dates, and events mentioned in two related narratives against local records, published and unpublished. They concluded, "Not one claim," major or minor, "found in these accounts has been disproven by independent records." Ibid., 118.

3. Philo, *Every Good Man Is Free*, 78 (trans. F. H. Colson, vol. 9 [Loeb, 1958]: 57).

4. *City of God* 16:8 (Saint Augustine, *The City of God against the Pagans*, trans. Eva Mathews Sanford and William McAllen Green, 5 [Loeb Classical Library; Cambridge, Mass.: Harvard University Press, 1965]: 42–45.)

5. Jean Marie Courtes, "The Theme of 'Ethiopia' and 'Ethiopians' in Patristic Literature," in *The Image of the Black in Western Art*, ed. Ladislas Bugner et al. (Cambridge, Mass.: Harvard University Press, 1979), vol. 2, pt. 1:22.

6. For black-faced Jews, see Bernard Blumenkranz, *Le juif médiéval au miroir de l'art chrétien* (Paris: Études augustiniennes, 1966), 22 (quote). For "Ethiopian demons," see *Image of the Black*, vol. 2, pt. 1:64, fig. 15; 65, fig. 17; 70, fig. 23; 71, fig. 24; and David Brion Davis, *Slavery and Human Progress* (New York: Oxford University Press, 1984), 89.

7. Paul H. D. Kaplan, *The Rise of the Black Magus in Western Art* (Ann Arbor, Mich.: UMI Research Press, 1985). For beautiful representations of this Wise Man, see *Image of the Black*, vol. 2, pt. 2: pp. 140–14, figs. 144–45.

8. Bartolemé de las Casas, *Apologética Historia de las Indias,* vol. 50 (vol. 13 of Nueva Biblioteca de Autores Españoles [Madrid: Bailly, Bailliere e Hijos, 1909]), 128.

Chapter 1: How the American Racial System Began

1. Omar ibn Saíd to Sheikh Hunter, n.d., c. 1831, trans. Alexander I. Cotheal and F. M. Moussa, in "Autobiography of Omar ibn Saíd, Slave in North Carolina," *American Historical Review* 30 (July 1925): 793.

2. Some distinction must be made between slavery in Christian and Muslim countries. Since most Christian lands did not practice institutionalized military slavery and employed their slaves nearly always in household service, Christians showed a stronger preference than the Muslims for female slaves. Also because of differences in family structure, law, and custom, Muslim slavery was more paternalistic. Slaves thus enjoyed more opportunities. The children of slave women in Christian countries, for example, derived their status from low-status mothers; in Muslim countries, from high-status fathers. See Daniel Evans, "Slave Coast of Europe," *Slavery and Abolition* 6 (May 1985): 47–48; Iris Origo, "The Domestic Enemy: The Eastern Slaves of Tuscany in the Fourteenth and Fifteenth Centuries," *Speculum* 30 (July 1955): 346–48. Compare with Orlando Patterson, *Slavery and Social Death: A Comparative Study* (Cambridge, Mass.: Harvard University Press, 1982), 263.

3. For further discussion, see Daniel Pipes, *Slave Soldiers of Islam: The Genesis of a Military System* (New Haven: Yale University Press, 1981).

4. The following discussion of the development of plantation production is based on Charles Verlinden, *Les origines de la civilization atlantique* (Paris: A. Michel, 1966), 160; idem, *Précédents médiévaux de la colonie en Amérique* (Mexico City: Instituto Panamericano de Geografía y Historia, 1954); idem, "Medieval Slavery in Europe and Colonial Slavery in America," in Verlinden's *The Beginnings of Modern Colonization: Eleven Essays with an Introduction,* trans. Yvonne Freccero (Ithaca: Cornell University Press, 1970), 39, 47. See also Philip D. Curtin's chapters "The Mediterranean Origins" and "Sugar Planting from Cyprus to the Atlantic Islands," in his *The Rise and Fall of the Plantation Complex* (Cambridge: Cambridge University Press, 1990), 3–28.

5. Verlinden, *Beginnings of Modern Colonization,* 31, 39; José Luís Cortes López, *La esclavitud negra en la España peninsular del siglo XVI* (Salamanca: Ediciones Universidad de Salamanca, 1989), 42, 62, 108.

6. A sampling of free male immigrants to early Virginia and Maryland found that only 3.2 percent admitted having an agricultural occupation. Robin Blackburn, *The Making of New World Slavery: From the Baroque to the Modern, 1492–1800* (London: Verso, 1997), 313.

7. The epidemics were most catastrophic in the tropical lowlands. See Philip D. Curtin, "Epidemiology and the Slave Trade," *Political Science Quarterly* 83 (1968): 200. There is no way to reconcile the findings of the demographic studies that estimate the size of the pre-Columbian population of the Americas, hence the magnitude of the collapse. For a conservative estimate, see Ángel Rosenblat, *La población indígena y el mestizaje en América,* vol. 1: *La población indígena, 1492–1952,* vol. 2: *El mestizaje de las castas coloniales* (Buenos Aires: Editorial Nova, 1954). Rosenblat's calculations are followed closely in Colin McEvedy and Richard Jones, *Atlas of World Population History* (New York: Penguin, 1978), 272–74, 291–93, 297. But Sherburne F. Cook and Woodrow Borah arrive at a population estimate for central Mexico, in 1519, that is

greater than Rosenblat's total for both continents. Hence they calculate a more catastrophic decline. See their *Essays in Population History: Mexico and the Caribbean*, vol. 2 (Berkeley: University of California Press, 1974), 180–81. According to one estimate, between 1492 and 1515 the Arawak population of Hispaniola fell from 500,000 to 32,000, a drop of 93 percent. See Mervyn Ratekin, "The Early Sugar Industry in Española," *Hispanic American Historical Review* 4 (1954): 5.

8. On the greater survival rate of Africans, see Philip D. Curtin, "The Atlantic Slave Trade, 1600–1800," in *History of West Africa*, ed. J. F. A. Ajayi and Michael Crowder, vol. 1 (New York: Columbia University Press, 1972), 253; idem, "Epidemiology and the Slave Trade," 200–201; James A. Rawley, *The Transatlantic Slave Trade: A History* (New York: Norton, 1981), 286–87, 308–9; Kenneth F. Kiple, *The Caribbean Slave: A Biological History* (Cambridge: Cambridge University Press, 1984), 161–62; Richard B. Sheridan, *Doctors and Slaves: A Medical and Demographical History of Slavery in the British West Indies, 1680–1834* (Cambridge: Cambridge University Press, 1985), 10.

9. For a discussion of the evolution and usage of the word "capitalism," see Maurice Dobb, *Studies in the Development of Capitalism* (London: Routledge and Kegan Paul, 1946), 1–32, esp. 7–8.

10. By the mid-1600s the Dutch merchant fleet had reached a capacity of 400,000 tons, or more than that of the Spanish, French, and British fleets combined. Jan de Vries and Ad van der Woude, *The First Modern Economy: Success, Failure, and Perseverance of the Dutch Economy, 1500–1815* (Cambridge: Cambridge University Press, 1997), 404.

11. This continuous expansion of the world market has come to be called globalism. See Alfred E. Eckes Jr. and Thomas W. Zeiler, *Globalism and the American Century* (Cambridge: Cambridge University Press, 2003), esp. 6.

12. See Immanuel Wallerstein, *The Modern World-System*, vol. 1: *Capitalist Agriculture and the Origins of the European World-Economy in the Sixteenth Century* (New York: Academic Press, 1974), vol. 2: *Mercantilism and the Consolidation of the European World-Economy* (New York: Academic Press, 1980).

13. See Wallerstein's chapter "Dutch Hegemony in the World-Economy," ibid., 2:36–71. See also Charles Wilson, *The Dutch Republic and the Civilization of the Seventeenth Century* (New York: McGraw-Hill, 1968), 55–56, 165; Jonathan Israel, *The Dutch Republic: Its Rise, Greatness, and Fall, 1477–1806* (Oxford: Clarendon Press, 1995), 271–75, 307–18.

14. On the coercive labor systems used in the sixteenth and seventeenth centuries, see Wallerstein, *Modern World-System*, 1:91–106, 2:171–75; Silvio Zafala, "The Evolving Labor System," in *Indian Labor in the Spanish Indies: Was There Another Solution?* ed. John Francis Bannon (Boston: Heath, 1966), 76–81. Maurice Dobb has a different explanation for the patterns of free and coerced labor. Labor was "free," he argues, in those areas where it was plentiful and cheap. In those areas where it was scarce and expensive, as on the Russian frontier and in the Americas, labor was coerced. See his *Studies in the Development of Capitalism*, esp. 57–58.

15. Charles Verlinden, the leading authority on medieval slavery, calls the late fifteenth century the "black period" of European slavery. See his "Schiavitù ed economia nel Mezzogiorno agli inizi dell'età moderna," *Annali del Mezzogiorno* 3 (1963): 37; idem, "Esclavage noir en France méridionale et courants de traite en Afrique," *Annales du Midi* 78 (1966): 335–43. See also Vicenta Cortes, *La esclavitud en Valencia durante el reinado de los Reyes Católicos*,

1479–1516 (Valencia: Publicaciones del Archivo Municipal, 1964), 16; A. C. de M. Saunders, *A Social History of Black Slaves in Portugal* (Cambridge: Cambridge University Press, 1982).

16. Cortes López, *La esclavitud negra*, 134, 178; Hugh Thomas, *The Slave Trade: The Story of the Atlantic Slave Trade, 1440–1870* (New York: Simon and Schuster, 1997), 806.

17. Antonio Dominguez Ortiz, "La esclavitud en Castilla durante la Edad Moderna," *Estudio de historia social de España* 2 (1962): 380–81.

18. On the demands of buyers of white slaves that the seller furnish them with a *Carta Servitutis,* certifying the slave to be of "unbeliever" or "heretic" origin, thus protecting the purchaser against a legal challenge to the sale, see Evans, "Slave Coast of Europe," 49.

19. José Antonio Saco, *Historia de la esclavitud desde los tiempos más remotos hasta nuestros días,* vol. 1 (Paris: Tipografia Lahure, 1875), vol. 2 (Paris: Imprenta de Jugelman, 1875), vol. 3 and vol. 4 (Barcelona: Imprenta de Jaime Jepús, 1877–79), 4:63; Colin A. Palmer, *Slaves of the White God: Blacks in Mexico, 1570–1650* (Cambridge, Mass.: Harvard University Press, 1976), 120, 223.

20. For a comparison of prices for white and black slaves, see Lucette Valensi, "Esclaves chrétiens et esclaves noirs à Tunis au XVIIIè siècle," *Annales: Economies, Sociétés, Civilisations* 2 (1967): 1280–81; Leslie B. Rout Jr., *The African Experience in Spanish America, 1502 to the Present Day* (Cambridge: Cambridge University Press, 1976), 16, 333–34 n. 53. On the ransoming societies and their influence on slave prices, see Charles Verlinden, *L'esclavage dans l'Europe médiévale,* vol. 1: *Péninsule Ibérique-France* (Brugge: De Temple, 1955), vol. 2: *Italie, Colonies italiennes du Levant* (Ghent: Université de Gand Recueil de Fac. de Phil. et Lettres, 1977), 1:156, 541–43; 2:261–62; Origo, "Domestic Enemy," 328–30; Domenico Gioffrè, *Il mercato degli schiavi a Genova nel secolo XV* (Genoa: Fratelli Brozzi, 1971), 51–52; and Fernand Braudel, *The Mediterranean and the Mediterranean World in the Age of Philip II,* 2 vols. (1966; New York: Harper and Row, 1973), 2:889.

21. Curtin, "Atlantic Slave Trade," 253; idem, "Epidemiology and the Slave Trade," 200–201; Kiple, *Caribbean Slave,* 161–62; Sheridan, *Doctors and Slaves,* 10.

22. For a somewhat different perspective on the development of racial prejudice, one that includes prejudice against such groups as Jews, see George M. Fredrickson, *Racism: A Short History* (Princeton: Princeton University Press, 2002).

23. Christopher Hill, *Reformation to the Industrial Revolution: The Making of Modern English Society,* vol. 1: *1530–1780* (New York: Pantheon, 1967), 57. For such raids as viewed by Turkish slave catchers, see Joseph Freiherr von Hammer-Purgestall, *Geschichte des osmanischen Reiches,* 10 vols. (Pest, Austria-Hungary: C. A. Hartleben, 1827–35), 3:167. See also Paul Baepler, ed., *White Slaves, African Masters: An Anthology of American Barbary Captivity Narratives* (Chicago: University of Chicago Press, 2000), 80–81.

24. In the words of the Nicholas brief of 1454, "subjugandi illorumque personas in perpetuam servituden," quoted by J. Margraf, who denied that these words constituted a papal blessing on the slave trade. See his *Kirche und Sklaverei seit der Entdeckung Amerikas* (Tübingen: H. Laupp, 1865), 187–88. See also John Francis Maxwell, *Slavery and the Catholic Church: The History of Catholic Teaching Concerning the Moral Legitimacy of the Institution of Slavery* (Chicester, Eng.: Rose [for] the Anti-Slavery Society for the Protection of Human Rights, 1975), 53; and Saco, *Historia de la esclavitud,* 4:36.

25. The concept of "Christian liberty" caused confusion in the status of slaves in Maryland and Virginia. See Helen Tunicliff Catterall, ed., *Judicial Cases Concerning American Slavery*

and the Negro, 5 vols., vol. 1: *Cases from the Courts of England, Virginia, West Virginia, and Kentucky* (1926; New York: Octagon, 1968), 55 n. 14, 58 n. 38.

26. The earliest example I have found of the racial form of the story of Ham among Europeans, alleging that the curse of Noah fell upon blacks, occurs in the mid-fifteenth century in negotiations between some Portuguese and Arabs over black slaves. See Gomes Eunnes de Azurara, *The Chronicle of the Discovery and Conquest of Guinea,* Hakluyk Society Publications, 1st ser., 95 (London, 1895), 54–55. For the use of nonracial forms of the same story by medieval Europeans to justify enslavement of fellow-whites, see [Andrew Horn], *The Mirror of Justices,* ed. William Joseph Whittaker (London: B. Quiritch, 1895), 77; Piero A. Milani, *La schiavitù nel pensiero politico dai Greci al basso Medio Evo* (Milan: A. Giuffrè, 1972), 292, 300, 309, 316, 355–57, 376–77 n. 16. On applying "Sambo" traits to Africans in Spain and Spanish colonies, see Cortes López, "La esclavitud negra," 391–92; Rout, *African Experience in Spanish America,* 22, 335 nn. 80–82.

27. For example, Kizlar Agasi Beshir (1650–1746), an Abyssian slave, served for many years as secretary of the treasury of the Ottoman Empire. The nineteenth-century Moroccan sultan Mulay Hasan was the son of a black mother. See William McKee Evans, "From the Land of Canaan to the Land of Guinea: The Strange Odyssey of the 'Sons of Ham,'" *American Historical Review* 85 (February 1980): 31.

28. Alexander von Humboldt, *Political Essay on the Kingdom of New Spain,* trans. John Black, vol. 1 (London: Longman, Hurst, Rees, Orme, and Brown, 1811), 246.

29. Montesquieu, *Lettres persanes,* 78 (*Oeuvres complètes,* vol. 1 [Paris: Gallimard, 1949], 249). Emphasis in the original.

30. For a general survey of the disintegration of the system of castas throughout Latin America, see vol. 2 of Rosenblat, *La población indígena.* For a more sharply focused view of the same process, see Gonzalo Aguirre Beltrán, *La población negra de México* (Mexico City: Fonde de Cultura Económica, 1972), 85, 104–5, 154, 172–73. See also Stafford Pool, "Church Law on the Ordination of Indians and *Castas* in New Spain," *Hispanic American Historical Review* 61 (1981): 637–50.

31. See Carl N. Degler, *Neither Black nor White: Slavery and Race Relations in Brazil and the United States* (New York: Macmillan, 1971), esp. 113–16, 227–29, 327. See also Robert Brent Toplin, *Freedom and Prejudice: The Legacy of Slavery in the United States and Brazil* (Westport, Conn.: Greenwood, 1981).

Chapter 2: Anglo Americans Adopt the Atlantic Racial System

1. So goes the social convention. In reality, "black" includes a variety of African, European, and Native American combinations, while about one-quarter of American "whites" have some fraction of sub-Saharan inheritance. See Robert P. Stuckert, "Race Mixture: The African Ancestry of White Americans," in *Physical Anthropology and Archeology,* ed. Peter B. Hammond (New York: Macmillan, [1964]), 192–97; John H. Burma, "The Measurement of Negro Passing," *American Journal of Sociology* 57 (1951–52): 587–89.

2. J. H. Lefroy, *Memorials of the Discovery and Early Settlement of the Bermudas or Somers Islands, 1515–1685,* 2 vols. (London: Longmans, Green, 1877), 1:115–16; Richard N. Bean and Robert P. Thomas, "The Adoption of Slave Labor in British America," in *The Uncommon Market: Essays in the Economic History of the Atlantic Slave Trade,* ed. Henry A. Gemery

and Jan S. Hogendorn (New York: Academic Press, 1979), 382; Susie M. Ames, *Studies of the Virginia Eastern Shore in the Seventeenth Century* (Richmond, Va.: Dietz Press, 1940), 101; Ross M. Kimmel, "Free Blacks in Seventeenth-Century Maryland," *Maryland Historical Magazine* 71 (1976): 20.

3. On the early Virginia death rate, see Edmund S. Morgan, *American Slavery, American Freedom: The Ordeal of Colonial Virginia* (New York: Norton, 1975), 159, and his entire chapter "Living with Death," 158–79; Beauchamp Plantagenet, *A Description of . . . New Albion*, in Peter Force, *Tracts and Other Papers relating . . . to the . . . Colonies*, 4 vols. (1836; Gloucester, Mass.: Peter Smith, 1963), vol. 2, no. 7, p. 7; William W. Hening, ed., *The Statutes of Virginia*, 13 vols. (Richmond: Samuel Pleasants, 1809–23), 2:515; Henry A. Gemery, "Emigration from the British Isles to the New World, 1630–1700," in *Research in Economic History: A Research Journal*, ed. Paul Uselding, vol. 5 (Greenwich, Conn.: JAI Press, 1980), 189. For a free Afro-Briton immigrant to Virginia, see Helen Tunnicliff Catterall, ed., *Judicial Cases Concerning American Slavery and the Negro*, 5 vols., vol. 1: *Cases from the Courts of England, Virginia, West Virginia, and Kentucky* (1926; New York: Octagon, 1968), 55 n. 14. For black indentured servants, see Barton H. Wise, "Northampton County Records in the 17th Century," *Virginia Magazine of History and Biography* 4 (1896–97): 407; T. H. Breen and Stephen Innes, *"Myne Owne Ground": Race and Freedom on Virginia Eastern Shore, 1640–1676* (New York: Oxford University Press, 1980).

4. Ames, *Studies of the Virginia Eastern Shore*, 82; T. H. Breen, "A Changing Labor Force and Race Relations in Virginia, 1660–1710," *Journal of Social History* (Fall 1973): 14; David W. Galenson, *White Servitude in Colonial America* (Cambridge: Cambridge University Press, 1981), 164–15.

5. R. H. Hilton, *The Decline of Serfdom in Medieval England* (London: Macmillan, 1969), 56–59; Leonard Cantor, *The Changing English Countryside, 1400–1700* (London: Routledge and Kegan Paul), 1987), 36–37, and his chapter "Agricultural Improvement: The Cultivated Landscape in the Seventeenth Century," 44–64.

6. James Horn, *Adapting to a New World: English Society in the Seventeenth Century* (Chapel Hill: University of North Carolina Press, 1994), 49.

7. Colin McEvedy and Richard Jones, *Atlas of World Population* (New York: Penguin, 1978), 279, 297. For a higher estimate of the British portion, see Marvin Harris, *Patterns of Race in the Americas* (New York: Norton, 1964), 82.

8. Alonso de Velasco to Philip III, August 22, 1611, in Alexander Brown, *The Genesis of the United States*, 2 vols. (1890; New York: Russell and Russell, 1964), 1:494–95; Marcus Wilson Jernegan, *Laboring and Dependent Classes in Colonial America, 1607–1783* (New York: Frederick Ungar, 1931), 45–52, 175–80. On the preference of immigrants for the northern settler colonies, see Galenson, *White Servitude in Colonial America*, 176. See also Richard S. Dunn's chapter "Death in the Tropics," in his *Sugar and Slaves: The Rise of the Planter Class in the English West Indies, 1624–1713* (New York: Norton, 1972), 300–34, esp. 333–34; A. H. Rutman and D. B. Rutman, "Of Agues and Fevers: Malaria in the Early Chesapeake," *William and Mary Quarterly* 33 (1976): 31.

9. English "real wages" fell to a fifty-year low at the beginning of the period of colonization. See Peter Bowen, "Agricultural Prices, Farm Profits and Rents," in *The Agricultural History of England and Wales*, vol. 4: *1500–1640*, ed. Joan Thirsk (Cambridge: Cambridge University Press, 1967–), 600. Compare with E. A. Wrigley and R. S. Schofield, *The Population History*

of England, 1541–1871: A Reconstruction (Cambridge, Mass.: Harvard University Press, 1981), 471; R. H. Tawney and Eileen Power, *Tudor Economic Documents,* vol. 3: *Pamphlets, Memoranda, and Literary Extracts* (New York: Barnes and Noble, 1962), 328–31, 335–37. See also Frank Aydelotte, *Elizabethan Rogues and Vagabonds* (New York: Barnes and Noble, [1967]), 63–71; R. H. Tawney, *The Agrarian Problem of the Sixteenth Century* (New York: Burt Franklin, [1912]), esp. 270–80. Robert J. Steinfeld notes, "Strictly speaking, before the eighteenth century, there was no unambiguously free labor in modern terms." Steinfeld, *The Invention of Free Labor: The Employment Relation in English and American Law and Culture, 1350–1870* (Chapel Hill: University of North Carolina Press, 1991), 102. On the tension between the free labor ideal and actual practices, see his chapter "The Freeborn Englishman and the Persistence of Traditional Service," ibid., 94–121.

10. John Cordy Jeaffreson, ed., *Middlesex County Records,* vol. 1 [1549–1688] (n.p.: Middlesex Records Society, [c. 1884]), 191.

11. Ibid., 1:103. In seventeenth-century England, it is said, "nearly three hundred crimes, varying from murder to keeping company with a gypsy, were punishable with death." Brown, *Genesis of the United States,* 2:529.

12. Brown, *Genesis of the United States,* 2:336–37. Since most had no money, many went to the plantations as "redemptioners." That is, in return for their passage, they agreed for the ship master to strike the best bargain he could for their labor. He could make his voyage more profitable by inflating his charge for their passage, which he could recover by adding to the years for which they were sold. One visitor to Barbados claimed that, in terms of the time they served, some redemptioners paid four or five times the cash price of passage. See Morgan Godwyn, *The Negro and Indians Advocate* (London: Printed for the Author, 1680), 170–71.

13. For prisoners who declined the commutation from death to transportation, see E. I. McCormack, *White Servitude in Maryland, 1634–1820* (Baltimore: Johns Hopkins University Press, 1904), 98. For a more typical petition, see Vincent T. Harlow, *A History of Barbados* (Oxford: Clarendon Press, 1926), 299.

14. Servants were flogged if the authorities found their complaints of ill-treatment insubstantial. Harlow, *History of Barbados,* 295–96 (quote), 302–5; Ames, *Studies of the Virginia Eastern Shore,* 86; Abbot Emerson Smith, *Colonists in Bondage: White Servitude in America, 1607–1776* (1947; New York: Norton, 1971), 255–56, 259, 265, 270; Galenson, *White Servitude in Colonial America,* 8–9, 145.

15. William Hand Browne et al., eds., *Archives of Maryland,* 72 vols. (Baltimore: Maryland Historical Society, 1883–), 1:72, 107. In other colonies laws were similar. See Force, *Tracts,* vol. 3, no. 2, p. 16; Lefroy, *Memorials of the Discovery,* 1:130.

16. Hening, *Statutes,* 2:299.

17. Lefroy, *Memorials of the Discovery,* 2:159–60; Aubrey Gwynn, "Documents Relating to the Irish in the West Indies," *Analecta Hibernica* (October 1932): 234; Browne et al., *Archives of Maryland,* 23:498–99.

18. Decades later, in 1677, Virginia lawmakers, concerned by the failing supply of white servants and wishing to make the colony more attractive to immigrants, passed a measure invalidating indentures signed while a previous one was still in force. The stated aim of this law was to prevent servants' being pressured into negotiating a new term while still subject to coercion by their masters. See Hening, *Statutes,* 2:388. The harsh legal codes of the colonies

must have functioned to extend the terms of servants. Ibid., 1:320; Thomas Dale et al., *Articles, Lawes, and Orders, Divine, Politique, and Martiall* (Force, *Tracts*, vol. 3, no. 2), esp. 10–16; Hilary McD. Beckles, *White Servitude and Black Slavery in Barbados, 1627–1715* (Knoxville: University of Tennessee Press, 1989), 80–83.

19. There "was never any such thing as perpetual slavery for any white man in any English colony," says Smith, *Colonists in Bondage*, 171. Jordan adds that no European servants, "no matter how miserably treated, served for life in the colonies, though of course many died before their term ended." Winthrop D. Jordan, *White over Black: American Attitudes toward the Negro, 1550–1820* (Chapel Hill: University of North Carolina Press, 1968), 63. During early colonization not all servants surviving their terms went free. Some had their terms continued for infractions of Dale's laws in Virginia or the code of Ecclesiastical Discipline in Bermuda. See above, n. 17. Others appear to have been coerced into accepting end-to-end terms.

20. William Bullock, *Virginia Impartially Examined . . .* (London: Whaley, 1649), 13–14; Smith, *Colonists in Bondage*, 10, 57–58; Galenson, *White Servitude in Colonial America*, 145; Peter H. Wood, *Black Majority: Negroes in Colonial South Carolina, 1670 through the Stono Rebellion* (New York: Norton, 1975), 40; James Curtis Ballagh, *White Servitude in the Colony of Virginia: A Study of the System of Indentured Labor in the American Colonies* (Baltimore: Johns Hopkins University Press, 1895), 91–92.

21. John P. Prendergast, *The Cromwellian Settlement of Ireland* ([c. 1865]; Dublin: Mellifont Press, 1922), 89–93; Patrick Francis Moran, *Historical Sketch of the Persecutions suffered by the Catholics of Ireland under the rule of Cromwell and the Puritans* (Dublin: M. H. Gill and Son, 1907), 341 (Grace quote), and see also Moran's chapter "Irish Exported as Slaves," 341–63. A Protestant minister who visited the West Indies was also shocked by the trade in servants and evidence of "spiriting." See Godwyn, *Negro and Indians Advocate*, 170–71. A recent study has found that from 1641 to 1654, war, famine, plague, and "transportation" reduced the population of Ireland by about 40 percent. See James Scott Wheeler, *Cromwell in Ireland* (New York: St. Martin's, 1999), 224–25.

22. Bullock, *Virginia Impartially Examined*, 14, 47; Lefroy, *Memorials of the Discovery*, 1:133; W. N. Sainsbury, "Kidnapping Maidens to Be Sold in Virginia, 1618," *Virginia Magazine of History and Biography* 6 (1898): 228–30. To be kidnapped for plantation labor was to be "Barbadosed." Alison Games, *Migration and the Origins of the Atlantic World* (Cambridge, Mass.: Harvard University Press, 1999), 77.

23. *Middlesex Records*, 3:259; see also 181–82, 254–55. A "setter" was a decoy or lure, who, by means of "sweetmeats" or some other attraction, persuaded children or young people to enter a house where they would be seized by "crimps," who cropped their hair or otherwise changed their appearance and held them prisoners until they could be sold to plantation agents. See Philip Alexander Bruce, *Economic History of Virginia in the Seventeenth Century*, 2 vols. (New York: P. Smith, 1935), 1:613–16.

24. Wrigley and Schofield, *Population History of England* 161–62, 402–3, 408, 418; John J. McClusker and Russell R. Menard, *The Economy of British America, 1607–1789* (Chapel Hill: University of North Carolina Press, 1985), 135; Leslie A. Clarkson, *The Pre-Industrial Economy in England* (New York: Schocken, [1972]), 48; B. A. Holderness, *Pre-Industrial England: Economy and Society, 1500–1750* (London: Dent, 1976), 9; Kristof Glamann, "European Trade, 1500–1750," in *The Fontana Economic History of Europe*, ed. Carlo M. Cipolla, vol. 2: *The Sixteenth and Seventeenth Centuries* (London: Collins, 1974), 431, 463; T. S. Ashton,

An Economic History of England: The Eighteenth Century (London: Methuen, 1966), 49–50; Ann Kussmaul, *A General View of the Rural Economy of England, 1538–1840* (Cambridge: Cambridge University Press, 1990), 174. Brian Fagan sees the beginnings of the agricultural revolution earlier, when farmers began gradually adapting to a cooler weather cycle by growing more forage and root crops. See his *The Long Summer: How Climate Changed Civilization* (New York: Basic Books, 2004), 248–50.

25. Ralph Davis, *A Commercial Revolution* (London: Historical Association, 1967), 7–8, 10–11; Maurice Dobb, *Studies in the Development of Capitalism* (New York: International Publishers, 1963), 146–47; J. H. Parry, "Transport and Trade Routes," in *The Economy of Expanding Europe in the Sixteenth and Seventeenth Centuries*, ed. E. E. Rich and C. H. Wilson, vol. 4 of *The Cambridge Economic History of Europe*, ed. M. Postan and H. J. Halakkak (Cambridge: Cambridge University Press, 1967), 206; Ralph Davis, *The Rise of the English Shipping Industry* (London: Macmillan, 1962), 15–20, 389–99; Holderness, *Pre-Industrial England*, 125–27; Charles Henry Wilson, *England's Apprenticeship, 1603–1763* (London: Longmans, 1965), 169.

26. Davis, *Commercial Revolution*, 10–11; Holderness, *Pre-Industrial England*, 125–27; and Wilson, *England's Apprenticeship*, 169.

27. J. H. Plumb, *The Growth of Political Stability: England, 1675–1725* (London: Macmillan, 1967); and Christopher Hill, *Reformation to the Industrial Revolution: The Making of Modern English Society*, vol. 1: *1530–1780* (New York: Pantheon, 1967), 173–83. Circumstances especially favorable to investment in Britain, and which attracted capital not only from Holland but also from all over Europe, were a stable, essentially one-party, business-oriented government; relative immunity from the disruptions of European armies; and a labor force comparable in skill to that of the Dutch but paid about 16 percent less. See Immanuel Wallerstein, *The Modern World-System*, vol. 2: *Mercantilism and the Consolidation of the European World-Economy, 1600–1750* (New York: Academic Press, 1980), 92, 111, 250–51, 268–69, 280–81; and Eveline Cruickshanks, *The Glorious Revolution* (London: MacMillan, 2000), 75–79. The tax rates in England were only about half those in Holland. See Jan de Vries and Ad van der Woude, *The First Modern Economy: Success, Failure, and Perseverance of the Dutch Economy, 1500–1815* (Cambridge: Cambridge University Press, 1997), 111, 141.

28. Wilson, *England's Apprenticeship*, 136; Ephraim Lipson, *The Economic History of England*, vols. 2–3: *The Age of Mercantilism* (London: A. and C. Black, 1956), 3:426–27; B. H. Slicher van Bath, *Agrarian History of Western Europe, A.D. 500–1850* (New York: St. Martin's, 1963), 327; Clarkson, *Pre-Industrial Economy in England*, 218; Holderness, *Pre-Industrial England*, 204; Wrigley and Schofield, *Population History of England*, 418.

29. Eli F. Heckscher, *Mercantilism*, trans. Mendel Shapiro, 2 vols. (1931; 2d ed. rev., New York: Macmillan, 1955), 2:158.

30. Quoted in Galenson, *White Servitude in Colonial America*, 189.

31. J. C. Jeaffreson, ed., *A Young Squire of the Seventeenth Century: From the Papers (1676–86) of Christopher Jeaffreson*, 2 vols. (London: Hurst and Blackett, 1878), 1:317–18. See also ibid., 2:5–6; Galenson, *White Servitude in Colonial America*, 154.

32. Hening, *Statutes*, 2:388. See also Browne et al., *Archives of Maryland*, 1:533–34; Catterall, *Judicial Cases Concerning American Slavery and the Negro*, vol. 4: *New England, the Middle States, and the District of Columbia*, 2, 49.

33. Gemery, "Emigration from the British Isles to the New World," 215. See also Dunn,

Sugar and Slaves, 70; Wood, *Black Majority,* 40–41. According to Russell Menard, "Chesapeake planters did not abandon indentured servitude, it abandoned them." Russell Robert Menard, "From Servants to Slaves: The Transformation of the Chesapeake Labor System," *Southern Studies* 16 (1977): 389; see also, 363, 371, 375–77 n. 36, 379, 355–90.

34. For the bad reputation the colonial labor system had in the British Isles, see Smith, *Colonists in Bondage,* 10; Wood, *Black Majority,* 40. On the declining supply of servants, see Ballagh, *White Servitude in the Colony of Virginia,* 91–92.

35. Philip D. Curtin, *The Atlantic Slave Trade: A Census* (Madison: University of Wisconsin Press, 1969), 119.

36. Ibid.; Hening, *Statutes,* 2:515; Elizabeth Donnan, ed., *Documents Illustrative of the History of the Slave Trade,* 4 vols. (1932; New York: Octagon, 1965), 3:2, 4:89.

37. Donnan, *Documents Illustrative of the Slave Trade,* 1:250, 445.

38. For authors who suggest psychological and cultural causes for racial stratification, see Carl N. Degler, *Neither Black nor White: Slavery and Race Relations in Brazil and the United States* (New York: Macmillan, 1971), 208; Jordan, *White over Black,* 7, 23. On narcissism as a cause, and the theory of "somatic norm image," see Harry Hoetink, *The Two Variants in Caribbean Race Relations: A Contribution to the Sociology of Segmented Societies,* trans. Eva M. Hooykaas (New York: Oxford University Press, 1967), 121, 120–60.

39. Donnan, *Documents Illustrative of the Slave Trade,* 1:125 n. 2. On the Dutch move from Brazil to the Caribbean, see de Vies and van der Woude, *First Modern Economy,* 400–404. See also Noel Deerr, *A History of Sugar,* 2 vols. (London: Chapman and Hall, 1949), 1:106–10, 160–63, 208. Also Richard Vines to John Winthrop, July 19, 1647, in *Winthrop Papers,* ed. Arthur Meier Schlesinger et al., vol. 5: *1645–1649* (Boston: Massachusetts Historical Society, 1947), 172.

40. Donnan, *Documents Illustrative of the Slave Trade,* 1:17, 105; Curtin, *Atlantic Slave Trade,* 116–19; James A. Rawley, *The Transatlantic Slave Trade: A History* (New York: Norton, 1981), 84–85.

41. Stanley L. Engerman, "The Slave Trade and British Capital Formation: A Comment on the Williams Thesis," *Business History Review* 46 (Winter 1972): 438.

42. Donnan, *Documents Illustrative of the Slave Trade,* 1:73, 111–12, 136 n. 6, 377–84, 410–13, 421–29, 445; 3:8–16. See also Curtin, *Atlantic Slave Trade,* 117. On the emergence of England as the leading slave trading nation, see Rawley, *Transatlantic Slave Trade,* 149.

43. On the growing economic advantage to planters in buying slaves over servants, see Governor Charles Calvert to Lord Baltimore, April 27, 1664, in *The Calvert Papers,* Peabody Fund Publication 28 (Baltimore: Maryland Historical Society, 1889), 249; Galenson, *White Servitude in Colonial America,* 119.

44. C. F. Boxer, *Women in Iberian Expansion Overseas, 1415–1815* (New York: Oxford University Press, 1975), 57, 136; A. J. R. Russell-Wood, *Fidalgos and Philanthropists: The Santa Casa da Misericordia of Bahia, 1550–1755* (Berkeley: University of California Press, 1968), 136–39, 143; Magnus Mörner, *Race Mixture in the History of Latin America* (Boston: Little, Brown, 1967), 44. For a general survey of development and disintegration of the system of racial castas in Latin America, see Ángel Rosenblat, *La población indígena y el mestizaje en América,* vol. 2: *El mestizaje de las castas coloniales* (Buenos Aires: Editorial Nova, 1954). For the process in Mexico, see Gonzalo Aguirre Beltrán, *La población negra de México* (Mexico City: Fonde de Cultura Económica, 1972), 85, 104–5, 154, 172–73. See also William L. Sher-

man's chapter "Indian Women and the Spaniards," in his *Forced Labor in Sixteenth-Century Central America* (Lincoln: University of Nebraska Press, 1979), 304–27.

45. While immigration had a high ratio of men to women even in the English colonies, women were less likely to remain unattached and hence had more children than those in Europe. As Adam Smith observed, "A young widow with four or five young children who, among the middling or inferior ranks of people in Europe, would have so little chance for a second husband, is [in America] frequently counted as a sort of fortune." Smith, *Wealth of Nations* (New York: Modern Library, [c. 1937]), 71. For the ratio of men to women, see Morgan, *American Slavery, American Freedom*, 310, 336; Herbert Moller, "Sex Composition and Correlated Cultural Patterns of Colonial America," *William and Mary Quarterly*, 3rd ser., 2 (April 1945): 114, 118–20, 128; Rawley, *Transatlantic Slave Trade*, 157.

46. Gemery, "Emigration from the British Isles to the New World," 189; Morgan, *American Slavery, American Freedom*, 180–84; Allan Kulikoff, *Tobacco and Slaves: The Development of Southern Cultures in the Chesapeake, 1680–1800* (Chapel Hill: University of North Carolina Press, 1986), 60–63.

47. Virginia DeJohn Anderson, "Animals in the Wilderness: The Development of Livestock Husbandry in the Seventeenth-Century Chesapeake," *William and Mary Quarterly*, 3rd ser., 59 (April 2002): 382, 387.

48. Smith, *Wealth of Nations*, 532. An observer in Pennsylvania claimed, "Poor People (both men and women) of all kinds, can here get three times the Wages for their Labour they can get in *England* or *Wales*." Gabriel Thomas, *An Historical and Geographical Account of the Province and Country of Pennsylvania and of West-New Jersey in America* (London: A. Baldwin, 1698), 28.

Chapter 3: The Construction of Planter Hegemony, 1676–1776

1. *The Republic* 9.578E (Loeb Library: *Plato The Republic*, trans. Paul Shorey, vol. 2 [Cambridge, Mass.: Harvard University Press, 1935]), 362–63.

2. George Fitzhugh, *Sociology for the South, or the Failure of Free Society* (New York: Burt Franklin, [1854]), 144.

3. C. Vann Woodward and Elizabeth Muhlenfeld, eds., *The Private Mary Chestnut: The Unpublished War Diaries* (New York: Oxford University Press, 1984), 41.

4. Drew Gilpin Faust, *James Henry Hammond and the Old South: A Design for Mastery* (Baton Rouge: Louisiana State University Press, 1982), 314–17; Orville Vernon Burton, *In My Father's House Are Many Mansions: Family and Community in Edgefield, South Carolina* (Chapel Hill: University of North Carolina Press, 1985), 186–87; Carol Bleser, *The Hammonds of Redcliffe* (New York: Oxford University Press, 1988), 10–11. Not all women of the planter class complied. Sarah and Angelina Grimké became abolitionists.

5. Antonio Gramsci, *Selections from the Prison Notebooks of Antonio Gramsci*, ed. and trans. Quintin Hoare and Geoffrey Nowell Smith (New York: International Publishers, 1971), 57–58; Roger Simon, *Gramsci's Political Thought: An Introduction* (London: Lawrence and Wishart, 1982), 22–23. On the way hegemonic power shapes a legal system, see Eugene D. Genovese, *Roll Jordan Roll: The World the Slaves Made* (New York: Random House, 1974), 26–27.

6. Edmund S. Morgan, *American Slavery, American Freedom: The Ordeal of Colonial Virginia* (New York: Norton, 1975), 346.

7. On a father's desire for his son to have "fresh land," see W. G. Standard, ed., "Abstracts of Rappahanock Co. Wills," *Virginia Magazine of History and Biography* 5 (1897–98): 285. See also Avery Odelle Craven, *Soil Exhaustion as a Factor in the Agricultural History of Virginia and Maryland, 1606–1860*, University of Illinois Studies in the Social Sciences 13, no. 1 (Urbana, [c. 1926]), 30–36, 56–57; Lewis Cecil Gray, *History of Agriculture in the Southern United States to 1860*, 2 vols. (Washington, D.C.: Carnegie Institution of Washington, 1933), 1:85.

8. Alexander Brown, *The Genesis of the United States*, 2 vols. (1890; New York: Russell and Russell, 1964), 1:481; Louis B. Wright, ed., *The Prose Works of William Byrd of Westover: Narratives of a Colonial Virginian* (Cambridge, Mass.: Harvard University Press, 1966), 184; John Lawson, *A New Voyage to Carolina* (London: n.p., 1709), 62–63, 79–80; Virginia DeJohn Anderson, "Animals in the Wilderness: The Development of Livestock Husbandry in the Seventeenth-Century Chesapeake," *William and Mary Quarterly*, 3rd ser., 59 (April 2002): 390.

9. Robert Beverly, *The History and Present State of Virginia*, ed. Louis B. Wright (1705; Chapel Hill: University of North Carolina Press, 1947), 318. As early as the 1630s, livestock and meat were exported from Virginia. See Alexander Bruce, *Economic History of Virginia in the Seventeenth Century*, 2 vols. (New York: Macmillan, 1895), 1:311. See also "A Perfect Description of Virginia," in Peter Force, *Tracts*, vol. 2, no. 8, p. 3. For the pioneer South's moment of herding prosperity, see J. F. H. Claiborne, "A Trip through the Piney Woods," *Publications of the Mississippi Historical Society* 9 (1906): 530.

10. Allan Kulikoff, *Tobacco and Slaves: The Development of Southern Cultures in the Chesapeake, 1680–1800* (Chapel Hill: University of North Carolina Press, 1984), 59–61. Winter forage was more precarious in Maryland. See Gloria Main, *Tobacco Colony: Life in Early Maryland, 1650–1720* (Princeton: Princeton University Press, 1982), 64. On the vast acreage required for open-range herding, see John Solomon Otto, "The Migration of the Southern Plain Folk: An Interdisciplinary Synthesis," *Journal of Southern History* 51 (May 1985): 191.

11. See Virginia's trespass law of 1662, in *The Statutes of Virginia . . .* , ed. William W. Hening, 13 vols. (Richmond: Samuel Pleasants, 1809–23) 2:96–97. Also see Maryland's 1674 "Act against the burners of fences," in *Archives of Maryland*, ed. William Hand Browne et al., 72 vols. (Baltimore: Maryland Historical Society, 1883–), 2:398–99.

12. Bernard Bailyn, "Politics and Social Structure in Virginia," *Seventeenth-Century America: Essays in Colonial History*, ed. James Morton Smith (Chapel Hill: University of North Carolina Press, 1959), 100–102.

13. Berkeley to "Mr. Secretary" [Thomas Ludwell], July 1676, in Henry Coventry Papers at Longleat, estate of the Marquis of Bath, vol. 77, fol. 145 (Microfilm, Library of Congress), as quoted in T. H. Breen, "A Changing Labor Force and Race Relations in Virginia, 1660–1710," *Journal of Social History* (Fall 1973): 4, 24 n 3.

14. See, for example, Hening, *Statutes*, 2:138–43.

15. On the numerous tenants and poor settlers in Maryland, see Aubrey C. Land, "Economic Base and Social Structure: The Northern Chesapeake in the Eighteenth Century," *Journal of Economic History* 25 (1965): 642, 648.

16. On the economy of Indians, see Charles Hudson, *The Southeastern Indians* (Knoxville: University of Tennessee Press, 1976), 289–90. See also "An Act Concerning Indians who keep hoggs . . . ," in Hening, *Statutes*, 2:316–17. Often, however, Indians appear to have treated wild livestock as game, like deer. See Browne et al., *Archives of Maryland*, 13:479.

17. Indian leaders protested these damages to the Council of Maryland. See Browne et

al., *Archives of Maryland*, 5:479–80. Even when the Indians built fences, settlers sometimes destroyed them. Ibid., 5:493. See also Gary B. Nash, *Red, White, and Black: The Peoples of Early America* (Englewood Cliffs, N.J.: Prentice-Hall, 1974), 129, 133.

18. Charles M. Andrews, ed., *Narratives of the Insurrections, 1675–1690* (New York: Barnes and Noble, 1915), 109.

19. For a study sympathetic to Berkeley, see Wilcomb E. Washburn, *The Governor and the Rebel: A History of Bacon's Rebellion in Virginia* (Chapel Hill: University of North Carolina Press, 1957); and, for one sympathetic to Bacon, see Thomas Jefferson Wertenbaker, *Torchbearer of the Revolution: The Story of Bacon's Rebellion and Its Leader* (Princeton: Princeton University Press, 1940).

20. See "Isle of Wight Grievances," in *English Historical Documents*, ed. David C. Douglas, vol. 9: *English Historical Documents, American Colonial Documents to 1776*, ed. Merrill Jensen (New York: Oxford University Press, 1969), 589–90. See also Stephen Saunders Webb, *1676: The End of American Independence* (New York: Knopf, 1984), 19; Kathleen M. Brown, *Good Wives, Nasty Wenches, and Anxious Patriarchs: Gender, Race, and Power in Colonial Virginia* (Chapel Hill: University of North Carolina Press, 1996), 154–55; Andrews, *Narratives of the Insurrections*, 108, 112; Warren M. Billings, *Sir William Berkeley and the Forging of Colonial Virginia* (Baton Rouge: Louisiana State University Press, 2004), 230–31; Morgan, *American Slavery, American Freedom*, 208.

21. Billings, *Sir William Berkeley*, 245. When the tide turned against the rebels some of the last-minute converts again switched sides to become "the most vindictive of loyalists." See Webb, *1676*, 41–42, 140–41.

22. People asked, "how shall wee know our enemyes from our Friends, are not the Indians all of a colour." Andrews, *Narratives of the Insurrections*, 112.

23. Browne et al., *Archives of Maryland*, 3:104, 13:479.

24. Nash, *Red, White, and Black*, 65.

25. Webb, *1676*, 18.

26. Billings, *Sir William Berkeley*, 236.

27. Morgan, *American Slavery, American Freedom*, 331.

28. Darrett and Anita H. Rutman, "Now-wives and Sons-in-law: Parental Death in a Seventeenth-Century Virginia County," in *The Chesapeake in the Seventeenth Century*, ed. Thad W. Tate and David L. Ammerman (Chapel Hill: University of North Carolina Press, 1979), 173.

29. Fithian, *Journal and Letters of Philip Vickers Fithian, 1773–1774: A Plantation Tutor of the Old Dominion*, ed. Hunter Dickinson Farish (Williamsburg, Va.: Colonial Williamsburg, Inc., 1943), 100.

30. Bertram Wyatt-Brown, *Southern Honor: Ethics and Behavior in the Old South* (New York: Oxford University Press, 1982), 185.

31. Carl Bridenbaugh, *Cities in Revolt: Urban Life in America, 1743–1776* (New York: Knopf, 1955), 216–17; Kulikoff, *Tobacco and Slaves*, 126–27.

32. Bruce, *Economic History*, 1:446.

33. Land, "Economic Base and Social Structure," 649, see also 639–54.

34. William Byrd II, for example, claimed that he had "every soart of trade amongst my own servants, so that I live in a kind of independence on every one, but Providence." Byrd to the Earl of Orrery, July 5, 1726, in *The Correspondence of Three William Byrds of Westover,*

Virginia, 1684–1776, ed. Marion Tinling, 2 vols. (Charlottesville: University of Virginia Press, 1977), 1:355. See also Edmund S. Morgan, *Virginians at Home: Family Life in the Eighteenth Century* (Williamsburg, Va.: Colonial Williamsburg Foundation, 1952), 53–54. A *South Carolina Gazette* survey, 1732–76, found slaves working in twenty-eight skilled trades. See Marcus Wilson Jernegan, *Laboring and Dependent Classes in Colonial America, 1607–1783* (New York: Frederick Ungar, 1931), 13.

35. It was not easy for poor people to dress in a proper European, "Christian" way, but to do so projected a strong sense of respectability. See Main, *Tobacco Colony,* 184; and on the inability of farm families to master skilled crafts, ibid., 175, 181–84.

36. T. H. Breen, *Tobacco Culture: The Mentality of Great Tidewater Planters on the Eve of Revolution* (Princeton: Princeton University Press, 1985), xii–xiv, 23, 29–32, 93–106, 118, 125, 133–41, 162–69, 193–203; see esp. 95–97.

37. William Byrd II to the Earl of Egmont, July 12, 1736, in Tinling, *Correspondence of the Three William Byrds,* 2:488. The Great Dismal Swamp, spanning the Virginia–North Carolina border, was a more frequent destination for escaped slaves. See Sally E. Hadden, *Slave Patrols: Law and Violence in Virginia and the Carolinas* (Cambridge, Mass.: Harvard University Press, 2001), 139–43, esp. 142.

38. On the rations of slaves, see Fithian, *Journal and Letters,* 51. On slave seizures of livestock, see Kulikoff, *Tobacco and Slaves,* 340; Robert Russell, *North America: Its Agriculture and Climate* (Edinburgh: A. and C. Black, 1857), 265.

39. Edmund S. Morgan, *Inventing the People: The Rise of Popular Sovereignty in England and America* (New York: Norton, 1988), 171.

40. Ibid., 169–73. See also James C. Bonner, "The Historical Basis of Southern Military Tradition," *Georgia Review* 9 (Spring 1955): 84. On southern military customs, see also Merton Dillon, s.v. "Patrols, Slave," in *Dictionary of Afro-American Slavery,* ed. Randall M. Miller and John David Smith (New York: Greenwood, 1988).

41. On Anglican orientation toward the gentry, see Fithian, *Journal and Letters,* 38. On control of these churches by aristocratic vestries, which were in fact hereditary, see Wesley M. Gewehr, *The Great Awakening in Virginia, 1740–1790* (Durham: Duke University Press, 1930), 31–33.

42. Quoted in Gewehr, *Great Awakening,* 240.

43. Quoted in Rhys Isaac, *The Transformation of Virginia, 1740–1790* (Chapel Hill: University of North Carolina Press, 1982), 162. For the unsuccessful challenge to slavery within the southern churches, see Donald G. Mathews, *Religion in the Old South* (Chicago: University of Chicago Press, 1977), 136–84.

44. Rev. Thomas Bacon, *Four Sermons, Preached at the Parish Church of St. Peter, in Talbot County, Maryland* (London: John Oliver, 1753), 18–19, 30.

45. Sydney V. James, *A People among Peoples: Quaker Benevolence in Eighteenth Century America* (Cambridge, Mass.: Harvard University Press, 1963), 230–33. For Methodism's early opposition, later temporizing, and final acquiescence on the slavery question, see Richard M. Cameron, "The New Church Takes Root," in *The History of American Methodism,* ed. Emory Stevens Bucke et al., 3 vols. (New York: Abington Press, 1964), 1:251–56.

46. "Class conflict between men of standing and ordinary planters lasted nearly a half century, until gentlemen finally attained a complete victory." Kulikoff, *Tobacco and Slaves,* 79. Other scholars equate the right to vote with political power. See Fletcher M. Green, *Con-*

stitutional Developments in the South Atlantic States, 1776–1860 (Chapel Hill: University of North Carolina Press, 1930), esp. 296–304; and idem, *Democracy in the Old South and Other Essays,* ed. J. Isaac Copeland (Nashville: Vanderbilt University Press, 1969), 65–110; Frank Lawrence Owsley, *Plain Folk of the Old South* (1949; Chicago: Quadrangle Books, 1965), 139; Robert E. and B. Katherine Brown, *Virginia, 1705–1786: Democracy or Aristocracy?* (East Lansing: Michigan State University Press, 1964), 239.

47. Adam Smith, *Wealth of Nations* (New York: Modern Library, [c. 1937]), 674.

48. William Byrd II to Earl of Egmont, July 12, 1736, in Tinling, *Correspondence of the Three William Byrds,* 2:488; William McKee Evans, "From the Land of Canaan to the Land of Guinea: The Strange Odyssey of the 'Sons of Ham,'" *American Historical Review* 85 (February 1980): 42.

49. Quoted in E. B. Washburne, *Sketch of Edward Coles, Second Governor of Illinois and the Slavery Struggle of 1823–24* (1882; New York: Negro Universities Press, 1969), 69.

Chapter 4: The Era of the American Revolution

1. For Johnson quote, see *The Political Writings of Dr. Johnson,* ed. J. P. Hardy (New York: Barnes and Noble, 1968), 132.

2. Compare with Galatians 3:26–28. Even earlier philosophers held that freedom was humankind's natural condition. See Eric Robertson Dodd, *The Ancient Concept of Progress and other Essays on Greek Literature and Belief* (Oxford: Clarendon Press, 1973), 101. Such ideas were central to early Christianity; see Orlando Patterson, *Freedom,* vol. 1: *Freedom in the Making of Western Culture* (New York: Basic Books, 1991), 323.

3. Robert Vaux, *Memoirs of the Lives of Benjamin Lay and Ralph Sandiford* (Philadelphia: Solomon W. Conrad, 1815), 24 (quote), 20–21, 23–24; C. Brightwer Roundtree, "Benjamin Lay (1681–1759)," *Journal of the Friends Historical Society* 33 (1936): 4, 12; David Brion Davis, *The Problem of Slavery in Western Culture* (Ithaca: Cornell University Press, 1966), 321–22, 324. On early antislavery Quakers, see also Thomas E. Drake's chapter "Voices Crying in the Wilderness," in his *Quakers and Slavery in America* (New Haven: Yale University Press, 1950), 34–47.

4. John the Baptist was an Essene, a rare group in antiquity who questioned slavery. On the Essenes and other ancient critics, see Patterson, *Freedom,* 1:152–53, 321, 430, and n. 31.

5. It is well known that Quakers played a central role in the movement against slavery. Less well known is that they played a central role in the Industrial Revolution. See Arthur Raistrick, *Quakers in Science and Industry . . . during the 17th and 18th Centuries* (London: Bannisdale Press, 1950). See also David Brion Davis, *The Problem of Slavery in the Age of Revolution* (Ithaca: Cornell University Press, 1975), 233; Paul Mantoux, *The Industrial Revolution in the Eighteenth Century: An Outline of the Beginnings of the Modern Factory System in England,* trans. Marjorie Vernon (1928; Chicago: University of Chicago Press, 1983), 465.

6. The Enlightenment awoke a dilemma: if human beings have "natural rights," what about slaves? Thinkers responded to this question in opposite ways: Benjamin Franklin said slavery was wrong; David Hume said slaves, being blacks, were intrinsically inferior. Jefferson said both things. For a sorting out of Jefferson's contradictory ideas, see Davis, *Problem of Slavery in the Age of Revolution,* 171–84; John Chester Miller, *The Wolf by the Ears: Thomas Jefferson and Slavery* (New York: Free Press, 1977).

7. This interpretation was fundamental to the thought of George Fox, the founder of the Quaker movement. See Rachel Hadley King, *George Fox and the Light Within* (Philadelphia: Friends Book Store, 1940), 58–59, 78, 84.

8. Mary Stoughton Locke, *Anti-Slavery in America from the Introduction of African Slaves to the Prohibition of the Slave Trade (1619–1808)* (1901; Gloucester, Mass.: Peter Smith, 1965), 36–37.

9. Ibid., 40–45; Donald G. Mathews, *Religion in the Old South* (Chicago: University of Chicago Press, 1977), 68–80. On the collapse of Methodist antislavery rules in Virginia, see Arthur Zilversmit, *The First Emancipation: The Abolition of Slavery in the North* (Chicago: University of Chicago Press, 1967), 155.

10. Jean R. Soderlund, *Quakers and Slavery: A Divided Spirit* (Princeton: Princeton University Press, 1985), 63–64, 70. At times Friends even disciplined critics of slavery. See Drake, *Quakers and Slavery,* 34.

11. King, *George Fox and the Light Within,* 30, 37, 42, 58–59, 61, 78; Frederick B. Tolles, *Meeting House and Counting House: The Quaker Merchants of Colonial Philadelphia* (Chapel Hill: University of North Carolina Press, 1948), 6.

12. On the paradox of the Quakers, the upward mobility of the persecuted and the private success of those concerned with public benevolence, see Raistrick, *Quakers in Science and Industry,* esp. 32–33, 42, 46–48.

13. On Quaker slaveholding in the mid-1700s, see Adolph B. Benson, ed., *The America of 1750: Peter Kalm's Travels in North America,* vol. 1 (New York: Dover, 1964): 106; Darold D. Wax, "Quaker Merchants and the Slave Trade in Colonial Pennsylvania," *Pennsylvania Magazine of History and Biography* 86 (1962): 145. On the influence of the slaveholding wealthy, see Soderland, *Quakers and Slavery,* 32–36, 43.

14. Lawrence Henry Gipson, *The British Empire before the American Revolution,* vol. 6: *The Great War for Empire: The Years of Defeat, 1754–1757,* vol. 7: *The Great War for Empire: The Victorious Years, 1758–1760* (New York: Knopf, 1959), 6:92–96, 7:46–48. On the furious backlash against Quakers and Catholics following Braddock's defeat, see Jack D. Marietta, *The Reformation of American Quakerism, 1748–1783* (Philadelphia: University of Pennsylvania Press, 1984), 150–51.

15. Gipson, *British Empire,* 7:52 n. 9.

16. *Pennsylvania Archives,* 8th ser., ed. Gertrude MacKinney et al., 8 vols. (n.p.: Bureau of Publications, 1931–35), 5:4245–46. On the tendency of the Indians to spare Quaker settlements, see Rayner-Wickenham Kelsey, *Friends and the Indians, 1655–1917* (Philadelphia: Friends on Indian Affairs, 1917), 75–76.

17. Soderlund, *Quakers and Slavery,* 43–46; Davis, *Problem of Slavery in Western Culture,* 330–31.

18. Abolition always had a class dimension, the temptation to invest in plantation commerce and African labor being greatest among those who could afford it. In Germantown, Pennsylvania, in 1688, a group of farmers and linen weavers declared: "we are against the traffick of mens-body. . . . we shall doe to all men, licke as we will be done ourselves: macking no difference of what generation, descent, or Colour they are. . . . In Europe there are many oppressed for Conscience sake; and here there are those oppressed wch are of a black Colour. . . . What thing in the world can be done worse towarts us then if men should robb or steal us away & sell us for slaves to strange Countries, separating housband from their wife

& children. . . . we who profess that it is not lawfull to steal, must lickewise avoid to purchase such things as are stolen, . . . If once these slaves (wch they say are so wicked and stubbern men) should joint themselves, fight for their freedom . . . ; will these masters and mastrisses tacke the sword at hand & warr against these poor slaves, . . . ? Or have these negers not as much right to fight for their freedom, as you have to keep them slaves?" Untitled document identified as a "protest" on April 18, 1688, entered by the "linen weavers and husbandmen of Germantown," listed by name, to the Quaker meeting of Philadelphia, quoted in *Pennsylvania Magazine of History and Biography* 4 (1880): 28–30.

19. By a curious irony, wars forced Quakers out of the slave-sugar-rum business just as this trade began to stagnate. They then began production of lumber, paper, glass, textiles, and iron just as these industries reached a takeoff point. See Tolles, *Meeting House and Counting House,* 97–100.

20. Raistrick, *Quakers in Science and Industry,* 32; Marietta, *Reformation of American Quakerism.*

21. Selwyn H. H. Carrington, *The Sugar Industry and the Abolition of the Slave Trade* (Gainesville: University Press of Florida, 2002), 5.

22. Allan Kulikoff, *Tobacco and Slaves: The Development of Southern Cultures in the Chesapeake, 1680–1800* (Chapel Hill: University of North Carolina Press, 1986), 73; Robert William Fogel and Stanley L. Engerman, *Time on the Cross: The Economics of American Negro Slavery,* 2 vols. (Boston: Little, Brown, 1974), 1:27–29.

23. *Virginia Historical Society Collections,* new ser., vol. 6: *Miscellaneous Papers, 1672–1865* (Richmond, Va.: Published by the Society, 1887), 14. On the cruelties of the interstate slave trade, see Walter Johnson, *Soul by Soul: Life inside the Antebellum Slave Market* (Cambridge, Mass.: Harvard University Press, 1999), esp. 34–37. Also Steven Deyle, *Carry Me Back: The Domestic Slave Trade in American Life* (New York: Oxford University Press, 2005), 16–20.

24. Elizabeth Donnan, ed., *Documents Illustrative of the History of the Slave Trade to America,* vol. 3: *New England the Middle Colonies* (1932; New York: Octagon, 1965), 186; H. J. Cadbury, "Another Early Quaker Anti-Slavery Document," *Journal of Negro History* 27 (1942): 211.

25. Leonard Woods Laboree, *Royal Government in America* (New York: Frederick Ungar, 1958), 62–63, 169–70, 227–28 n. 12; W. E. B. DuBois, *The Suppression of the African Slave Trade to the United States of America, 1638–1870* (c. 1896; New York: Social Science Press, 1954), 7–38.

26. DuBois, *Suppression of the African Slave Trade,* 44–52.

27. Julian P. Boyd et al., eds., *The Papers of Thomas Jefferson,* 24 vols. (Princeton: Princeton University Press, 1950–), 1:426. See also ibid., 1:130, 353, 414.

28. Julian P. Boyd, *The Declaration of Independence: The Evolution of the Text as Shown in Facsimiles of Various Drafts by Its Author, Thomas Jefferson* (Princeton: Princeton University Press, 1945), 20–21, 37.

29. Peter Force, ed., *American Archives: A Documentary History of the English Colonies in North America,* 4th ser., vol. 3 (Washington, D.C.: M. St. Clair Clark and Peter Force, 1840), col. 1385.

30. Benjamin Quarles, *The Negro in the American Revolution* (Chapel Hill: University of North Carolina Press, 1961), 119; James W. St. G. Walker, *The Black Loyalists: The Search for a Promised Land in Nova Scotia and Sierra Leone, 1783–1870* (New York: Africana Publishing Co., 1976), 3.

31. "To the most unobservant field hand it must have been plain that England had not the remotest idea of making the war a general crusade against slavery, especially since so many of her loyalist supporters would have protested bitterly." Quarles, *The Negro in the American Revolution*, 120.

32. Untitled anonymous response to Lord Dunmore's Proclamation, (Williamsburg) *Virginia Gazette* (Purdie), November 24, 1775, 2–3.

33. Quarles, *The Negro in the American Revolution*, 30–31; Gerald Mullins, *Flights and Rebellion Slave Resistance in Eighteenth-Century Virginia* (New York: Oxford University Press, 1972), 131–36.

34. Sally E. Hadden, *Slave Patrols: Law and Violence in Virginia and the Carolinas* (Cambridge, Mass.: Harvard University Press, 2001), 157.

35. Merton L. Dillon, *Slavery Attacked: Southern Slaves and Their Allies, 1619–1865* (Baton Rouge: Louisiana State University Press, 1990), 29–39. On the quick recovery of low-country planters, see Philip D. Morgan, "Black Society in the Lowcountry, 1760–1810," in *Slavery and Freedom in the Age of the American Revolution*, ed. Ira Berlin and Ronald Hoffman (Charlottesville: University of Virginia Press, 1983), 83, 111, 118–19.

36. Avery Odelle Craven, *Soil Exhaustion as a Factor in the Agricultural History of Virginia and Maryland, 1606–1860*, University of Illinois Studies in Social Science 13, no. 1 (Urbana, [c. 1926]), 30–36, 56–57, 160–61; Lewis Cecil Gray, *History of Agriculture in the Southern United States to 1860*, 2 vols. (Washington, D.C.: Carnegie Institution of Washington, 1933), 1:85; Robert Russell, *North America: Its Agriculture and Climate* (Edinburgh: A. and C. Black, 1857), 140–41, 154.

37. Rural New York also practiced mixed farming, and complaints there about slaves were similar. See Shane White, *Somewhat More Independent: The End of Slavery in New York City, 1770–1810* (Athens: University of Georgia Press, 1991), 28–30.

38. On George Washington's efforts to use his slaves productively, see John C. Fitzpatrick, ed., *The Writings of George Washington . . . ,* vol. 32: *March 10, 1792–June 30, 1793* (Washington, D.C.: Government Printing Office, 1939), 179, 203, 215.

39. Quoted in Jonathan D. Martin, *Divided Mastery: Slave Hiring in the American South* (Cambridge, Mass.: Harvard University Press, 2004), 30–31. In the same vein, see Fitzpatrick, *Writings of Washington*, 34:46–47. For a similar view of another large planter, see Marquis de Chastellux, *Travels in North America in the Years 1780, 1781, and 1782*, trans. and ed. Howard C. Rice, vol. 2 (Chapel Hill: University of North Carolina Press, 1963), 431–32.

40. W[illiam] Strickland, *Observations on the Agriculture of the United States of America* (London: W. Bulmer, 1801), 33.

41. Concerning the hopes that Patriots often pinned to the yeomanry, see Thomas Jefferson, *Notes on the State of Virginia*, ed. William Peden (1785; Chapel Hill: University of North Carolina Press, 1955), 164–65.

42. In 1781 twenty of Jefferson's own slaves deserted to the British. See Boyd et al., *Papers of Jefferson*, 6:224. Some of Washington's slaves also escaped. See Chastellux, *Travels*, 2:597–98.

43. Midori Takagi, *Rearing Wolves to Our Own Destruction: Slavery in Richmond, Virginia, 1782–1865* (Charlottesville: University of Virginia Press, 1999), 66.

44. Ira Berlin, *Slaves without Masters: The Free Negro in the Antebellum South* (New York: Vintage, 1976), 138.

45. Michael Tadman, *Speculators and Slaves: Masters, Traders, and Slaves in the Old South* (Madison: University of Wisconsin Press, 1999), 41.

46. As has been the case in other parts of the world, "abolition" has often been conflated with the repeal of laws regulating slavery. See Kevin Bales, *Understanding Global Slavery: A Reader* (Berkeley: University of California Press, 2005), 113.

47. Zilversmit, *First Emancipation;* Berlin, *Slaves without Masters;* Leon F. Litwack, *North of Slavery: The Negro in the Free States, 1790–1860* (Chicago: University of Chicago Press, 1961); Emory G. Evans, ed., "A Question of Complexion: Documents Concerning the Negro and the Franchise in the Eighteenth-Century Virginia," *Virginia Magazine of History and Biography* 71 (1963): 411–15.

48. Robert William Fogel and Stanley L. Engerman, "Philanthropy at Bargain Prices: Notes on the Economics of Gradual Emancipation," *Journal of Legal Studies* 3 (June 1974): 381.

49. Stanislaus Murray Hamilton, ed., *The Writings of James Monroe . . . ,* vol. 3 (New York: G. P. Putman's Sons, 1900), 353. In his worldwide study of slavery over many centuries, Orlando Patterson finds little evidence that emancipation resulted from the altruism of slave owners: "A master class never lost, but invariably gained by the change in status." Patterson, *Slavery and Social Death: A Comparative Study of Slavery* (Cambridge, Mass.: Harvard University Press, 1984), 294. See also Ira Berlin, *Generations of Captivity: A History of African-American Slaves* (Cambridge, Mass.: Harvard University Press, 2003), 35.

50. Gary Nash, *Race and Revolution* (Madison, Wisc.: Madison House, 1990), 30.

51. Berlin, *Generations of Captivity,* 104; *New Jersey Archives,* 3rd ser., Vol. 2: *Laws of the Royal Colony of New Jersey, 1703–1745,* ed. Bernard Bush (Trenton: New Jersey State Library, Archives, and History Bureau, 1977), 136, 140. Compare with *The Statutes at Large of Pennsylvania from 1682 to 1801,* vol. 4: *1724–1744,* ed. James T. Mitchell and Henry Flanders (n.p.: State Printer of Pennsylvania, 1897), 61–62. For a general treatment of the colonial black codes, see William M. Wiecek, "The Statutory Law of Slavery and Race in the Thirteen Mainland Colonies of British America," *William and Mary Quarterly* 3r ser., 34 (1977): 258–80. See also Duncan J. MacLeod, "Toward Caste," in Berlin and Hoffman, *Slavery and Freedom,* 224.

52. Deyle, *Carry Me Back,* 29–30.

53. Orville Vernon Burton, *The Age of Lincoln* (New York: Hill and Wang, 2007), 61.

54. Frederic Bancroft, *Slave-Trading in the Old South* (1931; New York: Ungar, 1959), 21, 27; White, *Somewhat More Independent,* 38, 144–45, 224 n. 33; Berlin, *Slaves without Masters,* 27.

55. Johnson, *Soul by Soul,* photo facing p. 116.

56. Helen Tunicliff Catterall, *Judicial Cases Concerning American Slavery and the Negro,* 5 vols., vol. 4: *New England, the Middle States, and the District of Columbia* (1926; New York: Octagon, 1968), 46, 64, 110, 114, 171, 271, 365, 379, 421, 478; Johnson, *Soul by Soul,* 130–31, and his chapter "Reading Bodies and Marking Race," 135–61.

57. Berlin, *Generations of Captivity,* 107.

58. Many owed their emancipation to a master's will stipulating, for example, that a slave was to be freed "having faithfully served my wife during her natural life," or that another was to be free "if he can pay my son or his heirs the sum of £4 per year for eighteen years." Quoted in Edgar J. McManus, *A History of Negro Slavery in New York* (Syracuse: Syracuse University Press, 1966), 149. See also White, *Somewhat More Independent,* 28–30.

59. *Hall v. Mullin* [1821], in Catterall, *Judicial Cases Concerning American Slavery,* 4:49–70; Johnson, *Soul by Soul,* 42.

60. Kidnapping freed people was an early form of organized crime. See Carol Wilson, *Freedom at Risk: The Kidnapping of Free Blacks in America, 1780–1865* (Lexington: University Press of Kentucky, 1994); Zilversmit, *First Emancipation,* 147, and also 151, 157, 208–9. On the warning that freed people organized, see White, *Somewhat More Independent,* 85. Also on kidnapping, see Dwight Lowell Dumond, *Antislavery: The Crusade for Freedom in America* (New York: Norton, 1961), 30, 51–52, 81. Slave traders targeted youth; see Fogel and Engerman, "Philanthropy at Bargain Prices," 393.

61. *Hamilton v. Cragg* [1823], in Catterall, *Judicial Cases Concerning American Slavery,* 4:71. For similar case, see *Crawford v. Moses* [1839], ibid., 1:194.

62. On preference of traders for the young, see Tadman, *Speculators and Slaves,* 25. On prices of males and females, see ibid., 288. On legal and illegal measures used to enslave freed people, see Ulrich Bonnell Phillips, *American Negro Slavery: A Survey of the Supply, Employment, and Control of Negro Labor as Determined by the Plantation Regime* (1918; Baton Rouge: Louisiana State University Press, 1969), 441–46.

63. Bernard Bailyn, *Voyagers to the West: A Passage in the Peopling of America on the Eve of the Revolution* (New York: Knopf, 1986), 128, 130, 152–53. Before the great famine, the Irish immigrants also were most often people of middling circumstances. The "relative prosperity" of people leaving for America was a "recurrent theme" of Irish newspapers. Ibid., 37 n. 7.

64. Jonathan A. Glickstein, *American Exceptionalism, American Anxiety: Wages, Competition, and Degraded Labor in the Antebellum United States* (Charlottesville: University of Virginia Press, 2002), 183.

Chapter 5: The Old South's Triumph

1. Richard Buel Jr., *In Irons: Britain's Naval Supremacy and the American Revolutionary Economy* (New Haven: Yale University Press, 1998), 244–53. However, the elimination of slavery was not painful to the northern economy. See Orlando Patterson, *Slavery and Social Death: A Comparative Study* (Cambridge, Mass.: Harvard University Press, 1982), 286.

2. According to Secretary of State James Madison, between 1803 and 1807 the British seized 528 American ships and the French 389. See Douglass Cecil North, *The Economic Growth of the United States, 1790–1860* (New York: Norton, 1966), 37.

3. Thomas C. Cochran, *Frontiers of Change: Early Industrialism in America* (New York: Oxford University Press, 1981), 42, 44, 97. New industries were taking root in the North. See Tench Coxe, *A View of the United States . . .* (Philadelphia: n.p., 1794), 124, 141–45, 148–49.

4. Cochran, *Frontiers of Change,* 6–7, 17–20, 50–51, 60–61, 68–70.

5. Henry Adams, *History of the United States* [during the Jefferson and Madison administrations, 1801–17], 9 vols. (1891–96; New York: Antiquarian Press, 1962), 3:44, 92–93 and 4:2.

6. On the "Essex Junto's" seeking closer relations with England, even secession from the Republic, see Timothy Pickering to Edward Pennington, July 12, 1812, in Henry Adams, ed., *Documents Relating to New England Federalism, 1800–1815* (1877; New York: Burt Franklin, n.d.), 390; and John Lowell to Timothy Pickering, December 3, 1814, ibid., 413.

7. "The Boston Illuminati," (Boston) *Independent Chronicle,* June 20, 1814, 2 (quote); Charles Warren, *Jacobin and Junto or Early American Politics as Viewed from the Diary of Dr. Nathaniel Ames, 1758–1822* (Cambridge, Mass.: Harvard University Press, 1931), 271.

8. "America and England: Preparations for War," (Boston) *Columbian Sentinel*, July 27, 1814, 2; "Boston Illuminati," 2; Warren, *Jacobin and Junto*, 259–71.

9. Adams, *History of the United States*, 8:15.

10. Ibid., 8:4, 122, 145–48, 267–68, 354.

11. Arsène Lacarrière Latour, *Historical Memoir of the War in West Florida and Louisiana, 1814–1815*, trans. H. P. Nugent (Philadelphia: John Conrad, 1816), 198–99; Andrew Jackson to Robert Hays, February 9, 1815, in *Correspondence of Andrew Jackson*, ed. John Spencer Bassett, 7 vols. (Washington, D.C.: Carnegie Institution of Washington, 1926–37), 2:162–63; Marquis James, *The Life of Andrew Jackson* (Indianapolis: Bobbs-Merrill, 1938), 253; Robert V. Remini, *Andrew Jackson and the Course of American Empire*, vol. 1: *1767–1821* (New York: Harper and Row, 1977), 290–92.

12. See Kent L. Steckmesser, *The Westward Movement: A Short History* (New York: McGraw-Hill, 1969), 134.

13. James G. Cusick, *The Other War of 1812: The Patriot War and the American Invasion of Spanish East Florida* (Gainesville: University Press of Florida, 2003).

14. Jackson to Gaines, April 8, 1816, in Bassett, *Correspondence of Jackson*, 2:239

15. Garçon is identified as a Choctaw chief in Hubert Bruce Fuller, *The Purchase of Florida* (Cleveland: Burrows, 1906), 230–31. Other accounts refer to him as an escaped slave. See Elena Sánchez-Fabrés Mirat, *Situatión de las Floridas en la segunda mitad del siglo XVIII (1783–1819): Los problemas de una región de frontera* (Madrid: Ministerio de Asuntos Exteriores, 1977), 289–90; and John Anthony Caruso, *The Southern Frontier* (Indianapolis: Bobbs-Merrill, [1963]), 365–67.

16. Captain Ferdinand Amelung to Jackson, June 4, 1816, in Bassett, *Correspondence of Jackson*, 2:243.

17. Hubert Howe Bancroft, *The History of the North Mexican States and Texas*, vol. 2 (vol. 16 of *The Works of Hubert Howe Bancroft*, 37 vols. [San Francisco: History Co., 1886–90]), 49–52, 73–76, 95–96, 149; William Ransom Hogan, *The Texas Republic: A Social and Economic History* (Norman: University of Oklahoma Press, 1946), 82–87, 293–95; Elgin Williams, *The Animating Pursuits of Speculation* (New York: Columbia University Press, 1949), 17–23; Charles W. Ramsdell, "The Natural Limits of Slavery Expansion," *Mississippi Valley Historical Review* 16 (September 1929): 154–55.

18. Steckmesser, *Westward Movement*, 216–20.

19. According to a later tradition, Davis reassured the demoralized Indiana troops by "pointing proudly to the gallant yeomanry of Mississippi, and saying: 'Stay and re-form behind that wall!'" Daniel R. Hundley, *Social Relations of Our Southern States* (1860; Baton Rouge: Louisiana State University Press, 1979), 200 (quote); William C. Davis, *Jefferson Davis: The Man and His Hour* (New York: Harper-Collins, 1991), 154–55; David Lavender, *Climax at Buena Vista: The Decisive Battle of the Mexican-American War* (Philadelphia: Lippincott, 2003), 202–3, 209–10, 241 n. 12.

20. Clement Eaton, *Jefferson Davis* (New York: Free Press, 1977), 63–64; James T. McIntosh et al., eds., *The Papers of Jefferson Davis*, vol. 3: *July 1846–December 1848* (Baton Rouge: Louisiana State University Press, 1981), 181–85; Davis, *Jefferson Davis*, 163.

21. In Texas this occurred only with annexation in 1846. The constitution of Texas had already legalized slavery, but the institution was no more secure than the insolvent and unstable republic itself. See Richard G. Lowe and Randolph B. Campbell, *Planters and*

Plain Folk: Agriculture in Antebellum Texas (Dallas: Southern Methodist University Press, 1987), 7.

22. James D. Foust and Dale E. Swan, "Productivity and Profitability of Antebellum Slave Labor: A Micro-Approach," *Agricultural History* 44 (January 1970); 56–57. Large producers had the advantage of owning ginning machinery. Weymouth T. Jordan, *Hugh Davis and His Alabama Plantation* (University, Ala.: University of Alabama Press, 1948), 134.

23. Cotton constituted more than 50 percent of exports, and tobacco another 15 percent. Slaves also produced most of the exported sugar, rice, naval stores, and hemp. Stuart Bruchey, comp and ed., *Cotton and the Growth of the American Economy* (New York: Harcourt, Brace, and World, [1967]), 2, 276.

24. For bankers, slaves were an attractive form of collateral because of their mobility. See Gavin Wright, *Slavery and the Development of the American Economy* (Baton Rouge: Louisiana State University Press, 2006), 70. See also James David Miller, *South by Southwest: Planter Emigration and Identity in the Slave South* (Charlottesville: University of Virginia Press, 2002), 91–93.

25. Harold D. Woodman, *King Cotton and His Retainers: Financing and Marketing the Cotton Crop of the South, 1800–1925* (Lexington: University Press of Kentucky, 1967), 140–41.

26. Leonard L. Richards, *The Slave Power: The Free North and Southern Domination, 1780–1860* (Baton Rouge: Louisiana State University Press, 2000), 130.

27. James H. Hammond, *Selections from the Letters and Speeches of the Hon. James H. Hammond* (1866; Spartanburg, S.C.: Reprint Co., 1978), 317.

Chapter 6: The Old South's Crisis and the Emergence of the White Solidarity Myth

1. Paul Goodman, *Of One Blood: Abolition and the Origins of Racial Equality* (Berkeley: University of California Press, 1998), 14; Leonard L. Richards, *The Slave Power: The Free North and Southern Domination, 1780–1860* (Baton Rouge: Louisiana State University Press, 2000), 57.

2. On the western limits of plantation agriculture, see Charles W. Ramsdell, "The Natural Limits of Slavery Expansion," *Mississippi Valley Historical Review* 16 (September 1929): 154–56. Slaves, however, had been successfully used in mining, the principal industry of the Far West. See "Gold Mining: A Forgotten Industry of Antebellum North Carolina," in *Democracy in the Old South and Other Essays by Flecher Melvin Green,* ed. J. Isaac Copeland (Nashville: Vanderbilt University Press, 1969), 39.

3. James H. Hammond, "Speech Delivered at Barnwell [Court House] S.C., October 29, 1858," *Selections from Letters and Speeches of the Hon. James H. Hammond* (1866; Spartanburg, S.C.: Reprint Co., 1978), 334–36.

4. On the South's slow population growth compared to growth in the North, see J. D. B. DeBow, *The Industrial Resources, Statistics, etc. of the United States and More Particularly of the Southern and Western States,* 3 vols. (1854; 3rd ed., New York: August M. Kelly, 1966), 2:109.

5. Ibid., 1:241.

6. The decline of open-range livestock production left the South with a dilapidated beef and dairy industry. See Cornelius Oliver Cathey, *Agricultural Developments in North Caro-*

lina, 1783–1860 (Chapel Hill: University of North Carolina Press, 1956), 172, 176, 178. See also Stanley W. Trimble, "Perspectives on the History of Soil Erosion in the Eastern United States," *Agricultural History* 59 (1985): 175.

7. "Address of Hon. C. C. Clay," *DeBow's Review* 19 (1855): 727.

8. Out-migration figures appear in James A. Dunlevy, "Regional Preferences and Migrant Settlement: On the Avoidance of the South by Nineteenth Century Immigrants," in *Research in Economic History: A Research Journal*, ed. Paul Uselding, vol. 8: *1982* (Greenwich, Conn.: JAI Press, 1983), 218–19. See also Ray Allen Billington, *Westward Expansion: A History of the American Frontier*, 4th ed. (New York: Macmillan, 1974), 305–6. Protest meetings were held proclaiming that slavery was not the cause of the South's economic problems. See Charles Henry Ambler, *Sectionalism in Virginia from 1776 to 1861* (1910; New York: Russell and Russell, 1964), 225.

9. See especially "Address of Hon. C. C. Clay," 727; James C. Bonner, "Profile of a Late Ante-Bellum Community," *American Historical Review* 49 (July 1944): 666. On the destructive legacy of plantation production, see William Gilmore Simms to James H. Hammond, January 28, 1858, in *The Letters of William Gilmore Simms*, ed. Mary C. Simms Oliphant et al., vol. 4: *1858–1866* (Columbia: University of South Carolina Press, 1955), 24.

10. Alfred G. Smith, *Economic Readjustment of an Old Cotton State* (Columbia: University of South Carolina Press, 1958), 34. See also William M. Mathew, *Edmund Ruffin and the Crisis of Slavery in the Old South: The Failure of Agricultural Reform* (Athens: University of Georgia Press, 1988), 11–12.

11. H. L. Clay to Clement Claiborne Clay, December 15, 1854, Clement Claiborne Clay Papers, Special Collections Department, William R. Perkins Library, Duke University. In 1860 Frederick Law Olmsted reported overgrazing and also soil exhaustion on the South's last frontier. See *A Journey through Texas; or, A Saddle-Trip on the Southwestern Frontier* (1860; New York: Burt Franklin, 1969), 63–64, 82–83.

12. DeBow, *Industrial Resources*, 1:241.

13. On the rise of antebellum poverty, see Wayne Flynt, *Dixie's Forgotten People: The South's Poor Whites* (Bloomington: Indiana University Press, 1979), 5. On antebellum white sharecroppers, see Marjorie Mendenhall, "The Rise of Southern Tenancy," *Yale Review*, new ser., 27 (1938): 111. See also Fabian Linden, "Economic Democracy in the Slave South: An Appraisal of Views," *Journal of Negro History* 31 (1946): 144; William L. Barney, *Secessionist Impulse: Alabama and Mississippi in 1860* (Princeton: Princeton University Press, 1974), 39; Charles C. Bolton, *Poor Whites of the Antebellum South: Tenants and Laborers in Central North Carolina and Northeastern Mississippi* (Durham: Duke University Press, 1994).

14. Mathew, *Edmund Ruffin*, 16, 184, 196, 203, 212. On the scarcity of agricultural journals in the South, see Lewis Cecil Gray, *History of Agriculture in the Southern United States to 1860*, 2 vols. (Washington, D.C.: Carnegie Institution of Washington, 1933), 2:788.

15. Gavin Wright, *Old South, New South: Revolutions in the Southern Economy since the Civil War* (New York: Basic Books, 1986), 21.

16. Some Virginians were not pleased with agricultural reform and the increasing use of free labor. The *Richmond Whig* suspected that behind this movement were the abolitionists, who were intent on "revolutionizing our social organization and establishing upon its ruins the corrupt, dangerous, anarchy-producing system of free society." Quoted in the *New York Daily Tribune*, March 18, 1857.

17. Edmund Ruffin, *Anticipations of the Future, to Serve as Lessons for the Present Time* (1860; Freeport, N.Y.: Books for Libraries Press, 1972), 12. For other southern comments on the negative side of the cotton boom, see James David Miller, *South by Southwest: Planter Emigration and Identity in the Slave South* (Charlottesville: University of Virginia Press, 2002), 91–93.

18. Indeed, as slavery declined in Maryland and Virginia, northern emigrants moved in. See Avery Odelle Craven, *Soil Exhaustion as a Factor in the Agricultural History of Virginia and Maryland, 1606–1860,* University of Illinois Studies in the Social Sciences 13, no. 1 (Urbana, [c. 1926]), 161.

19. Joseph W. Lesesne to Calhoun, September 12, 1847, in American Historical Association, *Annual Report* (1899), vol. 2: *Correspondence of John C. Calhoun,* ed. J. Franklin Jameson (Washington, D.C.: Government Printing Office, 1900), 1134.

20. Robert S. Starobin, *Industrial Slavery in the Old South* (New York: Oxford University Press, 1970), 11; Fred Bateman and Thomas Weiss, *A Deplorable Scarcity: The Failure of Industrialization in the Slave Economy* (Chapel Hill: University of North Carolina Press, 1981), 17. See also Gavin Wright's table, showing the slower rate of industrialization in the South. Wright, *Old South, New South,* 27.

21. Ruffin, *Anticipations of the Future,* 383–84. John C. Calhoun was similarly unfriendly but more ambiguous. See Theodore R. Marmor, "Anti-Industrialism and the Old South: The Agrarian Perspective of John C. Calhoun," in *New Perspectives on the American Past,* ed. Stanley N. Katz and Stanley I. Kutler, vol. 1: *1607–1877* (Boston: Little, Brown, 1969), 503. New York was a shock to a planter used to being treated with deference by the white poor and the blacks. See Charles S. Sydnor, *A Gentleman from the Natchez Region: Benjamin L. C. Wailes* (Durham: Duke University Press, 1938), 281.

22. H. W. Conner to Calhoun, January 12, 1849 in Jameson, *Correspondence of Calhoun,* 1188–89.

23. Frank Towers, *The Urban South and the Coming of the Civil War* (Charlottesville: University of Virginia Press, 2004), 197–98, 203.

24. As Claudia Dale Goldin has pointed out, the process of whitening was more advanced in the older and larger cities than in the new generation of some dozen new cities that began to develop in the 1850s. See her *Urban Slavery in the American South, 1820–1860: A Quantitative History* (Chicago: University of Chicago Press, 1976), 55.

25. On the problem of maintaining slavery in an urban setting, see Sally E. Hadden, *Slave Patrols: Law and Violence in Virginia and the Carolinas* (Cambridge, Mass.: Harvard University Press, 2001), 51–61. The rise of cities in medieval Europe had made serfs more difficult to manage. Southern cities also became a magnet for fugitives and created problems of discipline in surrounding rural areas. Richard C. Wade, *Slavery in the Cities* (New York: Oxford University Press, 1964), 209, 214–20. See also H. M. Henry, *The Police Control of the Slave in South Carolina* (1914; New York: Negro Universities Press, 1968), 44–48. In contrast to the authors of the above works, Claudia Dale Goldin argues, unconvincingly in my view, that slaveholders did not find it difficult or expensive to control slaves in cities. See her *Urban Slavery,* 2–5.

26. From 1840 to 1860 the South's ten largest cities had a total increase of white population of 444,000 and a decrease in black population of 682. Towers, *Urban South and the Coming of the Civil War,* 49.

27. DeBow, *Industrial Resources*, 1:241.

28. Charles C. Bolton and Scott P. Colclasure, comps., *The Confession of Edward Isham; A Poor White Life of the Old South* (Athens: University of Georgia Press, 1998), 19, 23, 26, 27 (quote).

29. The Old South was thus caught in the contradiction of having at the same time both a labor shortage and a labor surplus: a desperate demand for slave labor, an urban demand for skilled white labor, but in the rural countryside a surplus of unskilled poor white labor. In 1858 a cotton manufacturer in Florence, Alabama, complained of the "strange notion that our young men have, in believing that in training of the mind and hand to any kind of handicraft, causes them to lose cast[e] in society." "The Field for Southern Manufactures," *DeBow's Review* 24 (1858): 383.

30. On the frequently violated taboos on interracial fraternization and sexual relations, see Wade, *Slavery in the Cities,* 260, 321; "A Row," *Louisiana Gazette,* May 10, 1820. Dark secrets came to light in the courts. See Mark V. Tusnet, *The American Law of Slavery, 1810–1860* (Princeton: Princeton University Press, 1981), 14. See also James Hugo Johnston, *Race Relations in Virginia and Miscegenation in the South, 1776–1860,* (1937; Amherst: University of Massachusetts Press, 1970).

31. Frederick Law Olmsted found that the French recognized nine African-European combinations. See his book *A Journey in the Seaboard Slave States* (New York: Dix and Edwards, 1856), 583.

32. Wade, *Slavery in the Cities,* 124. James Henry Hammond claimed that the number of racially mixed was "infinitely small," except in the towns where the offenders were generally "natives of the North or foreigners." "Gov. Hammond's Letters on Slavery—No. 2," *DeBow's Review* 7 (1849): 494. But as he conceded in his will, he had contributed to that "infinitely small" number in the rural countryside. See Orville Vernon Burton, *In My Father's House Are Many Mansions: Family and Community in Edgefield, South Carolina* (Chapel Hill: University of North Carolina Press, 1985), 186–88.

33. Burton, *In My Father's House,* 185–89; Stephen David Kantrowitz, *Ben Tillman and the Reconstruction of White Supremacy* (Chapel Hill: University of North Carolina Press, 2000), 20.

34. But where slaves were numerous, free labor was weak indeed. See Broadus Mitchell, *William Gregg: Factory Master of the South* (Chapel Hill: University of North Carolina Press, 1928), 143.

35. An upper-class Southerner wrote in 1860, "although as a class the Poor White Trash are intensely proslavery, now and then one will find amongst them fierce abolitionists." Daniel R. Hundley, *Social Relations of Our Southern States* (1860; Baton Rouge: Louisiana State University Press, 1979), 274–75.

36. Gavin Wright traces the "Free Soil" tradition to the decline of serfdom in western Europe, where artisans advanced doctrines of "free soil" or "free air" to exclude coerced labor from cities and regions. See Wright, *Slavery and American Economic Development* (Baton Rouge: Louisiana State University Press, 2006), 40.

37. J. D. B. DeBow, a staunch defender of the Old South, did not minimize the troubles of the poor white. "Boys and girls, by thousands, destitute of both employment and the means of education, grow up to ignorance and poverty, and too many of them to vice and crime." He added that he had no "disposition to reproach the wealthy for the existence of such a state

of things," among which he prudently omitted slavery. See his *Industrial Resources*, 1:241. The Reverend George Pierce thought the "existing state of things," also corrupted young men of the upper classes, whom he described as "idle, dissipated, vicious with pistols in their pockets and the fumes of liquor in their brains." (Columbus, Ga.) *Soils of the South* 4 (April 1854): 170, quoted in Mathew, *Edmund Ruffin*, 189.

38. For the Old South's suppression of "unsound" opinions, see Clement Eaton, *The Freedom-of-Thought Struggle in the Old South* (1940; New York: Harper and Row, 1964), 36–37, 222–24, 272.

39. Samuel Langhorne Clemens, *Adventures of Huckleberry Finn* (New York: Bobbs-Merrill, 1967), 58.

40. For the persecution of a small group who opposed slavery, see Edwin Rogers Embree, "A Kentucky Crusader," *American Mercury* 24 (September 1931): 101.

41. President Andrew Jackson advised his postmaster general that postmasters should remove antislavery materials from the mails and publish the names of those who were to receive them. See Jackson to Amos Kendall, August 9, 1835, in *Correspondence of Andrew Jackson*, ed. John Spencer Bassett, 7 vols. (Washington, D.C.: Carnegie Institution of Washington, 1926–37), 5:360–61; Clement Eaton, *The Mind of the Old South* (Baton Rouge: Louisiana State University Press, 1967), 160. On Helper's *Impending Crisis* see also Orville Vernon Burton, *Age of Lincoln* (New York: Hill and Wang, 2007), 90–92.

42. A "Communication" in Robert J. Turnbull, *A South Carolinian, A Refutation of the Calumnies Circulated against the Southern and Western States* . . . (1822; New York: Negro Universities Press, 1969), 55; John S. C. Abbott, *South and North, or, Impressions Received during a Trip to Cuba and the South* (New York: Abbey and Abbott, 1860), 124.

43. According to John Adams, the "real cause" of abolition in Massachusetts was that "labouring white people who would no longer suffer the rich to employ these sable rivals so much to their injury." See "Letters and Documents Relating to Slavery in Massachusetts," in Massachusetts Historical Society, *Collections of the Massachusetts Historical Society*, 5th ser., vol. 3, p. 402.

44. Olmsted, *Journey in the Seaboard Slave States*, 589.

45. Although urban slaves were becoming less numerous, they were nevertheless the servants of the richest and most influential families. Wade, *Slavery in the Cities*, 20–21.

46. James Stirling, *Letters from the Slave States* (London: John W. Parker and Son, 1857), 250. Among American cities Charleston, during 1810–60, fell from fifth to twenty-second place. See Wade, *Slavery in the Cities*, 11.

47. Hugh Legaré to "My dear Sister," August 4, 1833, Legaré Papers, South Caroliniana Library, Columbia, S.C. Frederick Law Olmsted, visiting South Carolina in 1853, found that the "democratic theory of social organization is everywhere ridiculed and rejected, in public as well as in private, in the forum as well as the newspapers." Omsted, *Journey in the Seaboard Slave States*, 491.

48. See Dylan C. Penningroth's chapter "Slavery's Other Economy," in his *The Claims of Kinfolk: African American Property and Community in the Nineteenth Century* (Chapel Hill: University of North Carolina Pres, 2003), 45–78.

49. Barney, *Secessionist Impulse*, 41. See also Frederick Law Olmsted, *A Journey in the Back Country* (1860; New York: Burt Franklin, 1970), 137.

50. *Savannah Republican*, February 19, 1836, quoted in Wade, *Slavery in the Cities*, 85. "The

slaves and free negroes," the *New Orleans Daily Delta* of September 10, 1854, complained, "are daily growing more impudent and rebellious, and treason is nightly talked of, we doubt not, in these servile haunts, kept principally by unprincipled men, who do not even talk our language, and have no love for the prosperity of our institutions. Should a servile outbreak ever occur in the city of New Orleans . . . we will have to thank the keepers of the negro cabarets and club houses for it, within the precincts of whose damned halls, at the dead hour of midnight, heaven only knows what plots are hatched against our peace."

51. Anonymous letter to the editor, *Savannah Republican,* September 3, 1829. Some claimed also that the Sunday market benefited "the poorest class of white persons, who generally receive their weekly wages on the evening of Saturday." "Report . . . the Memorial of the Citizens of Savannah," ibid., July 8, 1829.

52. Ibid., August 28, 30, September 4, 1839, quoted in Wade, *Slavery in the Cities,* 254 and 321 n. 35. A South Carolina law irritated urban masters as well as shopkeepers, requiring masters to write out a pass for a servant sent out "on the most trifling errand." If purchases were to be made, each item had to be specified on the pass and the shopkeeper or vendor had to countersign each purchase. See Wade, *Slavery in the Cities,* 81. Such controls reduced the value of urban slaves.

53. J. D. B. DeBow noted that the country was becoming "more and more dependent on the town." "Country Life," *DeBow's Review* 29 (1860): 613–14.

54. Gray, *History of Agriculture,* 1:475–78. Among Black Belt whites, however, slaveholding was being concentrated into fewer and fewer hands. See Linden, "Economic Democracy in the Slave South," 178.

55. As plantations became larger and wealthier, non-slaveholders became more numerous and poorer. See Gavin Wright, *The Political Economy of the Cotton South: Households, Markets, and Wealth in the Nineteenth Century* (New York: Norton, 1978), 42.

56. One scholar has written that herdsmen abandoned plantation areas because they preferred land where they were "protected by the sterile, sandy soils of the piney woods and the rugged surface of the highlands" from the advancing agricultural frontier. Frank Lawrence Owsley, *Plain Folk of the Old South* (1949; Chicago: Quadrangle Books, 1965), 34. On the growing difficulties of open range herding, and the losses from starvation in winter, see Cathey, *Agricultural Developments in North Carolina,* esp. 175.

57. A Mississippi manufacturer proposed that if the poor whites were given jobs making "wool hats, shoes, and the coarse fabrics" for slaves they would feel bound to slavery and to the South. J. M. Weston to "Col. Claiborne," August 11, 1858, in J. F. H. Claiborne Papers, Southern Historical Collection, CB #3926, Wilson Library, University of North Carolina, Chapel Hill.

58. Bolton, *Poor Whites of the Antebellum South,* 45.

59. Walter Johnson, *Soul by Soul: Life inside the Antebellum Slave Market* (Cambridge, Mass.: Harvard University Press, 1999), 6.

60. Quoted in J. Mills Thornton, *Politics and Power: Alabama, 1800–1860* (Baton Rouge: Louisiana State University Press, 1978), 237, 220.

61. The *Charleston Mercury,* February 28, 1860, argued more logically that masters should be able to take slaves to areas where they might be used in mining. See Dwight Lowell Dumond, ed., *Southern Editorials on Secession* (1931; Gloucester, Mass.: Peter Smith, 1964), 40–48.

62. Ralph A. Wooster, *The People in Power: Courthouse and Statehouse in the Lower South,*

1850–1860 (Knoxville: University of Tennessee Press, 1969). On the shrinking number of slaveholders, see Wright, *Political Economy of the Cotton South,* 34. J. D. B. DeBow remained steadfastly optimistic: "The non-slaveholder knows that as soon as his savings will admit, he can become a slaveholder, and thus relieve his wife from the necessities of the kitchen and laundry, and his children from the labors of the field. . . . It is within my knowledge, that a plantation of fifty or sixty persons has been established from the descendants of a single female, in the course of the lifetime of the original purchaser." DeBow, *The Interest in Slavery of the Southern Non-Slaveholder* (Charleston, S.C.: Evans and Cogwell, 1860), 9. But, with prime field hands selling for $1,500, fewer and fewer plain people were able to benefit from such Malthusian fecundity.

63. Wright, *Political Economy of the Cotton South,* 35.

64. Ibid., 148.

65. Ibid., 35. Wright has also called attention to the similarity between the speculative or "subjective" equity of slaveholders and that which many Americans have in their homes. Though house buyers usually plan to live in their homes rather than sell them, they nevertheless maintain a keen interest in their homes' "equity." They realize, furthermore, that this self-worth depends heavily on what others do or think. Thus members of a white family, whether liberal or conservative, may feel themselves poorer upon seeing a black family moving in next door; and they may support conservative movements that promise to uphold real estate values. Ibid., 143, 148–49. See also Jonathan D. Martin, *Divided Mastery: Slave Hiring in the American South* (Cambridge, Mass.: Harvard University Press, 2004), 10–11.

66. A secessionist paper predicted that Lincoln's election would "reduce value of slaves one hundred dollars each." "The Terrors of Submission," *Charleston Mercury,* October 11, 1860.

67. See Bertram Wyatt-Brown, *Southern Honor: Ethics and Behavior in the Old South* (New York: Oxford University Press, 1982).

68. In 1860 one partner of a Broadway firm was reported to own twelve hundred slaves, another, three hundred. See Philip S. Foner, *Business and Slavery: New York Merchants and the Irrepressible Conflict* (1941; New York: Russell and Russell, 1968), 3–4.

69. For differing interpretations of one such incident, see Eaton, *Freedom-of-Thought Struggle,* 95–99; Herbert Aptheker, *American Negro Slave Revolts* (New York: International Publishers, 1969), 325–27. For similar atrocities see ibid., 141; and Olmsted, *Journey in the Back Country,* 447–48.

70. See Ronald T. Takaki, *A Pro-Slavery Crusade: The Agitation to Reopen the African Slave Trade* (New York: Free Press, 1971). Also on the African slave trade debate, see E. Merton Coulter, *Daniel Lee, Agriculturalist: His Life North and South* (Athens: University of Georgia Press, 1972), 83–87; "Southern Convention at Savannah," *DeBow's Review* 22 (February 1857): 217–18.

71. William W. Freehling, *The Road to Disunion,* vol. 2: *Secessionists Triumphant, 1854–1861* (New York: Oxford University Press, 2007), 178.

72. (Aberdeen, Miss.) *Sunny South,* June 3, 1858, quoted in Steven Deyle, *Carry Me Back: The Domestic Slave Trade in American Life* (New York: Oxford University Press, 2005), 82 (quote), 312 n.

73. "Proceedings: Late Southern Convention at Montgomery," *DeBow's Review* 24 (June 1858): 592; James H. Hammond to his brother, Marcus, July 23, 1859, and August 10, 1858, James Henry Hammond Papers, Manuscripts Division, Library of Congress.

74. M. W. Cluskey, ed., *Speeches, Messages and other Writings of the Hon. Albert G. Brown* (Philadelphia: J. P. Smith, 1859), 595. The *Charleston Mercury* on Febuary 28, 1860, asked if it was not likely that "the Anglo-Saxon race will, . . . occupy" Mexico and remove "the worthless mongrel races that now inhabit and curse the land?" Quoted in Dumond, *Southern Editorials on Secession,* 46.

75. According to a study of filibustering, almost "every year up to the Civil War, American adventurers would scheme to invade, or would actually invade some part of the Caribbean region." Robert E. May, *The Southern Dream of a Caribbean Empire, 1854–1861* (Baton Rouge: Louisiana State University Press, 1973), 29. For William Walker's activities in Nicaragua, see ibid., 91–92. See also William Walker, *The War in Nicaragua* (Mobile, Ala.: S. H. Goetzel, 1860); E. Bradford Burns, *Patriarch and Folk: The Emergence of Nicaragua, 1778–1858* (Cambridge, Mass.: Harvard University Press, 1991), 210.

76. Nicole Etcheson, *Bleeding Kansas: Contested Liberty in the Civil War Era* (Lawrence: University of Kansas Press, 2004), 2–4, 102–7.

77. William F. Samford to Clement Claiborne Clay, October 20, 1858, Clement Claiborne Clay Papers, Special Collections Department, William R. Perkins Library, Duke University.

78. The South Carolina textile manufacturer William Gregg originally planned to buy slaves, but he found that there were thousands of whites "seeking employment at half the compensation given to operatives in the North." Quoted in Mitchell, *William Gregg,* 24.

79. George Fitzhugh, *Sociology for the South, or the Failure of Free Society* (New York: Burt Franklin, [1854]), 144.

80. Richard Crallé, ed., *The Works of John C. Calhoun,* 6 vols. (New York: D. Appleton, 1854–57), 4:505–6. On the loss of political influence by the white poor during the 1850s, see Thornton, *Politics and Power,* 331–32.

81. (Vicksburg) *Daily Evening Citizen,* January 1, 1861, quoted in Barney, *Secessionist Impulse,* 43 n. 72.

Chapter 7: Emancipated but Black

1. On the wave of hysteria that followed the Harper's Ferry raid, see David S. Reynolds, *John Brown, Abolitionist: The Man Who Killed Slavery, Sparked the Civil War, and Seeded Civil Rights* (New York: Knopf, 2005), 416–18.

2. John G. Fee, *Autobiography of John G. Fee, Berea, Kentucky* (Chicago: National Christian Association, 1891), 130–31, 138. On the origins of the motto, see Acts 17:26. See also the recollections of Fee's grandson, Edwin Rogers Embree, "A Kentucky Crusader," *American Mercury* 24 (September 1931): 99, 102.

3. Leonard L. Richards, *"Gentlemen of Property and Standing": Anti-Abolition Mobs in Jacksonian America* (New York: Oxford University Press, 1970), 34–35, 96–97, 112, 114–22; Carter G. Woodson, "The Negroes of Cincinnati Prior to the Civil War," *Journal of Negro History* 1 (1916): 7; Leonard P. Curry's chapter "Race Riot: Prejudice Explodes," in his *The Free Black in Urban America, 1800–1850: The Shadow of a Dream* (Chicago: University of Chicago Press, 1981), 96–111; J. T. Headley, *Pen and Pencil Sketches of the Great Riots of New York City of 1834* (1882; New York: Arno Press, 1969), 83–95; Linda K. Kerber, "Abolitionists and Amalgamators: The New York City Riots of 1834," *New York History* 48 (January 1967): 28–39.

4. In an Ohio election for governor, each of the three candidates took pains to distance himself from a belief in racial equality. Still the *Daily Cincinnati Inquirer* for August 9, 1857, in an article entitled "The Issue—The Equalization of Whites and Blacks," announced that the contest would have "as its main issue, the immensely important social and political question whether the black or African race shall possess equal rights with whites."

5. Walter Johnson, *Soul by Soul: Life inside the Antebellum Slave Market* (Cambridge, Mass.: Harvard University Press, 1999), 6, 216.

6. *Hazard's Register of Pennsylvania* 14, no. 13 (September 27, 1834): 201. See also Noel Ignatiev, *How the Irish Became White* (New York: Routledge, 1995), 165.

7. Jonathan A. Glickstein, *American Exceptionalism, American Anxiety: Wages, Competition, and Degraded Labor in the Antebellum United States* (Charlottesville: University of Virginia Press, 2002), 9. For a scholar who stresses the responsibility, or "agency," of white workers in creating racial discrimination, see Bruce Nelson, *Divided We Stand: American Workers and the Struggle for Racial Equality* (Princeton: Princeton University Press, 2001), xxvi. See also David R. Roediger, *The Wages of Whiteness: Race and Making of the American Working Class* (London: Verso, 1991).

8. Industrialization began "not in the North but in New England." Gavin Wright, *The Political Economy of the Cotton South: Households, Markets, and Wealth in the Nineteenth ‹Century* (New York: Norton, 1978), 119. See also Marcus L. Hansen, "The Second Colonization of New England," *New England Quarterly* 2 (October 1929): 544. Passage on the lumber ships was only about one-sixth the fare to New York. Ibid., 545.

9. Employers sometimes ignored racial hierarchy in hiring. "Yet the interests of capitalists as a class . . . commonly lay in observing certain forms of labor-market segmentation . . . that divided and weakened" the working class. Glickstein, *American Exceptionalism, American Anxiety,* 277 n. 46.

10. Roediger, *Wages of Whiteness,* 25, 30. On the breakdown of the skilled crafts, see Orville Vernon Burton, *The Age of Lincoln* (New York: Hill and Wang, 2007), 25.

11. A popular playwright noted that his audiences came from "different countries or widely separated sections of the same country, [and] there is no bond of union among [them]." William Knight Northall, *Before and Behind the Curtain: Fifteen Years' Observations among the Theaters of New York* (New York: W. F. Burgess, 1851), 7. See also Ignatiev, *How the Irish Became White,* 41–42.

12. Even labor radicals were overwhelmed by the caste-like isolation of both the freed people in the East and the Chinese in the West. See Bruce Laurie, *Working People of Philadelphia, 1800–1850* (Philadelphia: Temple University Press, 1980), 76, 94, and especially his chapter "Radicals: Thomas Paine's Progeny," 67–83. A scholar who has explored extensively the failure of the radical vision concludes that early Marxists generalized on the experience of Western Europe while "American working-class experience will probably prove closer to the norm." Alexander Saxton, *The Rise and Fall of the White Republic: Class Politics and Mass Culture in Nineteenth-Century America* (London: Verso, 1990), 388–89.

13. Ignatiev, *How the Irish Became White,* 143–44. "It was safer and more expedient . . . to employ violence and act out their frustrations and hostilities against still more impotent and low-status African Americans, as well as against marginalized white abolitionists, than it was to directly challenge" those in power. Glickstein, *American Exceptionalism, American Anxiety,* 93.

14. Ignatiev, *How the Irish Became White*, 157–59.

15. Glover Moore, *The Missouri Controversy, 1819–1821* (Gloucester, Mass.: Peter Smith, 1967), 342; Robert Pierce, *The Missouri Compromise and Its Aftermath* (Chapel Hill: University of North Carolina Press, 2007), 3–4.

16. For abolition as a "foreign conspiracy," see [Calvin Colton,] *Abolition a Sedition by a Northern Man* (Philadelphia: George W. Donohue, 1839), 185. On the violent repression of free speech, see Mariett Martineau, *Society in America* (1837; New Brunswick, N.J.: Foundation Books, 1981), 202.

17. The historian George Bancroft said that the object of his work was "to follow the steps by which a favoring Providence, calling our institutions into being, has conducted the country to its present happiness and glory." Bancroft, *History of the United States of America from the Discovery of the Continent*, 6 vols. (1834; Boston: Little, Brown, 1879), 1:3.

18. Glickstein, *American Exceptionalism, American Anxiety*, 183.

19. Probably 2,000 slaves escaped the South each year, or some 20,000 for the decade of the 1850s. See Larry Gara, "Underground Railroad," *Dictionary of Afro-American Slavery*, ed. Randall M. Miller and John David Smith (New York: Greenwood, 1988), 746. Southern spokesmen alleged higher numbers for which they demanded compensation and severe measures to put down the abolitionists. J. F. H. Claiborn, for example, charged that during 1810–50, 100,000 slaves had been abducted with a loss to their owners of $30,000,000. Wilbur H. Siebert, *The Underground Railroad from Slavery to Freedom* (New York: Macmillan, 1899), 341. Such a number is not compatible with the slow increase of African Americans in the free states and Canada, nor with the fact that, while most fugitives were males, northern blacks continued to be predominantly female. See Larry Gara, *The Liberty Line: The Legend of the Underground Railroad* (Lexington: University Press of Kentucky, 1967), 16–17, 37–38. For a rare activist who kept records, see William Still, *The Underground Railroad: A Record of Facts, Authentic Narratives, Letters . . .* (Philadelphia: Porter and Coates, 1872). See also Stanley W. Campbell, "Fugitive Slaves," in *Encyclopedia of African American Culture*, 4 vols. (New York: Macmillan, 1995), 2:1077. For exciting escape accounts, see Fergus M. Bordevich, *Bound for Canaan: The Underground Railroad and the War for the Soul of America* (New York: HarperCollins, 2005).

20. Cotton alone accounted for more than 50 percent of American exports, and tobacco another 15 percent. These sales provided capital for the expansion of industry in the North. Stuart Bruchey, *Cotton and the Growth of the American Economy, 1790–1860* (New York: Harcourt, Brace, and World, 1967), 276.

21. J. D. B. DeBow, *The Industrial Resources, Statistics, etc. of the United States and More Particularly of the Southern and Western States*, 3 vols. (1854; 3rd ed., New York: August M. Kelly, 1966), 3:121–22. Gavin Wright estimates that by the late 1850s, out of thirty million Americans, about two million belonged to slave-holding families. Yet these families were five times richer than the average northern family; and they were about ten times richer than the three-quarters of southern white farming families who owned no slaves. See Wright, *Political Economy of the Cotton South*, 35. See also Douglass Cecil North, *The Economic Growth of the United States, 1760–1860* (New York: Norton, 1966), 40, 75; Robert Greenhalgh Albion, *The Rise of the New York Port (1815–1860)* (1939; Hamden, Conn.: Archon, 1961), 96.

22. Thomas Prentice Kettell, *Southern Wealth and Northern Profits . . .* (1860; University: University of Alabama Press, 1965), 98. According to Douglass C. North, the "surge of expansion" took place in 1843. North, *Economic Growth of the United States*, 176, 206.

23. It was to the Northeast that planters most often went for credit. All states chartered banks, but banking flourished in the great port cities where capital was accumulating. In the South, banks were organized not because of a surplus of capital but because of a clamor for loans. Cash-poor planters chartered cash-poor banks that often failed at the next downturn in the economy. See Harold D. Woodman's chapter "Bankers and Planters," in his *King Cotton and His Retainers: Financing and Marketing the Cotton Crop of the South, 1800–1925* (Lexington: University Press of Kentucky, 1968), 98–113. See also Thomas C. Cochran, *Frontier of Change: Early Industrialism in America* (New York: Oxford University Press, 1981), 112; Stanley Lebergott, "Labor Force and Employment, 1800–1860," in *Output, Employment, and Productivity in the United States after 1800,* Studies in Income and Wealth by the Conference on Research in Income and Wealth 30, ed. Dorothy S. Brady (New York: National Bureau of Economic Research, 1966), 131.

24. Philip S. Foner, *Business and Slavery: The New York Merchants and the Irrepressible Conflict* (1941; New York: Russell and Russell, 1968), 4.

25. This discussion of freed people draws heavily upon the work of Barbara J. Fields; see especially her chapters "Baltimore and the Problem of Slavery in the Cities" and "The Problem of Free Blacks in a Dual System," in her *Slavery and Freedom on the Middle Ground: Maryland during the Nineteenth Century* (New Haven: Yale University Press, 1985), 40–89.

26. Michael Tadman estimates that during the 1850s, more than a quarter million slaves were removed from the "slave exporting states." Some of these people were carried westward by their masters, but 60 to 70 percent were sold. See Tadman, *Speculators and Slave Masters, Traders, and Slaves in the Old South* (Madison: University of Wisconsin Press, 1989), 41, 44.

27. See Stephen Kantrowitz, "Savannah River Anti-Slave Traffick Association," in his *Ben Tillman and the Reconstruction of White Supremacy* (Chapel Hill: University of North Carolina Press, 2000), 21.

28. Sally E. Hadden, *Slave Patrols: Law and Violence in Virginia and the Carolinas* (Cambridge, Mass.: Harvard University Press, 2001), 52.

29. Charles C. Bolton, *Poor Whites of the Antebellum South: Tenants and Laborers in Central North Carolina and Northeastern Mississippi* (Durham: Duke University Press, 1994), 46–47.

30. Hadden, *Slave Patrols,* 55.

31. For poor whites prosecuted for playing cards with blacks or for other interracial activities, see Bolton, *Poor Whites of the Antebellum South,* 46–47.

32. Ira Berlin, *Slaves without Masters: The Free Negro in the Antebellum South* (New York: Vintage, 1976), 66–78, 89, 173–74, 303–6. The First African Baptist Church of Richmond was attended by both slaves and freed people. Madori Takagi, *Rearing Wolves to Our Own Destruction: Slaves in Richmond, 1782–1865* (Charlottesville: University of Virginia Press, 1999), 106.

33. A citizens' group's resolution charged that the growing number of freed people in Maryland was increasing slave discontent. See Howard L. Sacks and Judith Rose Sacks, *Way Up North in Dixie: A Black Family's Claim to the Confederate Anthem* (Washington, D.C.: Smithsonian Institution Press, 1993), 40.

34. Ira Berlin, *Generations of Captivity: A History of African-American Slaves* (Cambridge, Mass.: Harvard University Press, 2003), 235.

35. Takagi, *Rearing Wolves to Our Own Destruction,* 120–21.

36. In 1857, a Virginian urging the reopening of the African slave trade warned that "South-

ern soil is about to be transferred to the North." "Southern Convention at Savannah," *DeBow's Review* 22 (February 1857): 217.

37. Stanley W. Campbell, *The Slave Catchers: Enforcement of the Fugitive Slave Law* (1968; New York: Norton, 1970), 151.

38. The Cannon-Johnson gang kidnapped blacks in Pennsylvania and New Jersey and sold them in Louisiana. After a tenant discovered a chest of human bones on land belonging to Patty Cannon, she and her two partners, Ebenezer and Joe Johnson, were indicted for murder. The Johnson brothers escaped to the Deep South, and Cannon committed suicide before her case came to trial, but not before she called in a priest and confessed to eleven murders and taking part in at least twelve others. See Carol Wilson, *Freedom at Risk: The Kidnapping of Free Blacks in America, 1790–1865* (Lexington: University Press of Kentucky, 1994), 19–37. See also Johnson, *Soul by Soul*, 128–29.

39. Some leaders of this society opposed emancipation altogether. They saw colonization as a way of strengthening slavery by getting rid of troublemaking freed people. Eric Burin, *Slavery and the Peculiar Solution: A History of the American Colonization Society* (Gainesville: University Press of Florida, 2005), 14.

40. James G. Birney, a former agent of the society who had become an abolitionist, called the colonization movement "an opiate to the conscience." Quoted in Paul Goodman, *Of One Blood: Abolition and the Origins of Racial Equality* (Berkeley: University of California Press, 1998), 18. See also Dwight Lowell Dumond, *Antislavery: The Crusade for Freedom in America* (New York: Norton, 1961), 168.

41. For a critical edition of Walker's *Appeal*, see Herbert Aptheker, *"One Continuous Cry": David Walker's Appeal to the Colored Citizens of the World (1829–1830), Its Setting and Its Meaning* (New York: Humanities Press, 1965). See also Clement Eaton, "A Dangerous Pamphlet in the Old South," *Journal of Southern History* 2 (1936): 321–34. As a radical freedman who may have been in Charleston at the time of the Denmark Vesey conspiracy, Walker left a scant documentary trail. For a thorough exploration of this trail, see Peter P. Hinks, *To Awaken My Afflicted Brethren: David Walker and the Problem of Antebellum Slave Resistance* (University Park: Pennsylvania State University Press, 1997). See also Goodman, *Of One Blood*, 24–26; and Hadden, *Slave Patrols*, 47–48.

42. Aptheker, *"One Continuous Cry,"* 143.

43. While reports of his murder cannot be discounted, Walker probably died of consumption. See Hinks, *To Awaken My Afflicted Brethren*, 269–70.

44. "Walker's Appeal," *Liberator*, January 8, 1831; Robert H. Abzug, "The Influence of Garrisonian Abolitionists' Fears of Slave Violence on the Antislavery Argument, 1829–1840," *Journal of Negro History* 55 (1970): 14–28, esp. 18; John Demos, "The Antislavery Movement and the Problem of Violent Means," *New England Quarterly* 37 (1964): 501–26, esp. 504.

45. Benjamin Quarles, *Black Abolitionists* (New York: Oxford University Press, 1969), 19–20.

46. For a preacher invoking an ancient Christian doctrine of equality, see *Speech of Samuel J. May in the County Convention at Syracuse . . .* (Syracuse, N.Y.: Agan and Summers, 1851), 5. Compare with Augustine, *The City of God* 16:8 (Saint Augustine, *The City of God against the Pagans*, trans. Eva Mathews Sanford and William McAllen Green, 5 [Loeb Classical Library; Cambridge, Mass.: Harvard University Press, 1965]: 42–45).

47. Hadden, *Slave Patrols*, 1–7, 151, 171.

48. Norris v. Newton [1850], Helen Tunicliff Catterall, ed., *Judicial Cases Concerning American Slavery and the Negro*, 5 vols., vol. 5: *Cases from the Courts North of the Ohio and West of the Mississippi Rivers, Canada, and Jamaica* (1926; New York: Octagon, 1968), 35.

49. Wilson, *Freedom at Risk,* 32–33.

50. According to the Free-Soiler Salmon P. Chase, for example, if "both races were free they would naturally separate." Chase to C. H. and J. M. Langston, November 11, 1850, quoted in Gara, *Liberty Line,* 63.

51. Leon F. Litwack, *North of Slavery: The Negro in the Free States, 1790–1860* (Chicago: University of Chicago Press, 1961), 97–98, 103–4, 196–204.

52. Henry Fowler, *The American Pulpit: Sketches . . . of Living American Preachers* (New York: J. M. Fairchild, 1856), 374–75.

53. John Ashworth, *Slavery, Capitalism, and Politics in the Antebellum Republic,* vol. 1: *Commerce and Compromise, 1820–1850* (Cambridge: Cambridge University Press, 1995), esp. 1–8. "If there ever are great revolutions" in the United States, Alexis de Tocqueville predicted, "they will be caused by the presence of the blacks upon American soil. That is to say, it will not be the equality of social conditions, rather their inequality which may give rise thereof." Alexis de Tocqueville, *Democracy in America,* ed. T. P. Meyer (Garden City, N.Y.: Doubleday, 1969), 639.

54. Clement Eaton, *The Freedom-of-Thought Struggle in the Old South* (1940; New York: Harper and Row, 1964), 89–95, 162–66, 196–98.

55. Fredrick Law Olmsted, *The Cotton Kingdom: A Traveler's Observations on Cotton and Slavery in the American Slave States* (New York: Modern Library, 1984), 574.

56. J. M. Bolts, *Speech at the African Church, August 8, 1856* (Richmond: privately printed, 1856), 12.

57. Stephen Colwell, *The Five Cotton States and New York* (Philadelphia: n.p., 1861), 51–52.

58. Quoted in Reynolds, *John Brown, Abolitionist,* 429.

59. Quoted in Roy Franklin Nichols, *The Disruption of the American Democracy* (New York: Macmillan, 1948), 286.

Chapter 8: The Planter and the "Wage Slave"

1. "Republican Central Campaign Club . . . Speech of Hon. Thaddeus Stevens," *New York Daily Tribune,* September 28, 1860.

2. According to one large planter, the plantation system trained men "to command, to dominate and to carry themselves with [what the army would call] command presence." Leonard L. Richards, *The Slave Power: The Free North and Southern Domination, 1780–1860* (Baton Rouge: Louisiana State University Press, 2000), 26.

3. On Randolph of Roanoke, "the weirdest man to ever serve in Congress" and his famous epithet, see ibid., 85–86.

4. Glover Moore, *The Missouri Controversy, 1819–1821* (Gloucester, Mass.: Peter Smith, 1967), 342; Robert Pierce, *The Missouri Compromise and Its Aftermath* (Chapel Hill: University of North Carolina Press, 2007), 3–4.

5. Macon to Bartlette Yancey, March 8 and April 15, 1818, quoted in Albert Ray Newsome, *The Presidential Election of 1824 in North Carolina* (Chapel Hill: University of North Carolina Press, 1939), 15 nn. 29, 30.

6. Merrill D. Peterson, *Olive Branch and Sword: The Compromise of 1833* (Baton Rouge: Louisiana State University Press, 1982), 90–91; and Robert V. Remini, *Andrew Jackson and the Course of American Democracy, 1833–1845* (New York: Harper and Row, 1984), 43. On the weakness of nationalists who threatened the nullifiers with a Force Bill while acquiescing to their principal demand, see Richard E. Ellis, *The Union at Risk: Jacksonian Democracy, States' Rights, and the Nullification Crisis* (New York: Oxford University Press, 1987), 179–82.

7. See Jackson's address of December 7, 1835, in James D. Richardson, ed., *Messages and Papers of the Presidents,* vol. 3 (Washington, D.C.: Bureau of National Literature, 1897), 1383–85, 1390–91. On Jackson's vigorous public reaction to the nullifiers, see Michael O'Brien, *Conjectures of Order: Intellectual Life and the American South, 1810–1860,* 2 vols. (Chapel Hill: University of North Carolina Press, 2004), 2:844–49.

8. The system was a popular program even in certain parts of the South, such as non-slaveholding Appalachian Virginia. See Charles Henry Ambler, *Sectionalism in Virginia from 1776 to 1861* (1910; New York: Russell and Russell, 1964), 202, 219. See also Michael A. Morrison, *Slavery and the West: The Eclipse of Manifest Destiny* (Chapel Hill: University of North Carolina Press, 1997), 82–83, 98–99, 132–33.

9. Larry Gara, "Slavery and Slave Power: A Crucial Distinction," *Civil War History* 15 (1960): 13. Territorial expansion, or "Manifest Destiny," though ostensibly a national policy, had a noticeable southern accent. This may be seen in the contrasting policies in the 1840s toward northwestward and southwestward expansion. See Henry Wilson, *Rise and Fall of the Slave Power,* 3 vols. (New York: Houghton, Mifflin, 1872–77), 1:32.

10. For the views of a "cotton Whig," see [Calvin Colton,] *The Junius Tracts,* vol. 5: *Political Abolition* (New York: Greeley and McElrath, 1844), 5. Most Whigs thought that Manifest Destiny diverted attention from needed "internal improvements" and endangered North-South relations. See William J. Cooper, *The South and the Politics of Slavery* (Baton Rouge: Louisiana State University Press, 1978), esp. chapters 7 and 8.

11. J. D. B. DeBow, *The Interest in Slavery of the Southern Non-Slaveholder* (Charleston: Evans and Cogwell, 1860), 6. More recent works also stress the importance of the southern trade. See Robert Greenhalgh Albion, *Rise of New York Port (1815–1860)* (1939; Hamden, Conn.: Archon, 1961), 99, 101, 102. See also Douglass Cecil North, *The Economic Growth of the United States, 1760–1860* New York: Norton, 1966), 63, 67, 69.

12. Speech of Fernando Wood, January 6, 1861, quoted in "City Government . . . Message of the Mayor," *New York Times,* January 8, 1861. See also Samuel Augustus Pleasants, *Fernando Wood of New York* (New York: Columbia University Press, 1948), 99.

13. Samuel J. May, *Some Recollections of Our Antislavery Conflict* (Boston: Fields, Osgood, 1869), 127–28. See also Thomas Prentice Kettell, *Southern Wealth and Northern Profits . . .* (1860; University, Ala.: University of Alabama Press, 1965) 138; North, *Economic Growth of the United States,* 78–79.

14. On the anti-abolitionist orientation of northern commercial interests, see Leonard L. Richards, *"Gentlemen of Property and Standing": Anti-abolitionist Mobs in Jacksonian America* (New York: Oxford University Press, 1970), 54–55. Larry E. Tise, however, has found another source for this hostility. Old Federalists were alarmed by the "natural rights" views of abolitionists. These conservatives were thus anti-abolitionist *before* they became proslavery. Tise, *Proslavery: A History of the Defense of Slavery in America, 1701–1840* (Athens: University of Georgia Press, 1987), 285.

15. A southern clergyman urged that Fourth of July celebrations be confined "exclusively to the white population." Quoted in William W. Freehling, *Prelude to Civil War: The Nullification Controversy in South Carolina, 1816–1836* (New York: Harper and Row, 1965), 52.

16. See Larry E. Tise's chapter "Death of America's Revolutionary Ideology, 1776–1798," in his *Proslavery*, 183–203. On religion's forming a new reference point for political orientation, see David Montgomery, "The Shuttle and the Cross: Weavers and Artisans in the Kensington Riots of 1844," *Journal of Social History* 5 (Summer 1972): 412, 439.

17. Jonathan Glickstein, *American Exceptionalism, American Anxiety: Wages, Competition, and Degraded Labor in the Antebellum United States* (Charlottesville: University of Virginia Press, 2002), 3–5, 125.

18. A patriotic writer claimed that if "it were not for the slaves of the south, there would be but one rank." [Charles Jared Ingersoll,] *Inchiquin, The Jesuit's Letters during a Late Residence in the United States of America . . .* (New York: I. Riley, 1810), 120.

19. On the 1840 "log cabin and cider" election, see Charles Sellers, *The Market Revolution: Jacksonian America, 1815–1846* (New York: Oxford University Press, 1991), 361–62. On the extreme racial views introduced into elections by a New York publisher, see John H. Van Evrie, *White Supremacy and Negro Subordination* (New York: Van Evrie and Horton, 1868), 282–83.

20. Noel Ignatiev, *How the Irish Became White* (New York: Routledge, 1995), 195; Glickstein, *American Exceptionalism, American Anxiety,* 227–28.

21. "Pro-Slavery, Meeting of Irishmen in Pottsville," *National Anti-Slavery Standard,* March 24, 1842.

22. Whigs especially often argued that it was still possible for a man of humble origin to reach "the most elevated positions, or acquire a great amount of wealth." Calvin Colton, *Junius Tracts and the Rights of Labor* (New York: Garland, 1974), 111.

23. On the idea that all southern whites were upper class, see Richard Crallé, ed., *The Works of John C. Calhoun,* 6 vols. (New York: D. Appleton, 1854–57), 4:505–6. On the ideas of "wage slavery" or "white slavery" in Europe, see G. Franklyn, *Answer to the Rev. Mr. Clarkson's Essay on Slavery . . .* (London: Logographic Press, 1789), 203–4; and in the United States, Robert Walsh, *An Appeal from the Judgments of Great Britain . . .* (Philadelphia: Mitchell, Ames, and White, 1819), 414. It was thus to the well-established theory of wage slavery or white slavery that Calhoun, in the Senate, alluded in 1837, in his "positive good" defense of slavery: In the South, as "in few countries so much is left to the share of the laborer, and so little exacted from him, or where there is more kind attention paid to him in sickness or infirmities of age." Clyde N. Wilson et al., eds., *The Papers of John C. Calhoun,* vol. 13: *1835–1837* (Columbia: University of South Carolina Press, 1980), 396.

24. George Fitzhugh, *Cannibals All! or Slaves without Masters* (1857; Cambridge, Mass.: Harvard University Press, 1960), 15–18. On the planter critique of free labor, see Orville Vernon Burton, *The Age of Lincoln* (New York: Hill and Wang, 2007), 82–84.

25. Van Evrie, *White Supremacy and Negro Subordination,* esp. 303.

26. Robert Ernst, "The One and Only Mike Walsh," *New York Historical Society Quarterly* 36 (January 1952): 61. Another New Yorker who built his political career on working-class and immigrant votes and planter-class patronage was Fernando Wood. See Ignatiev, *How the Irish Became White,* 78–79.

27. Ernst, "One and Only Mike Walsh," 45–46, 58, 60–63 (quote, 61). Amy Bridges finds

that city "bosses did not use the police to help employers" but otherwise offered nothing to labor in exchange for their votes. See her *A City in the Republic: Antebellum New York and the Origins of Machine Politics* (Cambridge: Cambridge University Press, 1984), 153. I have characterized the planter-labor "alliance" (or the co-option of labor votes by the planters) as reactionary because it sustained planter policies without producing labor-friendly legislation. For a different view, see David R. Roediger, *The Wages of Whiteness: Race and Making of the American Working Class* (London: Verso, 1991), 74–77.

28. Sometimes this inconsistency was managed by placing "white slavery" in England rather than the American North. The play *White Slaves of England, or the Age We Live In,* for example, opening in Philadelphia in 1853, contrasted wretched conditions of English miners with the happiness of plantation slaves. See Harry Birdoff, *The World's Greatest Hit: Uncle Tom's Cabin* (New York: S. F. Vanni, 1947), 108, 121. See also Eric Lott, *Love and Theft: Blackface Minstrelsy and the American Working Class* (New York: Oxford University Press, 1993), 228–29.

29. Such "irrational" behavior is not unusual in time of crisis. With the outbreak of a war, for example, many young people respond not to self-interest, but to inherited ideology. They offer themselves as possible martyrs and bitterly denounce others who fail to do so.

30. Chase to C. H. and J. M. Langston, November 11, 1886, quoted in Larry Gara, *The Liberty Line: The Legend of the Underground Railroad* (Lexington: University Press of Kentucky, 1967), 63.

31. Harriet Beecher Stowe, *Uncle Tom's Cabin; or, Life among the Lowly* (1852; Garden City, N.Y.: Doubleday, 1960), 268.

32. On the prominence of clergymen as proslavery writers and as slaveholders, see Tise, *Proslavery,* 371 n. 5; and Stanley W. Campbell, *The Slave Catchers: Enforcement of the Fugitive Slave Law* (1968; New York: Norton, 1970), 67.

Chapter 9: King Cotton's Jesters

1. Robert Toll, *Blacking Up: The Minstrel Show in Nineteenth-Century America* (New York: Oxford University Press, 1974), 36.

2. Mary L. Gordon, "The Nationality of Slaves under the Early Roman Empire," in *Slavery in Classical Antiquity,* ed. M. I. Finley (Cambridge: W. Heffer, 1960), 174 [page 96 in original article]. On the representation of slaves in ancient drama, see Margarete Bieber, *The History of the Greek and Roman Theater* (1939; Princeton: Princeton University Press, 1971), 102 and fig. 392, 150.

3. On the comic servant in Europe, see [Isaac Bickerstaffe,] *The Padlock* (London: W. Griffin, [c. 1769]), 26–27. For early black characters on the American stage, see George C. D. Odell, *Annals of the New York Stage,* 15 vols. (New York: Columbia University Press, 1927–49), 1:151. See also Helen Langworthy, "The Theatre in the Frontier Cities of Lexington, Kentucky, and Cincinnati, Ohio, 1797–1835" (Ph.D. diss., State University of Iowa, Iowa City, 1952), 240; Alan W. C. Green, "'Jim Crow,' 'Zip Coon': The Northern Origins of Negro Minstrelsy," *Massachusetts Review* 11 (1970): 385–89.

4. On the importance of clowns in the Broadway circus and circuses generally, see Odell, *Annals of the New York Stage,* 4:420. See also Philip Graham, *Showboats: The History of an American Institution* (Austin: University of Texas Press, 1951), 24.

5. On the close parallel between the growth of Jim Crow comedy and abolition, see Constance Rourke, *American Humor: A Study of the National Character* (New York: Harcourt, Brace, 1931), 98. See also Eric Lott, *Love and Theft: Blackface Minstrelsy and the American Working Class* (New York: Oxford University Press, 1993), 90.

6. "Daddy Rice," *New York Times,* June 5, 1881. On competing versions of the origin of the Jim Crow act, one historian concluded that this one is perhaps "the most complete and most truthful." Odell, *Annals of the New York Stage,* 3:632. On the fame that the act brought to T. D. Rice, see Carl Wittke, *Tambo and Bones: A History of the American Minstrel Stage* (1930; New York: Greenwood, 1968), 25–25.

7. Odell, *Annals of the New York Stage,* 3:631 (quote); Lott, *Love and Theft,* 75; Langworthy, "Theatre in the Frontier Cities," 290, 292.

8. Odell, *Annals of the New York Stage,* 4:372. According to Joseph N. Ireland, "Jim Crow Rice" "probably drew more money to the Bowery treasury than any other American performer in the same period." *Records of the New York Stage,* vol. 2 (1867; New York: Burt Franklin, 1968), 55, 56 (quote).

9. Odell, *Annals of the New York Stage,* 4:74, 97, 220, 232, 238, 375, 486. See also William W. Clapp, *A Record of the Boston Stage* (Boston: James Munroe Co., 1853), 462.

10. A youth from a prominent banking family has recorded the depth of the crisis. See *The Diary of George Templeton Strong,* vol. 1: *Young Man in New York, 1835–1849,* ed. Alan Nevins and Milton Halsey Thomas (New York: Macmillan, 1952), 55, 60, 62.

11. The election of 1840 was "a legendary saturnalia of mindless pageantry." Yet the success of the Whigs in this election "established the middle-class mode of democratic politics that henceforth maintained bourgeois hegemony against every challenge." Charles Sellers, *The Market Revolution: Jacksonian America, 1815–1846* (New York: Oxford University Press, 1991), 361, 362.

12. Odell, *Annals of the New York Stage,* 4:674–76. Almost at the same time other troupes calling themselves "minstrels" sprang from obscurity to fame, and indeed "there were other companies which may have antedated the Virginia Minstrels." Wittke, *Tambo and Bones,* 47.

13. "Minstrelsy Is in the Ascendant," *New York Clipper,* March 17, 1860. See also Graham, *Showboats,* 24; Edmond M. Gagey, *The San Francisco Stage: A History* (New York: Columbia University Press, 1950), 4, 13, 31, 64–65; George R. MacMinn, *The Theatre of the Golden Era in California* (Caldwell, Idaho: Caxton Publishers, 1941), 23, 436 n. 13; Gary D. Engle, *This Grotesque Essence: Plays from the American Minstrel Stage* (Baton Rouge: Louisiana State University Press, 1978), xx.

14. In the 1850s Foster's reputation as a composer fell far short of the worldwide popularity of his songs, which were sometimes attributed to performers such as the famous Christy Minstrels. William W. Austin, *"Susanna," "Jeanie," and "The Old Folks at Home": The Songs of Stephen C. Foster from His Time to Ours* (New York: Macmillan, 1975), xi, 30–31; John Tasker Howard, *Stephen Foster, America's Troubadour* (1934; New York: Thomas Y. Crowell, 1953), 83, 179.

15. Toll, *Blacking Up,* 33.

16. Quoted in Robert C. Toll, *On with the Show: The First Century of Show Business in America* (New York: Oxford University Press, 1976), 95.

17. On the division of urban entertainment along class lines in the 1840s, see Lott, *Love*

and Theft, 72; Laurence W. Levine, *Highbrow/Lowbrow: The Emergence of Cultural Hierarchy in America* (Cambridge, Mass.: Harvard University Press, 1988). Even one of the greatest minstrel-song writers, Stephen C. Foster, reacted against the coarseness he saw in this form of popular culture. See Austin, *"Susanna,"* 202–3.

18. The extent to which minstrel performers and composers borrowed from African American music and dance may be an insoluble problem. It was the professionals, not the folk artists, who copyrighted songs and thus left the most documentation of their work, which was then widely popularized and reentered the stream of popular culture, both black and white. Certainly these talented professionals gave credit to their sources, but only in a general way, as to "street singers" or "steamboat hands." They did not give credit to particular individuals or groups, which would have compromised their claims to these valuable properties. See Dena J. Epstein, *Sinful Tunes and Spirituals: Black Folk Music to the Civil War* (Urbana: University of Illinois Press, 1977), xviii, 242.

19. On the *Banjo,* a minstrel boat on the Upper Mississippi during 1849–59, some players are reported to have been "Negroes, some White, yet all cork-blacked their faces." Graham, *Showboats,* 24. On the development, beginning about the 1830s, of an idealized concept of a "southern plantation," disseminated by popular fiction, see Francis Pendleton Gaines, *The Southern Plantation: A Study in the Development and Accuracy of a Tradition* (New York: Columbia University Press, 1925), 18. If one realm of the imagination was created about the "Old South," a later realm was created about the "Old West." American television sets once resounded with the thunder of hoof beats and the volleys of gunfire that echoed from this world that never was.

20. Walt Disney's Mickey Mouse, who first appeared in 1928 in *Steamboat Willie,* has been described as "the most graphic offspring of blackface minstrels' portrayals of the plantation slave. Black, wide-eyed, childlike, falsetto-voiced, and ever the clown, Mickey Mouse even takes his costuming from the burn-cork brotherhood: see the oversized white gloves, suspender buttons (minus suspenders), big feet, coy stance." Howard L. Sacks and Judith Rose Sacks, *Way Up North in Dixie: A Black Family's Claim to the Confederate Anthem* (Washington, D.C.: Smithsonian Institution Press, 1993), 158.

21. On the tensions that poverty created between husband and wife, see [James Dawson Burn,] *Three Years among the Working-Classes in the United States during the War* (London: Smith, Elder and Co., 1865), 84–85.

22. A number of successful minstrel stars achieved their first fame as boys or very young men playing "wench" roles. For pictures of some of the most popular of the antebellum female impersonators, see Edward LeRoy Rice, *Monarchs of Minstrelsy from Daddy Rice to Date* (New York: Kenny Publishing Co., 1911), 109. On the prevalence of these performers on the California frontier, see MacMinn, *Theatre of the Golden Era in California,* 432, 436–37. It appears that many of the "young ladies" in frontier theater were female impersonators. See Rice, *Monarchs of Minstrelsy,* 111. See also Graham, *Showboats,* 31–32.

23. MacMinn, *Theatre of the Golden Era in California,* 218 ("laugh-raiser"), 426 (Elph Horn quote). *The Female Forty Thieves* was performed in San Francisco; Philadelphia; New York, where it was a "brilliant success, running twenty-four consecutive nights"; and Boston, where it drew "tremendous houses." Ireland, *Records of the New York Stage,* 2:558 ("brilliant success); Clapp, *Record of the Boston Stage,* 477 ("tremendous houses").

24. Toll, *Blacking Up,* 68.

25. W. J. Rorabaugh, *The Alcoholic Republic: An American Tradition* (New York: Oxford University Press, 1979), 232–33; Ian R. Tyrrell, *Sobering Up: From Temperance to Prohibition in Antebellum America* (Westport, Conn.: Greenwood, 1979), 316–23.

26. On prostitution and theaters, see Toll, *On with the Show*, 6; Harry Birdoff, *The World's Greatest Hit: Uncle Tom's Cabin* (New York: S. F. Vanni, 1947), 94–95; Thomas F. Gossett, *Uncle Tom's Cabin and American Culture* (Dallas: Southern Methodist University Press, 1985), 269–70.

27. Alexander Saxton, *The Rise and Fall of the White Republic: Class Politics and Mass Culture in Nineteenth-Century America* (New York: Verso, 1990); 171; Engle, *This Grotesque Essence*, xxii.

28. Nathan Irvin Huggins, *Harlem Renaissance* (New York: Oxford University Press, 1971), 253. See also Huggins's perceptive chapter "Personal: White/Black Faces—Black Masks" (244–99), on the disempowering effects of racial stereotyping.

29. Saxton, *Rise and Fall of the White Republic*, 174–77.

30. The English journal *Punch* called the "Irish Yahoo" in the "lowest neighborhoods of London and Liverpool a creature manifestly between the Gorilla and the Negro." Quoted in Bruce Nelson, *Divided We Stand: American Workers and the Struggle of Black Equality* (Princeton: Princeton University Press, 2001), xxxviii.

31. On racial perceptions about the Irish, see James Pilgrim, *Katty O'Sheal* (New York: Samuel French, [1856?]), act 1, scene 1 (p. 3). The same blurring of these concepts may perhaps also be noted when blacks were called "smoked Irish." See Robert Cantwell, *Bluegrass Breakdown: The Making of the Old Southern Sound* (Urbana: University of Illinois Press, 1984), 262; and Dale T. Knobel, *Paddy and the Republic* (Middletown, Conn.: Wesleyan University Press, 1986), 123.

32. MacMinn, *Theatre of the Golden Era in California*, 434, 444; Graham, *Showboats*, 23; Lott, *Love and Theft*, 95.

33. Saxton, *Rise and Fall of the White Republic*, 172, 176–77; Toll, *Blacking Up*, 40.

34. Saxton, *Rise and Fall of the White Republic*, 172; Rice, *Monarchs of Minstrelsy*, 6; H. P. Phelps, *Players of a Century: A Record of the Albany Stage* (1880; New York: Benjamin Blom, 1972), 143–44.

35. Toll, *On with the Show*, 99–100; idem, *Blacking Up*, 67–68, 71–72.

36. Quoted in Saxton, *Rise and Fall of the White Republic*, 176.

37. Quoted in MacMinn, *Theatre of the Golden Era in California*, 432.

38. Foster, like most minstrel-song writers, "rarely used the ugly word 'slave.'" Rather slaves "*wanted* to live with their masters, just as children wanted to live with good parents." Toll, *On with the Show*, 93. See also, idem, *Blacking Up*, 34, 72, 76–80, 87, 99 nn. 9 and 10.

39. Noel Ignatiev, *How the Irish Became White* (New York: Routledge, 1995), 6–10.

40. According to Bruce Nelson, white workers were "developing plebian cultural forms that idealized the plantation South as a rural Arcadia." Nelson, *Divided We Stand*, xxvi.

Chapter 10: The War of the Cabins

1. [Simms], "Stowe's Key to Uncle Tom's Cabin," *Southern Quarterly Review* 8 (July 1853): 226.

2. "'Uncle Tom' on the Stage," *Liberator*, September 9, 1853.

3. Quoted in Forest Wilson, *Crusader in Crinoline: The Life of Harriet Beecher Stowe* (Philadelphia: Lippincott, 1941), 247. On the phenomenal public reception of *Uncle Tom's Cabin,* see Harry Birdoff, *The World's Greatest Hit: Uncle Tom's Cabin* (New York: S. F. Vanni, 1947), 19, 151; Carl Bode, *Antebellum Culture* (Carbondale: Southern Illinois University Press, 1970), 184–85; and Frank Luther Mott, *Golden Multitudes: The Story of Best Sellers in America* (New York: Bowker, 1947), 117–19.

4. There was indeed an antislavery subculture that attracted tiny audiences. See William W. Austin, *"Susanna," "Jeanie," and "Old Folks at Home": The Songs of Stephen C. Foster* (New York: Macmillan, 1975), 34; David Ewen, *All the Years of American Popular Music* (Englewood Cliffs, N.J.: Prentice-Hall, 1977), 62–69.

5. Alexander Saxton, *Rise and Fall of the White Republic: Class Politics and Mass Culture in Nineteenth Century America* (New York: Verso, 1990), 176, 182 (quote), and n. 33; George R. MacMinn, *The Theatre of the Golden Era in California* (Caldwell, Idaho: Caxton Publishers, 1941), 432.

6. Birdoff, *The World's Greatest Hit,* 96, 97. For a different perspective on Stowe, the view that she "played the race card" to heighten the drama of her story, see Linda Williams, *Playing the Race Card: Melodramas of Black and White from Uncle Tom to O. J. Simpson* (Princeton: Princeton University Press, 2001), 299–300.

7. It was the people in power who "could propagate and codify their beliefs." W. T. Lhamon Jr., *Jump Jim Crow: Lost Plays, Lyrics, and Street Prose of the First Atlantic Popular Culture* (Cambridge, Mass.: Harvard University Press, 1983), 11.

8. *Appendix to the Congressional Globe,* 29 Cong., 2 sess., p. 317.

9. It is perhaps no accident that in a dramatic rendition of *Uncle Tom's Cabin,* one of the characters of the novel is nearly white, as is his wife. See "Uncle Tom's Cabin at the National," *New York Herald,* September 3, 1852. On the stage, the "nearly white" Wilmot, defending his family, is allowed to shoot down their pursuers in the virile frontier manner much admired by American audiences. Had he been as black as Uncle Tom, such behavior would have been regarded as profoundly offensive, perhaps evoking memories of Nat Turner or even the Haitian Revolution.

10. Joan D. Hedrick, *Harriet Beecher Stowe: A Life* (New York: Oxford University Press, 1994), 90–91, 102–4, 106–8, 120–21, 208–9; Wilson, *Crusader in Crinoline,* 122–26, 136–37, 140–46, 180–90, 193–94, 211, 259–60. Stowe's brother Charles, a student at Lane, described the class ahead of him as "uncommonly strong, a little uncivilized, entirely radical, and terribly in earnest." Milton Rugoff, *The Beechers: An American Family in the Nineteenth Century* (New York: Harper and Row, 1981), 143. On the slavery debate and student revolt, see ibid., 145–51.

11. Austin, *"Susanna,"* 34; Ewen, *All the Years of American Popular Music,* 62–69.

12. Wilson, *Crusader in Crinoline,* 196. Neither Chase nor Stowe publicly confronted the issue of slavery itself, but rather free speech for abolitionists. But this meant little amid the hysteria of the time. See John Niven, *Salmon P. Chase: A Biography* (New York: Oxford University Press, 1995), 47–49.

13. Richard Moody, *America Takes the Stage: Romanticism in American Drama and Theatre, 1750–1900* (Bloomington: Indiana University Press, 1955), 61, 72. Stowe indeed had a real-life model for Uncle Tom, the Reverend Josiah Henson. Wilson, *Crusader in Crinoline,* 250. The old black uncle stereotype was already well established in the popular imagination. Stephen

Foster had earlier published his best-selling "Old Uncle Ned" and had conceived, though not yet published, "Old Black Joe." John Tasker Howard, *Stephen Foster, America's Troubadour* (1934; New York: Crowell, 1953), 137, 160; Robert C. Toll, *Blacking Up: The Minstrel Show in Nineteenth-Century America* (New York: Oxford University Press, 1974), 100 n. 17, 244.

14. Richard Yarborough, "Strategies of Black Characterization in *Uncle Tom's Cabin* and Early Afro-American Novel," in *New Essays on Uncle Tom's Cabin,* ed. Eric J. Sundquist (Cambridge: Cambridge University Press, 1986), 47–51; Eric Lott, *Love and Theft: Blackface Minstrelsy and the American Working Class* (New York: Oxford University Press, 1993), 222. Stowe adhered to a strain of nineteenth-century ideology that perceived blacks as fundamentally different, but not necessarily inferior to whites, a view George M. Fredrickson calls "romantic racialism." See his *The Black Image in the White Mind: The Debate on Afro-American Character and Destiny* (New York: Harper and Row, 1971), 110–11. See also Thomas F. Gossett, *Uncle Tom's Cabin and American Culture* (Dallas: Southern Methodist University Press, 1985), 64–86.

15. The "new labor historians" have shifted their focus from class conflict and power relationships to a close and sympathetic look at the everyday life of working people. Such history, however, can approach the subtitle of Stowe's *Uncle Tom's Cabin: Life among the Lowly.* An example is Robert W. Slenes, *Na Senzala, uma Flor* [a flower blooms in the slave quarter] (Rio de Janeiro: Nova Fronteira, 1999). The people of the quarter might have been slaves, but they had agency. They created a culture, distinctive speech and customs, and they planted flowers around their huts.

16. J. David Gillespie and Judi F. Gillespie, "Struggle for Identity: The Life of Jordan Chambers (A *Phylon* Document)," *Phylon* 40 (Summer 1979): 108–13. Illegitimacy also resulted in the enslavement of David Elias Sadgwar. Born in 1811 in Wilmington, North Carolina, the son of "a visiting French sea captain and the daughter of a prominent white family," Sadgwar was given to a black slave woman to rear. He thus grew up a "sociological black," the property of his foster mother's owner. His racial appearance on one occasion may have helped him escape, but did not prevent his being arrested in New York and returned to his North Carolina master. See Anne Russell, *Wilmington: A Pictorial History* (Norfolk, Va.: Donning, 1984), 25.

17. Stanley W. Campbell, *The Slave Catchers: Enforcement of the Fugitive Slave Law* (1968; New York: Norton, 1970), 115–16.

18. To sustain her indictment of slavery in *Uncle Tom's Cabin,* Stowe published the following year a 500-page collection of documentary materials. In a section consisting of advertisements for the recovery of fugitive slaves, she does not overlook such status-sensitive descriptions as that for one Mary Ann Paine, "a light mulatto woman" with "long, black, straight hair . . . ."; or "a negro boy named STEPHEN . . . a very light mulatto, with blue eyes and brownish hair . . . "; or Sam, who had "[l]ight sandy hair, blue eyes, ruddy complexion—is so white as very easily to pass for a free white man"; or Fanny, "white as most white women, with straight light hair, and blue eyes, and can pass herself for a white woman"; or William, who was "quite white, and would not readily be taken for a slave." See Stowe, *The Key to Uncle Tom's Cabin* (1853; New York: Amo Press, 1969), 351–52, 356, 362, 363.

19. Other antislavery writers exploited this vulnerability of antebellum society. See Richard Hildreth, *Archy Moore, the White Slave; or, Memoirs of a Fugitive* (1856; New York: Negro Universities Press, 1969), and the play of Dion Boucicault, *The Octoroon; or, Life in Louisiana*

[1859] in *The Black Crook and Other Nineteenth Century American Plays,* ed. Myron Matlaw (New York: E. P. Dutton, 1967), 201–56.

20. According to a Democratic newspaper, the runaway sale of *Uncle Tom's Cabin* was not due to its literary merits, but to the "widely extended sympathy, in all the North" for the "humbug and deception" that has "imperiled the peace and safety of the Union." "Uncle Tom's Cabin at the National," *New York Herald,* September 3, 1852.

21. The meteoric rise in exports from the Midwest during the 1840s and '50s, transforming the area into the world's most important food surplus region, was stimulated by (1) successive crop failures in Western Europe creating both a market for American grain and a flood of immigrants to grow it; (2) repeal of the British Corn Laws in 1846; and (3) the Crimean War in 1854, which interrupted Russian exports. On the redirection of this trade from the Mississippi River to the northeastern ports, see Robert Greenhalgh Albion, *The Rise of New York Port (1815–1860)* (1939; Hamden, Conn.: Archon, 1961), 119; Percy Wells Bidwell and John I. Falconer, *History of Agriculture in the Northern United States, 1820–1860* (Washington, D.C.: Carnegie Institution of Washington, 1925), 308–9; Douglass Cecil North, *The Economic Growth of the United States, 1790–1860* (New York: Norton, 1966), 105–10.

22. Birdoff, *World's Greatest Hit,* 17–19, 123; Mott, *Golden Multitudes,* 116–19; Gossett, *Uncle Tom's Cabin and American Culture,* 164–68; Bode, *Antebellum Culture,* 184–85.

23. Birdoff, *World's Greatest Hit,* 18, 23–24.

24. Ibid., 110–11, 214–24; George O. Willard, *History of the Providence Stage, 1762–1891* (Providence: Rhode Island News Co., 1891), 150; MacMinn, *Theatre of the Golden Era in California,* 206; Philip C. Lewis, *Trouping: How the Show Came to Town* (New York: Harper and Row, 1973), 61.

25. Birdoff, *World's Greatest Hit,* 1–9 (quote, 4); Lewis, *Trouping,* 70–71; Gossett, *Uncle Tom's Cabin and American Culture,* 268. "As the record stands" writes Richard Moody, "*Uncle Tom's Cabin* was one of the most important documents in American dramatic history." Moody, *America Takes the Stage,* 72. The pageantry of the street parade had been developed by traveling minstrel troupes. See Frank Costellow Davidson, "The Rise, Development, Decline, and Influence of the American Minstrel Show" (Ph.D. diss., New York University, New York, 1952), 103.

26. To "the genius of Mrs. Stowe more than to any other one cause, the origin of the Republican party may be assigned." Lurton D. Ingersoll, *The Life of Horace Greeley* (1873; New York: Beekman, 1974), 293. For the celebration of the Uncle Tom phenomenon in popular art, see Jo-Ann Morgan, *Uncle Tom's Cabin as Visual Culture* (Columbia: University of Missouri Press, 2007).

27. Quoted in Clement Eaton, *Freedom of Thought in the Old South* (New York: Peter Smith, 1951), 36–37.

28. "Notices of New Works: Uncle Tom's Cabin," *Southern Literary Messenger* 18 (October 1852): 631. This review appears to have been written by the editor himself, John R. Thompson. See Gossett, *Uncle Tom's Cabin and American Culture,* 189.

29. Langston Hughes, "Introduction to *Uncle Tom's Cabin,*" in *Critical Essays on Harriet Beecher Stowe,* ed. Elizabeth Ammons (Boston: E. H. Hall, 1980), 104.

30. Clement Eaton, *The Freedom-of-Thought Struggle in the Old South,* rev. and enl. (1940; New York: Harper and Row, 1964), 272.

31. The other documents found in Green's possession were a map of Canada and a picture

of a hotel in Niagara Falls, which were taken as evidence connecting him to the Underground Railroad. After he had served five years, the newly elected Civil War governor of Maryland pardoned him on condition that he leave the United States. In 1862, he left for Canada. See "Out of Jail," *Liberator*, July 4, 1862. See also Langston Hughes, "Introduction to *Uncle Tom's Cabin*," 104.

32. Frederick Law Olmsted, *A Journey in the Seaboard Slave States* (New York: Dix and Edwards, 1856), 616–17. See also his *A Journey in the Back Country* (1860; New York: Burt Franklin, 1970), 264.

33. Quoted in Gossett, *Uncle Tom's Cabin and American Culture*, 210. Surely among the less promising attempts at suppression were the reported efforts of schoolteachers to obtain pledges from their pupils to never read the scathingly condemned novel. See Edmund Wilson, "Harriet Beecher Stowe," in Ammons, *Critical Essays on Harriet Beecher Stowe*, 117.

34. Birdoff, *World's Greatest Hit*, 17, 21, 107–8.

35. For a study of these works see Thomas F. Gossett's chapter, "Anti-Tom Literature," in his *Uncle Tom's Cabin and American Culture*, 212–38.

36. See Saxton, *Rise and Fall of the White Republic*, 174–77.

37. Ibid.; Carl Wittke, *Tambo and Bones: A History of the American Minstrel Stage* (1930; New York: Greenwood, 1968), 51; Howard, *Stephen Foster*, 256; Austin, *"Susanna,"* xxvi, 33.

38. Toll, *Blacking Up*, 56. For the view that minstrel culture was developed by the white working class, see Bruce Nelson, *Divided We Stand: American Workers and the Struggle for Black Equality* (Princeton: Princeton University Press, 2001), xxvi.

39. "City Government for 1861 . . . Message of the Mayor," *New York Times*, January 8, 1861. The Wood family had lived in Kentucky, New Orleans, and Charleston before settling in New York, where they became millionaires and established their own political machine, Mozart Hall. Menahem Bondheim, *Copperhead Gore: Benjamin Wood's Fort Lafayette and Civil War America* (Bloomington: Indiana University Press, 2006), 4–5, 8–9.

40. Quoted in Birdoff, *World's Greatest Hit*, 21.

41. See his "Out of the Kitchen and into the Marketplace: Normalizing *Uncle Tom's Cabin* for the Antebellum Stage," *Journal of American Drama and Theatre* (Winter 1991): 5–28. On the failure of some "southern" versions of the play in the South, see Birdoff, *World's Greatest Hit*, 23.

42. Toll, *Blacking Up*, 91 (quote); George C. D. Odell, *Annals of the New York Stage*, 15 vols. (New York: Columbia University Press, 1927–49), 6:316–17. "As Barnum owned about a half dozen traveling menageries, he was afraid of sentiment in the South, and with admirable discretion avoided all the argumentative portions of Mrs. Stowe's work." Birdoff, *World's Greatest Hit*, 88. On Barnum's intensely antiblack and extravagant "humbug," or sensational, mode of "puffing," or advertising, see ibid., 88–89.

43. McConachie, "Out of the Kitchen and into the Marketplace," 15 (Topsy speech); Willard, *History of the Providence Stage*, 150. Also in 1853, Conway produced a lampoon of the Stowe novel, *Uncle Pat's Cabin*, starring the famous comedian Barney Williams, who had gotten his start in early youth playing "wench" roles in minstrel theater. Ireland, *Records of the New York Stage*, 2:610.

44. Ireland, *Records of the New York Stage*, 2:619; Odell, *Annals of the New York Stage*, 6:306.

45. Odell, *Annals of the New York Stage*, 6:326; Toll, *Blacking Up*, 91, 93 (quote), 99 n. 9.

46. Birdoff, *World's Greatest Hit*, 142.

47. Ibid., 113.

48. George L. Aiken, *Uncle Tom's Cabin* (1853), act 1, scenes 4 and 5 (*Uncle Tom's Cabin: Based upon the Dramatization by George L. Aiken*, rev. by A. E. Thomas [New York: D. Appleton-Century, 1931], 16–17).

49. Aiken, *Uncle Tom's Cabin*, act 1, scene 2 (*Uncle Tom's Cabin: Based on Aiken*, 10).

50. McConachie, "Out of the Kitchen and into the Marketplace," 11; Gossett, *Uncle Tom's Cabin and American Culture*, 262–69; Odell, *Annals of the New York Stage*, 6:237–38, 306–12. In treating the martyrdom of Uncle Tom, Aiken was faithful to the spirit of the novel as well as reaching out to his upstate New York audience. According to one scholar, "*Uncle Tom's Cabin* was the Protestant equivalent of the Roman Catholic mass, a dramatic re-enactment of the Crucifixion." See Hedrick, *Harriet Beecher Stowe*, 215.

51. H. P. Phelps, *Players of a Century: A Record of the Albany Stage* (1880; New York: Benjamin Blom, 1972), 286–88; Gossett, *Uncle Tom's Cabin and American Culture*, 269; Birdoff, *World's Greatest Hit*, 110, 117–18, 431.

52. Birdoff, *World's Greatest Hit*, 75.

53. Ibid., 95 ("Females of improper character"); Gossett, *Uncle Tom's Cabin and American Culture*, 271 ("a neat and comfortable parquette").

54. A contemporary commentator on theater called the Aiken production an "unprecedented success," bringing out "all classes of the community." Ireland, *Records of the New York Stage*, 2:608.

55. Arthur Herman Wilson, *A History of the Philadelphia Theatre, 1835–1855* (Philadelphia: University of Pennsylvania Press, 1935), 85–87.

56. Birdoff, *World's Greatest Hit*, 96–97, 434.

57. See Birdoff's chapter with this title in his *World's Greatest Hit*, 107–26.

58. Birdoff, *World's Greatest Hit*, 109–10.

59. Austin, "*Susanna*," 34; Ewen, *All the Years of American Popular Music*, 62–69.

60. Hans Nathan, *Dan Emmett and the Rise of Early Negro Minstrelsy* (Norman: University of Oklahoma Press, 1923), 244.

61. Ibid., 351–53.

62. On the complex origins of this "Dixie," see Saxton, *Rise and Fall of the White Republic*, 165–66, 181 n. 3.

63. For a book-length study on the origins of this "Dixie," see Howard L. Sacks and Judith Rose Sacks, *Way Up North in Dixie: A Black Family's Claim to the Confederate Anthem* (Washington, D.C.: Smithsonian Institution Press, 1993). On the relationship between professional composers and folk music, see also Dena J. Epstein, *Sinful Tunes and Spirituals: Black Folk Music to the Civil War* (Urbana: University of Illinois Press, 1977), xviii, 242.

64. Albert J. Beveridge, *Abraham Lincoln, 1809–1858*, vol. 1 (Boston: Houghton Mifflin, 1928), 536.

65. Nathan, *Dan Emmett*, 274. In 1861, "Dixie" reached the peak of its popularity in New York. See ibid., 270–71. Compare with Sacks and Sacks, *Way Up North in Dixie*, 158–59.

Chapter 11: The Republican Revolution and the Struggle for a "New Birth of Freedom"

1. See Jeffrey Rossbach, *Ambivalent Conspirators: John Brown, the Secret Six, and a Theory of Violence* (Philadelphia: University of Pennsylvania Press, 1982). See also Oswald Garrison Villard, *John Brown, 1800–1859: A Biography Fifty Years After* (1910; Gloucester, Mass.: Peter

Smith, 1965); Stephen B. Oates, *To Purge This Land with Blood: A Biography of John Brown* (New York: Harper, 1970); David S. Reynolds, *John Brown, Abolitionist: The Man Who Killed Slavery, Sparked the Civil War, and Seeded Civil Rights* (New York: Knopf, 2005).

2. See Tom Chaffin, *Fatal Glory: Narciso Lopez and the First Clandestine War Against Cuba* (Charlottesville: University of Virginia Press, 1996). According to the outstanding scholar of "filibustering" raids, virtually "every year up to the Civil War, American adventurers would formulate schemes to invade, or would actually invade, some part of the Caribbean region." Robert E. May, *The Southern Dream of Empire* (Baton Rouge: Louisiana State University Press, 1973), 29. A proslavery editor in Kansas published this call for his readers: "Scourge the country of abolitionism, freesoilism, and every other damnable ism that exists. Destroy their property, crops, and every article that would conduce to the support of any or every person who is known or suspected of acting, co-operating or sympathizing with abolitionism." *Squatter Sovereign,* September 9, 1856, call quoted without headline or title by Bill Cecil-Fronsman, "'Death to All Yankees and Traitors in Kansas': The *Squatter Sovereign* and the Defense of Slavery in Kansas," *Kansas History* (Spring 1994): 24. For Brown's own words about the double standard for judging proslavery and antislavery violence, see "The Harper's Ferry Outbreak . . . Speech of Old Brown," *New York Herald,* November 3, 1859.

3. Sally E. Hadden, *Slave Patrols: Law and Violence in Virginia and the Carolinas* (Cambridge, Mass.: Harvard University Press, 2001), 170–71; Wayne K. Durrill, *War of Another Kind: A Southern Community in the Great Rebellion* (New York: Oxford University Press, 1990), 20, 58, 59 (quote).

4. David Hunter Strother, "John Brown's Death and Last Words," ed. Boyd B. Stutler, *American Heritage* 6 (February 1955): 6–9. On the cast of characters witnessing Brown's execution, see Daniel Aaron, *The Unwritten War: American Writers and the Civil War* (New York: Oxford University Press, 1973), xiii.

5. A photocopy of this note appears in Villard, *John Brown,* facing p. 554.

6. Oates, *To Purge This Land with Blood,* 354.

7. A New York lawyer, who had no sympathy for abolitionists and who thought that Brown had been justly hanged, nevertheless noted that "his simplicity and consistency, the absence of fuss, parade and bravado, the strength and clearness of his letters, all indicate a depth of conviction that one does not expect in an Abolitionist. . . . One's faith in anything is terribly shaken by anybody who is ready to go to the gallows condemning and denouncing it." Entry for December 4, 1859, *The Diary of George Templeton Strong,* ed. Allan Nevins and Milton Halsey, 4 vols., vol. 1: *Young Man in New York, 1835–1849,* vol. 2: *The Turbulent Fifties, 1850–1859,* vol. 3: *The Civil War, 1860–1865,* vol. 4: *Post-War Years, 1865–1879* (New York: Macmillan, 1952), 2:474.

8. On the day of Brown's execution, the French novelist and poet Victor Hugo predicted that this event would "penetrate the Union with a secret fissure, which would, in the end, tear it asunder." Quoted in Reynolds, *John Brown, Abolitionist,* 409.

9. See John Niven, *The Coming of the Civil War, 1837–1861* (Arlington Heights, Ill.: Harlan Davidson, 1990); and Roy Nichols, *The Disruption of American Democracy* (New York: Macmillan, 1948), especially his chapter on the Charleston convention, 288–305.

10. Lincoln to James T. Hale, January 11, 1861, in Roy P. Basler, ed., *The Collected Works of Abraham Lincoln,* 9 vols. (New Brunswick, N.J.: Rutgers University Press, 1953–55), 4:172.

11. Lincoln's decision to provision Fort Sumter started a debate that still continues. Did

he already see war as inevitable and hence was he acting to rally the maximum support for the Union? For different views of his motives, see Charles W. Ramsdell, "Lincoln and Fort Sumter," *Journal of Southern History* 3 (1937): 259–88; David M. Potter, *Lincoln and His Party in the Secession Crisis* (1942; New Haven: Yale University Press, 1965), xxiii–xxxi; Kenneth M. Stampp, *And War Came: The North and the Secession Crisis, 1850–1861* (Chicago: University of Chicago Press, 1950); Richard N. Current, *Lincoln and the First Shot* (Philadelphia: Lippincott, 1963).

12. New York *National Principia,* May 4, 1861. The idea that the Civil War was "the second American Revolution" was elaborated and disseminated by Charles and Mary Beard in *The Rise of American Civilization,* 2 vols. in 1, rev. and enl. (1927; New York: Macmillan, 1934), 253. See also James M. McPherson, *Battle Cry of Freedom: The Civil War Era* (New York: Oxford, 1988), 452–53.

13. *Mobile Advertiser,* April 7, 1861, quoted in Silvana R. Siddali, *From Property to Person: Slavery and the Confiscation Acts, 1861–1862* (Baton Rouge: Louisiana University Press, 2005), 42–43.

14. Basler, *Collected Works of Abraham Lincoln,* 5:48–49.

15. The Cincinnati police shut down an African American recruiting center with the words, "you d—d niggers keep out of this; this is a white man's war." Peter H. Clark, *The Black Brigade of Cincinnati* (1864; New York: Arno Press, 1969), 4–5.

16. In the vast literature of the Civil War it is unusual to find a work that deals with military events without losing sight of the political and social issues for which the war was fought. A distinguished exception is McPherson, *Battle Cry of Freedom.* See also Allan Nevins, *The War for the Union,* 2 vols., vol. 1: *The Improvised War, 1861–1862,* and vol. 2: *War Becomes Revolution* (New York: Charles Scribner's Sons, 1960); Shelby Foote, *The Civil War: A Narrative,* 3 vols. (New York: Random House, 1958–74); Bruce Catton, *Centennial History of the Civil War,* vol. 1: *The Coming Fury,* vol. 2: *Terrible Swift Sword,* vol. 3: *Never Call Retreat* (Garden City, N.Y.: Doubleday, 1961–65).

17. See Virgil Carrington Jones, *The Civil War at Sea,* vol. 1: *January 1861–March 1862: The Blockaders,* vol. 2: *March 1862–July 1863: The River War,* vol. 3: *July 1863–November 1865: The Final Effort* (New York: Holt, Rinehart and Winston, 1960–62).

18. "In the early months of the war, the entire burden of heavy cannon production" for the Confederacy fell on the Tredegar plant in Richmond. Charles B. Dew, *Ironmaker to the Confederacy: Joseph R. Anderson and the Tredegar Iron Works* (New Haven: Yale University Press, 1966), 86–89 (quote, 86).

19. *The War of the Rebellion: A Compilation of the Official Records of the Union and Confederate Armies,* 128 vols. (Washington, D.C.: Government Printing Office, 1899), ser. 3, 2:2–3.

20. McPherson, *Battle Cry of Freedom,* 421; Jones, *War at Sea,* 2:188, 212–13, 218, 224.

21. E. B. Long with Barbara Long, *The Civil War Day by Day: An Almanac, 1861–1865* (Garden City, N.Y.: Doubleday, 1971), 261, 275. For a study of this Confederate offensive, see Joseph L. Harsh, *Confederate Tide Rising: Robert E. Lee and the Making of Southern Strategy, 1861–1862* (Kent, Ohio: Kent State University Press, 1998).

22. Clark, *Black Brigade of Cincinnati,* 6, 10, 16–20.

23. James L. Vallandigham, *A Life of Clement L. Vallandigham* (Baltimore: Turnbull Brothers, 1872), 208–10. Likewise Iowa state senator John J. Jennings hoped to see the advancing Confederate armies "conduct themselves with such vigor, *as to compel the North to yield to*

such compromises in the end as will secure to them their constitutional rights." Quoted in *Burlington* (Iowa) *Weekly Hawk-Eye,* June 14, 1862 (emphasis in the original). In New York, pro-Southern Democrats, headed by Mayor Fernando Wood, formerly of Charleston, organized a rally at Cooper Union, which passed a resolution opposing emancipation and affirming that "this is a government of white men and was established exclusively for the white race." Mark E. Neely Jr., *The Union Divided: Party Conflict in the Civil War North* (Cambridge, Mass.; Harvard University Press, 2002), 16. See also Jennifer Weber, *Copperheads: The Rise and Fall of Lincoln's Opponents* (New York: Oxford University Press, 2006), 53–54.

24. Frank Lawrence Owsley, *King Cotton Diplomacy: Foreign Relations of the Confederate States of America,* 2d. ed., revised by Harriet Chappell Owsley (1931; Chicago: University of Chicago Press, 1959), 28, 439; Wood Gray, *The Hidden War: The Story of the Copperheads* (New York: Viking, 1942), 128; Glyndon Van Deusen, *Horace Greeley, Nineteenth Century Crusader* (Philadelphia: University of Pennsylvania Press, 1953), 294–95.

25. Orville Vernon Burton, *Age of Lincoln* (New York: Hill and Wang, 2007), 155, 160.

26. Weber, *Copperheads,* 25, 49, 54, 80, 92; Robert F. Sterling, "Civil War Draft Resistance in the Middle West" (Ph.D. diss., Northern Illinois University, 1974), 57 and chapters 2 and 3.

27. Reinhard H. Luthin, *The First Lincoln Campaign* (Cambridge, Mass.: Harvard University Press, 1944), 10, 177, 187, 189.

28. See Hans L. Trefousse, *The Radical Republicans: Lincoln's Vanguard for Racial Justice* (New York: Knopf, 1969); idem, *Ben Butler: The South Called Him Beast* (New York: Twayne, 1963); idem, *Benjamin Franklin Wade: Radical Republican from Ohio* (New York: Twayne, 1963). See also John Niven, *Salmon P. Chase: A Biography* (New York: Oxford University Press, 1995).

29. Quoted in "Hon. Thad. Stevens Nominated for Congress by Acclamation," *Lancaster* (Pa.) *Exmainer and Herald,* September 10, 1862. See also Margaret Shortreed, "The Antislavery Radicals: From Crusade to Revolution, 1840–1868," *Past and Present* 16 (November 1959): 77, 86, and n. 48.

30. *Die Presse,* August 9, 1862, in Karl Marx and Frederick Engels, *The Civil War in the United States,* ed. Richard Enmale (New York: International Publishers, 1937), 200.

31. Nevins, *War for the Union,* 2:213, 484–91. Much of the impact of Republican policies occurred only after the war. See idem, *Emergence of Modern America, 1865–1868* (New York: Macmillan, 1927), 31–74. See also Stephen Salsbury, "The Effect of the Civil War on American Industrial Development" in *The Legacy of the American Civil War,* ed. Harold D. Woodman (New York: Wiley, 1973), 92–93.

32. See Philip S. Foner, *Business and Slavery: The New York Merchants and the Irrepressible Conflict* (1941; New York: Russell and Russell, 1968).

33. McPherson, *Battle Cry of Freedom,* 450–53; Salsbury, "Effect of the Civil War on Industrial Development," 92–93, 95. See also Nevins, *Emergence of Modern America,* 154.

34. The College Land Grant Act, or Morrill Act, July 2, 1862 (U.S. *Statutes at Large* 12 [1862]: 503–5). By 1873, nine existing colleges had been funded by the act to teach "agriculture and mechanical arts," and twenty-two new ones had been established. I. L. Kandel, *Federal Aid for Vocational Education: A Report to the Carnegie Foundation for the Advancement of Education,* Bulletin 10 (New York: n.p., [1917]), 99.

35. Adams noted the generous support that European governments gave to scientific investigations and pointed out that, while in Europe there were more than 130 astronomical

observatories, in the entire Western Hemisphere there was not even one. James D. Richardson, comp., *Messages and Papers of the Presidents*, vol. 2 (New York: Bureau of National Literature, 1897), 878–79.

36. Iver Bernstein, *The New York City Draft Riots: Their Significance for American Society and Politics in the Age of the Civil War* (New York: Oxford University Press, 1990), 29. A population survey made in 1865 indicates that the number of African Americans in the city had fallen by almost one-fourth since 1860. Ibid., 267.

37. Menahem Blondheim, *Copperhead Gore: Benjamin Wood's Fort Lafayette and Civil War America* (Bloomington: Indiana University Press, 2006), 50–51.

38. Gray, *Hidden Civil War*, 113. On the continuing violent threats of the Copperhead press, see ibid., 112.

39. Basler, *Collected Works of Abraham Lincoln*, 5:317–19.

40. See U.S. *Statutes at Large* 12 (1862): 589–92, 597; Hans L. Trefousse, *Lincoln's Decision for Emancipation* (Philadelphia: Lippincott, 1975); John Hope Franklin, *The Emancipation Proclamation* (Garden City, N.Y.: Doubleday, 1965); Steven Hahn, *A Nation under Our Feet: Black Political Struggles in Rural South from Slavery to the Great Migration* (Cambridge, Mass.: Harvard University Press, 2003), 90.

41. Hahn, *Nation under Our Feet*, 83.

42. Henry Wilson, *History of the Reconstruction Measures of the Thirty-Ninth and Fortieth Congresses, 1865–68* (1868; Westport, Conn.: Negro Universities Press, 1970), 104.

43. Mitchel [or "Mitchell"] to Edwin M. Stanton, May 4, 1862, in Ira Berlin et al., eds., *Freedom: A Documentary History of Emancipation, 1861–1867,* ser. 1, vol. 1: *The Destruction of Slavery,* ser. 1, vol. 3: *The Wartime Genesis of Free Labor: The Lower South,* ser. 2, vol. 1: *The Black Military Experience* (Cambridge: Cambridge University Press, 1982–), ser. 1, vol. 1:274–75.

44. *Burlington* (Iowa) *Weekly Hawk-Eye*, September 6, 1862.

45. Clark, *Black Brigade of Cincinnati*, 6.

46. Ibid., 6, 10, 16–20. Similarly, General David Hunter recruited blacks to defend the South Carolina Sea Islands, despite opposition in Congress. See Hunter to Stanton, June 23, 1862, in *War of the Rebellion,* ser. 3, 2:197.

47. On the political impact of the assault on Fort Wagner, see McPherson, *Battle Cry of Freedom,* 686–87; idem, *The Struggle for Equality: Abolitionists and the Negro in the Civil War and Reconstruction* (Princeton: Princeton University Press, 1964), esp. 89. See also John Greenleaf Whittier, quoted in Aaron, *Unwritten War,* 161 n.

48. *Burlington Hawk-Eye*, August 2, 1862.

49. Hammond to J. L. Orr, December 11, 1863, quoted in Orville Vernon Burton, "The Confederate Homefront: The Transformation of Values from Community to Nation in Edgefield, South Carolina," unpublished paper.

50. Boyd B. Stutler, "John Brown's Body," *Civil War History* 4 (1958): 254.

51. Ibid., 252–53.

52. Quoted in Reynolds, *John Brown, Abolitionist,* 466.

53. Entry of February 4, 1862, *Diary of George Templeton Strong,* 3:205.

54. Stutler, "John Brown's Body," 258–59.

55. *Atlantic Monthly* 9 (February 1862): 145. See also Merrill D. Peterson, *John Brown: The Legend Revisited* (Charlottesville: University of Virginia Press, 2002), 34–35.

56. Sen. Timothy Otis Howe (WS), Speech on Provisional Governments, January 10, 1866, *Congressional Globe,* 36 Cong., 1st sess., p. 163.

Chapter 12: Reconstruction

1. Speech by Representative Hamilton Ward of New York, December 13, 1866, *Congressional Globe,* 39th Cong., 1st sess., pt. 1, p. 118.

2. See Hans Trefousse's chapter "The Break with Johnson," in his *The Radical Republicans: Lincoln's Vanguard for Racial Justice* (New York: Knopf, 1969), 305–35; and Eric Foner, *Reconstruction: America's Unfinished Revolution, 1863–1877* (New York: Harper and Row, 1988), 228–39; Albert Castel, *The Presidency of Andrew Johnson* (Lawrence: Regents Press of Kansas, 1979), 26–29.

3. Johnson at a cabinet meeting is reported to have repeatedly questioned "whether any legislation was constitutional when eleven of the thirty-six states were not represented in Congress." John Niven, *Gideon Wells, Lincoln's Secretary of the Navy* (Baton Rouge: Louisiana State University Press, 1973), 523–24.

4. Edward McPherson, *The Political History of the United States of America during the Period of Reconstruction, April 15, 1865–July 15, 1870* (1871; New York: DaCapo, 1972), 9–10. In his address to Congress on December 4, 1865, Johnson said that with the adoption of the Thirteenth Amendment, "it would remain for the States, whose powers have been so long in abeyance, to resume their places in the two branches of the National Legislature, and thereby complete the work of restoration." *The Papers of Andrew Johnson,* ed. Paul H. Berson et al., vol. 9: *September, 1865–January, 1866* (Knoxville: University of Tennessee Press, 1991), 472. He thus seemed to imply that Southerners, by ratifying the amendment, could then, with their northern allies, negotiate whether "freedom" meant wage labor or serfdom, whether slaveholders were to be compensated for their losses, and whether the Federal and Confederate debts were equally valid. Foner, *Reconstruction,* 193–97; La Wanda Cox and John H. Cox, *Politics, Principle, and Prejudice: Dilemma of Reconstruction America* (New York: Atheneum, 1969), 159, 171.

5. Stephen Kantrowitz, *Ben Tillman and the Reconstruction of White Supremacy* (Chapel Hill: University of North Carolina Press, 2000), 3.

6. Orville Vernon Burton, *The Age of Lincoln* (New York: Hill and Wang, 2007), 292.

7. The freed people understood that planters, having control over land and food, thus had the means to shape the new types of labor. One told a journalist "without land, de ole massas can hire us or starve us, as dey please." Quoted in Whitelaw Reid, *After the War: A Tour of the Southern States, 1865–1866* (1866; New York: Harper and Row, 1965), 59. See also Fletcher Melvin Green, "Some Aspects of the Convict Lease System in the Southern States," in *Democracy in the Old South and Other Essays by Fletcher Melvin Green,* ed. J. Isaac Copeland (Nashville: Vanderbilt University Press, 1969), 271–87, esp. 273–74. See also Elizabeth Taylor, "The Origin and Development of the Convict Lease System in Georgia," *Georgia Historical Quarterly* 26 (June 1942): 113–28; David M. Oshinsky, *Worse Than Slavery: Parchman Farm and the Ordeal of Jim Crow Justice* (New York: Simon and Schuster, 1996).

8. On December 18, 1865, Carl Schurz documented this information in *Senate Document,* no. 2, 39th Cong., 1st sess., cited hereafter as Schurz Report.

9. McPherson, *Political History,* 107–9. One such Unionist explained to a journalist why

he had served four years as a Confederate colonel. Having just returned from Europe in the midst of the secession crisis, he said, "I was forced to raise a regiment in order to retain my influence in the community." See Reid, *After the War,* 43.

10. U.S. *Statutes at Large* 14 (1866): 27–30; McPherson, *Political History,* 78–81; Foner, *Reconstruction,* 243–47.

11. In an article entitled "The Suffrage Question," a contributor to the *New York Times* (December 22, 1868) thought expanded suffrage carried sinister implications: Beside 800,000 black voters, in the future another 800,000 Chinese and Mormons might receive the ballot, as well as 5,000,000 women. See also Foner, *Reconstruction,* 222–24; and William Gillette, *The Right to Vote: Politics and the Passage of the Fifteenth Amendment* (Baltimore: Johns Hopkins University Press, 1965), 23–25.

12. Foner, *Reconstruction,* 251–61. See also Joseph B. James, *The Framing of the Fourteenth Amendment* (1956; Urbana: University of Illinois Press, 1965); Benjamin B. Kendrick, *The Journal of the Joint Committee of Fifteen on Reconstruction* (1914; New York: Negro Universities Press, 1969).

13. U.S. Congress, House, Majority Report, *Memphis Riots and Massacres: Report No. 101* (serial no. 1274), July 25, 1866, 39th Cong., 1st sess., vol. 3, p. 36.

14. *New Orleans Riots: Report No. 16,* 39th Cong., 2d sess. (serial no. 1304); Gilles Vandal, *The New Orleans Riot of 1866: Anatomy of a Tragedy* (Lafayette: The Center for Louisiana Studies, University of Southwestern Louisiana, 1983); James G. Hollandsworth Jr., *An Absolute Massacre: The New Orleans Race Riot of July 30, 1866* (Baton Rouge: Louisiana State University Press, 2001).

15. Foner, *Reconstruction,* 28, 221–24, 240. On Iowa's "egalitarian moment," see Robert R. Dykstra, *Bright Radical Star: Black Freedom and White Supremacy in the Hawkeye Frontier* (Cambridge, Mass.: Harvard University Press, 1993).

16. McPherson, *Political History,* 191–94, 335–37.

17. For abstracts of ten southern constitutions adopted during 1867–68, see McPherson, *Political History,* 326–35.

18. Some antebellum offices were restricted to Protestants; see Fletcher M. Green, *Constitutional Development in the South Atlantic States, 1776–1860* (1930; New York: Norton, 1966), 94. See also Francis Newton Thorpe, ed., *The Federal and State Constitutions,* 7 vols. (Washington, D.C.: Government Printing Office, 1909), 2:724, 5:2812; and Foner, *Reconstruction,* 320.

19. Ira Berlin et al., *Freedom: A Documentary History of Emancipation, 1861–1867,* ser. 1, vol. 1: *The Destruction of Slavery,* ser. 1, vol. 2: *The Wartime Genesis of Free Labor: The Upper South,* ser. 1, vol. 3: *The Wartime Genesis of Free Labor: The Lower South,* ser. 2, vol. 1: *The Black Military Experience* (Cambridge: Cambridge University Press, 1982–), ser. 1, vol. 2: 135, 352, 471–472, 493, 535–44; William McKee Evans, *Ballots and Fence Rails: Reconstruction on the Lower Cape Fear* (1967; Athens: University of Georgia Press, 1995), 53–62; Edward Magdol, *A Right to Land: Essays on the Freedman's Community* (Westport, Conn.: Greenwood, 1977), esp. 165–70; Willie Lee Rose, *Rehearsal for Reconstruction: The Port Royal Experiment* (New York: Vintage, 1967), especially her chapter "'Squatter Rights' or 'Charitable Purposes,'" 272–96; Wayne K. Durrill, *War of Another Kind: A Southern Community in the Great Rebellion* (New York: Oxford University Press, 1990), 220–21.

20. Schurz Report, 19, 36. The southern elite, having reestablished their control over the land, now passed laws to extend their control over labor. These included fencing laws, end-

ing the open range; and laws restricting the traditional rights to hunt, fish, gather firewood and wild fruits and berries. See Foner, *Reconstruction,* 203 n. 53.

21. Foner, *Reconstruction,* 235–36. For less far-reaching efforts at land reform, see Burton, *Age of Lincoln,* 260.

22. The creation of homesteads from the largest plantations was also supported, by Representative George Washington Julian and Senator Charles Sumner. See Jonathan M. Wiener, *Social Origins of the New South: Alabama, 1860–1865* (Baton Rouge: Louisiana State University Press, 1978), 6.

23. In Indian Territory, for example, the Cherokee Nation lost 300,000 head of cattle to one side or the other. Lawrence M. Hauptman, *Between Two Fires: Americans in the Civil War* (New York: Free Press, 1995), 42.

24. Burton, *Age of Lincoln,*199.

25. Confederate currency was worthless, and in the South money of any kind was scarce. There was five times as much federal currency in circulation in Massachusetts alone than in the entire South. See Lawrence Goodwyn, *The Populist Moment: A Short History of the Agrarian Revolt in America* (New York: Oxford University Press, 1978), 22.

26. Wiener, *Social Origins of the New South,* 13–14.

27. Dwight B. Billings, *Planters and the Making of a New South: Class, Politics and Development in North Carolina, 1865–1900* (Chapel Hill: University of North Carolina Press, 1979), 87.

28. James C. Bonner, "Historical Basis of Southern Military Tradition," *Georgia Historical Review* 9 (Spring 1955): 84. For a fuller treatment of this tradition, see John Hope Franklin, *The Militant South, 1800–1860* (Boston: Beacon, 1965).

29. Henry Cooke to Jay Cooke, October 12, 1867, quoted in Ellis Paxton Oberholtzer, *Jay Cooke: Financier of the Civil War,* vol. 2 (Philadelphia: George Jacobs, 1907), 28.

30. To gain the votes required for the ratification of the Reconstruction amendments, the Republicans passed over women's rights. In reaction, some feminists no longer spoke out for the civil rights of blacks. Burton, *Age of Lincoln,* 260.

31. Allen W. Trelease, *White Terror: The Ku Klux Klan Conspiracy and Southern Reconstruction* (New York: Harper and Row, 1971), 113–17, 119, 129–31, 135–36, 150, 158, 175–77; Gillette, *Right to Vote,* 40.

32. U.S. *Congressional Globe,* 40th Cong., 3rd sess., pt. 2, 904.

33. Gillette, *Right to Vote,* 164–65.

34. Trelease, *White Terror,* 383–87; and see his conclusion: "Once the federal arrests and prosecutions fell off in 1873, it became ever clearer that terrorism was the surest and quickest road to victory in the South." Ibid., 420.

35. Foner, *Reconstruction,* 553–56, 587. Many Republican judges strongly advocated the right of property owners to use their property as they saw fit, even, as in businesses such as restaurants and hotels, the right to practice racial discrimination.

36. C. Vann Woodward, *Reunion and Reaction: The Compromise of 1877 and the End of Reconstruction* (New York: Doubleday, 1956), 7–9, 189, 239. Joel Williamson has shown, however, that the Republicans continued to give minimum attention to their southern wing. It was not until the Taft administration, 1909–13, that the purge of southern blacks was completed. Williamson, *Crucible of Race: Black-White Relations in the American South since Emancipation* New York: Oxford University Press, 1984), 357, 362.

Chapter 13: Between Slavery and Freedom

1. This number is for the 1880s and includes interest plus the "credit prices" that debtors paid for provisions. See Roger L. Ransom and Richard D. Sutch, *One Kind of Freedom: The Economic Consequences of Emancipation* (Cambridge: Cambridge University Press, 1977), 130, 240.

2. Jack P. Maddex Jr., *The Virginia Conservatives, 1867–1879: A Study of Reconstruction Politics* (Chapel Hill: University of North Carolina Press, 1970), 96, 146.

3. Steven Hahn, *A Nation under Our Feet: Black Political Struggles in the Rural South from Slavery to the Great Migration* (Cambridge, Mass.: Harvard University Press, 2003), 374–75, 382–83.

4. Ibid., 375–78, 381–82, 402–6; Carl N. Degler, *The Other South: Southern Dissenters in the Nineteenth Century* (New York: Harper and Row, 1974), 296 (quote).

5. Lawrence Goodwyn, *The Populist Moment: A Short History of the Agrarian Revolt in America* (New York: Oxford University Press, 1978), 74–77, 116–24.

6. See Goodwyn's chapter "The Alliance Develops a Movement Culture," *Populist Moment*, 20–54. See also ibid., 123–24.

7. Ibid., 74–80.

8. Lawrence Goodwyn calls the Alliance view of the crisis the "greenback critique of American finance capitalism," much of it derived from the short-lived Greenback Labor Party. Ibid., 13.

9. Alliance supporters campaigned for the "ten planks of Ocala." See *Documents of American History*, ed. Henry Steel Commager (New York: F. S. Crofts, 1946), 2:142–43.

10. Goodwyn, *Populist Moment*, 278–82.

11. Ibid.

12. Jeffrey J. Crow and Robert F. Durden, *Maverick Republican in the Old North State: A Political Biography of Daniel L. Russell* (Baton Rouge: Louisiana State University Press, 1977), 35–39.

13. J. Morgan Kousser, *The Shaping of Southern Politics: Suffrage Restructuring and the Establishment of the One-Party South, 1880–1900* (New Haven: Yale University Press, 1974), 485–87. For the lease controversy, see Crow and Durden, *Maverick Republican*, 99–116.

14. Quoted in Paul D. Escott, *Many Excellent People: Power and Privilege in North Carolina, 1850–1900* (Chapel Hill: University of North Carolina Press, 1985), 251.

15. Helen G. Edmonds, *The Negro and Fusion Politics in North Carolina, 1894–1901* (Chapel Hill: University of North Carolina Press, 1951), esp. 136–37, 153–54.

16. H. Leon Prather Sr., *We Have Taken a City: Wilmington Racial Massacre and Coup of 1898* (Rutherford, N.J.: Fairleigh Dickinson University Press, 1984), 49–50; Escott, *Many Excellent People*, 254–55.

17. Quoted in Crow and Durden, *Maverick Republican*, 130.

18. Glenda Elizabeth Gilmore, "Black Militia in the Spanish-American War," in *The War of 1898 and the U.S. Interventions, 1898–1934: An Encyclopedia*, ed. Benjamin R. Beede (New York: Garland, 1994), 53–54; idem, *Gender and Jim Crow: Women and the Politics of White Supremacy in North Carolina, 1896–1920* (Chapel Hill: University of North Carolina Press, 1996), 81–83; Willard B. Gatewood Jr., *"Smoked Yankees" and the Struggle for Empire: Letters from Negro Soldiers, 1898–1902* (Urbana: University of Illinois Press, 1971), 103, 110 n. 1.

19. Timothy B. Tyson, "Wars for Democracy," in *Democracy Betrayed: The Wilmington*

Race Riot of 1898 and Its Legacy, ed. David S. Cecelski and Timothy B. Tyson (Chapel Hill: University of North Carolina Press, 1998), 254.

20. Glenda E. Gilmore, "Murder, Memory, and the Flight of the Incubus," in Cecelski and Tyson, *Democracy Betrayed,* 83–90; and Stephen Kantrowitz, "The Two Faces of Domination in North Carolina, 1800–1998," ibid., 106–8.

21. Crow and Durden, *Maverick Republican,* 134; Prather, *We Have Taken a City,* 103–4.

22. Edmonds, *The Negro and Fusion Politics,* 125.

23. Kousser, *Shaping of Southern Politics,* 144. Disfranchisement was not a single law but an array of deliberately complex laws and regulations, a legal challenge to any one of which would require lengthy and expensive litigation that would eventually fail before a Supreme Court that had demonstrated its laissez-faire view of racial discrimination. A common device was to require voters to register. An applicant often had to convince a registrar appointed by the legislature of one's "literacy," one's ability to "interpret" the Constitution, and the like. See Kousser's chapter "A Good, Square, Honest, Law That Will Always Give a Good Democratic Majority," ibid., 182–223.

24. Quoted in ibid., 191.

25. Ibid., 191, 238–42.

26. Ibid., 193.

27. Stephen Kantrowitz, *Ben Tillman and the Reconstruction of White Supremacy* (Chapel Hill: University of North Carolina Press, 2000), 9.

28. C. Vann Woodward, *The Strange Career of Jim Crow* (New York: Oxford University Press, 1955), 54, 70–71.

29. See Pete Daniel, *The Shadow of Slavery: Peonage in the South, 1901–1969* (New York: Oxford University Press, 1973); David M. Oshinsky, *Worse Than Slavery: Parchman Farm and the Ordeal of Jim Crow Justice* (New York: Simon and Schuster, 1996).

30. Ransom and Sutch, *One Kind of Freedom,* 5, 198. Peonage, unlike slavery, was illegal or practiced under laws of dubious constitutionality. Also, widespread disapproval of the system made it possible on occasions for a victim to get help from authorities. In 1937, for example, a white Mississippi sheriff, on the complaint of a black worker, freed a woman held in chains by her employer. See Daniel, *Shadow of Slavery,* 174–75.

31. Willie Lee Rose, *Port Royal Experiment: The Port Royal Experiment* (New York: Random House, 1967), 229–35, 372–74; See W. E. B. DuBois's chapter, "Founding the Public School," in his *Black Reconstruction in America, 1860–1880* (1935; New York: Atheneum, 1969), 637–67.

32. Hahn, *A Nation under Our Feet,* 120, 230–34, 276–79, 461–62. African American schools and churches were often the targets of the white terror. During the Memphis "riots" of 1866, for example, a witness noted the "most intense and unjustifiable prejudice . . . seems to have been arrayed against teachers of color and against preachers to colored people. . . . these people were forced to flee from the city." U.S. Congress, House Majority Report, *Memphis Riots and Massacres: Report No. 101* (serial no. 1274), July 2, 1866, 39th Cong., 1st sess., vol. 3, p. 20. See also ibid., pp. 21, 36, 91–92.

33. The conservative constitutions reduced the number of white voters and virtually eliminated black ones. See C. Vann Woodward, *The Origins of the New South, 1877–1913* (Baton Rouge: Louisiana State University Press, 1951), 211, 342–43. In addition to the precipitous drop in the number of registered voters, there was a similar drop in the number of registered voters who actually voted. Whereas in presidential elections during Reconstruction, the turnout

of registered voters was more than 75 percent, by 1920 it had fallen to less than 20 percent. Numan V. Bartley and Hugh D. Graham, *Southern Politics and the Second Reconstruction* (Baltimore: Johns Hopkins University Press, 1975), 8–10. While the decline in voter participations in elections was sharpest in the one-party South, there was a less extreme decline in the two-party North and West. Ibid. See also Michael E. McGerr, *The Decline of Popular Politics: The American North 1865–1928* (New York: Oxford University Press, 1986), 51–52.

Chapter 14: The Age of Segregation at Its Zenith

1. "Between 1882 and 1946 almost 5,000 people died by lynching." Jacquelyn Dowd Hall, "'The Mind That Burns in Each Body': Women, Rape, and Racial Violence," in *The Powers of Desire: The Politics of Sexuality,* ed. Ann Snitow et al. (New York: Monthly Review Press, 1983), 329.

2. Speech of Albert Beveridge to the Middlesex Club, Boston, April 27, 1898. In Beveridge, *The Meaning of the Times and Other Speeches* (Indianapolis: Bobbs-Merrill, 1908), 43.

3. Clyde N. Wilson, ed., *The Papers of John C. Calhoun,* vol. 14: *1837–1839* (Columbia: University of South Carolina Press, 1981), 84–85.

4. While the market seemed endless for stories about the tragic war between brothers, one writer suggested a resolution: "All battles of the civil war were won by American soldiers. All the heroes of that war were Americans." Quoted in David W. Blight, *Race and Reunion: The Civil War in American Memory* (Cambridge, Mass.: Harvard University Press, 2001), 394. On the difficulties American writers have had dealing with Civil War, see Daniel Aaron, *The Unwritten War: American Writers and the Civil War* (New York: Oxford University Press, 1973).

5. Sheldon Van Auken, "The Southern Historical Novel in the Early Twentieth Century," *Journal of Southern History* 14 (May 1948): 164–71, 190–91. After Reconstruction and into the twentieth century no literary subject was more popular than southern romance, in which North-South reconciliation was a constant reoccurring theme, often expressed symbolically by love between a southern "belle" and a Yankee officer, sometimes the only noble Northerner in the story. Bronson Howard's *Shenandoah* (1889), for example, the most popular play since *Uncle Tom's Cabin,* "in the end made certain the future safety of the nation by uniting five (no less!) pairs of lovers whose loyalties had been divided by war." Paul H. Buck, *The Road to Reunion, 1865–1900* (1937; New York: Vintage, 1959), 242; see also 215–16.

6. On the "southern" point of view of early Hollywood and its influence on the representation of African Americans, see Thomas Cripps, *Slow Fade to Black: The Negro in American Films, 1900–1942* (New York: Oxford University Press, 1977); Daniel J. Leab, *From Sambo to Superspade: The Black Experience in Motion Pictures* (Boston: Houghton Mifflin, 1975); Donald Bogle, *Toms, Coons, Mulattos, Mammies, and Bucks: An Interpretive History of Blacks in American Films* (New York: Viking, 1973).

7. Nathan Irvin Huggins, *The Harlem Renaissance* (New York: Oxford University Press, 1971), 269, and on the persistence of the minstrel tradition of representing blacks, 275–86.

8. Arthur de Gobineau, *The Inequality of Human Races,* trans. Adrian Collins (New York: Howard Forting, 1967), 150; Richard Woolen, *The Seduction of Unreason: The Intellectual Romance with Fascism from Nietzsche to Postmodernism* (Princeton: Princeton University Press, 2004), 289–90; Michael D. Biddies, *Father of Racist Ideology: The Social and Political Thought of Count Gobineau* (New York: Eyebright and Talley, 1970).

9. Elazar Barkan, *The Retreat of Scientific Racism: Changing Concepts of Race in Britain and the United States between the World Wars* (Cambridge: Cambridge University Press, 1992), 66–69 (quote, 68). Eugenicists lamented the declining birthrate among women of "good stock" and accused feminists of luring them away from their traditional roles as child bearers. See Wendy Kline, *Building a Better Race: Gender, Sexuality, and Eugenics from the Turn of the Century to the Baby Boom* (Berkeley: University of California Press, 2001), 11, 14.

10. Madison Grant, *The Passing of a Great Race, or, The Racial Basis of European History* (New York: Scribner's, 1916), 49.

11. Theodore Lothrop Stoddard, *The Revolt against Civilization: The Menace of the Under Man* (New York: Scribner's, 1922), 253.

12. See "Unguarded Gates," quoted in Robert L. Beisner, *Twelve against Empire: The Anti-Imperialists, 1898–1900* (New York: McGraw-Hill, 1968), 12.

13. Beveridge, *Meaning of the Times,* 43. See also Richard Hofstadter's chapter "Racism and Imperialism," in his *Social Darwinism in American Thought* (Boston: Beacon, 1955), 170–200; R. J. Wilson, ed., *Darwinism and the American Intellectual: A Book of Readings* (Homewood, Ill.: Dorsey Press, 1967); Eric F. Goldman, *Rendezvous with Destiny: History of Modern American Reform* (New York: Vintage, 1958), 69–70; Eric T. L. Love, *Race over Empire: Racism and U.S. Imperialism, 1865–1900* (Chapel Hill: University of North Carolina Press, 2004), 191.

14. In the authoritative *Encyclopedia Britannica* one might read that because blacks suffered a "premature ossification of the skull, preventing all further development of the brain, many anthropologists have attributed the inherent mental inferiority of the blacks, an inferiority which is even more marked than their physical differences," s.v. "Negro," by A. H. Keane, vol. 17 (Chicago: Werner, 1893), 321.

15. Robert C. Weaver, "Racial Employment Trends in National Defense," *Pylon* 2 (4th quarter, 1941): 341–42; idem, *Negro Labor: A National Problem* (Port Washington, N.Y.: Kennikat, 1949); Gunnar Myrdal et al., *An American Dilemma: The Negro Problem and Modern Democracy* (New York: Harper, 1944), 1302 n. 2.

16. Bruce Nelson, *Divided We Stand: American Workers and the Struggle for Equality* (Princeton: Princeton University Press, 2001), 94–95; Beth Tompkins Bates, *Pullman Porters and the Rise of Protest Politics in Black America* (Chapel Hill: University of North Carolina Press, 2001), xx, 47, 257–58; Harvard Sitkoff, *A New Deal for Blacks: The Emergence of Civil Rights as a National Issue,* vol. 1: *The Depression Decade* (New York: Oxford University Press, 1978), 183.

17. August Meier and Elliott M. Rudwick, *From Plantation to Ghetto: An Interpretative History of American Negroes* (New York: Hill and Wang, 1966), 189; Nicholas Lemann, *The Great Migration and How It Changed America* (New York: Knopf, 1991); George W. Groh, *The Black Migration: The Journey to Urban America* (New York: Weybright and Talley, 1972), 50–51; Joe William Trotter Jr., *The Great Migration in Historical Perspective* (Bloomington: Indiana University Press, 1991).

18. Since the late nineteenth century, working people, native-born and immigrant, had become increasingly organized and assertive. They showed little faith in traditional Democratic-Republican politics but favored instead strikes and radical parties. World War I provided conservatives an opportunity to launch a fearful backlash. See William Preston, *Aliens and Dissenters: Federal Suppression of radicals, 1903–1933* (Urbana: University of Illinois Press, 1963).

19. George Hutchinson, *The Harlem Renaissance in Black and White* (Cambridge, Mass.: Harvard University Press, 1995), 212.

20. Martha Jane Nadell, *Enter the New Negro* (Cambridge, Mass.: Harvard University Press, 2004), 10–33.

21. Among Boaz's followers were Alfred Kroeber, Robert Lowie, Alexander Goldenweiser, Paul Radin, Melville Herskovits, Ruth Benedict, Margaret Mead, and Otto Klineberg. See Barkan, *Retreat of Scientific Racism*, 90–95. After World War I, scientists in the United States and elsewhere increasingly challenged and marginalized the advocates of scientific racism.

22. Glenda Elizabeth Gilmore, *Gender and Jim Crow: Women and the Politics of White Supremacy in North Carolina, 1896–1920* (Chapel Hill: University of North Carolina Press, 1996), 137.

23. Quoted in Goldman, *Rendezvous with Destiny*, 176–77.

24. According to a film critic, *The Birth of a Nation* "is almost universally recognized as a milestone in the development of world cinema. . . . It powerfully influenced all aspects of the film medium." Leab, *From Sambo to Superspade*, 25. See also Edward Wagenknecht and Anthony Slide, *The Films of D. W. Griffith* (New York: Crown, 1975), 59. On the film's run-away popularity, see Everett Carter, "Writing History with Lightning: The Significance of *The Birth of a Nation*," American *Quarterly* 12 (Fall 1960): 347; Richard Schickel, *D. W. Griffith: An American Life* (New York: Simon and Schuster, 1984), 214; Kenneth T. Jackson, *The Ku Klux Klan in the City, 1915–1930* (New York: Oxford University Press, 1996?), 3–4. For more general audience reactions, see Bogle, *Toms, Coons, Mulattos, Mammies, and Bucks*, 10. On the political importance of "rape" in the New South, see Diane Miller Sommerville, *Rape and Race in the Nineteenth-Century South* (Chapel Hill: University of North Carolina Press, 2004), 220. For an interpretation of this film that stresses the theme of race, the black/white contrast, as a device to enhance the dramatic impact of the story, see Linda Williams, *Playing the Race Card: Melodramas of Race and Black and White from Uncle Tom to O. J. Simpson* (Princeton: Princeton University Press, 2001), 109–29.

25. Herbert Shapiro, *White Violence and Black Response: From Reconstruction to Montgomery* (Amherst: University of Massachusetts Press, 1988), 49–55.

26. Quoted in Oscar Berland, "The Emergence of the Communist Perspective on the 'Negro Question' in America: 1919–1931," Part 1, *Science and Society* 63 (Winter 1999/2000): 411–32 (quote, 417); see also Part 2, *Science and Society* 64 (Summer 2000): 194–217.

27. "Labour cannot emancipate itself in the white skin where in the black it is branded." Karl Marx, *Capital: A Critique of Political Economy*, vol. 1 (1867; New York: Modern Library, 1906), 329.

28. Theodore Kornweibel Jr., *"Seeing Red": Federal Campaigns against Black Militancy* (Bloomington: Indiana University Press, 1999), 28; Harry Williams, *Black Responses to the Left, 1917–1929*, Princeton Undergraduate Studies in History 1 (Princeton: History Department, Princeton University, 1973), 92–93. Blacks who joined radical movements were at first mostly immigrants from the West Indies. See Winston James, *Holding Aloft the Banner of Ethiopia: Caribbean Radicalism in Early Twentieth Century America* (London: Verso, 1999), 122.

29. On the broadening vision of African Americans that began with the Great Migration, see Steven Hahn, *A Nation under Our Feet: Black Political Struggles in the Rural South from Slavery to the Great Migration* (Cambridge, Mass.: Harvard University Press, 2003), 468–72.

30. Langston Hughes, *I Wonder as I Wander: An Autobiographical Journey* (New York: Hill

and Wang, 1956), 172. For a broad view of the African American encounter with imperialism and the Russian revolution, see Glenda Elizabeth Gilmore's chapter "Jim Crow Meets Karl Marx," in her *Defying Dixie: The Radical Roots of Civil Rights* (New York: Norton, 2008), 15–66.

31. Quoted in Berland, "Emergence of the Communist Perspective," part 1: 421.

32. Isaac Deutscher, *Stalin: A Political Biography* (New York: Oxford University Press, 1949), 98–103, 228–29.

33. Joseph Stalin, *Marxism and the National Question and Other Writings* (New York: International Publishers, 1967), 12.

34. Berland, "Emergence of the Communist Perspective," part 1: 416–17.

35. "The Communist International Resolution on the Negro Question in the U.S." (A draft of this document was submitted by a subcommittee consisting of a Russian, N. Nasnov, who had visited the United States, four American blacks, and the occasional participation of three other Americans. The final resolution was based on this draft and the debates that followed it.) See Philip S. Foner and James S. Allen, eds., *American Communism and Black Americans: A Documentary History, 1919–1929* (Philadelphia: Temple University Press, 1987), 163, 189–96.

36. Ibid., 193. For an account of these debates from the point of view of a delegate who supported the "oppressed nation" formulation, see Harry Haywood, *Black Bolshevik: Autobiography of an Afro-American Communist* (Chicago: Liberator Press, 1978), 245–69.

37. Berland, "Emergence of the Communist Perspective," part 2: 208. See also Robin G. Kelley, *Hammer and Hoe: Alabama Communists during the Great Depression* (Chapel Hill: University of North Carolina Press, 1990), 28–29; Mark Solomon, *The Cry Was Unity: Communists and African Americans, 1917–36* (Jackson: University of Mississippi Press, 1998), 1, 127–28; Sitkoff, *New Deal for Blacks*, 1:157–59.

Chapter 15: Radical Challenge, Liberal Reform

1. Gavin Wright, *Old South, New South: Revolutions in the Southern Economy since the Civil War* (New York: Basic Books, 1986), 67, 76, 130, 206; Wayne Flynt, *Dixie's Forgotten People: The South's Poor Whites* (Bloomington: Indiana University Press, 1979), 65–67; Jacquelyn Dowd Hall et al., *Like a Family: The Making of a Southern Cotton Mill World* (Chapel Hill: University of North Carolina Press, 1987), 150. For traveler accounts of southern poverty in the 1930s, see David Eugene Conrad, *The Forgotten Farmers: The Story of Sharecroppers in the New Deal* (Urbana: University of Illinois Press, 1965), 16–18.

2. A Birmingham black Communist recalled that "the 'lower class of niggers,' as we were called in those days—and many of the 'better class ones' and some of the whites also would whisper to our people—they were saying, 'we are with you all' or 'I am in favor of what you all are working for, but know I cannot stick my neck out, but I am with you. Here is my little donation, but just keep what I say and do to yourself, and don't ever call my name to anyone.'" See Nell Irvin Painter, *The Narrative of Hosea Hudson: His Life as a Negro Communist in the South* (Cambridge, Mass.: Harvard University Press, 1979), 101.

3. Fred Beal, *Proletarian Journey: New England, Gastonia, Moscow* (New York: Hillman-Curl, 1937), 139.

4. *Gastonia Daily Gazette*, April 12, 1929, quoted in John A. Salmond, *Gastonia 1929: The*

Story of the Loray Mill Strike (Chapel Hill: University of North Carolina Press, 1995), 36 (quote), 194, and n. 25.

5. Quoted in Theodore Rosengarten, *All of God's Dangers: The Life of Nate Shaw* (1974; New York: Random House, 1984), 297–99, 304.

6. Painter, *Narrative of Hosea Hudson,* 83; Dan T. Carter, *Scottsboro: A Tragedy of the American South,* 2nd ed. (Baton Rouge: Louisiana State University Press, 1984); James Goodman, *Stories of Scottsboro* (New York: Pantheon, 1994); Harvard Sitkoff, *A New Deal for Blacks: The Emergence of Civil Rights as a National Issue,* vol. 1: *The Depression Decade* (New York: Oxford University Press, 1978), 145–49.

7. Mark I. Solomon, *The Cry Was Unity: Communists and African Americans, 1917–36* (Jackson: University of Mississippi Press, 1998), 122–23, 240, 294–95, 299; Robin G. Kelley, *Hammer and Hoe: Alabama Communists during the Great Depression* (Chapel Hill: University of North Carolina Press, 1990), 120–21, 170–71; Sitkoff, *New Deal for Blacks,* 1:158.

8. The Socialist leader Norman Thomas denied that the STFU was Socialist. He said that most of the members were Democrats who could not vote because of the poll tax. Conrad, *Forgotten Farmers,* 94.

9. Sitkoff, *New Deal for Blacks,* 1:163–64, 180; Kelly, *Hammer and Hoe,* 120–21.

10. John M. Glen, *Highlander: No Ordinary School, 1932–1962* (Lexington: University Press of Kentucky, 1988), 183–84.

11. Although the charges were later reduced or dropped, originally thirteen men and three women faced the death penalty for the murder of the police chief. For an account of the shootout by one who was present, see Beal, *Proletarian Journey,* 167–71. For other witnesses, see Glenda Elizabeth Gilmore, *Defying Dixie: The Radical Roots of Civil Rights* (New York: Norton, 2008), 89–90.

12. Also known as Ella May. After her separation from John Wiggins, she assumed her maiden name, as did eight of her nine children. See Salmond, *Gastonia 1929,* 50–51, 128.

13. Gilmore, *Defying Dixie,* 129–30.

14. Ibid., 106–97. See also Gunnar Myrdal et al., *An American Dilemma: The Negro Problem and Modern Democracy* (New York: Harper, 1944), 847.

15. Gilmore, *Defying Dixie,* 112.

16. Quoted in Neil Smith, *The Endgame of Globalism* (New York: Routlege, 2005), 82.

17. Anthony J. Badger, *The New Deal: The Depression Years, 1933–40* (New York: Noonday Press, 1989), 51–52, 114–16.

18. On the growing tensions within the Democratic Party, see Henry Lee Moon, *Balance of Power: The Negro Vote* (Garden City, N.Y.: Doubleday, 1949), 19.

19. Charles H. Martin, *The Angelo Herndon Case and Southern Justice* (Baton Rouge: Louisiana State University Press, 1976), 7–8; Solomon, *The Cry Was Unity,* 219, 359 nn. 31–32; Angelo Herndon, *Let Me Live* (New York: Random House, 1937), 238.

20. Herndon, *Let Me Live,* 228 (quote); Kelley, *Hammer and Hoe,* 13.

21. On a refugee from Gastonia who started large-scale protests in Winston-Salem, see Robert Rogers Korstad, *Civil Rights Unionism: Tobacco Workers and the Struggle for Democracy in the Mid-Twentieth-Century South* (Chapel Hill: University of North Carolina Press, 2003), 125–26. Clara Holden, driven out of Greenville, South Carolina, surfaced at Straight Creek, Kentucky, as an organizer in the Harlan County coal fields. See Gilmore, *Defying Dixie,* 130.

22. John A. Salmond, *The General Textile Strike of 1934: From Maine to Alabama* (Columbia: University of Missouri Press, 2002), ix, 45.

23. "Flying squadrons" began earlier with the anti-eviction riots in black Chicago. Youth bands, getting word of an eviction, would converge on the house, put the family's furniture back inside, and mobilize the neighborhood for a battle with the police. They would then distribute a leaflet about the eviction and the greed of the "rent hog." "When eviction notices arrived, it was not unusual for a mother to shout to the children, 'Run quick and find the Reds.'" St. Clare Drake and Horace R. Cayton, *Black Metropolis: A Study of Negro Life in a Northern City,* vol. 1 (New York: Harper and Row, 1962), 86–87.

24. Quoted in Hall et al., *Like a Family,* 332.

25. Indeed, angry workers broke up a Communist "solidarity" rally in Charlotte and the police are reported to have rescued the organizer.

26. At Herndon's Atlanta trial the prosecutor cried out to the jury: "Send this damnable anarchistic Bolsheviki to his death by electrocution and God will be satisfied that Justice has been done." See Solomon, *The Cry Was Unity,* 220, 359, and n. 35.

27. Salmond, *General Textile Strike,* 50, 240.

28. Ibid., 76.

29. Janet Irons, *Testing the New Deal: The General Textile Strike of 1934 in the American South* (Urbana: University of Illinois Press, 2000), 153. According to an article entitled "Many Mills Open: 80,000 of Strikers Still Out in South," *New York Times,* September 25, 1934, most of the strikers were locked out. See also Salmond, *General Textile Strike,* 215–16.

30. Bruce Nelson, *Divided We Stand: American Workers and the Struggle for Black Rights* (Princeton: Princeton University Press, 2001), 94–96; Beth Tomkins Bates, *Pullman Porters and the Rise of Protest Politics in Black America, 1925–1945* (Chapel Hill: University of North Carolina Press, 2001), xx, 47, 257–58; Sitkoff, *New Deal for Blacks,* 1: 183.

31. Herndon, *Let Me Live,* 318–19.

32. The CIO steel-organizing drive in Birmingham was headed by Noel R. Beddow, a lawyer. According to a local activist, Beddow was a "communist hater. But he had orders from Philip Murray and John L. Lewis and them, 'You got to work with these guys, cause they's good organizers. They's the ones that know how to organize, how to contact people.'" Quoted in Painter, *Narrative of Hosea Hudson,* 246.

33. On these New Deal programs, see Sitkoff, *New Deal for Blacks,* 1:67, 75, 202; Badger, *New Deal,* 175–77, 203–7, 227–35.

34. Sitkoff, *New Deal for Blacks,* 1:91, 95, 98; Myrdal et al., *American Dilemma,* 487–88.

35. Patricia Sullivan, *Days of Hope: Race and Democratic Party in the New Deal* (Chapel Hill: University of North Carolina Press, 1996), 60.

36. Irons, *Testing the New Deal,* 143.

37. Sitkoff, *New Deal for Blacks,* 1:52.

38. Sullivan, *Days of Hope,* 43.

39. Conrad, *Forgotten Farmers,* 80–81, 205–8.

40. Badger, *New Deal,* 199–200.

41. Wright, *Old South, New South,* 217, 236.

42. Sitkoff, *New Deal for Blacks,* 1:105.

43. Salmond, *General Textile Strike,* 71, 73; Gilmore, *Defying Dixie,* 180.

44. *Nation,* March 4, 1936, 270.

45. Sullivan, *Days of Hope,* 99–100.

46. George Brown Tindall, *Emergence of the New South, 1913–1945* (Baton Rouge: Louisiana State University Press, 1967), 557. See also the estimates of Ralph Bunch in Myrdal et al., *American Dilemma,* 488, 512–15; and estimates by Sitkoff in his *New Deal for Blacks,* 1:98.

47. "The Anderson affair," *Time,* April 17, 1939, 23; Harold L. Ickes, *The Secret Diary of Harold L. Ickes,* vol. 2: *The Inside Struggle, 1936–1939* (New York: Simon and Schuster, 1954), 612–17; Joseph P. Lash, *Eleanor and Franklin: The Story of Their Relationship Based on Eleanor's Private Papers* (New York: Norton, 1971), 525–28.

Chapter 16: The American Century, the American Dilemma

1. Henry R. Luce, "The American Century," *Life,* February 17, 1941, 63.

2. George Schuyler, "Views and Reviews," (Pittsburgh) *Courier,* December 21, 1940.

3. Dudley Taylor Cornish, *The Sable Army: Negro Troops in the Union Army* (New York: Norton, 1966), 288.

4. New Dealers feared that an unregulated economy would cause "chaos" and threaten harmony between the social classes. See John B. Kirby, *Black Americans in the Roosevelt Era: Liberalism and Race* (Knoxville: University of Tennessee Press, 1980), ix.

5. Harvard Sitkoff, *A New Deal for Blacks: The Emergence of Civil Rights as a National Issue,* vol. 1: *The Depression Decade* (New York: Oxford University Press, 1978), 111.

6. *Encyclopedia of American History,* ed. Richard B. Morris (New York: Harper and Row, 1970), 352, 359.

7. National Bureau of Economic Research, *Working Papers on Historical Factors in Long Run Growth,* no. 62: Peter Tamin, *The Great Depression* (Cambridge, Mass.: Published by the Bureau, 1994), 45. Compare with William Appleman Williams, *The Tragedy of American Diplomacy* (New York: Norton, 1972), 162–201, esp. 195. For the spike in exports to Italy and Japan during their wars in Ethiopia and China, see William O. Scruggs, "Oil for Italy," *Foreign Affairs* 14 (April, 1936): 524; and Robert Lincoln O'Brien, "The Need for World Markets," *Vital Speeches* 1 (June 1935): 601.

8. Walter White, after his 1941 interviews with the secretary of war and the secretary of the navy, reported their saying that Southerners held 50 percent or more of the top-ranking positions in the armed forces. White, *A Man Called White: The Autobiography of Walter White* (New York: Viking, 1948), 190–91.

9. Ibid., 187.

10. Luce, "American Century," 61.

11. Ibid., 65.

12. Beth Tompkins Bates, *Pullman Porters and the Rise of Protest Politics in Black America* (Chapel Hill: University of North Carolina Press, 2001), 155–56.

13. "The power of the new movement is mysterious. It has almost no organization, no big machine promotion and publicity. Yet it grips the people's imagination and holds their loyalty. Masses of the darker common people are looking to Randolph as the modern Messiah." Edwin R. Embree, *Thirteen against the Odds* (Port Washington, N.Y.: Kennikat, 1944), 225.

14. According to a spokesman for California-based Vultee Aircraft, "it is not the policy of this company to employ people other than of the Caucasian race." Robert C. Weaver, *Negro Labor: A National Problem* (Port Washington, N.Y.: Kennikat, 1949), 109.

15. These workers earned from four to eleven dollars for a work week that was often sixty hours or more. See George J. Stigler, *Domestic Servants in the United States, 1900–1940* (New York: National Bureau of Economic Research, 1946), 3, 7, 17, 20, 39. See also David Katzman, *Seven Days a Week: Women and Domestic Service in Industrializing America* (New York: Oxford University Press, 1978), 282–83.

16. Bates, *Pullman Porters,* 157.

17. Quoted in Joseph B. Lash, *Eleanor and Franklin: The Story of Their Relationship Based on Eleanor's Private Papers* (New York: Norton, 1971), 534.

18. Ibid. See also Paula F. Pfeffer, *A. Philip Randolph, Pioneer of the Civil Rights Movement* (Baton Rouge: Louisiana State University Press, 1990), 46–49.

19. Sitkoff, *A New Deal for Blacks,* 1:317 (quote), 383, citing *inter alias* the New York *Amsterdam News,* June 21, 1941; and the Baltimore *Afro-American,* June 21, 1941. Randolph in a later interview gave many more details about his exchanges with Eleanor Roosevelt. See Jarvis Anderson, *A. Philip Randolph: A Biographical Portrait* (New York: Harcourt Brace Jovanovich, 1972), 255, 374.

20. White, *A Man Called White,* 190.

21. Indeed, one scholar calls White "an old client; the power structure knew how to deal with him." Pfeffer, *A. Philip Randolph,* 48.

22. White, *A Man Called White,* 192; Kenneth Robert Jenken, *Walter White: Mr. NAACP* (Chapel Hill: University of North Carolina Press, 2007), 255–56.

23. "Reaffirming Policy of Full Participation in the Defense Program . . . Regardless of Race, Creed, Color, or National Origin" (Executive Order 8802), *Federal Register,* 6:125 (June 27, 1941), p. 3109.

24. Greg Robinson, *By Order of the President: FDR and the Internment of Japanese Americans* (Cambridge, Mass.: Harvard University Press, 2001), 4. Germans were not entirely silent. Beginning on February 27, 1943, there were several days of demonstrations in Berlin organized by non-Jewish wives and other relatives of Jews being deported. See Nathan Stoltzfus, *Resistance of the Heart: Intermarriage and the Rossenstrasse Protest in Nazi Germany* (New York: Norton, 1996).

25. As a result of the "dampening effect of Pearl Harbor" on protests, the New York *Amsterdam News,* which had been one of the staunchest supporters of MOWM, now took the position that a march would "play directly into the hands of Hitler"; and the NAACP adopted as its slogan, "Victory Is Vital to Minorities." Herbert Garfinkel, *When Negroes March: The March on Washington Movement for FEPC* (Glencoe, Ill.: Free Press, 1959), 81, 114, 200 n. 50.

26. Louis Ruchames, *Race, Jobs, and Politics: The Story of FEPC* (New York: Columbia University Press, 1953), 28–29.

27. Garfinkel, *When Negroes March,* 78. At a time when "war budgets ran off the edge of the page the president dug up a mere $80,000 out of his contingency to finance the FEPC's whole national show." John Beecher, "8802 Blues," *New Republic,* February 1943, 250.

28. Beecher, "8802 Blues," 250. On the FEPC's deluge of complaints and few successes, see Fair Employment Practices Committee, *Final Report,* June 28, 1946 (Washington, D.C.: Government Printing Office, 1947), 35. In the South much discrimination went unreported. For a somewhat better results in California, see ibid., 37.

29. The Republicans, with no "Jim Crow" bloc, called for an antilynch law, a permanent

FEPC, and the abolition of poll taxes. But blacks continued to support the man who had put bread on the table in hard times. See Kirby, *Black Americans in the Roosevelt Era,* 229.

30. According to a black journalist, "A. Philip Randolph was the outstanding leader of the period." Roi Ottley, *Black Odyssey* (London: John Murray, 1949), 279. See also Garfinkel, *When Negroes March,* 63. Compare with Louis Coleridge Kesselman, *The Social Politics of FEPC: A Study in Reform Pressure Movements* (Chapel Hill: University of North Carolina Press, 1948), 94–95.

31. Bates, *Pullman Porters,* 19.

32. Ibid., 164–66.

33. "Swinging wildly at Randolph, the administration hit the Negro." Beecher, "8802 Blues," 248.

34. Garfinkel, *When Negroes March,* 102.

35. Dominic J. Capeci Jr. and Martha Wilkerson, *Layered Violence: The Detroit Riots of 1943* (Jackson: University of Mississippi Press, 1991), 183–84; Timothy B. Tyson, "Wars for Democracy," in *Democracy Betrayed: The Wilmington Race Riot of 1898 and Its Legacy,* ed. David S. Cecelski and Timothy B. Tyson (Chapel Hill: University of North Carolina Press, 1998), 253–75.

36. Gunnar Myrdal et al., *An American Dilemma: The Negro Problem and Modern Democracy* (New York: Harper, 1944), 413, 415. See also Robert C. Weaver's chapter "The Color Bar Bends," in his *Negro Labor,* 28–40; and Garfinkel, *When Negroes March,* 114, 190, 191.

37. See Randolph's reply to the charge of receiving "Nazi funds." Garfinkel, *When Negroes March,* 84. For an attack on the "sensation-mongering Negro leaders," see Warren H. Brown, "A Negro Looks at the Negro Press," *Saturday Review of Literature,* December 19, 1942, 5–6.

38. Myrdal et al., *American Dilemma,* 821; Richard M. Delfume, "The 'Forgotten Years' of the Negro Revolution," *Journal of American History* 55 (June 1968): 94, 99–100.

39. Gavin Wright, *Old South, New South: Revolutions in the Southern Economy since the Civil War* (New York: Basic Books, 1986), 238, and his chapter "The New Economy of the Postwar South," 239–74; Jack M. Bloom, *Class, Race, and the Civil Rights Movement* (Bloomington: Indiana University Press, 1987), 63–68.

40. Walter White, *A Rising Wind* (Garden City, N.Y.: Doubleday, Doran and Co., 1945); Timothy B. Tyson, *Radio Free Dixie: Robert F. Williams and the Roots of Black Power* (Chapel Hill: University of North Carolina Press, 1999). See John Dittmer's chapter "We Return Fighting," in his *Local People: The Struggle for Civil Rights in Mississippi* (Urbana: University of Illinois Press, 1994), 1–18.

41. Mary L. Dudziak, *Cold War Civil Rights: Race and the Image of American Democracy* (Princeton: Princeton University Press, 2000), 52.

42. On the military and political concerns surrounding the decision to use the atomic bomb, see Samuel Walker, *Prompt and Utter Destruction: Truman and the Use of Atomic Bombs against Japan* (Chapel Hill: University of North Carolina Press, 2005), 105–6.

43. Some Americans prospered grandly, most rather modestly. See Studs Terkel, *"The Good War": An Oral History of World War Two* (New York: Pantheon, 1984); Michael C. C. Adams, *The Best War Ever: America and World War II* (Baltimore: Johns Hopkins University Press, 1994).

44. Adams, *Best War Ever,* 114–15; Bruce Nelson, *Divided We Stand: American Workers and the Struggle for Equality* (Princeton: Princeton University Press, 2001), 255.

45. Nelson, *Divided We Stand,* xxxiii.

46. Jeff Wood, *Black Struggle, Red Scare: Anti-Communism in the South, 1948–1968* (Baton Rouge: Louisiana State University Press, 2004), 31–32.

47. Gerald Horne, *Fire This Time: The Watts Uprising and the 1960s* (Charlottesville: University of Virginia Press, 1995), 5–7.

48. Harvey Schwartz, "A Union Combats Racism: The ILWU's 'Japanese-American Incident,'" *Southern California Quarterly Review* 62 (Summer 1980): 166 (quote), 175 n. 19.

49. Horne, *Fire This Time*, 7, 12. The decline of the Left has also been marked by the steady rise in the conversion of African Americans to Islam, often while serving in prison. By 2000, 32 percent of African Americans in New York state prisons were Muslims. Robert Dennin, *Black Pilgrimage to Islam* (New York: Oxford University Press, 2002), 166, 239, 261. For a broader view of the decline of the Left, see Patricia Sullivan, *Days of Hope: Race and Democracy in the New Deal Era* (Chapel Hill: University of North Carolina Press, 1996), 274–75; and Wood, *Black Struggle, Red Scare*, 31–32.

Chapter 17: The Black Freedom Movement

1. Gunnar Myrdal et al., *An American Dilemma: The Negro Problem and Modern Democracy* (New York: Harper, 1944), v–viii. Much of the strength of this study derives from Myrdal's able black collaborators, especially the young political scientist Ralph Bunch. See Walter Jackson, *Gunnar Myrdal and America's Conscience: Social Engineering and Racial Liberalism* (Chapel Hill: University of North Carolina Press, 1990), 21–31. The Myrdal project was a weapon of racial reformers, as was M. F. Ashley Montagu's *Man's Most Dangerous Myth: The Fallacy of Race* (New York: Harper, 1942).

2. As early as 1938, in the Gaines decision, the Court had ruled that the Missouri law, by providing a black law student with a stipend to study out of the state, had not offered him "equal" opportunity. John Hope Franklin and Alfred A. Moss Jr., *From Slavery to Freedom: A History of African Americans*, 7th ed. (New York: McGraw-Hill, 1994), 410.

3. Mary Dudziak, *Cold War Civil Rights: Race and the Image of American Democracy* (Princeton: Princeton University Pres, 2000), 85–86, 88. Randolph was often attacked by the established black leadership, including the NAACP, but he enjoyed great popular support. One poll showed that 70 percent of young black males agreed with Randolph. See Charles M. Payne, *I've Got the Light of Freedom: The Organizing Tradition and the Mississippi Freedom Struggle* (Berkeley: University of California Press, 1995), 430.

4. This strategy became more problematic as blacks registered to vote in unprecedented numbers. John Dittmer, *Local People: The Struggle for Civil Rights in Mississippi* (Urbana: University of Illinois Press, 1994), 27–28.

5. Dudziak, *Cold War Civil Rights*, 13.

6. Ibid., 56–60.

7. So long as the sounds that Louis Armstrong made came from his trumpet he had few problems. But in 1957 when Present Dwight D. Eisenhower seemed to falter in his constitutional duty to enforce the *Brown* decision in a school case in Little Rock, Arkansas, Armstrong canceled his tour of the Soviet Union, exploding, "the government can go to hell." A notice appeared in his FBI file: "Louis Sacho [*sic*] Armstrong is a communist. Why does State Dept. give him a passport?" Ibid., 66. See also Penny M. Von Eschen, *Satchmo Blows Up the World: Jazz Ambassador Plays the Cold War* (Cambridge, Mass.: Harvard University Press, 2004),

63. Compare with Thomas Borstelmann, *The Cold War and the Color Line: American Race Relations in the Global Arena* (Cambridge, Mass.: Harvard University Press, 2001), 122.

8. Borstelmann, *Cold War and the Color Line,* 77; Dudziak, *Cold War Civil Rights,* 44–45.

9. Dudziak, *Cold War Civil Rights,* 61–63.

10. Bennetta Jules-Rosette, *Josephine Baker in Art and Life: The Icon and the Image* (Urbana: University of Illinois Press, 2007), 35, 37, 70; Dudziak, *Cold War Civil Rights,* 67–70.

11. In Monroe, North Carolina, for example, two black boys, ages eight and ten, were arrested by police at gunpoint. They were supposed to have taken part in a "kissing game" played by a group of black and white playmates. They were accused of having kissed white girls. Tymothy B. Tyson, *Radio Free Dixie: Robert F. Williams the Roots of Black Power* (Chapel Hill: University of North Carolina Press, 1999), 90–101.

12. Carol Anderson, *Eyes Off the Prize: The United States and the African American Struggle for Human Rights* (Cambridge: Cambridge University Press, 2003), 106.

13. Borstelmann, *Cold War and the Color Line,* 93–94.

14. Jack M. Bloom, *Class, Race, and the Civil Rights Movement* (Bloomington: Indiana University Press, 1987), 105–6.

15. Quoted in Timothy B. Tyson, "Civil Rights Movement," in *The Oxford Companion to African American Literature,* ed. William L. Andrews, Frances Smith Foster, and Trudier Harris (New York: Oxford University Press, 1996), 147.

16. Parks had attended Highlander Folk School, and both she and the Montgomery Pullman porter organizer E. D. Nixon were veterans of the March on Washington movement. See Beth Thompkins Bates, *Pullman Porters and the Rise of Protest Politics in Black America* (Chapel Hill: University of North Carolina Press, 2001), 155, 187.

17. For an excellent treatment on how this played out among students, see William J. Billingsley, *Communists on Campus: Race, Politics, and Public University in Sixties North Carolina* (Athens: University of Georgia Press, 1999).

18. Numan V. Bartley, *The Rise of Massive Resistance: Race and Politics in the South during the 1950s* (Baton Rouge: Louisiana State University Press, 1969), 116–17; Bloom, *Class, Race, and the Civil Rights Movement,* 94–99.

19. Bloom, *Class, Race, and the Civil Rights Movement,* 313; William H. Chafe, *Civilities and Civil Rights: Greensboro, North Carolina, and the Black Struggle for Freedom* (New York: Oxford University Press, 1980), 62–63.

20. Elizabeth Jacoway, "An Introduction: Civil Rights and the Changing South," in *Southern Businessmen and Desegregation,* ed. Elizabeth Jacoway and David B. Colburn (Baton Rouge: Louisiana State University Press, 1882), 7, 11. On the contest between hard-liners and moderates, see Bartley, *Rise of Massive Resistance,* 320–39. The moderate former governor of Georgia, Ellis G. Arnall, emerged from retirement to declare, "You can't turn out into the streets a million school children, 48,000 teachers, 6,000 bus drivers, and 17,000 other school employees." Quoted, ibid., 334.

21. In May 1961, President John F. Kennedy was not pleased with the nightly TV drama. He was about to leave for Vienna for a meeting with Soviet Premier Nikita Khrushchev when he learned that a group of freedom riders were about to cross Alabama and Mississippi. He demanded of an aide who was supposed to have connections with activists, "Can't you get your goddamned friends off those buses? Stop them." But JFK had no such luck. He had to send in the FBI and to put pressure on local Democrats to maintain order. Quoted in Ray-

mond Arsenault, *Freedom Riders: 1961 and the Struggle for Racial Justice* (New York: Oxford University Press, 2006)), 164. See also Dittmer, *Local People,* 92.

22. The Mississippi campaign had been organized in 1962 by a coalition of the four major civil rights organizations: the Student Nonviolent Coordinating Committee (SNCC), the Congress of Racial Equality (CORE), the Southern Christian Leadership Conference (SCLC), and the National Association for the Advancement of Colored People (NAACP). See David R. Goldfield, *The Promised Land: The South since 1945* (Arlington Heights, Ill.: Harlan Davidson, 1987), 113. On the part of student volunteers in Freedom Summer, see Howard Zinn, *SNCC: The New Abolitionists* (Boston: Beacon, 1965), 242–54.

23. Payne, *I've Got the Light of Freedom,* 422, 424.

24. For overall studies of the black freedom movement in Mississippi, see ibid. and Dittmer, *Local People.* Also Kay Mills, *This Little Light of Mine: the Life of Fannie Lou Hamer* (New York: A Plume Book, 1993); Chana Kai Lee, *For Freedom's Sake: The Life of Fannie Lou Hamer* (Urbana: University of Illinois Press, 1999); and Barbara Ransby, *Ella Baker and the Black Freedom Movement* (Chapel Hill: University of North Carolina Press, 2005).

25. David J. Garrow, *Protest at Selma: Martin Luther King, Jr., and the Voting Rights Act of 1965* (New Haven: Yale University Press, 1978), 105–10.

26. Few citizens questioned either of the Cold War's sustaining myths: (1) that the Soviet Union, having just lost twenty million of its people and half of its industry in World War II, was about to launch a campaign of military expansion; and (2) that governments and movements throughout the world which favored economic development by state planning promoted "Soviet expansionism" and were a threat to American security.

27. Tyson, "Civil Rights Movement," 148.

28. Lance Hill, *The Deacons for Defense: Armed Resistance and the Civil Rights Movement* (Chapel Hill: University of North Carolina Press, 2004), 86. Perhaps the most effective use of conservative piggybacking was made by the Jesse Helms machine in North Carolina, which, rather than opposing civil rights as such, identified student activists as "communists." See Billingsley, *Communists on Campus.*

29. Martin Luther King Jr., *A Testament of Hope: The Essential Writings and Speeches of Martin Luther King, Jr.,* ed. James M. Washington (San Francisco: Harper, 1991), 248.

30. George W. Groh, *The Black Migration: The Journey to Urban America* (New York: Weybright and Talley, 1972), 63–69, 113–18; See also Nicholas Lemann, *The Promised Land: The Great Black Migration and How It Changed America* (New York: Knopf, 1991).

31. Hosea Williams, preparing marchers in Selma, Alabama, for what would be remembered as Bloody Sunday, told them, "I believe in the resurrection, but . . . resurrection comes *after* crucifixion . . . injustice must become the thud of club upon flesh, and this will echo around the world." Quoted in Goldfield, *Promised Land,* 118.

32. Hill, *Deacons for Defense,* 1.

33. Ibid., 1–2.

34. See Clayborne Carson's chapter "Racial Separation," in his book *In Struggle: SNCC and the Black Awakening in the 1960s* (Cambridge, Mass.: Harvard University Press, 1981), 191–211.

35. For other terms describing this conflict, see Pentagon Paper 19, in Neil Sheehan et al., *The Pentagon Papers, as Published by the New York Times* (New York: Quadrangle Books, 1971), 130–31.

36. The doves favored a blockade or quarantine of the island, while the hawks favored air strikes against Cuban missile sites. Shelton M. Stern, *Averting 'The Final Failure': John F. Kennedy and the Secret Cuban Missile Crisis Meetings* (Stanford: Stanford University Press, 2003), 130. See also ibid., 121–26, 424.

37. For a State Department debate between the two sides, see Fredrik Logevall, *Choosing War: The Lost Chance for Peace and the Escalation of the War in Vietnam* (Berkeley: University of California Press, 1999), 51. On Johnson's view of Kennedy, see also Robert L. Dallek, *Lyndon B. Johnson: Portrait of a President* (New York: Oxford University Press, 2004), 139.

38. For other dove initiatives by JFK, see Dallek, *Lyndon B. Johnson,* 17, 40, 43; Robert S. McNamara, *In Retrospect: The Tragedy and Lessons of Vietnam* (New York: Random House, 1995), 86–87.

39. Borstelman, *Cold War and the Color line,* 190; Dudziak, *Cold War Civil Rights,* 232.

40. McNamara, *In Retrospect,* 146–47. For a different view, a study that ascribes much more responsibility to McNamara himself and less to Johnson for the escalation of the war in Vietnam, see Gareth Porter, *Perils of Dominance: Imbalance of Power and the Road to War in Vietnam* (Berkeley: University of California Press, 2005), 182–84, 192.

41. Anthony Austin, *The President's War: The Story of the Tonkin Gulf Resolution and How the Nation Was Trapped in Vietnam* (Philadelphia: Lippincott, 1971), 345; John Galloway, *The Gulf of Tonkin Resolution* (Rutherford, N.J.: Fairleigh Dickinson University Press, 1970), 69–70; Logevall, *Choosing War,* 194–95.

42. Gerald Horne, *Fire This Time: The Watts Uprising and the 1960s* (Charlottesville: University of Virginia Press, 1995), 3.

43. U.S. National Advisory Commission on Civil Disorders, *Report of the National Advisory Commission on Civil Disorders* ("*Kerner Report*") (Washington, D.C.; Government Printing Office, 1968), 123–27, 143–45; Isabel Wilkerson, "New Studies Zeroing in on the Poorest of the Poor," *New York Times,* December 20, 1987; William Julius Wilson, "The Underclass: Issues, Perspectives, and Public Policy," in *The Ghetto Underclass: Social Science Perspectives,* ed. William Julius Wilson (1989; Updated ed., Newbury Park, Calif.: Sage, 1993), 42. On the limited educational opportunities of poor children, see Jonathan Kozol, *Savage Inequalities: Children in America's Schools* (New York: Crown, 1991).

44. King, *Testament of Hope,* 245.

45. Franklin and Moss, *From Slavery to Freedom,* 424–25, 493.

46. Hill, *Deacons for Defense,* 269, 271–72.

47. Archie Epps, ed., *Malcolm X: Speeches at Harvard* (New York: Paragon House, c. 1992), 10.

48. C. Eric Lincoln, *The Black Muslims in America,* 2nd ed. ([Boston:] Beacon, 1973), 211–13.

49. Franklin and Moss, *From Slavery to Freedom,* 124–25; Richard Brent Turner, *Islam in the African American Experience* (Bloomington: Indiana University Press, 1997), 224.

50. See Stokely Carmichael and Charles V. Hamilton, *Black Power: The Politics of Liberation in America* (New York: Vintage, 1967), 98–120. Jeffrey O. G. Ogbar, *Black Power: Radical Politics and African American Identity* (Baltimore: Johns Hopkins University Press, 2004), 90, 196. See also Angela Davis's manifesto, "I am a Communist Revolutionary," in *Off the Pigs! The History and Literature of the Black Panther Party,* ed. G. Louis Heath (Metuchen, N.J.: Scarecrow Press, 1976), 254–55.

51. On this debate see David L. Lewis, *King: A Critical Biography* (New York: Praeger, 1970), 358–60.

52. King, *A Testament of Hope,* 232.

53. On the global impact of Vietnam, see David Caute, *The Year of the Barricades: A Journey through 1968* (New York: Harper and Row, 1988).

54. Massimo Teodori, ed., *The New Left: A Documentary History* (Indianapolis: Bobbs-Merrill, 1969), 477–82. See also James L. Wood, *New Left Ideology: Its Dimensions and Development* (Beverly Hills, Calif.: Sage, 1975); Carl Oglesby, ed., *The New Left Reader* (New York: Grove Press, 1969); Maurice Isserman, *If I Had a Hammer . . . : The Death of the Old Left and the Birth of the New Left* (New York: Basic Books, 1987).

55. See *Bloody Sunday,* film by Paul Greenglass (Paramount DVD, 2003). Also Geoffrey Bell, *The Protestants of Ulster* (London: Pluto Press, 1975), 40, 52, 148; Alan O'Day and John Stevenson, eds., *Irish Historical Documents since 1800,* 213–14, 219–20.

56. Jac-André Boulet, "Les disparités de revenue sur le marche montréalais: Quelques éléments d'analyse," in *Économie et langue: Recueil de textes,* comp. François Villancourt (n.p.: Éditeur officiel du Québec, 1985), 160.

57. See Ogbar's chapter "Rainbow Radicalism: The Rise of Ethnic Radicalism," in his *Black Power,* 159–89.

58. When King had visited Los Angeles at the time of the Watts riot, he had been jeered with "I had a dream. I had a dream—hell we don't need no damn dreams. We want jobs." Hill, *Deacons for Defense,* 235.

59. The Johnson administration and the FBI were alarmed by King's opposition to the Vietnam War and his call for a Poor People's Campaign, as these positions challenged Johnson's publicly stated reluctance to escalate the war and his rhetorical support for his war on poverty. In effect, King and the SCLC were saying to the administration, "If you believe what you say you believe, come join us." See David J. Garrow, *The FBI and Martin Luther King* (New York: Penguin, 1981), 183–86.

60. The Black Panthers also suffered "an unprecedented assault from the FBI, and local police agencies. By 1971, the party had lost over twenty comrades to police gunfire and had expelled hundreds of others during its purge of suspected police agents." Ogbar, *Black Power,* 199. See also Huey P. Newton, *War against the Panthers: A Study of Repression in America* (New York: Harlem River Press, 1996).

61. Robert Finch as quoted in Robert Mason, *Richard Nixon and the Quest for a New Majority* (Chapel Hill: University of North Carolina Press, 2004), 26.

Chapter 18: The Racial System in the Age of Corporate Globalism, Technological Revolution, and Environmental Crisis

1. Martin Luther King Jr., *Where Do We Go from Here: Chaos or Community?* (New York: Harper and Row, 1968), 49–50.

2. Deirdre A. Royster, *Race and the Invisible Hand: How White Networks Excluded Black Men from Blue-Collar Jobs* (Berkeley: University of California Press, 2003), 190.

3. John Wright, ed., *New York Times 1998 Almanac* (New York: Penguin Reference Books, 1997), 281. The number of black-white marriages in the United States rose from 213,000 in 1993 to 663,000 in 2000. Renee C. Romano, *Race Mixing: Black-White Marriages in Postwar America* (Gainesville: University Press of Florida, 2003), 249.

4. Royster, *Race and the Invisible Hand*, 160–61, 177, 182, 184, 188. Resegregation has resulted in a process called "disaccumulation": as the neighborhood becomes poorer, the equity of homeowners declines instead of increases. Poorer health care results in more children born with light birth weight. These children also suffer from more water and air pollution and thus perform more poorly in schools, which themselves have deteriorated. See Michael K. Brown et al., *Whitewashing Race: The Myth of a Color-Blind Society* (Berkeley: University of California Press, 2003), 22–25.

5. See Jonathan Kozol, *Savage Inequalities: Children in America's Schools* (New York: Crown, 1991).

6. The myth of the level playing field goes back to the nineteenth century, popularized especially by Horatio Alger. Beginning in 1853, Alger published 120 books with a total circulation of at least 17 million. One hero of his success stories, "Ragged Dick," benefited from sound advice: "I hope my lad . . . you will prosper and rise in the world. You know that in this free country poverty is no bar to a man's advancement." *Ragged Dick and Mark the Match Boy* (New York: Collier Books, 1962), 6–7, 57, 69.

7. Dan T. Carter, *From George Wallace to Newt Gringrich: Race in the Conservative Counter-revolution, 1963–1994* (Baton Rouge: Louisiana State University Press, 1996), xiv, 58, 59, 118; J. Morgan Kousser, *Colorblind Injustice: Minority Voting Rights and the Undoing of the Second Reconstruction* (Chapel Hill: University of North Carolina Press, 1999), 6, 377.

8. Interview conducted as part of the "American Civilization" series of articles by Dennis Farney, *Wall Street Journal*, October 28, 1992, A12. See also C. A. Bowers, *Let Them Eat Data: How Computers Affect Education, Cultural Diversity and the Prospects for Ecological Sustainability* (Athens: University of Georgia Press, 2000).

9. Kozol, *Savage Inequalities*, 5; George Groh, *Black Migration: The Journey to Industrial America* (New York: Weybright and Talley, 1972), 117; William Julius Wilson, *When Work Disappears: The World of the New Urban Poor* (New York: Vintage, 1997), 199, 217–18.

10. The economist Adrian Wood, in a study of the relocation of manufacturing, calculated that in 1993 hourly "labor costs" (presumably wages plus benefits) in selected countries were: Germany, $24.9; Japan, $16.9; United States, $16.4; Britain, $12.4; South Korea, $4.9; Hungary, $1.8; China, $0.5. Colin Hines and Tim Lang, "The New Protectionism," *Nation*, July 15, 22, 1996, 29. The recent quantum leap in the ability of companies to relocate has created a race to the bottom as low-wage countries compete for industry. See Amy Breecher, "After NAFTA: Global Village or Global Pillage!" *Nation*, December, 1993, 685.

11. See Robert Pear, "Poverty, 1993: Bigger, Deeper, Younger, Getting Worse," *New York Times*, October 10, 1992; Richard N. Wolf, *Top Heavy: A Study of the Increasing Inequality of Wealth in America* (New York: Twentieth-Century Press, 1995).

12. Decreasing opportunities may explain two late twentieth-century trends: a drastic decline in marriage and a decline in home ownership. See Robert D. Ware and Christopher Winship, "Socioeconomic Change and the Decline of Marriage for Blacks and Whites," in *The Urban Underclass*, ed. Christopher Jencks and Paul E. Peterson (Washington, D.C.: Brookings Institution, 1991), 175–95, esp. 195. See also Katherine S. Newman, *Declining Fortunes: The Withering of the American Dream* (New York: Basic Books, 1993), 30–33.

13. Wilson, *When Work Disappears*, 26–27.

14. On the shredding of protection to black mothers, see Brown et al., *Whitewashing Race*, 100–101. Some of the less helpful proposals for managing this problem are calls for strict measures to jail "deadbeat dads" and to require "welfare mothers" to find jobs.

15. See especially Carter, *From George Wallace to Newt Gingrich*, 64. See also David Zucchino, *The Myth of the Welfare Queen* (New York: Scribner, 1997), and Robert Mason, *Richard Nixon and the Quest for a New Majority* (Chapel Hill: University of North Carolina Press, 2004), 47–50.

16. Not only were blacks more likely than whites to be arrested, but they fared worse in court. In the 1990s blacks constituted 15 percent of those less than eighteen years of age, but were 26 percent of those arrested, 44 percent of those "detained in custody," and 58 percent of those admitted to adult prisons. See Brown et al., *Whitewashing Race*, 40–41.

17. "In 1985 roughly 800,000 people were arrested on drug charges; by 1989 the number of annual narcotics busts had shot up to almost 1.4 million." Christian Parenti, *Lockdown America: Police and Prisons in Time of Crisis* (London: Verso, 1999), 58. See also Mike Davis, *City of Quartz: Excavating the Future of Los Angeles* (New York: Vintage, 1992), 277, 268–316. On the reluctance of employers to hire inner-city workers, "particularly blacks," see Joleen Kirschenman and Kathryn M. Neckerman, "'We'd Love to Hire Them, But . . . ': The Meaning of Race for Employers," in Jencks and Peterson, *The Urban Underclass*, 203–31; see esp. the authors' conclusion, 230–31 (the phrase "particularly blacks" appears on 230).

18. The international narcotics trade has been estimated at a half trillion dollars a year. Alfred E. Eckes Jr. and Thomas W. Zeiler, *Globalization and the American Century* (Cambridge: Cambridge University Press, 2003), 257. "Yet by some estimates money laundering is a $1.5 trillion a year operation and the foundation of the criminal underworld. Some of the best-known U.S. banks, including Bank of America and Chase Manhattan, have such weak controls that they have become unwitting links in the scheme." Editorial, "Banks Wearing Blinders," *Los Angeles Times*, February 8, 2001, B10. A Mexican civil servant, when asked how it was with his modest salary he was able to buy a bank in Texas and a mansion in Connecticut, replied, "A politician who is poor is a poor politician." Charles Bowen, *Down by the River: Drugs, Murder, Money, and Family* (New York: Simon and Shuster, 2003), 75.

19. Ellis Cose, "Casualties of War," *Newsweek*, September 6, 1999, 20; Dina R. Rose, *When Neighbors Go to Jail: Impact on Attitudes about Formal and Informal Social Control* (Washington, D.C.: Department of Justice, 1999), 1–3; Norm Stamper, *Breaking Rank: A Top Cop's Exposé of the Dark Side of American Policing* (New York: Nation Books, 2005), 54.

20. Seymour Melman, "From Private to Pentagon Capitalism," in his *The War Economy of the United States: Readings on Military Industry and the Economy* (New York: St. Martin's, 1971), 1–7; Sidney Lens, *The Military Industrial Complex* (Philadelphia: Pilgrim Press, 1970). The military budget for 2004–5 was higher than the combined military budgets of the sixteen nations having the next highest military budgets, almost all of whom were at the time either U.S. allies or seeking to become U.S. allies. Taxpayers were funding some fifteen global intelligence agencies and 400,000 troops occupying bases in 141 countries.

21. Neil Smith, *The Endgame of Globalization* (New York: Routledge, 2005), 198.

22. Royster, *Race and the Invisible Hand*, 190.

23. Kousser, *Colorblind Injustice*, 344–45.

24. Ibid., 5, 26, 65–67.

25. Groh, *Black Migration*, 117.

26. "American Identities for Sale," a documentary by Draggan Mihailovich on *60 Minutes, Wednesday*, and broadcast April 20, 2005, transcript, New York: CBS News, 2005, p. 2.

27. Editorial, "Modern-Day Slavery," *New York Times*, September 9, 2000, A14 (quote);

Kevin Bales, *New Slavery: A Reference Handbook* (Santa Barbara, Calif.: ABC-CLIO, 2000), 24; idem, *Disposable People: New Slavery in the Global Economy* (Berkley: University of California Press, 2004); idem, *Understanding World Slavery: A Reader* (Berkeley: University of California Press, 2005), 64, 135.

28. Eckes and Zeiler, *Globalization and the American Century*, 241; *The World Almanac and Book of Facts: 2005* (New York: World Almanac Books, 2005), 128.

29. "Busting High-Tech Wages," *Hightower Lowdown,* October 2003, 2–3. On the growing discrimination of employers against older workers, see John Helyar, "50 and Fired," *Fortune,* May 16, 2005, 78–80, 83–84, 86.

30. George Groh has remarked that in 1929 some Wall Street investors might have saved themselves some losses if they had been reading Chicago's black *Defender*. See Groh, *Black Migration*, 60.

31. Ralph Peters, "Our Soldiers, Their Cities," *Parameters: Journal of the U.S. Army War College* (Spring 1996): 43 quoted in Mike Davis, *Planet of Slums* (London: Verso, 2006), 203 [Peters article available online at http://www.carlisle.army.mil/usawc/parameters/96spring/peters.htm, accessed August 15, 2008]. A UN report found that Los Angeles had 100,000 homeless, the most of any city in the First World, while Mumbai (Bombay) with a million had the most of any city in the Third World. Ibid., 36.

32. Julian L. Simon, *The Ultimate Resource* (Princeton: Princeton University Press, 1996), 54, 59. Some neoliberals have thought that the collapse of the Soviet Union spelled not only the end of the Cold War but also the "end of history," ensuring the infinite growth of the free-market economy. For a discussion of this idea, see Kenneth M. Jensen, ed., *A Look at "The End of History?"* (Washington, D.C.: United States Institute of Peace, 1990).

33. A study of more than a dozen "complex" societies has found that when the poor continue to grow poorer, the ideological consensus that sustains the society becomes severed and the government can no longer govern. See Joseph A. Tainter, *The Collapse of Complex Societies* (Cambridge: Cambridge University Press, 1988), 248, 150–51.

34. See especially Richard Heinberg's chapter "The End of Cheap Energy," in his *Power Down: Options and Actions for a Post-Carbon World* (Forest Row, Can.: Clairview, 2004), 17–54. See also Kenneth S. Delfeyes, *Hubbert's Peak: The Impending Oil Shortage* (Princeton: Princeton University Press, 2001), 1, 176–85; Paul Roberts, *The End of Oil: On the Edge of a Perilous New World* (New York: Houghton Mifflin, 2004).

35. Jared M. Diamond, *Collapse: How Societies Choose to Fail or Succeed* (New York: Viking, 2005), 509.

36. See James Gustave Speth, *Red Sky at Morning: America and the Crisis of the Global Environment* (New Haven: Yale University Press, 2004); Herman B. Daly, "Sustainable Growth? No Thank You," in *The Case against the Global Economy and for a Turn toward the Local,* ed. Jerry Mander and Edward Goldsmith (San Francisco: Sierra Club Books, 1996), 197–206; Robert Goodland, "Growth Has Reached Its Limits," in ibid., 207–17. For a collection of essays generally critical of the idea that continuous economic expansion is sustainable, see James Gustave Speth, ed., *Worlds Apart: Globalization and the Environment* (Washington, D.C.: Island Press, 2003). On infinite growth on a finite planet, see interview of Prabhu Guptara, a director of the Bank of Switzerland, on American Public Media, "Marketplace," May 18, 2005, transcript (Livingston, N.J.: BurrelleLuce Transcripts, 2005), 6.

37. Such forms of culture do not rise to popularity spontaneously. See "The Merchants of

Cool: A Report on the Creators and Marketers of Popular Culture for Teenagers," directed by Barak Goodman; produced by Barak Goodman and Rachel Dretzin; correspondent and consulting producer, Douglas Rushkoff; online at www.pbs.org/wgbh/pages/frontline/shows/cool/view (accessed June 10, 2008).

38. Henry Wilson, *History of the Reconstruction Measures of the Thirty-Ninth and Fortieth Congress, 1865–68* (1868; Westport, Conn.: Negro Universities Press, 1970), 104.

Index

abolitionists/abolitionism, 104, 106–7
affirmative action, 238
African Blood Brotherhood, 197
Afro-Britons, 25
Afro-Portuguese yeomen, 95
Agricultural Adjustment Act (AAA), 206–7
agricultural revolution in England, 25–26, 29
Aiken, George L., 139, 140
"alambristas" (through the barbed wire immigrants), 243
Aldrich, Thomas Bailey, quoted, 193
amendments to Constitution: 13th, 185; 14th, 166–67, 185; 15th, 173–74, 185; and "palace revolution," 224
American Antislavery Society, 122
American Civil Liberties Union (ACLU), 200, 205
American Dilemma, An: The Negro Problem and Modern Democracy (Myrdal et al.), 222
"American exceptionalism," 24, 114, 115
"American System," 110, 111, 112, 144
Anderson, Marian, 208
Anti-Comintern Pact, 204
Anti-Communist Christian Association, 219
antislavery Uncle Tom plays, 139–40
Apalachicola River, 70–71
apocalypse of American natives, 15
Appeal (pamphlet, Walker), 103
aristocratic critique of capitalism, 116–17
armed forces, racial integration of, 236
Army of Northern Virginia, 152
Ashworth, John, 107
asiento, 32

Atlantic racial system, origin of, 16–17
Atlantic slave trade/African slave trade: English domination of, 29; upsurge of, 31–33; opposition to, 7, 74; movement to revive, 89–90
Augustine, Saint, quoted, 8

Bacon, Nathaniel, 40
Bacon, Thomas, quoted, 47
Bacon's Rebellion, 39–42
Bailey, Gamaliel, 132, 137
Baker, Josephine, 224
Balthazar (black "wise man"), 9
banks/bankers, 110, 117, 155
Baptists, 46, 52
Barbados, 27, 28
Barnum, P. T., 141
Bay of Pigs, 320
Berea College, 94
Berkeley, Gov. William: quoted, 39; mentioned, 40, 41, 42
Bermuda, 28
Bethune, Mary McLeod, 208
Beveridge, Albert, quoted, 189
Birmingham, Ala., 208, 227, 228, 229
Birney, James, G., 132, 133
Birth of a Nation (film), 191, 195
Black Brigade of Cincinnati, 159
black church: as rival view of religion, 102
black codes, 42, 59, 108, 149, 159
Black Legion, 204
Black Panther Party, 232, 234
"black power," 230, 236
Black Sea region, 18
Black Shirts, 201, 204, 207
black urbanization, 194
"Bloody Sunday" (Selma, Ala.), 228
Boaz, Franz, 194

Bogalusa, La., 219–20

Bridges, Harry, quoted, 220

British Board of Trade, 55

British commercial network, 66

Brotherhood of Sleeping Car Porters
(BSCP), 215–16

Brown, Albert G., quoted, 91

Brown, John: his raid on Harpers Ferry,
Va., 147; execution of, 148; mentioned,
149, 158, 159, 161

Brown v. Board of Education (1954), 224,
226

Bryan, William Jennings, 180

Buena Vista, battle of, 72–73

Bullwinkle, Alfred Lee, 201

business class in antebellum South, 83–85

Byrd, William, III, quoted, 45

Cadiz, Spain, 18

Caldwell, Andrew, 134

Calhoun, John C., 116, 118; quoted, 190–91;
mentioned, 206

Cameron, Paul Carrington, 171

Canada, 142, 154, 157, 233

Cannon-Johnson gang, 102

capital growth/capital accumulation:
driven by plantation production,
99–100, 112, 113

Carter, Robert "King," 44

Castas (color-defined status groups), 22,
24, 23

Catholics, 195, 205

Chambers, Jordan (white slave), 7, 134

Charleston, S.C.: mob scandalized by
white slave in, 7; small middle class in,
84; despotic police (quote about), 107;
sale of *Uncle Tom's Cabin* in, 137; 1860
Democratic national convention in, 149;
attack on Fort Sumter in, 150

Charlotte, N.C., 203

Chase, Salmon P., 118, 133

Chestnut, Mary, quoted, 37

Child, Lydia Maria, 161

Christian Recorder (Philadelphia), quoted,
189

Christian vision of liberation, 148, 160–62

Cincinnati, Ohio, 94, 132–33, 152, 159

Cincinnati Whig, 94

Civil Rights Act of 1866, 166

Civil War: Confederate offensive in,

152–53; Confederacy enacts first conscription in North America, 152; crisis
of the Union, 153, 156, 158; and conscription in the North, 154, 157, 158; memory
of, 191

Clay, Clement C., quoted, 77

Clay, Henry, 144

cognitive elite, 238–39

Cold War/cold warriors, 218, 219, 223, 228,
236

College Land Grant Act, 156

colonial courts, 25, 30–31

"color blind" discrimination, 238

color line, origin of, 33–34

Colored Farmers' Alliance, 178

Comintern (Communist International),
195, 197

commodification of labor, 96–98

Communists (American): early views
of, 196; and the question of a "a Negro
Nation," 197–98; their challenge in the
South, 99–101; marginalized by New
Deal, 101–3; their influence on labor
movement, left and liberal groups,
204–6

Communist University of the Toilers of
the East, 196

concentration of land ownership in antebellum South, 77

Congress of 1860: near riot in, 108

Congress of Industrial Organizations
(CIO), 205

Connor, Eugene "Bull," 208

conservative orientation of show business,
129, 138–39

conspiracies of servants and slaves in colonies, 27–28

Constitutional Unionists, 87

Continental Congress, 1

Conway, Henry J., 138–39

Cook, Henry, quoted, 172

Cook, Jay, 172

co-option of Uncle Tom story by conservatives, 138–39

"copperheads" (Peace Democrats): response to Confederate successes, 152,
153, 154, 157; response to Union successes, 155, 156, 157

Cornish, Rev. Samuel, 106

corporate hegemony, emergence of, 190

Cossacks, 95
counterrevolution in post–Civil War South, 165–66
coup d'état in Wilmington, N.C., 181–82
Cox, Rev. Samuel, 106
Cragg, James, 61
credit, 45, 176
Creek Indians, 70
crime: in England of 1600s, 27; and race, 141–42
"crimps" (English labor recruiters), 28
crisis of Chesapeake agriculture: and African slave trade, 54
crisis of 1876–77 (contested presidential election), 174
Crittenden Compromise, 149
crop liens/crop lien system, 170, 176
Cuba: invaded by "filibusters," 90, 147; Ultras demand annexation of, 148; and Lincoln, 149

Daily Evening Citizen (Vicksburg), quoted, 92
Daily Post (Cincinnati), 94
Dalmatian coast: export of white slaves from, 18
Danville, Va.: "race riot" in, 177
Darwin, Charles, 192
Daughters of the American Revolution (DAR), 208
Davenport, Charles Benedict, 192
David Walker's *Appeal. See Appeal*
Davis, Jefferson, 72, 73, 143
Deacons for Defense and Justice, 220
DeBow, J. D. B., quoted, 76, 112
Declaration of Independence and the "palace revolution," 223
decline of slavery in South's border states, 78–79, 86
democracy in Chesapeake proto-South, 49
Democratic Party (1900s): dominated by "the Slave Power" 109, 112, 113; 1860 break-up of, 148; and post-Reconstruction political system, 190; and New Deal, 201, 206
Democratic Republicans, 68
Democratic National Convention (1860), 148, 149
demagogues in South, 184
demographics and the "color line," 33–34

Depression of 1837, 123
Deutches Theatre, 141
Diamond, Jared, quoted, 246
disease threat in New World, 25, 26
disengagement/détente: 1963 failure of, 230
disfranchisement: of black southerners and poor whites, 182–83; of "illegal" immigrant part of working class, 243
dissenter churches, 46–47, 52–53
domestic slave trade, rise of, 58, 60
"doughfaced" leaders, 110, 113, 151; as allies of planters, 156
Douglass, Frederick, 108
"doves"/disengagement/détente, 230
Dred Scott decision of Supreme Court (1857), 93
DuBois, W. E. B., 223
Dunmore, Lord Edward, 55, 56
Dutch Republic/Netherlands: early technological ascendancy, 16; transfer of its investments to England, 29–30; and Caribbean sugar boom, 32

education: College Land Grant Act, 156; free schools in Reconstruction South, 168; and college for black veterans of World War II, 218
elections: of 1840, 123; of 1860, 148–49; of 1868, 173; of 1936, 211; of 1948, 222
Emmett, Daniel Decatur, 124, 142, 143
encomienda and *hacienda* labor systems, 17
endogamy: of English settlers, 33; of African slaves, 33–34
"enemies of the faith": as Old World justification for enslavement, 7, 14
English Revolution, 25–26
Enlightenment, 31
environmental crisis, 246
environmentalists/"greens," 246
Erie Canal, 112
Eisenhower, Dwight D., 225, 242
Essenes, quoted, 8
Ethiopian Regiment, 56
Ethridge, Mark, 215
eugenics, 192, 193
every-white-man-a-master movement, 89–90
executive orders: #8802 (fair employment), 214–15, 224–25; #9066 (interning

Japanese Americans), 215; #9981 (integrating armed forces), 222

exports: and antebellum capital accumulation, 113

extended family in South, 43–44

Fair Employment Practices Committee (FEPC), 215

family: southern extended family, 43–44; fragile family of the working poor, 239–40

Farmers' Alliance, 178–79

Farmer's Register, 78

fascist threat pre–World War II, 204

Federal Bureau of Investigation (FBI), 202

Federalist Party, 68

Fee, Rev. John, 94, 248

filibuster campaigns, 90–91, 154

Finch, Robert, quoted, 234

First Emancipation, 59

Fithian, Philip, quoted, 44

Fitzhugh, George, quoted, 36, 116

Florida, acquisition of, 70–71

"flying squadron" strike (1934), 203–4

foreign policy of the early United States, 67

Forrest, Nathan Bedford, 165

Fort Macon, 182

Fort Pillow, 159

Fort Sumter, 150

Fort Wagner, 159

Foster, Stephen C., 124, 129, 138

Framell, Dennis, 134

Franklin, John, 133

Fredericksburg, battle of, 153

free citizen's defense of slaveholders, 36–37

free coinage of silver, 180

Freedom Democratic Party of Mississippi, 228

Freedom Riders, 227

"Freedom Summer," 228

freed people/quasi freed people (antebellum), 48

Free-Soil movement, 81–83, 118

French and Indian War/Seven Years War, 49, 53

Fugitive Slave Act of 1850, 134

Fur and Leather Workers Union (FLWU), 205

"furnishing man," 176

fur traders, 40, 49

Fusion challenge, 180–83

Gadsden Strip, 91

Galton Society, 192

Garçon, Choctaw chief, 71

Garrison, William Lloyd, 103–4

Gastonia, N.C.: Communists lead textile strike in, 199–200; "flying squadron" strike begins in, 203

General Agreement on Tariffs and Trade (GATT), 238

German American Bund, 204

Gettysburg, battle of, 157

global economy, 238

global warming, 246

Glorious Revolution, 29–30

Gobineau, Count Arthur de, 192

gold bug politics, 183

Goldwater, Barry M., 231

Gone with the Wind (film), 191

Goodloe, Daniel R., 137

Gore, Christopher, 68

Grace, Rev. John, 28

Gramsci, Antonio: his theory of hegemony, 37–38

Grant, Madison, quoted, 192

Grant, Ulysses S., 173

Great Awakening, 52

Great Depression, 201, 204, 236, 245–46

Greeley, Horace, 153

Green, Samuel, 137

Greenbackers, 175

"greens." *See* environmentalists

"Green Springs Faction," 40

Greenville, S.C., 201

Gruening, Ernest, 194

Guinea Coast, 18

Halka (opera) 211

Hamer, Fannie Lou, 228

Hamitic myth, 21

Hammond, James H., quoted, 74, 108, 160

Harlem Renaissance, 194

Harper's Ferry, Va., 94, 147, 148

"hawks" (of 1812), 68; (of 1963), 230, 233

Hayes, Rutherford B., 174

hegemony: theory of, 37–38; emergence of planter hegemony, 38; and the defense of slavery, 82–83

Helper, Hilton Rowan, 83

Hendricks, Kelly Yale "Red," 203
Herndon, Angelo, 201
Herrenvolk democracy, 47
Highlander Folk School, 200
Holden, Clara, 201
Hollywood, 191, 195
Homestead Act, 155, 156
Horne, Gerald, 219
hospitality and power in Chesapeake proto-South, 44
House Un-American Activities Committee, 224
Howard-Fox Troup, 139–40
Howe, Julia Ward, and *Battle Hymn of the Republic,* 161
Hubbard, David, 86
Huckleberry Finn, 83
Huggins, Nathan Irwin, quoted, 126–27
human family, ancient vision of: and the Essenes, 8; persistence of concept, 10; and the American Revolution, 51; and the Quakers, 53; as organizing idea for change, 248
"human nature"; as explanation of the racial system, 2
Humboldt, Alexander von, quoted, 22
Hutchinson family: antislavery singers, 142, 144

ideology of slavery: race replaces religion in, 7, 19
immigrants: employers hire instead of free blacks, 61; and New England, 96; and ethnic conflict, 97–98; and minstrel show, 127–28; and wage levels, 143–45; during Civil War, 156; and "scientific racism," 193
Impending Crisis, The (Helper), 83
indentures, 25
Indians. *See* Native Americans/American natives/Indians
industrialists' employment practices: discrimination in favor of whites, 61, 96, 193
Industrial Revolution: and abolition of slavery, 51; in antebellum America, 66–67, 96, 113
Informational Revolution, 238–39
infrastructure of colonies: control of by gentry, 44–45

inner city riots, 216, 220, 231
"inner light" doctrine, 9, 52, 53
integration of armed forces, 222, 226, 227, 229–30
International Labor Defense (ILD), 205
International Longshoremen's and Warehousemen's Union (ILWU), 219–20
internationalists: on eve of World War II, 213
Irish immigrants: appeal of minstrels for, 127–28, 129
"isolationists": on eve of World War II, 212
industrial evolution in the South, 171–72

Jackson, Andrew, 69; quoted, 71; mentioned, 111
Jacksonian democracy/Jacksonian movement, 115, 150
Jacksonian nationalism, 98
Japan: and attack on Pearl Harbor, 215
Japanese Americans: target of Klan in 1919, 195; interned during World War II, 215
Jefferson, Thomas, quoted, 50, 55, 70
Jews, 195, 205, 220
"Jim Crow": minstrel character, 121; as icon for segregation, 196
Jim Crow army, 212
Jim Crow bloc in twentieth-century Democratic Party, 206, 212, 215
job market: fragmented by ethnicity and race, 115
Johnson, Andrew, 164
Johnson, Lyndon B., 228, 230
Johnson, Dr. Samuel, quoted, 50
judicial backlash to civil rights reforms, 242–43
justification of slavery, 7, 19

Kansas, 147
Kennedy, John F., 230
Kennedy, Robert F., 234
Kettell, Thomas Prentice, 118
kidnappers: of servants for English plantations, 28–29, 31; of freed people in the North, 102
King, Martin Luther, Jr., 127, 128; quoted, 232, 234, 235, 238
King Cotton: the power of, 74

kinship in the Chesapeake proto-South, 43–44
Knights of the Golden Circle, 154
Know Nothing Party, 115
Ku Klux Act, 174
Ku Klux Klan, 165, 195, 201, 202, 204, 220

Lane Theological Seminary, 132
Lawrence, Kans., 91
Lay, Benjamin, 51
Lee, General Robert E., 148, 152
legal protection of labor: in England, 27, 30; in English colonies, 25, 27–28, 30–31
Legaré, Hugh, quoted, 84
Legree, Simon: icon of cruel overseer, 21, 136, 141
Lenin, V. I., 197
level playing field myth, 238
Liberator, 121–22
Liberty Party, 118
Lincoln, Abraham: quoted, 62; reaction to "Dixie," 143; and the secession crisis, 149–50; and French mediation plan, 153; and Radical agenda, 155; and compensated emancipation, 158; and Preliminary Emancipation Proclamation, 157–58
Lincoln Memorial concert of 1939, 208–9
Little Rock, Ark., 227
Lope de Vega: author of play *Slave of Her Lover,* 7
Lopez, Narciso, 147
Loray Mill, 199–200
Loyalists, 56
Luce, Henry R., quoted, 210, 213
Lucy, Autherine, 226
Luddites, 245
Lundy, Benjamin, 104
lynching, 179, 189, 194

Macon, Nathaniel, 111
Madison Avenue, 191, 236
Maine, 69, 128
Malcolm X, quoted, 232
Manifest Destiny, 91, 111
march on Montgomery (1965), 228
March on Washington Movement (MOWM), 213–16
market-driven, color-defined slavery, 20–21
marl and agricultural reform, 78

maroons, 95
Marx, Karl: quoted, 155; mentioned, 192, 196
Marxism and the National Question (Stalin), 197
Maryland: decline of slavery in, 79
Mason-Dixon Line, 65
"massive resistance" movement, 226
May, Samuel J., 113
McCarthy, Joseph, 219
McConachie, Bruce, quoted, 138
McGuire, Tom, 138
McKay, Claude, quoted, 196
McKinley, William, 182
McNamara, Robert S., quoted, 231
mechanization of southern agriculture, 207, 229, 239
medieval view of slavery, 7
Mediterranean slave trade, 17–18
Memphis massacre of 1866, 167
Mexican War, 72–73
middle class: and globalism, 244–45
migration westward during Civil War, 156
"military industrial complex," 242
military slavery, 14
Militia Act of 1862, 154, 158
minstrel show: description of, 100; racial message of, 119, 128; primary audience of, 122–24; issues addressed by, 125; gospel of success, 126–27; politics of, 127–28, 129, 138–39
minstrel stereotype of northern free black, 128
missile crisis, 230
Missouri Compromise: results from crisis of 1819–20, 98, 110
Mitchel, General O. M., quoted, 159
Mobile, Ala., 79
Mobile Advertiser, quoted, 151
Moniuszko, Stanislaw, 211
Monroe, James, quoted, 59
Monroe Doctrine, 153; and the Civil War, 154
Montesquieu, quoted, 23
Montgomery bus boycott, 225, 227
Morgan, Edmund S., quoted, 38, 46
Morgan, J. P., 181
Morris, Gov. Robert Hunter, 53
Muslim slaves; expelled from Santo Domingo and Mexico, 18

muster day: in Chesapeake proto-South, 46
Myrdal, Gunnar, 222

Napoleon III: invades Mexico, 153
narcotics trade, 241
Narrative of the Life of Frederick Douglass (Douglass), 133
National Association for the Advancement of Colored People (NAACP), 194, 200, 205, 216, 223, 226
National Era (newspaper), 137, 138
National Principia (New York newspaper), 150
National Recovery Act (NRA), 203, 206
national security state/warfare state, 242
Nation of Islam, 232
Native Americans/American natives/Indians: apocalypse of, 15; and Virginia pioneers, 40, 41, 42; and French and Indian War, 53; and War of 1812, 70–71
Naval Expansion Act of 1938, 211
Nazi Party, 204
"Negro Fort," 71
neo-liberals/libertarians, 245
Netherlands. *See* Dutch Republic
New Deal/New Dealers, 201–2, 207, 211, 212
New Deal legacy, 219, 236
New England, 26, 66–69, 96
"new immigrants," 193
"new left," 233
New Jersey, 78
"new Negro," 196
New Orleans, 69, 80, 82, 83, 167
New York, 94, 112, 141, 157, 194
Nicaragua, 91
Nixon, Richard M., 234
"normalization" of *Uncle Tom's Cabin*, 38–139
North Atlantic Treaty Organization (NATO), 220
Northern Ireland, 228, 233
northernization of southern cities, 79–80
North-South racial consensus, 83, 193
Nullification Crisis, 110
nullifiers in South Carolina, 111

O'Connell, Daniel, quoted, 129
Old Basil, 60
"old left," 196, 233

Olmsted, Frederick Law, quoted, 107, 137
Omar ibn Saíd, 13
oppressed nations, theory of, 195–98
organized labor: weakness in antebellum years, 97; and Communist influence, 199–201, 205; and "flying squadron" textile strike, 203–4
Original Knights of Ku Klux Klan, 229
out-migration from antebellum South, 77

"palace revolution"/reform from above, 222
Parks, Rosa, 225, 234
paternalism, 14
Patriots, 9, 56
Paul, Saint, quoted, 8
peace time draft, 211
Pearl Harbor, 213, 215
pellagra/malnutrition, 170, 199
Pennsylvania, 53
Pentagon, 242
peonage, 165, 176, 184
Peters, Major Ralph, quoted, 245
Pettigrew, Charles, 147
"piggybacking" (a political tactic), 132, 135, 231
Philanthropist (newspaper), 132
pioneer herdsmen, 39, 40, 43, 56, 65
"place" of blacks: as critical racial idea, 129
plain whites/yeomanry, 41–42, 43, 57
plantation expansion within South, 117
plantation export economy, 73–74
Plato, quoted, 36
Plessey v. Ferguson (1896), 184
pogroms/"race riots": mob attacks on minority neighborhoods, 196
politics of irrationality, 86, 89
Poor People's Campaign, 234
poor whites, increase of, 78, 80, 85–86, 170
Populist (or People's) Party, 179–80
Portuguese, 32
post–Civil War national power structure, 170–71
post-industrial economy, 237–39
poverty: in late antebellum South, 78; in late twentieth century, 241
Presidential Reconstruction, 165–66
Prophet, the, 68
"Prussian Road" to South's industrialization, 172

"pure whites"/Anglo Saxons/Nordics/Aryans, 192, 193

Quakers/Society of Friends: and the "inner light" 9, 52, 53; and technology, 51; first organized abolitionists, 52; their capital accumulation, 53; their nonviolence/opposition to war, 53

race riots, 94, 165, 177
racial blending/"race mixing," 81, 237
racial consensus/hegemonic racial ideas, 82–83
racial ideas: anti-Africans slave trade lore, 21; no white man a slave, no black man fully free, 19–20; white solidarity myth, 92, 119; blacks useful and happy as slaves, miserable and dangerous when free, 61–62, 128–29
racial laws, 42–43, 103, 183, 184
Radical Reconstruction, 166–69
Radical southern constitutions, 168, 176
Radicals' political collapse (1868), 173
railroads, 79, 135–36, 156–57
Randolph, A. Philip, 213; quoted, 214; mentioned, 215, 218, 222, 233
Rankin, John, 133
ransoming societies, 19
Readjusters, 175, 177–78
real estate speculators on southern frontier, 40, 41, 71–72
realignment of social classes, 38, 144
rebellions in colonial Chesapeake region, 38–41
Rebel property, 150–51, 154, 159
"red summer" of 1919, 195, 197
Reconstruction acts (1866), 168
redistricting and race, 243
Registry of Servants Act, 30
Reich, Robert, quoted, 238
rescue riots, 102–3
retailers of drugs, 241
reverse discrimination, 238
revolutions of 1848, 191–92
Rice, T. D.: creator of "Jim Crow" character, 121, 139, 141
Richmond, 152, 153
Robeson, Paul, 224
Roosevelt, Eleanor, 208; quoted, 214; mentioned, 223

Roosevelt, Franklin D. (FDR): quoted, 201, 214; mentioned, 201, 203, 206, 211, 225
"Roosevelt Depression" of 1937, 211
Royal Africa Company, 29
Ruffin, Edmund, 78–79; quoted, 79; mentioned, 148
Russell, Daniel L., 180–82
Russian Revolution, 195–98

Savannah Republican, quoted, 84
Saxton, Alexander, 138
scandal of the white slave, 7, 134–35
scandalous paradox, 95
"scientific racism," 191–93
Scottsboro Case, 200, 202, 205, 220
Second American Revolution, 149, 150
Second Bull Run, battle of, 152
Second Reconstruction, 234
segregation: in antebellum North, 105–6, 118; and the "palace revolution," 225
Semi-Colon Club, 132
Seneca Falls Women's Rights Convention, 125
service workers: growth of in post-industrial America, 239
"Shameful Matches Act," repealed, 30
sharecroppers, 165, 170, 200, 207
Share Croppers Union, 200
Sharp, Sarah, quoted, 28–29
Shaw, Nate, quoted, 200
Shelby plantation, 133
Shuttlesworth, Rev. Fred, 234
Simms, William Gilmore, quoted, 130
Slave of Her Lover (Lope de Vega play): as medieval view of slavery, 7
"Slave Power, the"/King Cotton establishment: description of, 3–11; mobilized culture in defense of South's slavery, 109, 112
slavery: in Old World, 14; in New World, 13, 14; medieval view of, 7, 8, 9; impact on of market capitalism, 2, 13, 14, 16, 21; redefined by color (race), 13, 14, 19, 20, 22; becomes key to antebellum economy, 65–66, 73, 100; widens inequality among free people, 37
slave trade: trans-Saharan, 21; Mediterranean, 15, 17, 18, 19; Atlantic, 15, 18, 20, 31; and ideology of enslaveable "other," 19, 20, 21; spread of anti-African lore by, 14;

growth of Atlantic trade in 1500s and 1600s, 31; entrance of all maritime powers in, 33; English come to dominate, 31; slave trade to English Colonies, 31; internal slave trade in antebellum South, 58, 60, 61, 73

Slavs: source of white slaves, 17–18; as origin of the word "slave," 17; victims of Sambo stereotype, 17

Smith, Adam, quoted, 34, 48

Socialists, 200

Social Security Act, 206

Society of Friends. *See* Quakers

soil exhaustion in South, 66, 78, 79, 91

songs: of antislavery protest, 133, 141, 142, 144; of Dixie, 142–44; celebrating John Brown, 160–61

Southern Christian Leadership Conference (SCLC), 232, 233, 234

southern cities (antebellum), 79–82, 83–85

Southern Conference for Human Welfare (SCHW), 208

"southernization" process, 42

Southern Literary Messenger, 136, 137

Southern Manifesto, 226

southern pioneers: their livestock production, 39, 40, 41, 42, 43; their quick recovery from War for Independence, 65

Southern Tenant Farmers' Union (STFU), 200

Soviet Union, and segregation, 212

Spanish Council of the Indies, 32

speculators, on frontier land, 40, 70, 71, 72

"spirits" (kidnappers), 28

squatters, on frontier land, 40, 41

Stalin, Joseph, 197, 202–3

Stalwarts (Republican faction), 173

State Department, 224, 225

Stevens, Thaddeus: quoted, 109, 154; mentioned, 169

Stoddard, Theodore Lothrop, 193; quoted, 193

Stowe, Calvin, 132, 133

Stowe, Harriet Beecher: quoted, 118, 130–31; mentioned, 143, 144

street gangs, and politics, 97, 177

"sturdy beggars" (English vagabonds), 26

success, as political ideal, 114

sugar boom, 32–33

Sumner, Charles, quoted, 173

Supreme Court: and Civil Rights Act of 1866, 166; and "palace revolution," 222, 223, 224, 225

"swing voter," 222

Talmadge, Eugene, quoted, 207

Taney, Chief Justice Roger B., quoted, 93

tariffs, 111, 155

Taylor, Zachary, 109

Tyler, John, 116

technology and abolition, 152–52

Tecumseh, 68

Tennessee Valley Authority (TVA), 217

Texas, 72, 179

textile industry, 66

textile strike of 1928 (Gastonia, N. C.), 199–200

textile strike of 1934 (flying squadrons), 203–4

Third North Carolina Volunteers, 182

Thirteenth Amendment, 185

Tonkin Gulf Resolution, 231

"totem pole" of "scientific racism," 194

trade unionism, 115, 204–5

"traffic, the," 83, 84, 101

Transport Workers Union (TWU), 205

Truman, Harry S., 222

Truman Doctrine, 223

Truth, Sojourner, 108

Tubman, Harriet, 108

Turner, Nat, 104–5

Tuscaroa War, 42

"ultras," 86–88

"Uncle Tom," 133

Unemployment Councils, 199, 201

"underground railroad," 133

Union League, 175–76

Union's crisis of 1862, 153, 156, 158

Union war bonds, 155

"united front" against fascism, 104–5

United Nations (UN), 223

United States Information Agency (USIA), 223, 224

universal human family concept, 8; and American Revolution, 50–51; persistence of, 162, 248

Universal News Reels, 224

Upper North, 135–36, 139–40, 144

urbanization of blacks, 193–94

Urban League, 214
urban street gangs, 97
Uzbekistan, 196

Vallandigham, Clement L., quoted, 153
Van Evrie, John, 116
Vicksburg, 152
Vicksburg Daily Evening Citizen, quoted, 92
Vietnam War, 230
vigilance committees, 104
villeins (English serfs), 25, 26
Virginia dynasty, 67
Virginia Minstrels, 120–21
Voice of America, 223, 224
voluntary emancipation and gradualism, 59–61
voter registration drive in South, 208, 228
Voting Rights Act of 1965, 228

Waddell, A. M., quoted, 182
wage (or "free") labor, origin of, 16
"wage slave"/"white slave," 116–17
Walker, David, 103, 104
Walker, William, 91, 147
Wallace, George, 241
Wallace, Lewis, 159
Waller, John, 46
Wallerstein, Immanuel, 16
Walsh, Michael, 116, 118
"war hawks" of 1812, 68
"war of the cabins," 141–42
"war on crime," 241
"war on poverty," 230
warfare state/national security state, 240–41
Washington, D.C., 67; capture by the British (1814), 69, 161, 174, 214, 228; Poor People's Campaign, 233–34
Washington, George, 54; quoted, 57
Watson, Thomas, 201
Watts uprising of 1965, 231
Welch's National Amphitheatre, 137
welfare state versus warfare state, 242
Wellington, Duke of, 69
"wench" characters in minstrel show, 125

West Indies, 26
"Whig oligarchy" (in England), 29
westward limit of plantation production, 76, 77
Whig Party, 112, 115; Whigs as Republicans, 166
White, Chief Justice Edward, quoted, 195
White, Walter, 214
white chauvinism, 197
White Citizens' Councils, 226
white moderates, and Civil Rights movement, 226–27
"white primary," 184
white servants, 25
white slavery, "disappearance" of, 20
white solidarity, 175, 176–77, 218
white solidarity myth, emergence of, 92, 115, 117, 119, 147
Wiggins, Ella May, 201, 203
Williams, Aubrey, 214
Wilmington, N.C., 180, 182
Wilmot, David, quoted, 132
Wilmot Proviso, 132
Wilson, Woodrow, 194, 211
Winston, Joan, 27
"wisdom of the market," 245
Wise, Rabbi Stephen, 205
women's liberation movement, 233
women's rights convention in Seneca Falls, N. Y., 125
Wood, Benjamin, 157
Wood, Henry, 138
Wood, Fernando, 113, 118, 138
working poor, 239–40
World War I, 193–94
World War II, 216, 217, 218; compared to Vietnam War, 231, 236
Wormley bargain, 174, 175, 225
Wright Gavin, quoted, 87
Wright, Sir James, 56

Yamasee War, 42
yeomen. *See* plain whites

"Zip Coon": minstrel show stereotype, 128

William McKee Evans is professor emeritus, California State Polytechnic University, Pomona. His articles include "From the Land of Canaan to the Land of Guinea: The Strange Odyssey of the 'Sons of Ham,'" which appeared in the *American Historical Review* (February 1980). Professor Evans is the author of *Ballots and Fence Rails: Reconstruction on the Lower Cape Fear* and *To Die Game: The Story of the Lowry Band, Indian Guerrillas of Reconstruction.*

The University of Illinois Press
is a founding member of the
Association of American University Presses.

Composed in 10/13.5 Adobe Minion
with Akzidenz Grotesk display
by Celia Shapland
at the University of Illinois Press
Designed by Copenhaver Cumpston
Manufactured by Sheridan Books, Inc.

University of Illinois Press
1325 South Oak Street
Champaign, IL 61820-6903
www.press.uillinois.edu

DATE DUE

APR 19 2017			
GAYLORD			PRINTED IN U.S.A.